A Little Cha... last day.

to pickup! for pickups. mainly.

Like a relay race with one runner.
Kate jumping from carriage
to carriage to desk to bath.
lights up, lights down, Marie-Claire
here, now gone (...) [Such a
sweet future in which grasping
temporary fields — is that OK?]
* (late night in same stuff)
Au revoir to Kate. She moves
swiftly and cleanly on — total
commitment to everything. Me, her
children, this film, that next film.
The kids baked beans-throwing party.
~~ruthless emotional commitment.~~
)8O Wrap Party ruthless emotional detachments
which turned out to be a
joyous thing.
Chiswick House. Great venue.
A bar and two other adjoining
rooms — drink, talk or dance.
and people genuinely happy to
be there, wanting to be there.

But all these sudden goodbyes to
people who have shared the inside
of your head, heart, insecurities,
triumphs, have laughed, starred and
yawned with you .... now the
strange absence.

Madly, Deeply

Madly, Deeply

the diaries of
ALAN RICKMAN

EDITED BY ALAN TAYLOR

HENRY HOLT AND COMPANY

NEW YORK

Henry Holt and Company
Publishers since 1866
120 Broadway
New York, New York 10271
www.henryholt.com

Library of Congress Cataloging-in-Publication Data is available.

ISBN: 9781250847959

Our books may be purchased in bulk for promotional, educational, or business use. Please contact your local bookseller or the Macmillan Corporate and Premium Sales Department at (800) 221-7945, extension 5442, or by e-mail at MacmillanSpecialMarkets@macmillan.com.

First published in the U.K. by Canongate

First U.S. Edition 2022

Designed by Meryl Sussman Levavi

Printed in the United States of America

3   5   7   9   10   8   6   4

Contents

Foreword

The most remarkable thing about the first days after Alan died was the number of actors, poets, musicians, playwrights and directors who wanted to express their gratitude for all the help he'd given them.

I don't think I know anyone in this business who has championed more aspiring artists nor unerringly perceived so many great ones before they became great. Quite a number said that, latterly, they had been too shy to thank him personally. They had found it hard to approach him.

Of all the contradictions in my blissfully contradictory friend, this is perhaps the greatest—this combination of profoundly nurturing and imperturbably distant.

He was not, of course, distant. He was alarmingly present at all times. The inscrutability was partly a protective shield. If anyone *did* approach him with anything like gratitude or even just a question, they would be greeted with a depth of sweetness that no one who didn't know him could even guess at. And he was not, of course, unflappable. I could flap him like nobody's business and when I did he was fierce with me and it did me no end of good.

He was generous and challenging. Dangerous and comical. Sexy and androgynous. Virile and peculiar. Temperamental and languid. Fastidious and casual.

My list is endless. I am sure you can add to it.

There was something of the sage about him—and had he had more confidence and been at all corruptible, he could probably have started his own religion. His taste in all things from sausages to furnishings appeared to me to be impeccable.

His generosity of spirit was unsurpassed and he had so much time for people that I used to wonder if he ever slept or ever got time for himself.

A word not traditionally associated with Alan is gleeful. But when he was genuinely amused he was absolutely the essence of glee. There would be a holding back as the moment built and then a sudden leaning forward and swinging round of the torso as a vast, impish grin flowered, sometimes accompanied by an inarticulate shout of laughter. It was almost as if he was surprised by himself. It was my life's mission to provoke those moments.

I remember Imelda Staunton nearly killing him by telling him a story about my mother and an unfortunate incident with some hashish. I've never seen him laugh more, before or since. It was a bit like watching someone tickling the Sphinx.

One Christmas Eve party I had a sprig of mistletoe hanging up at home. I was loitering under it and turned to find Alan bearing down on me. I lifted my chin up hopefully. He smiled and approached. I puckered. He leaned in under the mistletoe and a sudden change came over his face. His eyes started to glitter and his nostrils quiver. He lifted up a hand, reached in and pulled a longish hair out of my chin.

'Ouch,' I said.

'That's an incipient beard,' he said, handing me the hair and walking off.

That was the thing about Alan. You never knew if you were going to be kissed or unsettled. But you couldn't wait to see what would come next.

The trouble with death is that there is no next. There is only what was and for that I am profoundly and heartbrokenly grateful.

The last thing we did together was change a plug on a standard lamp in his hospital room. The task went the same way as everything we have ever done together. I had a go—he told me to try something else—I tried and it didn't work so he had a go. I got impatient and took it from him and tried again and it still wasn't right. We both got slightly irritable. Then he patiently took it all apart again and got the right lead into the right hole. I screwed it in. We complained about how fiddly it was. Then we had a cup of tea. It took us at least half an hour. He said afterwards: 'Well, it's a good thing I decided not to be an electrician'.

I am still heartbroken that Alan is gone, but these diaries bring back so much of what I remember of him—there is that sweetness I mentioned, his generosity, his championing of others, his fierce critical eye, his intelligence, his humour.

Alan was the ultimate ally. In life, art and politics. I trusted him absolutely.

He was, above all things, a rare and unique human being and we shall not see his like again.

EMMA THOMPSON

Introduction

Moviegoers caught their first sight of Alan Rickman in 1988 in the action thriller *Die Hard*. At the age of forty-two, antediluvian by Hollywood standards, he was cast as Hans Gruber, a Teutonic terrorist who has seized control of a Los Angeles skyscraper and taken hostages. So far, so unremarkable; expectations for the film were modest and early reviews mixed. This, though, did nothing to dent its popularity at the box office, which grew by word of mouth. Starring Bruce Willis as an NYPD detective, Gruber's nemesis, *Die Hard* alerted audiences around the globe to the talented Mr Rickman whose devil-may-care interpretation of a psychopath stole the show and received a deluge of plaudits. As a *New Yorker* critic later noted, Gruber 'likes nice suits, reads magazines, misquotes Plutarch. No one ever looked so brilliantly uninterested while firing a machine gun or executing a civilian. As portrayed by Rickman, Gruber seems to possess a strange fatalism, as if he expects to lose, and to die, all along.'

Lord Byron quipped that after the publication of his poem *Childe Harold* he awoke one morning and found himself famous. The same might be said of Alan Rickman and *Die Hard*. Until then his career had largely been forged in Britain, most notably at the Royal Shakespeare Company, where, in 1985, he stood out in plays such as *Les Liaisons Dangereuses*. But before then, in 1982, he appeared on BBC television in a series adapted from Anthony Trollope's Barchester novels. Perfectly cast as the Reverend Obadiah Slope, a slimy hypocrite with a toe-curling smile, Alan demonstrated that he was as at home on-screen as he was on the stage. Global stardom may have taken its time to embrace him but there was surely never any doubt that it would eventually do so.

Blessed with a voice that could make fluctuations on the stock market sound seductive and a delivery that was hypnotically unhurried, it was obvious that Alan had a natural gift for acting. To him, it was more a vocation than a profession and he was irked by those who sought to disparage it and in awe of anyone who devoted their life to it. As his diaries demonstrate, acting is not merely a means of escape—in itself a wondrous thing—but a portal to a greater understanding of what it means to be human.

However, it was not how he originally sought to make a living. Born in 1946 in the London working-class suburb of Acton, Alan Sidney Patrick Rickman was the second of four children—three boys and one girl. His father, Bernard, was a factory worker who died when Alan was eight. It was thus left to his mother, Margaret, who worked as a telephonist, to bring up the family. He was educated at a local primary school and Latymer Upper, which counts among its alumni the actors Hugh Grant and Mel Smith.

He met Rima Horton when she was fifteen and he was a year older; both were keen on amateur dramatics. Friends for several years, they became a couple around 1970 and remained together for the rest of Alan's life, marrying in 2012.

On leaving school he attended Chelsea College of Art and Design, graduating in 1968. After a few years working as a graphic designer, he won a scholarship to the Royal Academy of Dramatic Art. It was at RADA, where he was recognized as one of the top students, that his future life was defined. As he wrote in 1974: 'Fine acting always hits an audience with the force and oneness of the well-aimed bomb—one is only aware of the blast or series of blasts at the time—afterwards you can study the devastation or think about how a bomb is made.'

Alan's apprenticeship was served in repertory theatre, in towns and cities like Sheffield, Birmingham, Nottingham and Glasgow, where he could hone his craft and gain experience. It was his equivalent of a Swiss finishing school and gave him a solid bedrock on which to build. It meant, too, that when he made the breakthrough as a star he never lost touch with his roots or his sense of perspective. Following *Die Hard*, he was in constant demand. First came *Robin Hood: Prince of Thieves*, in which he was unforgettable as the Sheriff of Nottingham: 'That's it then. Cancel the kitchen scraps for lepers and orphans, no more merciful beheadings, and call off Christmas.'

Always wary of being typecast, especially as a villain, his next role was in the romantic comedy *Truly, Madly, Deeply*, opposite Juliet Stevenson. She was one of a number of female actors whom he counted as close friends. In 1995, he appeared in *An Awfully Big Adventure*, an adaptation of Beryl Bainbridge's novel of the same title, and *Sense and Sensibility*, which Emma Thompson adapted from Jane Austen's classic novel. *Galaxy Quest*, a parody of *Star Trek*, which has since acquired cult status, required him to play an alien, while in *Dogma* he was an angel who has the voice of God. Alan was nothing if not versatile. Other roles included Rasputin, Anton Mesmer, Éamon de Valera and Hilly Kristal, owner of the legendary New York punk rock club CBGB. The first decade of the new century was devoted largely to the *Harry Potter* series of eight films. He played Severus Snape, the famously grumpy professor with a ready wit, a part with which he became synonymous, and which reduced considerably the average age of his burgeoning fan base. On learning that I was editing Alan's diaries, my eight-year-old granddaughter was suitably—and unusually—impressed.

As the diaries demonstrate, Alan was ever eager to test himself and rarely chose an easy option. He set his bar high and if he suffered fools it was through clenched teeth. He demanded as much of himself as he did of others. A case in point is the 1998 production at the National Theatre of *Antony and Cleopatra*, with Helen Mirren as the voluptuous enchantress of the Nile and Alan as her befuddled, besotted suitor. In another existence, he might have devoted himself to directing. His production of Sharman Macdonald's play *The Winter Guest*, in the theatre and as a movie, remained among his proudest achievements. *My Name Is Rachel Corrie* was another such highlight. Based on the journals and letters of the eponymous heroine, who was killed by an Israeli armoured bulldozer while protesting against the demolition of Palestinian homes, the show, which he co-wrote with the journalist Katharine Viner, was 'postponed' on the eve of its transfer to New York because of alleged anti-Israeli bias. It was a charge Alan vehemently denied. Less controversial was the movie *A Little Chaos*, about a gardener (Kate Winslet), who is employed by Louis XIV of France (Alan). Long in gestation, it finally appeared in 2014.

Given such a catalogue of credits, it might be assumed that Alan's dedication to his work eclipsed all else. Nothing could be further from the truth. He was devoted to his family and friends and was renowned for his gregariousness, kindness, honesty and generosity. Should anyone attempt to pay for a meal they were often rebuffed with two words, 'Harry' and 'Potter'. Few were the days he did not dine out. When not in London, he was often in New York, where he and Rima had an apartment, or the Tuscan town of Campagnatico, where they restored a house. Favoured holiday destinations were the Caribbean and South Africa. If not on stage himself, he was assiduous in attending shows in which his peers were appearing. It was his habit to take notes and offer advice, which was mostly received in the manner in which it was given. Brian Cox recalled that, while they were performing in the 1980 television adaptation of Zola's *Thérèse Raquin*, Alan told him that he was being 'rather slow in picking up your cues'. 'Alan,' replied Cox, 'do you realise how long it took you to say that? You call me slow. You—you are the master.'

Such testimony is legion, as was the love Alan engendered. It is worth bearing in mind that when in his diaries he is critical of friends it was born of love. Moreover, we can safely assume that what he wrote he was also prepared to say face to face.

Why he kept a diary is unclear. Diarists come in all shapes, and their reasons for recording their lives are similarly diverse. Some people want to bear witness to earth-shattering events while others are content to detail what appears to be trivia but which, with the passage of time, acquires enduring significance. We do not know whether Alan would like to have seen his diaries published but he did receive invitations to write books which could have drawn upon the material in them. What we do know is that once he started writing a diary it became addictive. From 1972, he kept a pocket diary in which he noted appointments, anniversaries, opening nights and addresses. Twenty-seven of these remain. In 1992, he started to produce a much fuller account of his life and work and bought diaries from a local stationer's which gave him a page per day to play with. These number twenty-six volumes, several of which are colourfully and beautifully illustrated. In addition, there is a notebook, kept from the mid-1970s to the mid-1980s, to which he added whenever he felt the urge. He made his last entry on 12 December 2015, by when he knew he did not have long to live.

Madly, Deeply is a distillation of more than a million words. It tells the story of what it meant to be one of the most fêted and admired actors in the decades immediately before and after the dawn of the third millennium. There are highs and lows, glowing reviews and bad, performances that were a joy and others when it seemed that everything that could go wrong did. After the applause and encores Alan would repair to a favoured late-night haunt where, surrounded by well-wishers and fellow actors, he would unwind and think about the show just gone and the shows yet to come. Reading this book is as close as we can get to being there ourselves and to encountering the real Alan Rickman. What a privilege it is to spend time in his company.

ALAN TAYLOR

Diaries

1993–2015

1993

13 JUNE

Quiet pleasure of preparing food for friends.

1pm Michael G., Christopher and Laura Hampton, Danny & Leila [Bertrand] Webb, Jane and Mark and Rima and Lily.

The sun emerged and we spilled into the garden.

20 JUNE

Patrick Caulfield [English painter] who says he hates painting but it's how he earns a living. 'The horror of walking into this small room. Important to do something. Doesn't matter what. Just something.'

21 JUNE

Arrive home, switch on BBC2—Pina Bausch.[1] The Real Thing. (After reading another article in *The Face* about Hot Young Things.) She has such a graceful determined truthfulness. And Robert Lepage[2] pays homage. Of course.

23 JUNE

12ish Midland Bank to talk of possible house purchase.

1ish David Coppard [A.R.'s accountant]—movies, taxes, arrangements, expenses. How does he retain his charm?

4ish Belinda Lang & [her husband] Hugh Fraser—Lily's birthday. But she's sick. Apparently I upset Elaine Paige on Election Day. My casual cruelty again.

---

[1] German dancer and choreographer (1940–2009)
[2] Canadian playwright (1957–)

24 JUNE

Finish Christopher Hampton's *Nostromo* script. How do you cram that book into a movie? Maybe he has . . . I don't know.

A morning on the phone—How few real conversations there are. Mainly a desire to present a moving target.

12 Gym. I'm not sure about all this.

4 Take Mum to Goldsborough Apartments. She's a brave soul. Feel myself *persuading* her. It's probably not the real answer.

25 JUNE

→ The gym.

This is hard work.

pm Talk to Christopher of *Nostromo*, *Sunset Blvd*—Andrew Lloyd Webber in tears some days ago. 'I'll postpone 6 months and bring in Hal Prince.' Trevor Nunn says I need 30 secs of dialogue in this scene. 'What about?' 'I don't mind.'

26 JUNE

6pm Coliseum. *Macbeth* . . . A strange mixture of Argentinian Fascism & *Dr Finlay's Casebook*.

Peter Jonas,[1] David Pountney [opera director] & Mark Elder [conductor] all saying au revoir [to English National Opera]. A world I know little about, sitting among fanatical applauding Tories. Jonas made speech about the Arts & NHS. I wanted to cheer. The audience went a bit quiet. The quiet of dissent.

28 JUNE

A race against time. Reading scripts before lunch w. Belinda and Hugh—traumatised because their nanny has given notice, but typically, Belinda puts a delicious lunch on the table, immaculately, on time, being told at 11.30ish it's 12.30 lunch not 1pm. She's been ill and in the studio and looks $1m.

10.30 *Sleepless in Seattle*—Halfway through I think 'I was in this movie.'[2]

1 JULY

Dinner with Richard Wilson—wonderful food at L'Accento—*Something's* certain.

Carol Todd calls . . . Delicate stages on Riverside.

Roger[3] calls. He's, shall we say, not hopeful.

---

[1] British arts administrator and opera company director (1946–2020)
[2] He wasn't.
[3] Roger Spottiswoode, British film director (1945–)

2 JULY

3.40am Awake trying to locate one worthwhile, nameable emotion that deserves this sleeplessness. The dream was of walking down one's own corridor at night, in the dark, trying to work out the geography only with my hands—finding doors that should have been locked, not.

(NB Hand this to the nearest amateur psychiatrist.)

4 JULY

am Driving through the Lake District to Ruskin's house.

5ish—Ferry back across the lake.

6.58 to Euston.

Really good to see Roger & Charlotte Glossop[1] again and now their wonderful, loving children.

They had a real, simple, generous, open attitude to work and life. Not a single deception or selfishness. They've built their dream and are living it. And giving it to others. Such an antidote to the shenanigans of this week.

5 JULY

12 Juliet Stevenson arrives—a flurry of lost keys, inability to get men on the phone etc.—in other words, as ever, late.

But it's fun to work through the show with two bright lights like these.

Juliet has, of course, been clamped.

6 JULY

3.30 Interview for Radio Sussex—this is why I don't want to do them any more. A man who talks of 'paddies' and thinks one-person shows are the salvation of British theatre.

8 JULY

3.30 Flight to Berlin.

Lance [W. Reynolds, producer] on the flight, Wieland [Schulz-Keil, producer] drives me to the hotel and then to the restaurant—I can't let go with them; I'm pulling on the reins all the time until they sign.

9 JULY

Fittings with Birgit [Hutter, costume designer]—instantly an angel full of the right ideas. Wigs & makeup need to be shown.

5.05 Flight to London.

---

[1] Husband and wife Roger Glossop and Charlotte Scott, owners of the Old Laundry Theatre, Bowness

7ish—script to Mary Elizabeth Mastrantonio and Pat O'Connor[1] wants to party; but for some strange reason they're off to Ireland for a week (they only just got here).

14 JULY

It seems sometimes to be in the stars that some days are peaceful and some are manic.

9am David comes to deliver a bookcase and mend a cupboard, Steve comes to fix the stereo, Janet comes to clean, Ruby [Wax] to show some outtakes and the phone rings and rings and rings.

If it isn't the Riverside lunch; it's not a Riverside lunch it's a dinner; did I read the Rudkin script?[2] Can we go to Stroud? Who can come, who can't?

8pm Supper with Louise Krakower [film director].

9.50 *Groundhog Day*.

Nearly. Not quite Capra. But a relief.

15 JULY

A day which led to Riverside shenanigans. And a 7pm dash with the proposal. Jane [Hackworth-Young] screwed up or screwed us in a big way. What's underneath this? If it turns out to be Jules Wright I shall screw *her* to every sticking place I can find.[3]

16 JULY

As for Riverside we wait and see. Ditto *Mesmer*.

I think Deborah Warner[4] has the right idea. Only do what you want to, make yourself a unique entity—then you get invited to Salzburg & Bruno Ganz. 200 extras and five horses to do *Coriolanus*.

---

[1] Irish theatre director (1943–)

[2] David Rudkin, English playwright and screenwriter (1936–)

[3] In the summer of 1993, Alan, together with theatre producer Thelma Holt and Catherine Bailey, a film producer whom he had known since RADA, attempted to take over the running of Riverside Studios in West London, which was in financial difficulties. Alan, as the most high-profile of the triumvirate, bore the brunt of the media coverage. Jules Wright, an Australian theatre entrepreneur who ran the Women's Playhouse Trust and had been a member of the Riverside board, made a rival proposal. According to *Time Out*, London's listing magazine, she had been offered the role of artistic director. What became known, inevitably, as 'Rivergate' grew increasingly contentious, culminating in a feisty encounter between Alan and Wright (28 November 1993). In the end, the ambitious bid by Alan and associates was rejected, Wright withdrew hers, and William Burdett-Coutts, who made his name running the Assembly Rooms at the Edinburgh Fringe, was appointed director of Riverside Studios, a position he held for twenty-seven years.

[4] British theatre director (1959–)

18 JULY

Home to phone message saying Jules Wright has been given Riverside and then a call from Roger Spottiswoode telling me the latest *Mesmer* horror stories. Is this a big test? What sense can one make of the Riverside situation? I am writing this not angry (yet—that will arrive in a big way if we discover anything untoward) just numb from the endless pursuit and advancement of the mediocre in this country.

19 JULY

Most of today picking up the telephone receiver.

Mesmer seems to be breathing again. A cheque has been sent—was it signed? Misspelt? Something must delay it, surely.

Jules Wright has Riverside, no she doesn't, yes she does, were we read? Maybe not. Is [Jane] H.-Y. a traitor or innocent stroke power-mad? At all events it's not coming to us although we don't know if there's any money to run the place.

20 JULY

Maybe today a corner was turned and for that I guess I'm grateful in the middle of all this shite.

Malcolm & Sweet Pea [assistants to Thelma Holt] were so practical and focused—it was very moving—they'd laugh if I said so to their faces.

Somehow we got through it all—all those letters without mentioning Jules Wright by name—as yet. Then Thelma returned and the room is filled with humanity and good humour.

Returning home I discover that J.W.'s proposal is all of 4 pages. 'Put-up job' says Rima without a pause. Her certainty is often hilarious.

10.30ish—Billboard Cafe. Juliet [Stevenson], Mary McGowan, Lindsay Duncan & [her husband] Hilton McRae. Acquainting them of the day's facts creates focus, strength & purpose. We'll see, we'll see, we'll see.

Somewhere in here *Mesmer* careers crazily on. Faxes, phone calls, entreaties, promises, demands. Questions. Somehow no answers. Plus I'm offered £50,000 a week to do *Slice of Sat Night*[1] in West End. MAD MAD MAD.

21 JULY

More phone calls.

Letters being answered.

Thelma got tough.

---

[1] *A Slice of Saturday Night*, musical by the Heather Brothers

Time Out continues to ferret.

Michael Owen[1] backs off.

Andreas [A.R.'s personal trainer] shows me a daunting new regime for the gym.

22 JULY

To the gym and then take Arwen to lunch—Café Tempo, King's Road. Can't really begin to deal with how easy it is for me and how hard for her to walk up a flight of stairs. The image of her flat on her face on the floor of the taxi will stay with both of us. Thank God she, me and the taxi driver could laugh.

23 JULY

Diaries—funny things. Having to record people as a collection of initials. For the record J.W. = Jules Wright; a dangerous, manipulative person.

26 JULY

And Riverside brews on . . .

A letter from a friend of J.W. in the *Standard*. Write the reply on the plane. Just shows how quickly it can be done. The prospect of seeing Peter Sellars'[2] production of *The Persians*, a sudden 'yes', some phone calls and I'm out the door with a hold-all and on the way. To Salzburg.

The journey to Heathrow really is the best.

Then to Munich, and cool hi-tech airport. 100 miles of corridor later and there is a driver. £100 later and I'm in Salzburg for the last ½ hour of *The Persians*. Now I'm mentally photographing every second to make it count. Fifi [Fiona Shaw] is there at the end. It's always good to see her. She's one great Yes to life.

27 JULY

To Festspielhaus for *Coriolan*. Staggering venue. Hildegard's[3] model now full, unbelievable size. A sudden strange desire to be in it. And we almost are, in the 3rd row. 200 extras, horses, flames; epic but ambiguous too. Bruno Ganz is the one for me. Seems not to be an actor at all. At the party I meet him. Shy, courteous, quiet, slight. Of course. Peter Stein[4]—a whole ball game of his own. As Deborah found. Brave show. Cowardly audience.

---

[1] Arts editor, *Evening Standard*
[2] American theatre director (1957–)
[3] Hildegard Bechtler, German set and costume designer (1951–), wife of Bill Paterson
[4] German theatre director (1937–)

28 JULY

Deborah and Fiona Shaw have certainly found their power. But there's a sense of panic somewhere—what do they do with it? Stories of Stein's abrasiveness when confronted by Deborah's self-sufficiency.

Sod the diet—Bratwurst, potatoes & sauerkraut for lunch. Mozart museum—the girl playing the instruments pretends to speak French badly in order to surprise us how *well* she speaks it. And English.

Find Fifi & Deborah at the theatre. Have tea. F. worrying about her production of *Hamlet*, her film career, our agent, the play she's due to do at the National Theatre. I can see reasons for all the concerns but what a waste of her extraordinary energy. Talk of this and more with Catherine Bailey on the plane. A remarkable woman. Hits the ball smack in the middle of the bat, but all heart too. Home. Did that all happen?

29 JULY

Back home to articles in *Time Out* and the *Evening Standard*. All very energising and focusing. If all the energy and focus can shift to the other side of the river then, great. Keep talking.

Jurassic Park—what the hell is the plot? Great dinosaurs.

→ 8pm *Lust* w. Denis Lawson. Reminded me a lot of *Lock Up Your Daughters* in 1974. Even *less* direction here.

30 JULY

Spoke with Stephen Tate—*Observer*. Talking with journalists always leaves me feeling uneasy and a little like those tribes who don't like having photos taken because they're giving away their souls. But today there is a strong sense of colliding with one's destiny.

31 JULY

Woke up from a dream where Rima and I are going for a week's holiday in a remote country cottage. To get there first we have to tramp through a muddy field to a farmhouse—on the right there is a kind of hen coop. Our instructions are to shoo the hens off the mattress they are running around on, shake it & take it off to the cottage. As we approach, we can hear après-sex giggling. We peer in. There in the straw are a pair of 75-year-olds, dressed, but lying amongst the eggs and hens, grinning.

Work with Tara Hugo [American singer and actor] for her New York opening. I do love transforming things like this—or maybe it's just pointing a spotlight on a fine talent with more accuracy. At all events the process is a mystery to me. Where does the insight come from? Part of it is cumulative, but most of it is a gift still shrouded in mist.

1 AUGUST

Riverside report in *Observer*—lazy journalism so the points are more bluntly made than they should have been.

3 AUGUST

10.30 To ICM [talent agency] to sign deal memo. I wish these things were more about common sense—it's embarrassing to think that discussions have to take place about the size of one's name, whether they'll pay for the laundry, how many bottles of Evian water etbloodycetra. Of course, if they try to rip me off . . .

Then Rima and I go shopping for her Jamaica trip. Keep feeding her and obtaining regular cups of coffee and it's fun in Knightsbridge.

5 AUGUST

Kristin Milward [old friend of A.R.'s from RADA] comes for lunch. Now I think it's time for something drastic. If there's no magic pill, then maybe she should work in another country. England does not recognise or reward her qualities.

8 AUGUST

At home watch last part of *Kinnock*. Neil is wrong to feel such failure. With the same instinct which told me too that he would lose the April 9th election I also know that this country had developed such a meanness of spirit—a refusal, however unspoken, to think of others' problems, that the balance was tipped and he could have done *nothing* more. He has made it possible for others to win by the hugest personal sacrifice.

Livingstone,[1] Skinner[2] et al. are wrong because they spend their lives so consumed by politics they cannot put their fingers *truly* to the wind. Their professionalism makes them lose touch with their innocence.

9 AUGUST

4pm to Thelma's office for preliminary chat about Riverside before N.N. arrives. Present—Thelma, me, Claire, Margaret Heffernan,[3] and after a while Catherine Bailey. We discuss avenues of approach and Margaret is her

[1] Ken Livingstone, British politician (1945–)
[2] Dennis Skinner, Member of Parliament for nearly half a century (1932–)
[3] American entrepreneur (1955–)

always blindingly clear self. Doorbells ring, people enter and leave without seeing each other, which is clearly the object, if not the plan. N.N. is basically saying—take Riverside off our hands and it's yours—if you can manage without funding and at a peppercorn rent. He's an accountant. Theatre stories (Thelma!) don't resonate. At one point we are sitting plotting around an invisible cauldron as Ian McKellen stops at the door. Thelma immediately enlists him and nearly says too much too soon.

10 AUGUST

To Vienna for costume fittings and I didn't even argue. I should have.
     Coffee and lemon cake in famous Austrian or Viennese coffee house.
     Back to London.

12 AUGUST

Damning and fairly unprecedented report in *Standard* re Riverside. Talk about things fadging.
     3 Roger & Gillian[1] to talk of the movie script. [Dennis] Potter reluctant to rewrite.

15 AUGUST

All afternoon—the simple but back-breaking pleasure of creating a flower-bed.

16 AUGUST

7.45 *Gormenghast*—Lyric Theatre.
     Wonderful things, but no wonder I never read the book. For fans.

17 AUGUST

3pm Doctor for film insurance check-up. Ironic, with this streaming cold. He throws me by asking which character I would choose above all others to play. There's no answer, because as ever, it all depends on the script.

19 AUGUST

A phone call from Peter James [theatre director] wanting some assurances for the Riverside board meeting tomorrow. Strange not being able to say everything to an old friend.

20 AUGUST

9.30 Royal Festival Hall with Belinda Lang and Mary Elizabeth Mastrantonio for Steve Reich concert. Almost dreading some esoteric wank—it turns

---

[1] English actor Gillian Barge (1940–2003), playing Frau Mesmer

out to be real food for thought on many levels. Of how many pieces of music can it be said 'it has genuinely clarified the Middle East conflict for me'?

Belinda had come prepared with a mental list of things to think about if it had been dreadful.

21 AUGUST

8 → Lindsay Duncan & Hilton McRae with R. & Robin Ellis[1] & Caroline Holdaway [designer] & Fatima[h Namdar, photographer]. I guess we must have had a wonderful evening—because when we left after eating great food, talking, talking and standing round the piano singing Dylan etc. together it was 3am.

22 AUGUST

Walking out of the Caprice to find a cab, cat and mouse with a photographer who clearly wants a 'pissed off' picture. He certainly has a 'pissed off' back of my head.

23 AUGUST

am—and now it's William Burdett-Coutts for Riverside. He wants to talk. OK, but at this point—about what, whilst that board is still in place . . .

Pat O'Connor comes over—I've spoken with Christopher Hampton again about *Carrington* and I really don't know whether or not to do it.

8pm to Hampstead for *Marvin's Room* with Allan Corduner[2] and Dalia.[3] Another of those American plays which *insist* that you feel something. I don't think anger & frustration is what they had in mind. My mind feels totally shut down by the experience. Alison [Steadman] & other fine actors compromised by atrocious direction.

24 AUGUST

1pm Patio, lunch with Diana Hawkins & Sue D'Arcy re press for *Mesmer*. This side of it, I'm told, is necessary. It is also, finally, humiliating. Not their fault—actors as product.

30 AUGUST

10am-ish because of the [Notting Hill] carnival barricades and no taxis → Kensington Hilton and first rehearsal of *Mesmer* . . . Script obstacles to be overcome but encouraging to see how often Potter is on the button.

---

[1] British actor (1942–)
[2] British actor (1950–)
[3] Dalia Ibelhauptaitė, Lithuanian film and opera director (1967–)

1 SEPTEMBER

9.30 Rehearse.

At least Roger is completely transparent—if there's a problem it inhabits his entire frame—and with Mayfair[1] etc. there are problems . . .

2 SEPTEMBER

8.15 To Laura Hampton's apartment. Champagne & stories of family skulduggery and on to—

9pm Norma Heyman [film producer]—*Sleepless in Seattle* party. Names, names—Meg Ryan, Nora Ephron, Neil Jordan, Andrew Birkin,[2] Michael Caine, Alan Bates, Edna O'Brien, Stephen Frears, Lindsay & Hilton, Jon Robin Baitz.[3]

5 SEPTEMBER

2.30 To Mum.

She's tired and needs a holiday. But always levelling. I'm off to Austria— she needs a new adaptor for the sewing machine.

6.10 Fly to Vienna. One of those flights. Baby crying = tense mother. Drunk English businessman = resentful stewardess etc., etc.

6 SEPTEMBER

1pm Auditions for character sensitively known as 'Bosom'—2 out of 3 actresses turn up with 'Bosom' well to the fore. Humiliating for all concerned.

2.30 Find Simon McBurney[4] & Gillian Barge and Richard O'Brien. Simon's friend Johannes takes me on a whizz-tour of Vienna & its coffee houses. Also tells me of time when seven friends committed suicide (3 of them at one funeral after another).

8 SEPTEMBER

First day's shooting *Mesmer*.[5]

There are Slovaks from Bratislava and Hungarians. The crew is German-Hungarian. I miss not being able to barter rudenesses. Am reduced to being an observer. Apart from continuing script negotiations.

---

[1] Production company
[2] English screenwriter (1945–)
[3] American playwright (1961–)
[4] English actor (1957–)
[5] Directed by Roger Spottiswoode, with a script by Dennis Potter and a score by Michael Nyman, *Mesmer* tells the story of the eighteenth-century maverick physician Franz Anton Mesmer, who used unorthodox healing practices based on animal magnetism.

11 SEPTEMBER
Rehearse with actors for 'Afflicted' scene. Austrians, Germans and Hungarians. The scene is, thankfully, moved to a more helpful location.

Lunch with Johannes and Simon and on to the Annie Leibovitz exhibition—she's a very good graphic designer with an even better address book; her earlier pictures of parents, grandmother are infinitely more interesting. Hundertwasser,[1] however, is an architect of delight. The museum & the apartment block are extraordinary . . . He creates uneven floors to give a 'melody of the feet'.

12 SEPTEMBER
Major 'Afflicted' day. A spat with the producers who, of course, want something for nothing—in this case the Austrian actors (although the Hungarians are paid a pittance because their standard of living is so much lower). Interestingly, I am accused of blackmail—I pointed out that a ton load of moral blackmail would descend on my head to perform (not to mention the fact that so far I am working unpaid).

This makes the atmosphere sound blacker than it is—no, just boys will be boys.

The work is exhausting but pretty good. I suspect that one of the Hungarians is better than most if not all of us. He certainly solved the opening of the scene.

Lunchtime meeting with Roger brings uncomfortable déjà vus.—'Alan is undirectable'—Howard Davies.[2]

Dinner at MAK—Roger Spottiswoode and Amanda Ooms[3] are clearly having a fling—I hope the old keel is kept even.

13 SEPTEMBER
Kissing scene.

Too much like a commercial—no danger.

More Afflicted. There are some terrific actors in this group—particularly amongst the Hungarians. English actors just don't *look* like that. It makes me want to hand over the costume and say 'Let me watch *you*.'

An interesting discussion w. R.S. & W.S.-K. They say 'Great! We got this, that & the other'; I say, 'Yes but totally on the level of actors'—not with our 'concentration and command' (it's in the text for fuck's sake, don't they *ever* read it?).

---

[1] Friedensreich Hundertwasser, Austrian visual artist and architect (1928–2000)
[2] British theatre director (1945–2016). He worked with A.R. early in his career at the RSC.
[3] Swedish actor (1964–)

14 SEPTEMBER

No process in the afternoon and so—the spatzing is unavoidable. I want to be *directed* not whinged at. (But I think I must be a bit of a nightmare with my 'certainties'.)

Rima phones to tell me Harold Innocent[1] died at the weekend. A piece of my life—and in a way it's selfish to at least be sure we had met and talked recently.

15 SEPTEMBER

Called in from day off . . . Argument I still don't understand with R.S. The scene plays as I had imagined (more or less). Does that mean he didn't get what he wanted or that I was right anyway and hadn't explained myself properly?

16 SEPTEMBER

Long scene—major concentration required. Someone is watching over us meteorologically if not financially. The sun shines, the wind blows—on cut. A bit frightening really. Mesmer—is he monitoring this? The battle goes on for me *not* to.

17 SEPTEMBER

Last day in Vienna for the time being.

A request to write about Jules [Wright] for *Vogue*. I don't know about that. What does it smack of? Having to be more than honest in print. Why?

Birgit's party—she is a genuinely beautiful person in every way. Looks, spirit, the whole shebang. Amazing food. Some good talk. A bit of a sense of being circled by descending wasps, mosquitoes, feathers, brick walls etc. But it was 2.45 when I got back so it must have been good.

Chris [set designer] thought I was 36. I did not disillusion him.

19 SEPTEMBER

Fly to Berlin 7pm. Walk around town . . . Get lost . . . Time stands tapping its feet on days like this. Waiting to go somewhere else and when you get there, not know where you are.

21 SEPTEMBER

To . . . breakfast with Amanda, Gillian and Wallace Shawn[2] who we found in the lobby. He's doing a show tonight at the Berliner Ensemble. He talks in his

---

[1] English actor (1933–1993)
[2] American actor and writer (1943–)

haltingly carefully phrased way of Eastern Europe, of people coming up to him in the streets of Manhattan and offering him film parts in Amsterdam, or asking him to read a script. He talks of his office suffusing him with guilt whenever he enters it—some scripts have lain there since '86—and of going out to buy a piece of paper when he has to write [a] letter—and he talks of never making an unplanned move.

22 SEPTEMBER

One of those days—a bit too tiring—vaguely stressful—I'm always surprised at how easily I can buy into that instead of working against it. It's the dog with a slipper syndrome. Difficult scenes in the morning because of an actor with no real process and R.S. with no notion of teaching him.

Roger tells me Wieland called him from his meeting in London—there were 23 lawyers present, all on our payroll. Wingate[1] liked the footage—are we supposed to be pleased or is it OK for me to feel insulted that he wished & was allowed to see it?

Dinner with Gillian Barge—one of the greatest pleasures of this film is working with her (finally) and getting to know her.

23 SEPTEMBER

The devil was crawling around today making me antsy. Tiredness is a factor along with a lack of real discussion which is why it was well-motored by Simon this afternoon.

The madness has to be located and shown.

Meanwhile the dreaded press and even in the unit publicist the unstoppable desire to compare one job with another—was X more difficult than Y? No, X=X and Y=Y. Don't be lazy.

Tonight I was fuming. The co-star[2] is tired from something or other, so rehearsals are curtailed. No discussions.

24 SEPTEMBER

And a continuation today. Extraordinary how the set picks up and absorbs and dances lightly round an atmosphere especially between two actors. Difficult scene, fury with the director not abated. So—a decision to remain apart as much as possible = chill factor on set all day.

---

[1] Roger Wingate from Mayfair Entertainment, one of the film's backers
[2] Amanda Ooms

It's wrong when an actress is treated like a piece of Dresden rather than a professional.

But we finish one scene and rehearse another. With difficulty. But we get there. Onward.

27 SEPTEMBER

A day at the top of a flight of stairs—throwing Simon [McBurney] down, or sliding down the bannisters (and ripping my pants).

10ish Gillian finished so late and is being called early—I have to talk to someone. This is slavery (exploitation). Supper with her and Jan Rubes,[1] Czechoslovakian, charming and likes dirty jokes.

28 SEPTEMBER

A day almost entirely on my own. Walking along Kurfurstendamm to buy shoes (the wrong ones) and then Savignyplatz for some more (the right ones). Finding a new part for the electric razor and speaking German to do it. Photographing the bag lady who was sitting by a ton of rubbish (not hers) in plastic bags . . .

Gillian called when she came back from the set—we had room service in my room & talked of Stratford & Stratfordites (and of her not being able to spell Oedipus in a P. Brook rehearsal).

29 SEPTEMBER

I think it's called a relatively jolly day on the set.

A letter from Amanda—heartfelt words. A rushed but honest response.

Paris Bar after work. Gillian, Tom, Roger, Amanda, Simon.

(1) There are difficult days ahead on this script. (2) There are cross-currents amongst these people that would confound a mini-series. Or a Feydeau farce.

1 OCTOBER

In the end some very good work is on film, but blood is on the carpet. I fought, kicked and screamed—or rather some mesmeric force did the kicking and screaming—I *hope* in protest at the way we were being asked to 'make an effect work'. I don't know who is right or wrong. I am difficult, temperamental, uncommunicative; others are sentimental, effect-driven, undisciplined. But in the end something that is OK.

---

[1] Czech-Canadian opera singer and actor (1920–2009)

2 OCTOBER

Long, difficult day. The scene is designed around a lighting effect. I rest my case.

On arriving, I announced that today I was a marionette—I would be very well-behaved. Ironic laughter.

3 OCTOBER

A day off.

To the Xenon and *The Piano* w. Gillian & Tom.

For half of it I thought it was a slightly coldly accurate rendition of the script. But somehow it kicked in. Holly Hunter was wonderful. They all were. An inspiration and (currently) a vindication. I envy Tom the innocence of crying in the street afterwards.

4 OCTOBER

7pm pick up tickets for 7.30 show of *Clockwork Orange* at the Volksbühne. I can see what the cavils might be but they are so impressive. The atmosphere in the theatre is very charged—the actors are in physical danger quite often; buckets of blood, flour, water, whatever descend at regular intervals—and the anger at the East German sellout is transparent. What the hell do they do with *Lear* and *Othello*?

5 OCTOBER

Shenanigans is the alternative title to this film. Who the fuck is telling the truth???

Good work goes on. But so does the skulduggery. And I'm *so* tired of it.

An interview with *Cinema* tests one's responses more than somewhat . . .

6 OCTOBER

Sitting in front of a mirror all day. However much I look at my face under such circumstances I never see the full horror that photographers manage to capture. How do we edit that out? I rake my features looking for all the bumps, cavities and lines that litter the contact sheets . . .

Tantrums at the end of the day—pushed into a way of playing a scene by not rehearsing it first, and then having an instinct sat on rather than explored.

7 OCTOBER

The sound stage next to us is shooting *The Neverending Story*—how ironic.

6pm Wrap Berlin party.

–Good to dance again.

I seem to be functioning in short sentences today.

9 OCTOBER

Talk to Rima, bless her, she always can make me laugh.

10 OCTOBER

8.15 *Last Action Hero*.

I went with no axes grinding but it's a very bad movie . . .

11 OCTOBER

Sometimes the emotional commitment to a piece of work keeps itself invisible, often for a long time, until it is threatened—and then complete immobility happens—a kind of nervous exhaustion descends.

I walked to a shop, had a coffee and a sauna, listened to some people on the phone—all so defensive, all hiding their own untruths.

13 OCTOBER

8.15 pick-up for 9.50 flight to Vienna and car to Sopron—Hungary.

Pleasure at pastures new is very much tempered by the tensions and insecurities attached to this job—every day there's some new financial drama—will I ever know the truth underneath all this? However the town has a great, impersonal beauty—it knows it has been here forever, it tolerates the twentieth century with its teenagers in backpacks and jeans. After all it knew satins and bows.

The snooker was fun. On every level Miss O swims in selfishness. What price freedom and personality when there's little curiosity?

No sound in the street. Odd moments of plumbing in the hotel. A dog barks. The wind blows. 2am wide wide awake. Why am I having to fight idiotic battles about hotel rooms?

14 OCTOBER

Sitting in a carriage in the wrong order in the wrong environment, and a scene which should be unbroken is done in two parts.

Still no answers, still no certainty. And today, no food. The town remains beautiful, the hotel—especially the bathroom—makes me think of visits to my grandmother. No matching towels in those days. Other crew members are not so lucky—they've gone out to buy shoes to wear in their showers.

What the hell has this year been about? The push to direct? The punishment is beginning to feel a little unrelated to the crime.

15 OCTOBER

A carriage ride with a coachman who learnt today how to drive . . .

Some hilarious moments. Pizza Bar lunch in full 18th C. costume.

16 OCTOBER

Splat! Most of the day face down in the mud. Refreshing in an odd kind of way.

17 OCTOBER

Today was a real Sunday in Sopron. Quiet streets, church bells. I didn't go on a driving trip—I was v. well-behaved and worked. And walked—to the cemetery. A very moving place—here family is everything. The poor graves with simple home-made wooden crosses as powerful as the granite slabs. Every corner were the women. Cleaning, planting, looking after their memories.

18 OCTOBER

Wet. Wet. Wet.

Cold. Cold. Cold.

Carriages, freezing hands, crane shots.

Cold banana soup for lunch.

Shorter days, earlier darkness. Home by 6.30.

19 OCTOBER

Caroline Holdaway and I play out Ball Scene. Having woken at 3am and stayed awake until the 5.30am pick-up—the brain and the mouth were not on the best of terms. And it rained. And cars honked and people talked. But we did it—Caroline at all times impeccable manners and good humour. I did not.

Catherine [Bailey] & the BBC [*Late Show*] crew arrive. Odd mixing friends and work like this. It means extra control but extra requests.

To the Forum with a whole bunch and then the Billiard Club. Talking with Roger—my selfishness when working takes my breath away—Elemér[1] has his own story this week. Others have their vulnerable points. Where on earth do I get this appalling certainty?

20 OCTOBER

Thinking of what I might say to *Omnibus*/Whatever—British theatre (Establishment) is marooned behind the proscenium. For the most part in the hands of untrained, smartass young directors who have ambitions but no heart or politics and whether they realise it or not are being steered to success by their actors and designers. They cast only from preconceptions so that there is no

---

[1] Elemér Ragályi, Hungarian cinematographer (1939–)

real challenge to the actor whose performance has been predicted from the outset. This applies everywhere—I would be happy to pick up the gauntlet if only someone would fling it. Few people are prepared to ask any really big questions of us (actors) without the security of thinking they already know the answer.

21 OCTOBER

The day is like a media circus—

1. David Nicholson from *The Times*—seductive questioner—his pupils have different sizes—really, he wanted the dirt on religious mania.

2. Murray H.—took photographs. (Boring ones.) NB Snowdon.

3. Someone from *Sight and Sound* ferreting.

4. The Crew on the Hunt.

We play the scene.

We also have a screaming match about the fact that the extras are given rolls as a midday meal. Food was duly served in the evening.

22 OCTOBER

A let's-get-it-done day threaded with Amanda's unhappiness and tiredness—Blanche DuBois is in a hazy distance.

The BBC2 crew films on and on. Till 2am when we went back to the Billiard Hall.

23 OCTOBER

To the Hilton and the Film Ball.

Ghastly. These things always are except on the people watching level. Found David Thewlis, met Julie Brown[1] (*Raining Stones*). Oases in a very noisy desert.

Playing hard-to-get = a practised innocence. I suppose it's better than a complicated involvement. Certainly with nightmare woman.

24 OCTOBER

My back is killing me. Seven weeks of accumulated tension is finally expressing itself.

25 OCTOBER

Why was I dreaming about having got myself a Saturday job at Woolworth's??

26 OCTOBER

The Diva quotient is stepped up. Not however the Hungarian actresses. Thank you once again the west. The Hungarians first commit. However inorganic and time-wasting the process may be.

---

[1] American actor (1958–)

Later at the Forum we all start to relax—*wonderful* goulash supper and then at a strange nightclub (six customers and a girl in UV bikini) it all comes out. They really were never talked to (they did, however, put up huge barriers and stamped a bit—*not* the Hungarian thing). But basically it is all about trusting actors and allowing being open—all the old things. Somehow, Roger takes it all smack on the chin. And then says 'I have learned something tonight.' *Infuriating*, but extraordinary in his openness.

27 OCTOBER

And then you discover that he remembers nothing of last night.

We part in a flurry of flowers as I throw them into the back of their minivan. Lots of hugs and blown kisses—they were great, those women, and impossible. One moment inspired—the next, screaming for makeup. 'Das ist immoglich!!'[1]

5 NOVEMBER

Shooting the last scene became something of a nightmare. Again—no process.

Some reserves of toughness and concentration groped for.

This crew is amazing. Such quietness and support. By 6.30am we were a small band and the room was filled with unnameable feelings. 'CUT' and Mesmer speaks no more.

8 NOVEMBER

The last day of shooting. Happy, sad.

I sat, breathing it all back in. I spoke a bit, forgot to stand up, forgot to have it interpreted—probably it was too short.

Monumentally moving was the flower given by every member of crew to Amanda and I standing at the top of a flight of white marble stairs as they fanned out below. At times I feel so close to that girl.

Goodbyes. Kisses. Hugs. People coiling wires. Unscrewing lamps. Loading. Kisses. Slamming doors.

9 NOVEMBER

6.40[pm] Flight to London. This time it feels like I've been away forever.

10 NOVEMBER

. . . to Chelsea & Westminster Hospital to see the newest child and Ruby's third. It is so hard to believe but she has done it. And this time (the child she

---

[1] 'That is impossible!'

was thinking of auctioning) there she is, breast feeding. The room is filled with flowers—something very grotesque from the orchid world from Joan Collins looms in a corner. I took her a ready-cooked chicken. She fell upon it.

11 NOVEMBER

Paris.

The most beautiful day. Blue, clear skies and clean hard sunshine. Out to Versailles—a scene I fought to keep in the film. Strange to see Beatie[1] walk towards us as Marie Antoinette in full sail. Roger is furious/sulking. He never wanted a French actor for Louis—Serge [Ridoux] really does have a strong accent. Roger breaks the lens cap on the BBC's camera . . . The scene is done for a crowd of tourists and to a backing of gunfire . . . A burst of late sun gives us an extraordinary last show and we move to L'Abbaye Hotel in Paris . . . Go to collect Roni[2] & Isabelle H[uppert] for dinner with the rest of us . . . A pleasant evening. Roger and I fittingly finish with a row about my character, my work methods, did they have sex etc., etc.

12 NOVEMBER

Another glorious day. Slightly messy, unfocused walking around. Buy some clothes for Rima . . . Grab a sandwich. Back to the hotel for a long, ghastly drive to the airport—nearly miss the plane.

17 NOVEMBER

3ish Royal Court Theatre Production meeting. Educative to hear people talk this way. Actors as meat on a West End slab. Main topic of respect—the investors (largely same people as in the room), the project, the risk. Hmm. The Royal Court.

18 NOVEMBER

6.45 Planet Hollywood for Juliet's David Bailey film [*Who Dealt?*]. Bailey is truly endearing even when the film breaks down. I would like to work with him. He's bonkers.

19 NOVEMBER

11ish Waldorf Tea Room w. William Burdett-Coutts, Thelma and Catherine [Bailey]. I felt particularly inarticulate because I felt I was staring at a com-

---

[1] Beatie Edney, English actor (1962–)
[2] Lebanese director Ronald Chammah (1951–), married to Isabelle Huppert

pletely unacceptable position. Everything negative—nothing to offer, just waiting for our input. Why should we?

21 NOVEMBER

3ish An attempt to see *Remains of the Day*. Sold out. A pleasant hour's mooching around Waterstones instead.

23 NOVEMBER

We go to Victoria Palace for an Arts Rally and then to the Houses of P to lobby MPs. Standing in the cold with Ken Cranham,[1] Sylvestra Le Touzel,[2] Stephen Daldry, Harriet Walter. Cameras poke around—the *Sun* pretends to be the *Guardian*. Gordon Brown comes out and says hello. Go in—why have I never visited before? Someone in a white bow tie gives you a green card to fill in. But now we're off to a committee room. Dennis Skinner speaks to us—brilliantly. My MP is not available.

7pm National for *Machinal* . . . Extraordinary staging of fitfully interesting and boring play with Fifi as Ringmaster. Some moments of her most brilliant work—some when a forklift could not have shovelled it off the page.

11 → Sandra & Michael Kamen.[3] Star spotting—Annie Lennox, George Harrison, Eric Clapton. Some live music. Left Ruby getting the info from Pattie Boyd . . .

28 NOVEMBER

To the Royal Court for 7.30 Max Stafford-Clark leaving show. Very well organised, brilliantly MC'd by Richard Wilson and Pam Ferris, full of good things especially Lesley Sharp's[4] piece from *Road*. Nice to see Gary Oldman on stage.

Afterwards the inevitable encounter with Jules Wright who seems, perhaps understandably, a touch crazed.

29 NOVEMBER

I go to Savoy—cameras, bucks fizz, Tim Spall (thank God). Eat bits of the meal, daringly drink a little white wine, watch the dessert melt. The generator blows. Waiting waiting. Miriam Margolyes tells Jewish jokes. Make speech—though so quiet you feel the criticism every second. Escape.

---

[1] Kenneth Cranham, Scottish actor (1944–)
[2] British actor (1958–)
[3] American composer Michael Kamen (1948–2003) and his wife, Sandra Keenan-Kamen
[4] English actor (1960–)

3 DECEMBER

12.45 → To Berlin for Felix Awards.

David Puttnam and Jeremy Thomas [film producer] on the plane. David shows me a speech he is to deliver. Being awake to opportunities = people went to *Jurassic Park* because they wanted to = don't make art films with no reference to audience. My protests re allowing an artist to have their voice fell on *very* deaf ears. I said he should get ready for the boos.

9pm Messages left—don't understand. Dinner at Florian with Wieland—he has a nimble tongue and a good heart. We move on to the Mirror Tent—very funny trio is performing. On leaving bump into Denis Staunton & friends including Michael Radcliffe. We tumble into a boys' own bar across the road for tequila. Talk of Burgess, Vidal, Volksbühne, Stein, Faust, Schiller, Baal and, at one point, Doris Day.

4 DECEMBER

The ceremony was its usual interminable self. The more one goes [to such events] the more ridiculous it all is. Except for the winners I guess—a base instinct that always responds when encouraged.

As do others, of course, in the face of all common sense. A considered 'no' should be controlling one but this devilish urgent 'yes' propels one forward—Food, Drink, Sex.

4am Florian with it all swimming around me as earlier were Antonioni, Wim Wenders, Louis Malle, J.-J. Armand, [Volker] Schlöndorff, Frears, etc., etc . . . Otto Sander[1] is a new friend.

6 DECEMBER

6.45 Taxi brings Mum, Pat and Michael to take us to Prince Edward Theatre for *Crazy for You*. Birthday outing, stupid plot, wonderful choreography, endlessly inventive and not at all corny. Of course it's all a bit of a Chinese meal.

9 DECEMBER

Who could write the script for today?

11.30 Graham Wood comes to take photographs for *The Times*—I'm not sure what I feel about these pictures. Sometimes you trust the process, sometimes not.

Ruby arrives—in a bad way. I can only keep talking, hoping to put up some skittles she can't knock down.

---

[1] German actor (1941–2013)

Emma Thompson phones—would I take part in a charity performance? R[obert] Lindsay is ill. Prince of Wales. OK.

8 St James's Palace in a tie. Rehearse in the taxi. A run-through—sort of. Do it. With panache. Prince of Wales is a good guy, I think. An awful lot of 'ushering' went on and I was steered in to meet HRH. Loathsome.

Savoy Grill with Emma. A very easy, enjoyable meal with an easy enjoyable person. She says 'fuck' a lot. Much laughter.

11 DECEMBER

1.30 [Ruby's daughter] Madeleine's party. Smarties ground into the carpet. Paper hats being snatched off little heads. Fights to blow out the candles. Grown-ups standing around a very low table watching the children at their first party, remembering theirs. As many tears and tantrums as smiles.

13 DECEMBER

And now the Fascists are in Russia.

While Rome burns—I go Xmas shopping with Ruby—she's on the mobile phone, looking at exhibits in the V&A, picking up earrings, putting them back, buying a Noddy toy for John Simpson, worrying about the service charge, window shopping while driving & over lunch the arrows of perception come shafting out. We talk, too, of the depression the world is in.

pm—writing Christmas cards—a strange exercise when there are about 150 of them and there's no time for a real message.

17 DECEMBER

8am Special delivery from Buckingham Palace. OK. But why at 8am? (Prince of Wales saying thank you.)

25 DECEMBER

Christmas morning is always a favourite time. The calm, coffee, orange juice, presents, quiet streets.

Around 12 Mum, Michael, Sheila, John, Sarah & Amy[1] come over and the turkey panic has already begun. The temperature goes up and down and eventually the bird is cooked in 3½ hours rather than the 5 hours we had expected. Turkey panic is replaced by potato panic. Vegetable panic lurks in waiting.

Somehow, it all (except the completely forgotten stuffing) arrives on the

---

[1] Michael is A.R.'s younger brother. Sheila is their sister and John her husband. Sarah is their brother David's eldest daughter. Amy is one of Sheila and John's two daughters.

table and is scoffed. Now for present panic. Does it fit? Do they like it? It does. They do.

Pictionary. Noise. *Morecambe & Wise* wind down.

27 DECEMBER

The central heating completely fucked. Yellow Pages brings rescue.

30 DECEMBER

3 hours' sleep. A sluggish taxi to Gatwick. An extremely welcome up-grade to first class to Antigua. I might have known we'd be punished.

I'm writing this in the restaurant at Antigua airport. Our flight was over-booked with a party of West Indian OAPs who were sitting very tight in their seats. So it's off with our luggage amidst a lot of 'This is completely unacceptable' and 'No, I don't want to stay in Antigua tonight.' Eventually we fly to St Kitts on the 7pm . . . and then we scramble on to a 6-seater for the 10 min ride to Nevis. Dinner poolside at the hotel.[1] Lots of Americans surrounded by bamboo.

On the plane watched *In the Line of Fire*—unbelievable *Die Hard* rip-off. Adversaries on the phone to each other, falling from a skyscraper etc., etc.

31 DECEMBER

Discovering Nevis. Drove round the island. Afternoon on a lounger. Script. Snooze. Coke. 7.30 Champagne in the Great House . . . At the end of this year, the feeling is of being a silent sandwich filling.

---

[1] Nisbet Plantation Beach Club

1994

Caribbean — *Mesmer* — Los Angeles earthquake — Golden Globes —
Ninagawa — Yukio — Anthony Sher — Harold Innocent's memorial
service — Los Angeles — Dublin — *An Awfully Big Adventure* — RADA —
Eddie Izzard — Michael Nyman — Nelson Mandela — John Smith —
Paris — *The Winter Guest* — Wimbledon — Paris —
Bettina Jonic — Tuscany — *Mesmer* in Montreal — Dublin — Vienna —
Dennis Potter's memorial service — Edinburgh and Glasgow

1 JANUARY

Nevis Island, Caribbean.

Properly blustery for a New Year's Day. When it got too windy on the beach
we set off to look for some lunch. Charlestown shut, locked, deserted. On
to the race track picking up a couple of totally incurious hitchhikers. At the
track, a huge rickety old grandstand, chicken being fried in what looked
like old buckets, an announcer saying 'I hope it'll be a good clean race.' A
13-year-old jockey from Antigua wins the second race. Rima wanted to back
Linda. She didn't. It won. Hilary the taxi driver buys us a couple of beers, a
guy realising I'll never reverse the car out of its gap does it for me. Coffee
and cake back at the hotel and a chat with Patterson the maître d', who's a
sharp cookie, and tells us restaurant and beach gossip. Dinner is Claus' West
Indian night . . . A good chat with the flute/saxophone player in the bar. He
plays some sweet jazz and gets a request for 'My Way'.

2 JANUARY

Time to explore after the faxed copy of the *NY Times* with its somewhat idiosyncratic crossword has been dealt with . . . The Beachcomber Bar with its
handpainted sign right next to the nightmarish 4 Seasons. America swallows
up another culture and turns it (literally) into a golf course with pedalos and
lounge bars and grills and happy hours. Coffee at the Fort Ashby—just about
standing up amidst the swamp vegetation—is a humanising experience
afterwards. Watch the sunset. Rum punch, palm fronds, leaves & sailing
boats in silhouette, peach-coloured clouds. A sight that never disappoints.

Lobster and steak Bar-B-Q. Talk to the Rhodesian mother and daughter. Rima wonders dreamily if we will meet anyone of a left-wing persuasion. Forced to converse with 'The Fascists' again over dinner. She likes Rima's voice, tells us of English people who admire Rommel. She's German and bemoans today's rain, though it means she's had 'a very good day' (nudge, nudge). He manages to look lascivious and coy at the same time, and says (as he did previously when socialism was mentioned) 'Sorry, I don't seem to be able to hear you—heh! heh.'

3 JANUARY

All day the push pull of sinking into the hotel life or kicking on and discovering the real island, the people, the surprises. I prefer a world that contains Sylvia's Fashions and Muriel's Giftique to one with a 4 Seasons and a Benetton at almost every stop sign.

4 JANUARY

A day spent chasing the sun and running from the rain. After that scariness with ignition key. The car wouldn't start, we're on a dirt track. Thank goodness for the man at Fort Ashby who just said (rightly) 'turn the handle a little'.

Alexander Hamilton Museum. I learnt a bit about soil erosion and why we plant trees, not much about AH.

1ish. Unello's on the Waterfront. Patterson spoke of the fabled slow service. Actually it was quite speedy, but the waitress did have to spit out a lump of ice before she could take our order.

Tonight the tree frogs were silent. What do they know?

8 JANUARY

7.15 Montpelier—excellent dinner. Would have been perfect if only I'd had a handgun for the other guests: 'Of course communism was always bound to fail.'

9 JANUARY

Packing. Tea in the Great House. Down to the airport. Faff around. Bucks are passed. An innocent chaos. Finally Carib Air takes Rima off for a 3 hour wait at Antigua airport. Poolside Bar-B-Q for one. An odd experience, eating alone. Doesn't bear too much repetition. Say some farewells to this extraordinary staff. They are all such individuals. Not cowed. Nisbet can pride itself on that if not on our bathroom.

10 JANUARY

The freedom and emptiness of waking alone in a king-sized bed.

Breakfast and a solo-completed crossword. Amazing. Pay the bill. A philosophical moment as one's life flashes before one—when was the moment crossed over into *this* territory of signing over *this* kind of cash. (For a holiday.)

Swim/walk along the beach. To the airport again . . . Man with impossible toupee under sky-blue cap. Group of sexy Dutch with impossible tans. Tightrope walking with delays—a calm lack of announcements . . . A rush to the Miami plane. Is the luggage on board? Meet Leonard Nimoy & his wife. Marcia Firesten[1] arrives in a pick-up truck. A moment to remember and heave the case out at the Sunset Marquis.

11 JANUARY

LA—and a morning with the remote control. The Lorena Bobbitt[2] trial is fairly compulsive viewing. Jaw dropping in its content and the coverage—the world is as it is and this trial fills the TV screens. Eventually a car is delivered and Marcia comes—we go for some lunch—the car is all automatic locks and windows and push buttons—and *too big*. One of those cars that drives you.

A wander round clothes and shoe shops—*everything*; roads, lights, noise, clothes is weird after 10 days in Nevis.

12 JANUARY

1pm Cousin Ian picks me up and takes me on a tour of his life in LA. His new coffee shop in the Valley, his house, his new interior design shop in Beverly Hills. They're a great couple he and Wilma and they deserve the best—there is a simple gutsiness and clarity about them that was a tonic today.

8pm Dinner at the Grill with Judy [Hoflund, A.R.'s manager] and Roger. He'll show the film tomorrow, is clearly concerned that I'll misjudge everything but he's full of tiny smiles and Judy is encouraged. But it's so hard to discuss anything with someone so defensive.

13 JANUARY

Marcia comes over with a copy of Ruby's *Hello* magazine—she gets away with it.[3]

---

[1] American actor (1955–)
[2] She cut off her husband's penis while he was asleep.
[3] 8 January 1994 edition, cover with Ruby Wax and baby: 'First Photos of Zany Comedienne at Home with Her Family and New Baby Marina'

Big Time screening room to see rough cut of *Mesmer*. So hard to watch. Everyone else seems to be very positive—I think there is a lot of work to do to find its rhythm, to reclaim its wit and craziness and also to make the story clearer. What I look and sound like is too late to import. I am in shock, really.

14 JANUARY

More sleeplessness thinking about the film. I need to spend time with Roger in the editing room. Talking with him, it seems at least a possibility.

11.30 To UTA [United Talent Agency] and talk with Judy. I'm feeling vulnerable which doesn't help, but we did try not to bullshit—and really land on what we think and feel about the film, and other projects around. They want me to stay in LA at the moment. I want to run to the bus stop. Talk about 'show business thins the mind'.

Tea and sympathy with Ant Minghella at the Hotel. He is doing similar mental spring cleaning.

16 JANUARY

6 To Francine's[1] to watch the ACE awards—a platform, people in black with their fucking red ribbons come on, go off, come on, go off, nominate, announce, present, say thank-yous. Same as all the others.

9ish. More people in black at the restaurant party given by HBO. Michael Fuchs[2]—rudeness to remember. Kiefer Sutherland says hello as does Brian Dennehy. K.S. seems to have a truly sweet nature.

17 JANUARY

Just before 9am—although time has lost all meaning since 4.30am when the world seemed to come off its hinges. The bed, the walls, the hotel, the street shook for what seemed like forever. I was filled with a strange mixture of total panic and total calm—holding on to the bed (stupidly) which was like a plant in a thunderstorm. When it all went quiet, some sort of rational thought returned, at the same time as the realisation that there was total blackness. I started to think of standing in doorways and then of finding some shoes. The shoes came first then the thought that I would look pretty stupid naked plus sneakers. I found (somehow groping around) some underpants—focusing bizarrely on whether or not I had them on back to front (who gives a shit!)—jeans & T-shirt. Then my brain kicked in and I

---

[1] Francine LeFrak (1948–), American theatre producer and philanthropist
[2] Then chairman of HBO, which—according to the *LA Times*—he ran 'like a Marine boot camp'. He was fired in 1995.

thought maybe I should get the hell out of there. Scrabbled around for keys, money, Filofax. People outside in nightwear, blankets, gathering in the hotel lobby. Eventually groped in basement to car and drove in black streets to see if Francine was OK. Came back down the hill to a hotel now producing coffee. The rest of the day was surreal. The staff somehow carried on serving, cleaning, hoovering. At lunchtime I drank cappuccino in the sunshine all the time not knowing what next? Continued all day as people approached the evening with a quiet tension.

18 JANUARY

Woke just in time for 3 or 4 major aftershocks. Whoopee. The irony of watching all this on TV is that the scenes of homelessness generally involve Spanish Americans and working people whereas at the hotel room service lives on . . .

19 JANUARY

Here was an odd LA day. Some kind of total exhaustion set in—probably from being held in a suspended animation like everyone else in this city. Watched 'quake broadcasts most of the day—eventually managed to turn my mind to a script. In the meantime a couple of 5.0 aftershocks focus the brain in half a second.

9.15 Le Dome—coffee and wine with Pam & Mel Smith. D.P. racy as ever. LA is depressing me.

21 JANUARY

9.30 Talk through the film with Roger. I'm still scared he'll knock the corners off . . .

1pm To the Bel Air Hotel (I wonder if it's too nice) for lunch with Christopher Hampton. Dan Day-Lewis jogs by, sweating. We chat about Jack & Pat O'Connor. Leave a rude note for Emma Thompson. Look at Christopher's room—the voyeur's lunch. My relationship with this town is an ever-changing thing . . .

22 JANUARY

Table tennis by the pool with Jon Amici (I can't keep up with the roller coaster of his amours) and then a swim.

Trip to the clothes shops (somewhat deserted) to buy something to wear tonight. Found and bought something to wear *not* tonight.

So it's off to the Golden Globes. An award show and all that that suggests. Genuinely funny speeches from the *Seinfeld* crew . . .

23 JANUARY

Too many rumours flying around about further earthquakes; too many nights alone to make the rumours dissolve. Somehow I've arrived at the decision to get on the plane to London. Emma Thompson's on the plane and gets me upgraded. So more nattering (the perfect word and she's easy, warm and lovable with it) and some fitful sleep.

24 JANUARY

The smallest bump or sound makes me jump. I've never known such delayed action. The wheels going down, the scrape of a chair. Emma and I have plotted some future work together. It has to be the right play at the right time and maybe we'll produce it ourselves. Which sounds like a sentence from *Swish of the Curtain*[1] but I'm jet-lagged.

Phone calls, unpacking. London makes me lethargic—jet lag aside. (Except when the scrape of a chair upstairs makes me reach for the nearest support. How long will *this* last?)

26 JANUARY

The phone call with [Roman] Polanski only confirms his charisma and intelligence—charisma on the phone! I don't know . . .

I hate it when my head, heart and aspirations are filled to the brim only with career. The rest of me hangs around like a jacket on the back of a door-knob.

27 JANUARY

The builders are here this week, plastering, repairing cracks, dust everywhere.

Desultory days. Can't think properly. A strange reluctance to make phone calls. Talking to friends feels like a duty.

Indecision is, as ever, at the root of it all.

And so many No's—Bee Holm's film *Awfully Big Adventure*, the Rankin film, *Jack and Sarah*, directing *The Tin Soldier*,[2] running Nottingham Playhouse. Fate is running around throwing hands in the air.

28 JANUARY

8pm *Dead Funny* at Hampstead.

More actors in search of a director. Authors should not direct their own work in the theatre. This could be wonderful if it put its Reeboks on. Supper

---

[1] Children's book (1941) by Pamela Brown
[2] Stage adaptation of *The Steadfast Tin Soldier* fairy tale by Hans Christian Andersen

with Beatie and Zoë [Wanamaker] afterwards. Treading carefully is OK, but things can still be hugely improved so I risk some fairly strong suggestions.

29 JANUARY
pm To Harvey Nichols to look for Rima's birthday gift. Too late, too rushed, too hungry.

6ish To visit Mum whose eye is daily improving. Then home for Rima's fave rave *Casualty* . . .

And then watch *Remains of the Day*—a gloriously crafted film with [Anthony] Hopkins quite wonderful. A lesson. Emma needs to work with someone who will ask her to dig rather than skim.

30 JANUARY
9am And the painters are banging about upstairs. I know they want to finish but . . .

31 JANUARY
Funnily enough, when the pressure's on I can either knuckle down in a major way, or pull the sheets over my head am, and pm hit the shops. Today—the latter. And scripts remain unread.

1 FEBRUARY
Builders, dust, dishwasher—repair, tiling, replastering, dust, dust, visitors.

2 FEBRUARY
And the jet lag goes on—this weird displacement of mind and body, the sudden sleeps, the 5am waking and know that it lasts for another couple of weeks. This body wreaks its proud revenge.

Paola Dionisotti[1] calls. A real conversation with a friend as opposed to the empty automated words that mostly drift down the telephone wires.

3 FEBRUARY
10.30 Paola picks me up and we trek out to Clapham and the *Peer Gynt* rehearsal room. Great to see Ninagawa's[2] smiling face and all the others with Thelma. Many a pang as I stand in the rehearsal room thinking what if . . . Ninagawa and I both say, 'Next time.'

4pm Stephen Poliakoff brings a new draft of his next film—walking up and down, throwing an orange in the air and completely unaware of either.

8ish Louise, Ruby, Ed, Stephen join Rima and I for one of our Henrietta's

---

[1] Italian-British actor (1946–)
[2] Japanese theatre director Yukio Ninagawa (1935–2016)

'Quick Cuisines'.[1] Brilliant fast food. And a fast evening. Ruby very much on form—achingly funny.

5 FEBRUARY

5pm to Oxford with Allan C. [Corduner] and Judy Parish to see Rowan Joffé's play. Jokingly, we say we are hitching ourselves to his coattails while we can—it may not be such a joke; the play is more of a movie script (his future?) but its underpinning is brave and original and Rowan himself hangs on to his charm.

6 FEBRUARY

More paint, dust, tea making.

Rima phoned. She was in a car crash. Instant fears. She's OK.

7 FEBRUARY

Rima comes by with a limp but she's in one piece! 'Thank God' are the only words that flow naturally.

6ish to Beach Blanket Babylon with Mike Newell to talk about *Awfully Big Adventure*—basically fine words can be found to justify the casting that satisfies the financiers. I dunno . . .

Supper amidst dust and furniture that's crammed and out of place. Unsettling.

9 FEBRUARY

11.30 Kristin Milward comes by—to Cherries [local café] to escape dust and drilling and fumes. She brings some Stollen or 'v. moreish cake'. She's still planning her Bosnia trip. We talk of maverick spirits.

Talk with Stephen Poliakoff to tell him I don't want to do his new film. I am so tired of saying no. *He* won't take no for an answer.

12 FEBRUARY

This space is filled with mops, buckets, cleaning fluids, dusters, vacuum cleaners and sweat.

13 FEBRUARY

8.30 Rik and Barbara Mayall's housewarming. A big Victorian novel of a house with nooks and crannies for days. Red balloons and hearts hanging everywhere—at one point, in a corner, is almost all of TV comedy. Rik, Ade Edmondson, Ben Elton, Ruby, Jennifer Saunders (Dawn & Lenny having left). They all have such focus (or seem to).

---

[1] *Quick Cuisine* by Lewis Esson, Henrietta Green and Marie-Pierre Moine (1991)

14 FEBRUARY

A layer of snow and England grinds to a halt. 'I won't be able to take any of the side roads,' says the cab driver, daring me to get in at all. 'Just take me to Knightsbridge,' is final enough for him to discover sheepishness and me— piss elegance.

Over there, England strikes again. Tara [Hugo]'s second opening at Pizza on the Park. No lights, no sound is the norm but NO pianist? We rehearse a cappella (in some ways simpler . . .).

Lunch at Harvey Nichols (avoid the vegetarian menu).

Some pm shop wandering.

8.30pm Back to P on the P. Tara takes 2 Beta Blockers and is just behind the beat all evening but the vowels are thrillingly relaxed. Otherwise . . . brilliant. Back to chez moi for cheese, gherkins, pickled onions and assorted fridge remains.

16 FEBRUARY

Last knocking from the builders. Could we finally say 'The dust has settled'?

Read Tony Sher's screenplay—it could make an amazing film but it's his film and does it have enough money & the right people attached?

Talk to Juliet—always the easiest thing . . . from Morocco to *Death and the Maiden*—would be easy to talk for hours (which of course she does). Hanging pictures at 2am—a welter of indecision and small holes all over the walls.

17 FEBRUARY

Spoke with Tony Sher. We'll meet next week sometime which means [I must] find some time to read it again. When I think of the yeses and nos and the maybes of this last year the mind boggles. All I have are my instincts but they are appallingly diluted and redirected by second guessing other people's opinions.

Today is the 6pm meeting with Stephen P. about his new film. I'm trying to be [as] honest and direct as possible but I'm not quite sure what it is I want to say. There's a big hole in my perceptions just now.

18 FEBRUARY

Ivy 12.30—lunch with Irene, Paul Lyon-Maris [A.R.'s agent], Mark Shivas [TV producer], talk of directing, producing; restaurant full of industry faces as London apes LA. Sometimes one could wish for an earthquake to hit the odd specially chosen table.

24 FEBRUARY

Flying by the seat of my pants.

A 10am rehearsal and already I'm watching the clock. At 11.15 get a taxi to Covent Garden for Harold [Innocent]'s memorial service in St Paul's. David G has organised it brilliantly. Sit down in the shivering cold with Barbara Leigh-Hunt,[1] Noel Davis[2] and Derek Jacobi. The church is full (thank goodness) and the service was perfect—funny, beautiful singing, lots of applause. Harold would have loved it. I read John Donne and Christy Brown—Harold might have wanted the Donne louder.

25 FEBRUARY

6pm 47 Park Street to meet Sydney Pollack. True warmth, intelligence, charm. I could happily sign on the dotted line.

26 FEBRUARY

12.30 Flight to Los Angeles. Arrive 3.30—Take Amanda [Ooms] to Polka Dots and Moonbeam for swift shopping blast—she has only sweaters. She, of course, could drop the proverbial sack over her head and make it sing.

To the Sunset Marquis—I'm now on a stay awake jag. Shower, whisky sour. Picked up for 8pm screening. Familiar faces, strange faces. *Mesmer* is now a love story and I seem to have one rhythm, one voice pitch, one expression. Truly disturbing what can be done in an editing room . . . And ultimately very depressing. And at 3.30am it keeps you awake.

27 FEBRUARY

Breakfast with Amanda—much mulling over the night before. As she says, you can make small critical noises but afterwards there's just a kind of emptiness.

28 FEBRUARY

10am Walk the eggshell-strewn path and talk about the film with Roger who is, understandably, defensive but open as ever. If he could bottle it, etc., etc.

1 MARCH

11.30 To UTA office to be filmed with Judy Hoflund—take 3 of walking in and saying Hi sort of stuff. Somewhere on tape there however is some actionable stuff about *Mesmer*.

---

[1] British actor (1935–)
[2] British actor (1927–2002)

2 MARCH

A hopeless phone-call with Roger who thinks I'm a crazed actor. His openness is matched by his stubbornness.

4 MARCH

9am To Greg Gorman [photographer] for a day of photos with Amanda and Frances and Diana & Greg's crew. Everything so professional; people working together to find something. And we did . . . The irony is the way the day was suffused by my growing anger at my work being compromised. Putting the clothes on again was strange enough.

Back to the hotel for a drink—stories of people telephoning to find I had checked out . . . Question marks to Judy . . . A stretch limo to the airport.

9pm Flight to London.

5 MARCH

4pm-ish Arrive home and start getting ready to go out, plus putting laundry in the machines and reading mail . . .

Taxi to Barbican for Ninagawa's *Peer Gynt*. How can I judge on this kind of jet lag? But some beautiful moments inside a general lack of resonance.

6 MARCH

1pm Belvedere with Rima, Ruby, Ed, Mr & Mrs Wax & the children. The full picture of Wax en famille is something no film script could dream up. Ruby sits laughing amidst it all—a great advert for Prozac.

Back to their house for tea and furniture-rearranging.

Belinda rings & offers Chinese food. Perfect. Horror stories of her play reduce me (along with jet lag) to silence. Rima makes up for it with brilliant defence of *family benefits*. I love her for that. Things balance out.

7 MARCH

9am Drive to Heathrow for 10.50 flight to Dublin. Waste £200 in upgrading my seat.

8 MARCH

First day on *Awfully Big Adventure*.

One of the hardest scenes comes first. Maybe not such a bad thing. Remember to keep a forward energy. Too much time means too much thinking. Alun Armstrong and Rita Tushingham already looking settled in. Not so wardrobe. Some frightful last minutery going on.

9 MARCH

Afternoon and evening we planned tomorrow's bed scenes and shot the first kiss. Georgina[1] brave and focused as ever. I constantly forget she is 17. No allowances *at all* are necessary. A phenomenal luxury.

Back to the hotel for a yawning supper. So tired I am sure I answered the phone in my sleep. Halfway through the call I came to, realising that I was talking to Gillian Barge and arranging lunch on Saturday. I must ask her for her recollections of speaking to a lunatic.

10 MARCH

All morning bonking (screen type), humping, exhausting. Life definitely not mirroring art—if anybody had sex in that position they would break their wrists second time out.

12 MARCH

Hangover.

3pm Motorbike lesson. 20 minutes to discover clutch control on something that reminds me of a big dangerous horse.

13 MARCH

7.40 pick-up. And off to the docks. A wonderful stormy day is perfect for the scene. Life only gets difficult when it's a question of the double not being a double. My attempt to save the day meant skidding off the motorbike and a swollen knee. Later face down twice in the water—freezing and, strangely enough, very wet. Plus much running & intenseness means writing this at 9.30pm and tired through to the bones.

Later—the back pains, the knee pain, the sneezing . . .

15 MARCH

Back to the docks to face a new devil—that fucking motorbike. It has a brain or certainly a will. It got fed up with my increasing confidence and started to rev itself with a higher gear completely unaided. But it's like a horse that wants to go.

4.45 Flight to London. Roger comes by with *Mesmer* tape. I watch on fast forward for an hour. We go for dinner to L'Accento. What was I eating? I was concentrating only on trying to explain myself. But this is a brick shit-house wall.

---

[1] Georgina Cates, English actor (1975–)

17 MARCH

9.30 Goldcrest [Studios].

Work the afternoon on an even keel and then an explosion as the end of the film descends towards Mills and Boon.

Finish at 6.45 and go to the Riverside for *3 Lives of Lucie Cabrol*.

18 MARCH

11am Marcia Firesten and Allan Corduner's wedding.

I managed not to laugh, mainly because it made me very reflective. Thank goodness religion didn't come into it, because that would have made me v. uneasy.

Back to Allan's for some champagne—I think he's almost believing it all—or enjoying the dress up, maybe.

20 MARCH

Dublin.

The day passes in the trailer. 'Oh well that's filming' is said all day. Called at 10.15am. Not used. Released at 9pm. Not enough to read. Trying not to overeat—all trousers are currently too tight. On a trip back from the food van with another black coffee there's Alan Devlin[1] coming towards me. Alun Armstrong joins us. 3 Alans. Devlin fights a constant battle with the bottle. Wonderful aggressive wit, vulnerability pouring from his eyes. 'Look at you two! Wearing dodgy coats and you're winning.'

Dinner later at the Trocadero with Roger. Easy & warm. What's the point of arguing? Should have asked to see all the cut material.

22 MARCH

All day in the Gaiety Theatre bar which is pretending to be a Xmas party venue. Balloons, streamers, turkey dinners, heat, dancing, playbacks, mimed fun. A good intimate chatty atmosphere as actors got to know each other, sitting ironically enough in the seats of the dress circle. Only our profession would put itself so mercilessly under the public microscope.

9.30 Watching the Oscars . . . Funny and serious by turn. We are our own worst enemies when we take ourselves *that* seriously. But then the world wants to film it. Apes picking fleas from each other.

---

[1] Irish actor (1948–2011)

25 MARCH

Captain Hook day. As I said to Mike Newell, there are 3 people operating here—me, Captain Hook & O'Hara all with different centres and mine (the one pulling the other two's strings) is definitely the shakiest. So, haltingly we move towards something that looks vaguely confident. Amazing to feel the 'audience's' confidence grow with you.

27 MARCH

. . . to work or to hang around for 5 hours is the question. Sometimes the silence of producers goes beyond bad manners and enters the realm of cowardice. Finishing a compromised scene at 10pm and being called at 7.15am should not go unremarked. Irritations fade by going to La Stampa. Bob Geldof is there who is all the things one thought—impassioned, articulate, attractive and (as you start thinking what *could* you be . . . ?) wasted.

29 MARCH

The BBC films all day. Beryl Bainbridge arrives. Caught napping with her. Competition has seriously reared its ugly little head. The character [of Captain Hook] distances me somewhat, but oh boy some of these young actors only have ambition to fall back on. A spiky, unsprung cushion.

pm Rima arrives and a big lump of me settles. Thank God we laugh together. She's here in time to see Patti Love[1] fly on as Peter Pan. Unmissable.

31 MARCH

Captain Hooking all afternoon and into the evening. It's a bit like bursting a balloon. Finally at 9.30 → Gate Theatre for second half of *The Seagull*—directing at its dangerous worst—good and wonderful actors floating, floating in nowhere land . . . Patti, Rima & I end up drinking tea at the hotel & discussing The Diva [Georgina Cates].

1 APRIL

The bug bites—a sore throat to win prizes.

Time to hang around in dressing gowns with room service.

Or sit in a corner in the lounge with some tea & chicken sandwiches.

Or watch TV and answer mail.

Or have dinner in the downstairs restaurant—'as a concession we are allowing 2 guests to share ½ bottle of wine'—Good Friday in Dublin.

The Diva bounds in—she's 'gone with Judy' . . . [2]

---

[1] British actor (1947–)

[2] She signed with A.R.'s manager, Judy Hoflund

6 APRIL

The alarm earns its keep at 5.30am and Rima's off to London. An hour or so of fitfulness and get in the taxi for Cork Airport and Dublin . . . To the hotel. To coffee with Conor McDermottroe.[1] To buy some Irish music tapes. To the Olympia. Hello to Prunella Scales—detailed, complicated actress and the person is slow to reveal herself, too. Like persuading some petals to open a bit more. There is a great deal of self-containment on this set. Ms Scales, Mike N., The Diva, me . . .

7 APRIL

Well here was a strange day—when a growing mood becomes a dangerous corner. Do the reverse shot with Prunella—walking into a close up flirts with awful self-consciousness.

8 APRIL

My shot of the day. Walk up a few steps. Stop. Turn. Look. Look away. The simplest tasks can make you feel like an unoiled robot.

16 APRIL

Some more [motor]bike-riding.

4.30 Tea at the Shelbourne with Carolyn Choa[2] and, eventually, Anthony Minghella. Talk of *Wisdom of Crocodiles*, and 4W[3] which is now No 1 in the States . . .

Later, Fiona Shaw and Denis and the 3 of us go to Café en Seine (Cafe Insane as Denis calls it). Very good time had by all. Fiona thinks I'm mad not to do the Rudkin film. Heigh ho. To the set . . . Everyone's in a nearby pub getting plastered. Dick Pope [cinematographer] is getting furious at the wasting of his time and talents.

17 APRIL

On standby all day. Which means room service, packing, wrapping gifts until 5pm → to the set for the unit photograph. Slightly joyless occasion. There's a feeling of frustration now. Too much good work, too little time—scenes are having to be lost or curtailed. Goodbye to some of the actors—there are people who inspire articulacy, wit, humour, warmth. There are people who freeze all those qualities in the mind pyre.

---

[1] Co-producer of *An Awfully Big Adventure*
[2] Married to Anthony Minghella
[3] *Four Weddings and a Funeral*

18 APRIL

On standby till 1pm. Buy some brandy for Tony Hopkins. NB My driver is not Sir A. Baggot Street is not so far away ... why have I not wandered up and down it before? Lunch on the set. A last-dayish atmosphere. Quiet and caring. Bang my head against some rubber and then to the Aquarium. Freezing water; a frogman; grabbing my ankles; eyes open; blood on the forehead; staring. It takes a while.

9pm Olivier Awards. How far away it all seems. On to Trocadero—silly ideas are shall we say not tolerated.

Diva Junior is in the hotel bar with her aunt. She's chatty but with pointed eyes.

On to Trocadero ... There with Joan Bergin [costume designer], Fifi and Conor. I think we eventually had a real conversation but Fi is not about to accept any criticism—maybe she's right, but can any of us be *that* sure?

19 APRIL

10.45 → flight to London.

An overall ache is developing, not emotional, just a reaction to the Aquarium dunking.

20 APRIL

The photos from Diana for Dennis Potter arrive.

In amongst the customary evasion of focus, I went to see Judy Daish [agent] for her to deliver the pictures. She talks of Potter, he's finished his current work, is very weak. I would like to be proud of my connection with him—I can only hope that his strengths and darkness comes through sub-liminally. Maybe when the music is there. I wrote thank you for giving me more than a 'faint sense of perfection'.

22 APRIL

8 Ruby's birthday party.

She arrives so happily amidst apparent chaos with Ed's perfectly balanced calm at her side. The children are opening up—is it just because they feel more secure? Jennifer Saunders, Ade Edmondson, Zoë Wanamaker, Joanna Lumley, Suzanne Bertish,[1] Tira, Henrietta, John Sessions. And the inevitable late night row ...

[1] English actor Suzanne Bertish (1951–)

24 APRIL

12.30 To Ruby's for bagels and smoked salmon. Many children underfoot, in arms and on shoulders. Or playing Nintendo games—mere oblivion!

Carrie Fisher is there, funny and fast. Steve asks Jennifer S. what she does. Ruby doesn't know what to wear for the BAFTA awards tonight. Something that works in a close-up, I suggest.

25 APRIL

2.30 Picasso.

Mind-blowing exhibition. Fiona Shaw & I wander around ashamed of our little lives and minute aspirations. It's like Picasso was *permanently* plugged in and the socket switched on. Endless invention, humanity, passion. On the page those are just words—in the exhibition rooms they are all *tangible*.

27 APRIL

7am Watching South Africa put up new flags and crawl over the trip wires and out of the tunnel.

1pm To RADA for the first programme of the evening. Young actors trot through their paces for an assortment of people with paper and biros. Tick, cross, tick. Back in the building after 20 years. How can it have been that long? . . . The Vanbrugh, hideously altered, now presents a cliff-face to the action where once was a theatre. Maybe my role as council member will be more reactionary than I thought.

28 APRIL

Have been asked to do Mamet's new play *The Cryptogram*. Have said no. The part seems wrong. Suggest Eddie Izzard. This meets with general approval. But he will need persuading—talk to him & suggest reading the play together. He says OK. I feel like a producer—it's a good feeling.

4pm Stephen Poliakoff comes over to discuss the screenplay. With himself. I know my place. Sit quietly and wait for the odd space, jagged though it may be, to present itself. He has a new scene in mind to hook me back in.

29 APRIL

4pm Peter Barnes[1] and Dilys Laye[2] come by. Peter's wife Charlotte [Beck] died on Wednesday. She had a unique spirit—electric, shining, fiercely protective. In the end it fought itself in schizophrenia. Peter says she willed herself

---

[1] English playwright (1931–2004)
[2] English actor (1934–2009)

to die. Peter is clearly shaken by it all. I'm reminded to value all the strong friendships in my life.

6 Amanda [Ooms] comes by to look at the Greg Gorman pictures. She, of course, is so beautiful in all of them that she can afford to just glance.

30 APRIL

12ish → Abbey Road to hear some of Michael Nyman's score for *Mesmer*. Roger & Wieland there. No one introduces anyone . . . but the music sounds like a motor, an engine.

1.30 Lindsay & Hilton's to read *The Cryptogram* with Eddie Izzard. Bob Crowley [theatre designer] there too.

10.30 Abbey Road. Watch *Eurovision* with Nyman. The juxtaposition is very enjoyable. I should have put money on the Irish song[1] a month ago.

1 MAY

Call Mum and a Feydeau [farce] is commenced with taxis. Eventually she gets here and we spend a peaceful afternoon as she does crosswords, fills in competition forms, watches TV. She's looking very good and makes her own amusement in such an easy, self-contained way. I brood with equal ease. Rima gets back from canvassing. I make some supper. Mum tells stories of her children and shows photos.

3 MAY

Talk to Liz. She saw *Mesmer* in Paris with James Ivory & the actor [Daniel Mesguich] who is to play Mesmer in his movie.[2] I am genuinely shocked at *another* lack of courtesy.

4 MAY

Lindsay calls and Eddie Izzard got the job!! I feel a real sense of achievement. Now keep all fingers crossed for the next few weeks.

5 MAY

Local elections. St Mary's School; bright-eyed & bushy tailed.

12.30 for 1pm → The Ivy for lunch held by the *Evening Standard* for Peter Brook. *Very* starry: left to right, me, Michael Owen, Felicity Kendall, Peter Ustinov, Editor [Stewart Steven], Mrs Steven, Tom Stoppard, Deborah Warner, Oliver Sacks, one of his patients, Vanessa Redgrave, Sir John Gielgud, Peter Brook,

---

[1] 'Rock 'n' Roll Kids' by Paul Harrington and Charlie McGettigan
[2] *Jefferson in Paris*

Trevor Nunn, Fiona Shaw. Ustinov effortlessly funny—stories he remembers in gruesome detail of watching *Tonight We Improvise*.

6 MAY

The British electorate today announce their dissatisfaction with the Tory Party for they vote for someone else. The days of voting FOR anything long gone. Labour now basically in charge of the country's councils as the government staggers about.

7 MAY

3.30 Royal Court with Rima & Pauline Moran[1] for Howard Barker's *Hotel Nightfall*. Totally impenetrable as far as I was concerned but (of course) not boring and heavy with irony. Why do I not know what was going on? Am I getting stupider?

9 MAY

Dreaming vividly again. Pure sex. No weirdness, just unadulterated. Should be a video.

9pm Watching Mandela walk into Parliament!

10 MAY

South Africa has a Black president and is a free country. It was like watching a film.

6pm A drink with Greg Mosher [theatre director] and Eddie Izzard. Eddie seems to be glowing with the challenge.

11 MAY

5 Home, change for Labour Party European Gala Dinner. John Smith, Robin Cook, Tony Blair all say hello, pass Barbara Castle on the stairs. 'If I win the raffle, let me know.' I did win a prize at the raffle. 2 books. Many an encounter, many a speech. The whole thing seemed pleasant and perfunctory. Gordon Brown looking *sooo* bored. John Prescott bid £3,500 for some Orwell first editions. Any mention of Neil gets huge applause. (Glenys' mum had died during the evening.) Smith's speech the *best* I've heard him make. Ben Elton fast *and* funny.

12 MAY

John Smith is dead. Last night I spoke with him. He talked of feelings of the impossibility of taking on the leadership of a country but then he sees (as I did)

---

[1] English actor (1947–)

Mandela and thinks his own problems or insecurities are minute. His speech *was* excellent. We all know how he *would* have been a great leader. Looking along the platform and amongst the audience at the complexities of Beckett, Prescott, Brown, Blair all I see now is his clarity, intelligence & warmth.

13 MAY

It occurs to me watching breakfast TV and most tributes, prophecies and analyses that the sense of 'What is John Smith doing?' was very much connected with the British media's love affair with negativity. The more John Major screws up the more the banner headlines scream. John Smith's competence and humour and quiet strength didn't sell newspapers until they became his epitaph.

Tea with Ruby. Or rather 'would you read these scripts?'

14 MAY

Reading scripts. More No's.

Phone calls.

Answering mail. And still the requests for money pile up. People don't know what else to do now.

To the dry cleaners in the rain.

Watching the cup final.

Reading.

Making supper.

Watching TV. Roger calls back. He's finished the film. Doesn't know about the screening in Paris. Is, understandably, pissed off. And now what? with this saga.

19 MAY

3.30 Stephen Poliakoff. Hard to be objective with a terrier's teeth sunk into your trouser leg.

20 MAY

Watching John Smith's funeral on TV, as I get ready to be photographed—this life stuffed with weird juxtapositions. The solemn and the frivolous. Maybe it infected my mood because Andreas Neubauer, the photographer, had to wait quite a while to get anything alive. He'd worked hard, too. The hotel was a good location—orange bedspread and poppy wallpaper and various Ortonesque corridors.

2.30 To Tower Bridge and Wharfland. Peeling doors, rusting railings—even a dead rat in one spot. Gradually I could feel my face muscles yield and I think towards the end of a long day he got some photographs.

21 MAY

12.30 Flight to Paris. Straight out to find Irié's shop. Rima chooses clothes and I. is there, too. Charming and shy as ever. Fortunately, given the armful of items, he also comes armed with a discount.

Then some Paris wandering. Shoe shops, coffee bars—chairs pointing outwards at the world—it is a city where you need never be embarrassed by being alone in a café.

22 MAY

Breakfast—always more fun in hotels . . . Watch Margaret Beckett being very impressive on the *Frost* show. Rima thinks she shouldn't be dumped as Deputy.

23 MAY

1pm The French House dining room—lunch with Terry Hands.[1] I used to find him so alarming—for his part he describes my big failing while at the RSC as due to my 'diffidence, lack of anger'—there's a connection there somewhere . . . Whatever I may think of some of his past work—visual ornateness, too much leather—he loves actors and understands them.

24 MAY

8pm Dinner with Ruby, Shere Hite and Kirsty Lang[2] at the Neal Street Restaurant. Incredibly snotty receptionist and over-attentive staff. Very good food. Great conversation—Europe, Feminism, the names of SH's brothel (Hite Site—mine; SH Gives Blow Jobs Here—Ruby's).

30 MAY

8 To the Thai restaurant with Dexter[3] and Dalia. I must try not to be sucked into other people's problems when all it does is drain my energy.

1 JUNE

11am Dexter F. comes by to collect money for mortgage. We organise it via telegraphic transfer—this, however, is England so it's not possible without encountering Mr and Mrs Jobsworth at occasional turns.

Sharman Macd.[4] and Robin Don [theatre designer] come by & we go to 192 to talk of *Winter Guest* and its possible mounting at the Tramway in

---

[1] English theatre director (1941–2020)
[2] British journalist (1962–)
[3] British artist and theatre designer Dexter Fletcher (1966–)
[4] Scottish writer and actor Sharman Macdonald (1951–)

Glasgow. Must avoid the temptation to talk this play into the ground—it's a fragile, enigmatic creature.

2 JUNE

11ish Ruby comes by.

1pm Dentist. When was bleach this expensive? Not to say stinging. Or I was stung.

7.30 *Happy Days* [by Samuel Beckett] at the French Institute.

Angela Pleasence[1] & Peter Bayliss. She's had a rough ride with Simone Benmussa[2] but whatever the rights and wrongs you cannot have a situation where an actress *this* talented is so scared that she is *this* inaudible. Afterwards Pasta Restaurant SW7 we talk of it all. She'll pitch it up tomorrow. Otherwise who are we doing it for? What a great play, though.

3 JUNE

The poetry of ordinary speech—Justin Webb interviewing two WW2 (June 6 is D-Day 50 years) veterans on *Breakfast News* asks them 'Is it always with you, can you ever put it out of your mind?' Ernest says it's hard when you go to cemeteries with all your mates around you. Ron says 'I like it in the graveyards. I want to go to where my best mate is buried. He was killed right in front of me. He turned to me and said "What a day, Blanco!" Bang. Gone. Just like that.'

6 JUNE

8ish To Ruby—we cook some pasta. She gives me her point of view or not—which basically is that I procrastinate to an awesome degree—true but not as negatively as she suggests. She who casts out people weaker than she. I know what she means but can she be right (to live like that)?

7 JUNE

Write to Brian Friel—say no to his play.

pm—in the local hardware shop looking for spray for black fly when I hear the radio announcement of Dennis Potter's death. I assume he might have approved of the juxtaposition.

9 JUNE

7.30 *A Month in the Country*. Helen Mirren a beacon amidst the fog. So unselfish, so unaffected by the quicksand she is standing in.

---

[1] English actor (1941–)
[2] Algerian-born writer and theatre director (1931–2001)

12 JUNE

A peaceful, sunny quiet day. Rima marking exams in the garden. Me pottering about.

Eventually reading scripts of *Persuasion* and *Madness of George*. Both no.

Eventually watch the Euro Election results. Labour pulling seats now. The ironic sight of Glenys K. winning her seat with Neil on her arm. 15 years of telling people it's OK to be selfish shites. Now a little common sense is winnowing upwards as we realise it's no way to live a life, but meanwhile Glenys & Neil are in the wake. I ought to feel jubilant. I feel resentful.

14 JUNE

Phone call from Roger Sp. in LA. The *Mesmer* saga runs and runs. Clearly Mayfair are philistines—the Louis & Maria A. scene is to their minds 'disgusting'. Where's the love story? Did they not notice the name Dennis Potter on the script?

15 JUNE

→ to 192 for some lunch and to send flowers to Juliet who's had a girl after days in labour—9lbs of agony.

20 JUNE

Desultory days.

Some phone calls arranging future plans.

Listening to the answering machine and not picking up.

The first day of Wimbledon.

Eventually—not going to the Red Fort (Indian restaurant). Feeling somewhat used.

A day like this is no way to live one's life but may be necessary breathing space, an opportunity to create some focus.

25 JUNE

From the nasty little man in the tailor's—'This is rather difficult why do you buy jackets like this if they are impossible to alter—please could you stand over there, no not there you are in my light—would *you* like to do the alteration?' Answer—no, but (gathering everything up) I'll ask someone else. Thank you.

29 JUNE

If a day can be schizophrenic then this was it. Margaret[1] rings to say Mum is being taken into hospital. It is like suddenly finding yourself in the freezer.

---

[1] A.R.'s mum's neighbour

And then practicality kicks in. A few phone calls, taxi to the house. Taxi to Hammersmith Hospital. Michael is in the waiting room of Casualty. Mum in a cubicle with an oxygen mask. Breathing is hard but otherwise OK. A lot of questions, a lot of waiting. The woman in the cubicle opposite in response to her daughter's 'Can I get you anything, Mum?' says 'A dose of poison.' Good old emotional blackmail lives on. Eventually to the ward. Nurses incredibly caring and gentle. More questions. Yes she looks after herself. Yes she gets her own meals. A piece of toast for breakfast, a ham sandwich for lunch, yes a cooked meal in the evening, maybe chicken and chips. All pretty levelling. So appropriate that I leave to go to a First Night. *The Cryptogram* . . . Afterwards we escape the crush and go to Orso.

1 JULY

1pm Orso lunch for Thelma CBE. Thelma's diary would be compulsive reading. 'Going to the theatre with Gore Vidal. After 10 mins he wanted to leave. I said, "You can't leave you're famous and everyone will notice." "Oh," he said. In the interval I said, "Look everyone's staring at you," they weren't of course, but he stood there nodding and smiling . . .'

To the hospital where my mother's stories are echoing up the ward as I arrive . . .

2 JULY

Decide against the 1pm matinée of *Millennium Approaches*[1] in favour of watching Martina Navratilova. I should have known. She lost. I'd like to meet her—in the interview afterwards she talks of finding out what she may do as a 'productive human being'. She's not just a serve and volley person.

3 JULY

Yesterday's whim is now fact. 7am Marcy Kahan [playwright] arrives. 7.15 the taxi and off for the 8.30 flight to Paris.

Lunch at La Closerie des Lilas w. Susanna S., Isabelle DuBar & Laurent. Really wonderful—duck with lime & figs. Pinch some of Rima's lamb—also worth flying over for.

And on to L'Odeon for the 3pm performance of *Orlando* with Isabelle Huppert directed by Robert Wilson.[2] Truly one of the most extraordinary acting feats I've ever seen—freedom of spirit and technical mastery in complete harmony.

---

[1] *Angels in America: Millennium Approaches* by Tony Kushner
[2] American director (1941–)

In the dressing room after Isabelle as open, charming, clear-sighted & unsentimental as ever.

A slightly dazed wander in Luxembourg Gardens afterwards, a coffee, citron pressé, ice cream. Airport. Fly home.

4 JULY

1.30 Car picks me up to take me to Beaconsfield. National Film School. Watch *Hudsucker Proxy*. Coen Bros' supposed homage to *It's a Wonderful Life*, *His Girl Friday* etc. In the end, it's a sluggish & directionless pastiche—Tim Robbins warm and friendly at the centre, Jennifer Jason Leigh being brilliant and cold on the outskirts. Talk of this and much else with a roomful of screenwriting course applicants afterwards. It's an exercise in keeping on the subject, not letting it be 'And what do you eat for breakfast?' Mostly it succeeds but on leaving one of them asks me how he can get a script to Bruce Willis.

6 JULY

3pm RADA—30-odd students about to step out of the womb. Can't think too much about being in Room 14 with boot firmly on the other foot. Everything in their faces from open and charmed to reluctant and sceptical. Somehow, as always, we get on to politics. And Hollywood. And the theatre. I liked them on the whole, and shaped a few thoughts that were previously v. muddled.

7 JULY

9.30 To Belinda and Hugh for their Northumberland Place street party. England at its weirdest. Bring your table out into the street and have a dinner party with dozens of others but don't introduce anyone.

9 JULY

8pm (After finding gifts at Waterstone's) Glenys Kinnock's birthday party at the Viceroy of India—great as I'm starving. Dancing Indian girls. Around and about—Ian McKellen, Michael Foot, Folletts K. & B.,[1] Harriet Harman, Gordon Brown etc., etc. At one point I saw Michael Foot with his stick walking past the very uptight Tony Blair in a beige suit. Labour Party bookends.

14 JULY

Taxi to RADA for 2.30 council meeting. First one—Lord A.[2] is chairman. I sit between Sir Anthony H. & Sylvia Syms.

Move on to the 4.30 AGM—a nightmare with the American witch

---

[1] British novelist Ken Follett (1949–) and his wife, British Labour politician Barbara Follett (1942–)
[2] Richard Attenborough (1923–2014)

woman—who is she?—her first associates meeting but she dictates, bosses and just plain talks. People bail out. At the end I go with Paul to look at the props room. Impressive man & organisation. On the way out I encounter the Stepford wife. A hideous scene on the pavement. She invokes the spirit of Thatcher, Reagan, Churchill. So why bother? Why get angry? What can you say to 'Students should pay their own way—Communism is dead etc., etc'. It finishes with her saying 'Grow up' & me saying 'Wake up' as she misses a taxi. Ha ha ha.

15 JULY

7–7.30 To the hospitality room at the BBC & then to the gallery for Ruby's taping.

Some inspired madness between her and Tony Slattery and some of the old less welcome bullying [of] your guest.

To the Patio for supper—tiredness and too much bad wine must have meant I was talking total gibberish to the ever-patient Peter Richardson.[1]

16 JULY

← and also means waking up with a hangover—still dizzy, keep the head facing forward . . .

17 JULY

The World Cup final looks all wrong from the beginning—the stands in the Pasadena Rose Bowl are not high enough for drama, we are reminded of a game in the park. It all comes down to a penalty shootout so the drama makes a comeback but how to live with it if it was you who missed?[2]

20 JULY

Sometimes phone calls should be taped—speaking to Bettina Jonic[3] this morning, in 45 minutes a whistlestop tour of Helen Weigel,[4] Lotte Lenya[5] (Weigel stopped the first performance of *Happy Days* by reading a treatise instead of singing), Samuel Beckett, separate rooms, then separate entrances for Suzanne his wife but she it was who banged on doors with *Godot*. Ionesco talking of slicing his wife up to be sure she died before him (she's still alive).

These are stories to listen to on hot, desultory days which are otherwise

[1] British director (1951–)
[2] Brazil beat Italy on penalties, 3–2.
[3] Croatian-born singer (1938–2021)
[4] German actor (1900–1971)
[5] Austrian singer (1898–1981)

filled with picking up registered mail (photographs by Andreas Neubau-er—I remember this session, who is this person?) being home for Gerry the plumber to fix the water pressure, eating too many sweet things.

21 JULY

The life mind and times of a Piscean. While half of me is saying—no, don't go, it's a mistake, the other half is ironing the shirt and ordering a taxi. To Museum of the Moving Image for the Cinema 100 launch and a line-up for Prince Charles. Juliet, Jeremy Irons, Richard E. Grant, Joan Plowright, Rita Tushingham, Dickie A., Sir John Mills. Chit chat and mineral water before-hand. Then Charles arrives—does the semi circle with, incredibly, some-thing relevant to say to everyone; a cinema show & speeches, then lunch and talk with A. Yentob & Colin McCabe.[1] David Puttnam comes from the 'coronation' of Tony Blair and tells me my name is down to speak at a debate at the party conference.

To the hospital to steer Mum to some safe harbour. Ruby arrives and makes everyone laugh; we go to the River Cafe with Ed, Alan Wanzenberg [old friend of Ruby's] & Jed [his partner]. And suddenly from nowhere there is Irène Jacob. With Rufus Sewell. And a movie team. Much laughing from our table—Ruby's stories never fail. Talk to Judy Hoflund later—she's preg-nant. 'Don't worry—I was back at work after 10 days last time.'

Worry? Me?? Today has been stuffed with after images. Jeremy's doing *Die Hard 3*. Irène didn't do *Mesmer*. Richard E. did do *Jack & Sarah*. Rufus is doing *Carrington*.

1 AUGUST

A morning of sudden, ferocious energy. Watching myself make things happen. In a few phone calls appointments with architects, tickets at the National, wheelchairs ordered and delivered and finally a trip to Glynde-bourne is arranged—for today—get ready in an hour & a half and get to Victoria Station (in black tie).

Meet Fiona & Deborah—one of the major terrible twos in the art world. Hildegard joins and we're on the train to Glyndebourne. When you get there—there it all is—a bit of little Olde England still determinedly putting out its collapsible chairs, sandwiches, champagne (one guy all alone with his Fortnum hamper, another group with a fucking flower arrangement). I kept

---

[1] English academic and film producer (1949–)

thinking 'someone with a machine gun will appear any minute'. The cows ambled around trying different groups.

Don Giovanni—of course full of wonderful challenging ideas but the singers so far from fulfilling those ideas as actors that I worry for Deborah's non-ability to self-criticise. And Fiona's. And probably mine if caught in a situation like this. Some of it was just embarrassing—the chorus doing the Twist in clothes from *La Dolce Vita*.

Chase home. Speed bath.

10 AUGUST

4 hours' sleep before the 7.45 pick-up drive to Heathrow and the 10.10 flight to Pisa → train to Pisa Central → train to Grosseto. Beautiful walled town, public holiday, everything's shut, walk around the shuttered windows, snooze at the hotel, go out for some dinner (if anything's open) find the obviously annual relay race around the old town going on (the blue team won), the whole town watching, families everywhere, little children running around or sitting on laps in cafés (even at midnight) totally *included*. A practised sixth sense leads us to the big open-air pizzeria, red wine, salad, coffee, perfect.

Family of four at one table—Mama blowing on forkful of pizza before putting it in younger daughter's mouth. All around tables of 6, 8, 10 people—no muzak, just chatter. And a clean white tablecloth for every new set of customers.

11 AUGUST

Breakfast in the room before wandering to Café Canducci to meet Dalia who runs up looking tanned and wearing a straw hat. We go find Harriet Cruickshank [film producer] & Duncan MacAskill [artist] and take a rip off taxi ride to Talamone (by sea) for beer and lunch. Taxi back, get out before Polizei spot that 5 of us are on board. Back to hotel for snooze, Dalia to take shower and arrange 7pm pick-up to go to Castiglione. The taxi driver has a friend with a boat and there the magic begins . . .

We sail right *into* the sunset towards Elba. As the sun disappeared—throwing the rocks and tower into the blackest against pinkest relief—the crescent moon sharpened and a flock of birds seemed suddenly released to say hello. We thudded back to the Darsena Ristorante for wondrous fish, salad, salmon carpaccio, french fries, lemon sorbet, espresso, local wine. An extraordinary evening is completed with 100mph dash back with Giofreddo the cab driver and dancing in the square. Old, young, blondes, bald heads all smiling and moving to the music at midnight. Very, very special hours.

12 AUGUST

11.45—Bus to Siena. Peaceful, empty air-conditioned motorway trip through postcard Tuscany to this glorious town. The first view of Piazza del Campo vies with Piazza Navona or rounding the bay to Sydney Harbour. Sit under brown umbrellas as the sand for the horses blows about—crostini, spaghetti pomodoro, salad, happiness . . . Total harmony of window against brick, roof against wall, doorway against bleachers (there for the horse races—July 2, August 16; one can only imagine the pulse rates). Climb the tower of the town hall—dizzy-making in every respect. On to the Duomo—like being in a vast Licorice Allsort—and San Domenico, rush, rush for the bus which is 25 mins late but never mind because the drive home is everything van Gogh waded through. Breathtaking is a word that gets slung about, but here it's apt. And in the middle of it all people just go about their lives in the most direct uncomplicated way, it seems. And talking, talking, talking.

14 AUGUST

To Saul Zaentz[1] and Annette for lunch with them, Anthony M., Barbara, Carolyn, Max [the Minghellas' son], Michael Ondaatje, Judy Daish, Angy, Dalia, Maria B.[2] More idyll, more food, more swimming, much laughter. Saul & Angy real wits. We all set out for Batignano and *Don Giovanni*. Dexter is there with Steve & little Jack (after we have failed to get into the local restaurant). We all sit under the stars . . . We've had the tour of the convent—now we're sitting in the audience. This production is of course so different from Glyndebourne—the name Maria Bjornson would tell you that—but really rich and enjoyable in its own way. Sue Blane [costume designer] was there (and Leon Brittan . . .). It was all another neon-lit element in a great week. Holidays . . . Saul and Annette drive us back to the Bastiani at 1.30am. Tired but happy but full of *English Patient* thoughts. Timing, timing. 'Night and day, I slave away . . .'

16 AUGUST

Get up and out by 9am and down to Grosseto Station to discover that the 9.35 to Pisa is actually 9.25. Maria Bjornson & Rachel at another ticket window so we wander back to Café Carducci. Maria talks of disillusion, maybe

---

[1] American film producer (1921–2014)
[2] French theatre designer Maria Bjornson (1949–2002)

temporarily relieved by working with Dalia, and for once being included in the process. The old story . . .

Some meandering—buy a teapot from a great old shop in a side street and eventually get back to the station for the 12.38. Dalia's there with armfuls of luggage I had vowed to have nothing to do with. Stagger on to the train, stagger off at Pisa, leave it all in left luggage, go look at Tower/Duomo/Baptistry. Pisa is a very haphazard, resentful sort of place. Any old fencing will do, very ordinary food, lots of horrible souvenirs. The inside of the cathedral however is staggering (word du jour). How many gobsmacking churches are there? Pisa Airport → London → a pile of mail.

19 AUGUST

4pm Catherine [Bailey] and Rosie come to talk about the *Mesmer* documentary which I just watched. It's good, but at the moment one scene *has* to be removed to save my blushes and other people's feelings. *Never* say this is off the record, someone will use it anyway. The film needs more facts and a more definite point of view.

20 AUGUST

Sometimes the sensation of being a personal launderette service—friendship must not become a space for indulgence. Listening to casting problems, rehearsal problems, photograph problems. There is a point at which they walk away stronger and you are exhausted. This cannot be right . . .

21 AUGUST

→ to the Odeon Kensington. Long queue. Rescued by Alice Pollock[1] and we're in to see *The Last Seduction*—great reviews, Linda Fiorentino, etc., etc. Bodes well. But a deeply cynical, joyless, diminishing piece of work and we decide to leave. An espresso is more rewarding.

25 AUGUST

To Toronto 1pm.

What with packing, telephone calls (including one with the carbonated Hilary Heath . . . [2]), I managed to leave jackets and trousers behind. Now, either some nimble use of jeans and T shirts is required or the even nimbler use of the Amex card.

---

[1] Casting director Patsy Pollock's daughter
[2] English actor (1945–2020)

28 AUGUST

Montreal.

11 First screening of *Mesmer*. A full house in the Imperial—a beautiful theatre—tiered and red-plushed. Speaking in French turns out to be less alarming than the prospect was.

Then a day of interviews begins and with it the battle to be honest, informative, but *guarded* . . .

9.30 Second screening of *Mesmer* . . . Watch some of it from the circle. Immediately depressing sense of what it could have been.

29 AUGUST

A wander to the Musée des Beaux Arts—Lichtenstein and de Lempicka—it's Monday, the museum is closed. As a comfort sweet, I toy with the idea of spending $1200 on a jacket. The temptation is resisted. I really haven't seen Montreal on this trip and anyway junkets tend to dull your curiosity—you might get excited and the guard would drop and that would never do.

Mesmer has been received extraordinarily well. Seconds out. Round 2.

5.30 Montreal airport. Charles Dance there—a genuinely nice man.

1 SEPTEMBER

One of these really lousy days when you think 'what have I done?'

Today also brings an invitation to appear on *Question Time*. The very definition of 'you must be joking' . . .

4 SEPTEMBER

Sweeping up leaves is good therapy for almost everything. Dalia calls—she comes over to supper. Duck, roast potatoes. One forgets that one duck *just about* feeds two people.

5 SEPTEMBER

8pm Elizabeth & Alessandro Lunardi[1] come over and when Rima (eventually) gets back from the town hall we go to the Ivy. A fine feast. Talk of Italy and Italians. Walk on Waterloo Bridge. Home.

6 SEPTEMBER

Early morning letter-writing as a result of a 5am wake-up as a result of brooding over builder's bills, tax, etc., etc. (Oh for a Tuscan farmhouse, a glass of wine and a piece of cheese.)

---

[1] Italian-American architect and designer

The phone rings and Andras [co-producer on *Mesmer*] brings news of a Best Actor Award from Montreal. This is heart-warming as it makes Mayfair look more and more, shall we say, misguided.

Il Gallo D'Oro lunch with Hilary Heath—still a girl really, with a big heart and conversation like a jack-knife.

Later to 12 Upper A.[1] More details with Peter [Mishcon, architect] & Brian D. [builder]. Now we have to slow these spiralling thousands.

7 SEPTEMBER

The walls we are surrounded by—the objects we fill the spaces with—the lives they all describe.

Taking my mother from a house stuffed with collected bits of furniture, pieces of paper, magazines, old biros neatly lined up with emery boards and a teaspoon—off to Chartwell House; purpose built for the elderly genteel. It's all on one level and the staff are terrific. It keeps me reassured and guilty—a rare combination. We'll see.

12 Upper Addison is another phenomenon. Vast sums being spent on fastidious details—a millimetre here, a maple strip there.

My own home (it's Wednesday and Janet has been) looks like a film set. Abandoned for the night. Waiting for a story. And then a letter from Rima's dad, living in a home. Calling it an asylum—being caught naked on the lavatory. Lights out at 9pm.

8 SEPTEMBER

Most of the day spent at Chartwell House. My life is in such clear-cut strands at the moment. Career, Architect, Subsidence, Other People's Careers, Relationships. Seemingly in that order. Today was almost exclusively about my mother. Just spending time in this new environment, calling the doctor, testing her hearing, wrapping her up and taking her and her wheelchair for a walk to get the prescription, looking on helplessly at today's pain and her fury at it. I don't know what I become under these circumstances—a kind of amorphous bundle of past and present. I have to kick myself towards the phone to attend to some of the other members of the above list. The strands. Later Eileen [A.R.'s cousin] and boyfriend and 2 daughters come by. Some of my childhood, cousins, aunts & uncles, swim before me. Then Rima arrives and reduces me to silence for the rest of the evening. Is this control, depression or exhaustion?

---

[1] 12 Upper Addison Gardens, a flat A.R. had bought in Holland Park

9 SEPTEMBER

10.30 De Lane Lea [Studios] (in not the best mental state) for a screening of *Awfully Big Adventure*. Just Mike Newell, the sound engineer and me. It's a mosaic, or an attic of a movie. Jumbled and intense, full of dark corners and sudden hilarious surprises. God knows what America will make of it—or if they will know *how* to watch it. You can't be passive—the audience has to work a bit. Maybe its kaleidoscopic quality is a little too hard to watch and it could linger a little more often. At all events it has a bundle of good performances—I can't tell about Hugh [Grant], Georgina or me. Too much sense of competition, or the memory still hangs in the air. But Ms Cates suffers from *only* functioning from her sense of the story. She listens to nothing, responds to nothing. She's a butterfly inside her own glass case, watching herself bat around.

A car to Heathrow and then, appropriately enough, to Dublin. Conor's at the Davenport Hotel. We eat something, then I bump into Shelagh Stephenson[1]—a Guinness at Davy B's[2] then to the Peacock for *Asylum Asylum* by David O'Kerry—really good writing, direction, acting.

10 SEPTEMBER

Sleep late then go into town to meet Conor . . . Background information from last night's play fills out the whole experience. The neurotic actor, the mean actor, the actress who always goes straight home.

To the airport—bliss, I'm in the back seat and can spread across three seats. Taxi to Chartwell House, find Rima and Mum. Home to get ready for *Lady Windermere's Fan*. Me, Rima, and Belinda and along the row Raine Spencer.[3] All I could think about was poor sod in the seat behind all that hair.

12 SEPTEMBER

3.30 to 12UA. Something sheepish in the air—as well there might be when I finally discover where the bill is going, that is into the stratosphere.

13 SEPTEMBER

Take Mum home from Chartwell House, leaving her to think about all the options.

Home to find Gilly working in the garden . . . we won a Residents' Association award for the front garden . . .

---

[1] English playwright and actor (1955–)
[2] Davy Byrne's pub
[3] Daughter of Barbara Cartland and stepmother of Princess Diana (1929–2015)

Marcia arrives. Rima arrives. We go to the Lyric Hammersmith to *The Picture of Dorian Gray*. It's Neil Bartlett's first show of his tenure and we speak at the top of a flight of steps, so I'm all in favour, wishing it well and all that but try as I might, it either stays resolutely on the stage or flies straight over my head. No contact is made.

21 SEPTEMBER
Andreas comes over. My function is to listen, challenge and supply possible leads as to an escape from his current hell. So easy to slip into bullshit when talking to someone who is bereaved. The English are well-trained. Years of . . . rehearsing platitudes. At least we talked about Briny and about how he was feeling—and laughed. In the end, having been over the spiritual/ philosophical sand dunes, he went off to audition for a vodka commercial.

25 SEPTEMBER
Lunch at the Connaught with Rima and ever-generous Richard Wilson. A day of shifting sands with old friends. Lunch involves wearing a tie and paying £35 for a piece of fish (plus, I suppose, silverware, French waiters, flowers on the table and oak panelling). Nearby a table-full of Wodehouse refugees—in fact a room full of regulars. Except us. The thing I really hate about wine waiters is their insistence on refilling the glass after one's every mouthful.

29 SEPTEMBER
am 12UA. To discuss skirting boards.

1 OCTOBER
11ish To Books Etc., to find a gift for Denis Lawson. Robert Evans' autobiography[1] fits the bill.

2 OCTOBER
The Sunday papers carry previews of tomorrow's *Late Show* Special (already rubbished by yesterday's *Guardian*)[2] and the sensation increases during the day of having been silently mugged. I have to recognise the dangers of actors talking about themselves (unless you have an American accent—an hour's profile tonight of Dennis Hopper produces no sharpened claws—if you are

---

[1] *The Fat Lady Sang*
[2] BBC documentary (*Truly, Madly, Alan Rickman*) focusing on the making of *Mesmer* and A.R.'s career to date

English get the Elastoplast ready) but are we always to be so patronised, can we *never* talk about our work without being forced to trivialise it?

4 OCTOBER

7.30am and the phone rings, clearing my head . . .

As a result of which the day has a lightness that is mostly energising, a little dizzy-making. Mostly, people responded well to last night's programme—I swerved away from the newsprint.

6pm Groucho Club to meet with Peter Richardson and Stephen Fry to talk of the film project. Stephen looks ashen—he's been experiencing the Rottweiler element in the press. A kind of blooding.

6 OCTOBER

Last night and today thinking of yesterday's delivery of the 2 inch thick file of Mayfair's objections. Looming large is their complaint that at one point 'Tears did not spring to my eyes'—how do you take this nonsense seriously?[1]

Watched the *Imagine* film and wept a bit with all the others at the end. As one girl was saying 'We grew up with them.' And Lennon was so articulate esp in the face of Al Capp & the *NY Times* woman. Not a lazy answer anywhere. An enviable grown-up man.

10 OCTOBER

Difficult days. Judy says *Winter Guest* can go into rehearsal December 16. Everyone is thrilled. What *is* this I feel. Hijacked?

1.15 RADA Council meeting. Attenborough is an extra special man. Courteous to a fault, aware of every nuance in the room, and open enough to be excited by the idea of staying with Nelson Mandela. On an obsessive day like this he is an object lesson in how to live your life in all directions at once.

12 OCTOBER

6.30 20th C. Fox screening room. *An Awfully Big Adventure* shown to British Screen Investors. I am surrounded by people nervous of their own opinions. The film is too long and the opening is difficult & at the moment I don't know if there is an audience who knows how to watch it.

---

[1] Alan seemed ideally suited to the role but as filming progressed discord grew as representatives of Mayfair Entertainment International, one of its principal backers, voiced their dismay, claiming among other things that the star was not sufficiently erotic. Others disagreed: Alan won the Best Actor award at the 1994 Montreal Film Festival, and the *Atlantic*'s critic said, 'He's not just brilliant; he's great, bold to the point of folly.' Arbitration followed and thereafter Mayfair withdrew funding.

13 OCTOBER

1pm Lunch at La Fenice with Judy Daish. The maître d' is as rude as ever. We talk through a running order for Dennis Potter's memorial service. It comes together fairly easily—on the page. Such ironies . . .

14 OCTOBER

Ladybird, Ladybird at the Lumière. About 5 mins in I was folding my arms and starting to raise an eyebrow. What is this film about?? It's too easy to attack the social services and I don't think we are given all the facts. Crissy Rock[1] engages sympathy and never loses it, really. But *of course* it makes almost everything else ultimately look foolish.

15 OCTOBER

8 To Ruby and Ed for a brief glimpse of Ruby's interview with Madonna. But who's doing all the talking? Guess. Finally, some very funny moments.

16 OCTOBER

To Mum who is immovable and vulnerable.

This is not a great day to be sure of what-it's-all-about. I can see obligations, old patterns and not sinking in superficiality but where, exactly, is the nourishment?

17 OCTOBER

8.20 *Forrest Gump*. I had sworn I wouldn't go. I went and it was as horrific as I had thought but in a totally different way. A clear attempt had been made to dilute the sentimentality, but along the way the film has its cake, eats it and spits it out with Vietnam, 'unnamed viruses' etc.

Late—Malabar—where Ruby's waters once broke.

18 OCTOBER

4ish 12UA. The bill is soaring. I should be getting angry now—what is the point? A major school of buck passing is going on and *still* the job has to be finished.

20 OCTOBER

1pm Joyce Nettles for lunch at L'Accento. The first time I've worked with a casting director like this. I don't quite feel the ground beneath my feet.

And on to the *Carrington* screening—just what the doctor might *not* have chosen to order. This is like a sustained mugging.

---

[1] Christine Rock, English actor (1958–)

21 OCTOBER

pm 12UA, Paint colours . . . Blood red springs to mind . . .

23 OCTOBER

To 12UA. An attempt to get some lower estimates.

To the Odeon West End—cast and crew screening of *Awfully Big Adventure*. Tapping on windows to be let in; Mike N. & Philip H[inchcliffe, producer] oblige, Hilary [Heath]'s on a landing with Ms Cates. I find it impossible to be other than cool. The film looks beautiful on a big screen.

24 OCTOBER

To 12UA. A tiling crisis. Who? How much? When? With a bit of affronted dignity threading through it. Colours are starting to go on now and *starting* to look great.

25 OCTOBER

Vienna.

To the cinema for the [*Mesmer*] screening. I can't watch. Roger and I find a bar—he depressed the life out of me with stories of Mayfair and their philistinism.

29 OCTOBER

8.45 *Pulp Fiction*—Brilliant and empty. Original and repetitious. Like reading a v.v. classy comic—if you're going to be a gangster, that is . . .

31 OCTOBER

am Spent poring over Mayfair's legal statements. Bullshit is the horse-blanket shroud—safety instead of discovery.

8 → Go to the Ivy. Dinner with Malcolm McLaren & Michelle Guish [casting director]. VV entertaining. And NO BULLSHIT!!

1 NOVEMBER

9am Dennis Potter's memorial service at St James's, Piccadilly. At the beginning the Rev. Donald Reeves seems like he's without any trace of humour—dangerous. But no, eventually his true colours show and by the time the service starts his full colours are flying and we are told to sing 'Roll Along Prairie Moon' again because we could do better. The hour passes full of the most wonderful words and music from Potter to Hazlitt, from Imelda Staunton singing 'Roses of Picardy' to Mozart's 'Kyrie'. [Michael] Grade,

[Alan] Yentob & Trodd[1] were wonderfully funny, Grade knowing we might break down at any moment from the rehearsal, Trodd recalling Potter's mournful statement that one thing preoccupied him about death. That Trodd might speak at his memorial service.

2 NOVEMBER

And another 9am. This time lawyers, tables, water, papers, thin smiles. The thinnest from me to Scorer[2] as I went into the room.

A tremendously nerve wracking experience—justifying my right to interpret a script—what decade is this? In the end I found a speech from somewhere near my gut and with no erms and aahs. I can only hope it was Potter, pausing briefly from laughter to lend a bit of a helping hand. Spent the rest of the day feeling demeaned and soiled, and terribly, terribly sad. I can only assume the utter symmetry of these two days has some greater purpose.

3 NOVEMBER

To ICM. Whip through some transparencies. Present myself with my Montreal award while eating half a sandwich.

Home to get things up on *Winter Guest*—casting, meetings etc.

4 NOVEMBER

Middayish—to 12UA. The bedroom is the wrong colour *again*. Not my fault, this time.

10 NOVEMBER

Boot on the other foot day—interviewing young actors for *The Winter Guest*. Trying to be open to them—not difficult since Joyce Nettles has arranged a great selection—all *so* different. At this point only ½ an idea who to cast.

11 NOVEMBER

3pm Ruby—of course I should have known. She wanted help to sharpen a new show.

12 NOVEMBER

7.15 Camden Grand.

With my newly crafted speech to introduce Tony Blair to a full house. I'm nervous, he's last-minute adjusting. Ben Elton does a brilliant set about 'garnish'—which is exactly what we are it occurs to me now. Blair's off the

---

[1] British television producer Kenith Trodd (1936–)
[2] Ian Scorer, founder of Mayfair Entertainment International

minute his speech is over to talk to Indian businessmen at the House of Commons—'same speech?' I wittily enquire. 'You need a mental lap-top.' 'I've got one,' he says. His speech is a touch lazy, not truly geared to the audience and woolly round the edges. Kinnock, however, is dazzling—received like a hero. 'Bless them,' says Glenys, who at the end looks into the audience with such a private loving admiration as Neil is in the wings singing 'Happy Days' with the gospel choir. Maybe Blair's detachment will make him a successful leader. But Neil remembers to bring his heart like his front door keys.

15 NOVEMBER

5.30 Plane to Edinburgh. Collected by Scott [Thomas, film editor]. Taken to the Youth Theatre (W. Lothian) workshop. Have to be very animal in picking kids but there are a definite trio . . . Drinks with Scott in hotel bar & → Caledonian Hotel. Luxury and a club sandwich.

16 NOVEMBER

Train to Glasgow and . . . on to RSAMD for a day of hello, sorry, come in, this is the story, what did you think about, would you mind reading . . . The building is a disgrace—who came up with this echoing hospital as somewhere to study voice, music, movement?

Writing this, I have subliminal memories of people who seemed righter, more talented than others. The boot very much on the other foot. Even more so at the end of the day when going in to talk to maybe 100 students.

Train back to Edinburgh. Completely knackered. All that politeness.

17 NOVEMBER

10.30 Royal Lyceum.

At least they had made a pot of coffee. I discover these things matter. And courtesy, and openness. And no bullshit. More talent—more questions. It could go in several directions.

Lunchtime at the Traverse café with Elizabeth Millbank who introduces herself. A much-admired actress—she reminds me I suggested her to Howard Davies a few years ago. She's *certainly* open—like meeting an old friend. And she introduces me to Philip Howard [then associate director] who shows me around this stunning new theatre—Lyceum, Usher Hall, Traverse, a curve of culture.

6.45 Another W. Lothian Youth Theatre workshop—less successful but

Scott's enthusiasm is a plus, as is dinner in a Thai restaurant with his girl-friend & friend of. People at an adjacent table stare a lot and eventually get a friend to phone the restaurant to check if I am me. At this point tiredness makes me wonder . . .

18 NOVEMBER

Edinburgh.

Phone call from LA is from *such* another world—can they cannibalise me even more from *Die Hard* for *DH3*?

20 NOVEMBER

Thank you to the middle-of-the-night pissed joker who rewrote my break-fast order so that I had fish and pineapple juice delivered at 7.20am instead of toast and coffee at 8.30 . . .

21 NOVEMBER

11.45 To the Almeida to talk with Joyce and Sharman about the Scotland trip. This bit is hard—playing a sort of God with people's lives. Just deciding is difficult enough.

Watching the annual *Evening Standard* Drama Awards on TV. Grace and disgrace so close together. Disgraceful, really, this need to back slap but if it has to happen accept with the grace of Peter Brook.

23 NOVEMBER

Arwen Holm phones to tell me of a nasty little piece in the *Telegraph* saying how unsmiling I was in the local deli.

25 NOVEMBER

Thanksgiving party at Sandra & Michael Kamen's. All I wanted was an auto-graph book—Kate Bush, Bryan Adams, David Bowie, Stevie Winwood.

26 NOVEMBER

9.15 Joyce and a taxi to go to Heathrow for the 11am flight to Glasgow and on to the Athenaeum for the workshop at the Scottish Youth Theatre. A two hour whip around Sean, Douglas, Anthony, Andrew, Brian, David, John-Ross and John.[1] All wonderful, all different. I'm a little too tired to

---

[1] Auditioning for parts in *The Winter Guest*

be inspired but thank God for Joyce who fills the parents with confidence. After, Christian Zanone[1] and family come in to talk it all through.

One of those days that has no rules—time passes too quickly, a lot of it one would like to rewind or re-do. But there it was—a great sprawling, hopeful splurge of a day.

27 NOVEMBER

Royal Albert Hall—Elton John and Ray Cooper. Elton really *fills* that great space, helped, it turns out, by Ray Cooper who plays drums like a dancer might. But the secret with both of them is relaxation.

2 DECEMBER

Supper at home for Lindsay, Hilton, Jane, Mark, Allan and Fifi. I am feeling so distracted but manage to tap dance here and there. And anyway it's a room full of people you could have a breakdown in front of, which is always reassuring.

Later—a bottle of champagne or a port—midnight visit to 12UA. Fifi sitting in the bath.

4 DECEMBER

7.45 Curzon West End for the Almeida Fund Raiser of *Vanya on 42 Street*. No one, sadly, told me it was a Mayfair film. Scorer walks towards me, hand sort of outstretched. 'Some day, we must sit down and talk.' 'About what?' I manage. 'The truth,' he replies.

7 DECEMBER

8pm Sandra & Michael Kamen—impossible, really, to believe—violins, cello, flute, oboe, harp and eventually Nigel Kennedy in the Kamen front room playing Bach and Brahms for maybe 10 of us. A wonderful guilty treat.

9 DECEMBER

2.30 Michael Kamen—who has the *shortest* attention span. He's so gifted he's finished before he's started and bored with it before we got properly interested. Hard to infiltrate that rhythm. But melodies pour out of him.

11 DECEMBER

To 12UA with Dalia, vacuum, mops and buckets. Honest toil to add to the dishonest expense. It could hardly redress the balance but a bit . . .

---

[1] Scottish actor who played Alex

12 DECEMBER

Taxi to St George's Theatre for first day rehearsals of *The Winter Guest*. Fiddling with text, cuts, gathering of information for John and Anthony[1] (who turns out over lunch to be a big fan of Frank Capra & Orson Welles as well as Tarantino . . .). So they can write their essays and diaries.

pm John-Ross and David arrive. Certainly 4 temperaments which is great—but they seem to feed into each other really well.

And why don't we all go to the theatre together. And, why not (eventually) make it *Les Misérables*—a show, I thought, I would never see. Surprisingly it is played with 100% high octane energy and commitment. Bully for them. But still—watching the Red Flag waving at all these £30 a head multinational audience members is a weird sight.

13 DECEMBER

St George's Theatre.

Alternating boys all day—four very different personalities emerging.

John-Ross—Nirvana, Guns N' Roses, Science Fiction, Baseball cap. Great at immediacy.

John W.—Wise and kind beyond his 12 years—almost seems the oldest at times. Very talented. A born actor. Quiet and complete concentration.

Anthony—His school says he's trouble. When? He's complex—he likes Capra, Welles, and doesn't concentrate easily but only because we got there hours ago. Does a great Alan Partridge impression.

David—The one to open up. A bit walled in. Brave soul. Cursed with weak heart. Growth deficiencies. Great talent, too much technique. Will hold it all together.

Good hearts all of them.

18 DECEMBER

3ish to Mum. She's now sitting at her command centre—phone, letters, Mills & Boon (though not just love stories . . .), crosswords, compilations all within easy reach in a semi-circle of diversions. A still fierce instinct to keep her mind going—'I'm not going to that club over the road—all old people, effing and blinding.'

---

[1] The cast of the stage version of *The Winter Guest* included several young Scottish actors, among them Christian Zanone, John-Ross Morland, Anthony O'Donnell, David Evans and John Wark.

19 DECEMBER

10.30 First day of rehearsals for grown-ups. A test when finally you have to say something—fortunately Robin's set speaks volumes and inspires confidence. And so, we trawl through the day, looking for clues, a shape, ambiguities. Christian and Arlene[1]—their first day in London, in a play, knowing no one. Arlene is rescued from her B&B by Sharman.

6pm Almeida wine bar for interview with Duncan Fallowell of the *Observer*. He's intelligent and comes in from all angles but of course it's the negative standpoint—difficult, rebellious, maverick. Heigh ho.

Later and Rima at the drop of a crossword tells me in detail the plot of *Richard III*.

23 DECEMBER

Said no to *Richard III*. What strange days these are.

Christmas shopping.

24 DECEMBER

Michael comes around at 8.30 and we eat something before going (with Dalia who comes at 11.45) to All Saints for the Midnight Mass—carols, candles, a crib, somebody drunk crying on a shoulder by the door, all the hymns, as usual, way too high, and this organist clearly on 33⅓ rpm. But it formalises the day, and that's good—I want something to come at me not to be always looking, probing, hoping, reaching.

25 DECEMBER

Getting to bed at 2am meant a bit of a scrabble for baths, breakfast and unwrapping before David arrived at 12. But it's my favourite part of Christmas Day—just two of us enjoying things in the same way, complementary rhythms. And it's fine up to and during lunch—Chris[2] a phenomenon of organisation. The more alcohol that's consumed, however, the more the tensions appear, the greater the sense of hideous impending temperament about to explode on the suburban scene. The accident of families . . . which takes people, makes siblings of them, staples on some relationships and children and gathers them into a room for one day to enjoy themselves. And we *do*—there's a lot of uncomplicated love around all mixed up with other emotional luggage. Finally—the two of us home again and a cup of tea. All's well . . .

---

[1] Arlene Cockburn, Scottish actor who played Nita
[2] Christine, David's wife

31 DECEMBER

A year has passed . . . which has included the earthquake, *Mesmer*itus, Potter's memorial, *Awfully Big Adventure*, nudging Tara Hugo and Eddie Izzard into other places, the rebirth of Upper Addison, growing pains but *growing* of *Wisdom of Crocodiles* and the Richardson/Fry script, *Don Giovanni*, Paris, Italy, RADA Council. And *The Winter Guest* bridges the years. Bigger marks on other graphs, of course—Mandela, Rwanda, Smith, Blair. But good to be looking forward.

1995

2 JANUARY

Breakfast with the Richardson household, a quick visit to the archetypal country kitchen next door and then everyone bundled into the car to Newton Abbott and the 12.02 to Paddington.

The stretch of coast at Dawlish where the railway line runs right along the beach is really magnificent. As I was saying tonight (see below), my head is filled with Famous Five-ish images of rockpools and starfish, short trousers and sticks.

Back home a wander around area. A bit of final (!) Christmas shopping. Maybe tonight will be quietly preparing to go away. Maybe not. Dalia is followed by Julian Sands and Evgenia [Citkowitz, his wife] and then the four of us have a happy, chatty evening over brilliant Malaysian takeaway (or rather bring to).

Far too late to bed. There will be a price to pay.

3 JANUARY

There was.

7am car to King's Cross, 7.50 train to Leeds. Pullman trains now like a Forte's hotel corridor.

The theatre is filled with friendliness and it's good to see the boys again. John and David, watchful as ever, John-Ross and Anthony both on another planet. They have retained a lot in the gap but there's certainly work to do.

pm with Christian and Arlene, whose faces light up as they make discoveries about energy, tension, playing together. And some wonderful work from Sheila and Sandra[1] in the evening. Now there's time, space and *light* to work in this kind of detail.

---

[1] Scottish actors Sheila Reid (1937–), who played Lily, and Sandra Voe (1936–), who played Chloe

4 JANUARY

10.30 for the tour of the building.

11.30–12 Finally the company is together and we read the play for the first time. Some of it wonderful—the boys, so open, unaffected. Other areas so closed and complicated. But that's the stuff of this & next week.

5pm production meetings & wardrobe talks. Easy to be decisive in these situations—colours, shapes.

7pm Into the rehearsal room with Phyllida [Law] and Siân Thomas[1] and the best kind of detailed character building.

Sharman and I go to Pizza Express for red wine & no cheese. Sharman trawling for resonances, reconciliations—things to end a play with.

5 JANUARY

This was a wonderful day's work. Starting with the boys—first moving through the scenes and watching particularly John-Ross finding new life away from the script and David leaving his old safety nets behind.

Then working gradually through the play, putting scenes together for the first time—and it works. Still some fingers crossed about music, lights, sound but the play opens up all day long.

7pm Arlene, so still and gifted beginning to enjoy the work. Christian beginning to enjoy it a little less—which is good.

7 JANUARY

Scrabble through some scenes this morning (this is how *not* to work) Sharman behind me in a flap as we approach taxi time. But we make the train—Siân, Sharman & me chit chat & read our way back to Kings X . . . Letters, cheques, take down the Xmas cards, phone calls, washing.

8 JANUARY

To Ruby & Ed with Christmas gifts. Esp. Madeleine's jewel box, which she was last seen kissing, before taking it to bed. As Rima said, apart from anything else, maybe it's one of the few things she got not made of plastic.

9 JANUARY

7.50 train to Leeds. The man opposite with a stomach dented by the table 2 feet in front of him, tucking into sausages, eggs, the lot. 'Could I have more potato, please?'

10am with the boys—all excited by their weekend purchases. Sunglasses,

---

[1] British actor (1953–)

things to scare me, and for John a big fat copy of *Les Misérables*—'It was only three quid.'

10 JANUARY

First major run-through produces all the pluses and minuses.

Sharman has written a play filled with complex resonances, ironies, jokes, sadnesses which the actors illuminate and inhabit miraculously most of the time. The danger is of it falling for its own beat and the added problem is that some of its darker passages are in the mouths of 12-year-olds and the writing is (technically) beyond them. The question is how to teach them to lie???

12 JANUARY

Press conference—20-odd journalists. The clever ones sit quietly taking notes while the idiots ask questions.

14 JANUARY

The run has its now usual quota of wonderful things and places where the pace threatens towards slow motion. But they are heroes and if the boys can hold it together and Arlene & Christian can find some joy then I can just direct and not be a social worker.

19 JANUARY

2.45 Dress rehearsal.

First preview—which went *so* well all things considered. David and John-Ross enjoying themselves hugely. Everyone else putting it all together. What a business this is.

20 JANUARY

Next morning—and I've gone right off changing anything.

And the news is—the press are coming on Monday . . . I hope they remember to pack their full quota—brain cells, antennae, hearts.

2.45 Dress rehearsal. Which at this stage feels a bit unnecessary. But not for John & Anthony. Hard to strike the balance at this stage—either lots of notes and extra rehearsals or just push the boat out and let it be.

Second preview—As ever the gremlins poking about seeing where they can get a toehold . . . Something in the general air seems to capsize on second nights. But the audience loved it and John and Anthony were full of wonders. As long as confidence doesn't turn to something overblown.

23 JANUARY

I watched the show from the box. But mostly quietly. No notes. It's all going down there—the audience is cool but not cold. A bit of first-night judging. They're too aware of the event. David does a brilliant bit of rescue work, John-Ross nearly brings the kittens on ½hr too soon but basically all is well. All also piled into Pizza Express for a happy couple of hours. Four kids completely *part* of an adult group—wonderful to watch.

24 JANUARY

Up at 8.30 for the 10.15 flight to Dallas. Streaming with a cold—main preoccupation being to get a large box of tissues for the flight.

3.45 Dallas → Salt Lake City

7pm *An Awfully Big Adventure*. Showered and changed in 8 minutes. A drive into town to a 200 seater cinema . . .

Later, a fairly embarrassing Q&A—by now I'm so tired I don't recognise words any more and then on to the Barking Frog for Mexican food . . . It's like a crazy children's party without the hats and balloons. Also paranoid. The film. My place in it all. Heigh ho.

25 JANUARY

The good news is the faxed reviews from the London papers. They are wonderful which is wonderful.

9pm *The Usual Suspects*—10 mins in realised it was a script that had been chasing me. I slept through a lot of it. Seemed like a director's calling card.[1] Gabriel Byrne has the warmest smile. Tim Roth hangs like a snake over his chair.

26 JANUARY

10am Farcical press call. Begins to be clear that America will be fascinated by the Diva. Once again the *Telegraph* shows its tawdry little fangs.

Find Danny Boyle—his face shining with the acclaim, promise and *arrival* of it all.[2]

30 JANUARY

Los Angeles.

7pm Drive to LAX. Of course, find the *Observer* review—is this paranoia but why? Do we have to be over the page, without a picture but definitely *with*

---

[1] The director was Bryan Singer.
[2] *Shallow Grave* had been recently released.

Michael Ratcliffe's prejudices? It *can't* be right to focus ⅓ of a review on the boys' diction and West Yorkshire Playhouse's snowbound service . . .

9.10 Flight to London.

2 FEBRUARY

12 Longish notes session but the train needs to be picked up and put back on the tracks.

Lunch. Rehearse. 4.05 train. I felt like a carrot in a tin of sardines. They're all mobile—phoning, laptopping, looking through the balance sheets. I read a script.

Evening at home . . . Write to Angela—Donald Pleasence [her father] died today. He taught me my first big lesson in how to upstage on camera—wait till the other actor in a two-person scene has a big speech, then move during it—they have to cover you. Wicked man. But vulnerable and gentle. And brilliant.

4 FEBRUARY

Got to get down to the gym.

Later . . . With Jools Holland on TV and a real treat with Johnny Cash, June Carter, Carleen Anderson, Pops Staples and Mazzy Star.

5 FEBRUARY

8 L'Accento with Rima, Dexter & Dalia. Dinner as therapy session. Hoping that if things are said often, clearly & loudly enough you can hack past defences and conditioning if only because underneath it he knows the truth of 'I've been there too.'

7 FEBRUARY

1.10 train to Leeds . . . At the theatre all is well—apart from John-Ross's cold. But he is uncomplaining. Sheila has dyed her hair red, 'I had to do something—coming off stage as Lily every night.' They give a beautiful performance—this piece of work is dead right for *now*. A kind of nostalgic celebration of the seven ages.

8 FEBRUARY

A curious melancholy is descending. I feel with the play as if the job is over, really. All I can do is get out the dustpan and brush from time to time—anything more radical hits barriers of youth or habit. This at the same time to saying no to work offers is not too good for peace of mind.

Emma Thompson phones. OK I'm [going to] meet him.[1]

---

[1] A.R. is referring to Ang Lee.

9 FEBRUARY

Snowdon calls to invite me to the Dorchester lunch he gives each year for Oliver Messel.[1]

10 FEBRUARY

Answer machine says *Mail on Sunday* about to print something actionable. Lawyers alerted. *Everything* passes through the brainbox.

11 FEBRUARY

10am Paul Lyon-Maris phones. Of course, it was *Mesmer*. It is alleged I was aloof. It is alleged I made 57 changes. It is alleged Roger talked of 'brilliant, argumentative, hubris'. May they try.

John Lewis to buy interesting things like a kettle, a toaster, an ironing board. Take things to UA. Some day this flat will be finished. Furnished. Fun-ish.

12 FEBRUARY

The *Mesmer* piece in the *Mail on Sunday* colours the day plus lunch talk of other films. This *cannot* be the sum of my life. And I *cannot* stoop to the Mayfair level of verbal foot-stamping.

13 FEBRUARY

Talk to Emma. 'Her people' and 'my people' now. Lawyers loom in yesterday's press. As Sharman writes—I don't know. I don't know. I don't know.

4ish To Mum. Monstrous piece of machinery called mobile staircase now dominates the hall.

This morning Ruby rang to do her I'm-back-from-my-travels-and-wait-til-you-hear-this monologue. It included telling of inviting Carrie Fisher to view her trailer (like Ms F. had never seen one). WHO, incidentally is on the cover of the *Sunday Times Magazine*, WHO incidentally wants to do a feature (yes? no?) AND which contains a wonderful piece of writing by Zoë Heller about her mother. Ruby, Carrie F. & Zoë H.—sometimes it is too weird that one's life is splayed endlessly across a double page spread.

14 FEBRUARY

11am To Lord Snowdon to look at *Mesmer* negatives. A man of total charm and a touching need to show his latest work in this month's *Vanity Fair*. He also talks of his annoyance with the BBC over the Sellers[2] documentary &

---

[1] English artist and stage designer (1904–1978)
[2] *Arena: The Peter Sellers Story* (BBC2, 1995)

using private film footage of him & 'Princess Margaret' & the general invasions that go on (he had seen Sunday's paper). His pictures from the film were good, too. Not, however, of Amanda—you can see how pissed off she was. Sometimes you just have to do as you're told ('move your little finger up—too much—now down—that's it').

18 FEBRUARY
Most of today broodingly affected by the Yorkshire press clippings which were sent from West Yorkshire Playhouse. What I took to be directness, they call rude, intimidating etc., etc.—so the headlines are all Truly Madly Badly etc., etc., etc. God forbid they shouldn't have an angle . . . But maybe I've learned a lesson. Just smile and deflect.

Watching the Sellers *Arena* programme later, you realise that it is now necessary to rationalise and reduce him down to 'nutter' rather than really focus on what was clearly (watching some *Strangelove*) genius, and how it is nurtured . . .

21 FEBRUARY
A birthday arrives again. But I'm not counting any more. Other people are, though. My brother's card arrives amongst the others like a folded couple of pages from the *Sun*—full of yearly warnings of fading powers . . . in dayglo and exclamation marks.

24 FEBRUARY
Watching news of Stephen Fry's Great Escape.[1] Ian McK. writes a well-worded letter to one of the broadsheets. In many ways what Stephen has done took great courage. I remember crawling on stage with the knives still in me—I don't recall any great sense of the honour and dignity of it all—just pain. And as time goes on, a real bewilderment that critics and journalists can take such seeming pleasure in such cruelty . . . It occurs to me that if faced with an end-of-the-world choice of companion, Stephen Fry or certain drama critics—no contest.

28 FEBRUARY
A week after the cold—flu strikes. People say 'I've got flu'—mostly they haven't. *This* is flu. The legs ache, eyes hurt, head pounds. Bed is the best place. Whenever you get up, the legs totter.

And it spreads itself through the body.

---

[1] He walked out of his lead role in Simon Gray's *Cell Mates* and fled to Belgium.

A talk with Duncan Heath.[1]

A chat with Catherine Olim.[2]

I can't work it out at all. What message am I being given?

1 MARCH

Early am—vomiting in the dark. And the morning rushing to the toilet . . . A day in bed is what the body craves and gets. Janet comes and hoovers around me.

8 MARCH

First thing an inventive cab driver brings me to the Almeida 15 mins late for the rest of the technical.

1pm another series of red lights and jams before meeting Bernardo Bertolucci & [casting director] Celestia Fox for what? His Tuscany film.[3] He's nice enough but I can see all sorts of little judgements being made every 5 seconds.

10 MARCH

12.30 Meet Christian to listen to his RADA audition pieces. One of which is Angelo [*Measure for Measure*]. Here he is, 17 years old doing the speech I left RADA with.

Preview 2.

A slowish audience turns out to have been listening carefully.

11 MARCH

4pm—matinée. With it all the way. Some notes afterwards and then the bar starts filling up with Geraldine McEwan, Catherine, Dalia, Dexter, Saffron Burrows,[4] Alan Cumming, Lindsay Duncan, Hilton. They all loved it, tough audience that they were. Full of ice-cream-carton-scrapers, foot re-arrangers, cough experts. Except by the end you realise that everyone else has been listening hard.

14 MARCH

7pm—press night.

No one in their wildest imaginings could have wished for anything better. Everything came together in some very special way. Every single actor was

---

[1] British talent agent (1947–). He was A.R.'s agent during the early part of his career.

[2] A.R.'s publicist

[3] *Stealing Beauty* (1996)

[4] British actor and model (1972–)

in the middle of the racquet. We had even *nearly* sorted out the lighting and the audience was filled with friends.

Supper for 95 (it seemed) afterwards—and I was told that someone had felt the play & the audience become one unit tonight. Which *will* do.

18 MARCH

3pm To Ang Lee. He gets the Sensibility, what's the Sense? How to play, how to shoot Brandon 'the only strong man in the story'. I said 'I'll be doing it, you'll just have to shoot it.' On the way out, there's Imogen Stubbs on the way in.

19 MARCH

2 more good reviews for *Winter Guest*. We press on.

At home later watching Martin Amis—I hope he laughs sometimes, is easy sometimes. Rima says he writes 'Men's Books'.

23 MARCH

Things in a bag and the car comes to take me to Heathrow for the 6.55 flight to Berlin. I wish these lounges weren't so devoted to the bored & boring. Perhaps there could be a door marked Eccentrics and Weirdos Only.

24 MARCH

am—Goes very fast. Print and radio interviews [for *Mesmer*]. I'm not sure I gain anything by fighting the labels, but fight I have to.

On the whole, though, the day is filled with more or less intelligent questioning. And, amazingly enough, no question about age or private life.

3pm Back for TV interviews. 'What is an actor?' . . . 'I don't think this film will be a great success' (!?!!)

25 MARCH

Quiet sleepy trip home.

8.30 to the Almeida, to watch the company sounding a bit tired. Good work but corner-cutting and David, dangerously, starting to 'act' again. The theatre is packed but way too hot from the matinée. This fragile, unpredictable piece . . . like my life at the moment. →

26 MARCH

→ And the row goes on. I *am* a bully. But it's only a noise I make to get rid of the silence.

8.30 John and Nina Darnton's [American journalists]. Dinner with Tony &

Cherie Blair, Jon Snow & his wife, Helena Kennedy & Iain Hutchison, Hugo Young & [his wife] Lucy Waring, Arthur Sulzberger[1] & Gail.

Like high-altitude oxygen I imagine—hearing Tony Blair ask Hugo Young 'what should we be doing?' Jon Snow desperate to banish titles . . . Tony Blair v. impressive and committed when relaxed (not to say informal—he was upset to find himself the only man without a tie). I had similar agonies about wearing one—he had assumed I would be an ally. I would like to talk more to Cherie Blair—intelligent but not pushy. Blair and I talk of the misuse of celebrities. He obviously has respect for Major—but then he's not remotely vindictive.

28 MARCH

3am–6.30am Madness. Watching the Oscars. Some of the most tasteless, graceless moments on recent television. *Forrest Gump* elevated. *Pulp Fiction* dumped. What does it all mean? That the Academy voters have an average age of 95 says Judy Hoflund.

Later . . . *Sense and Sensibility* deal now more or less done. With some relief.

30 MARCH

Oliver Messel suite at the Dorchester for Lord Snowdon's lunch. Glorious day, glorious room and balcony, champagne before, good chat around the table with Polly Devlin,[2] Joan Juliet Buck,[3] John Wells[4] (Bird & Fortune improvist on *The [Rory] Bremner Show*). One of life's treats.

3.30 To Shepperton for makeup and costume tests. Emma, Imelda [Staunton], Imogen in the trailer—and Kate Winslet—first impression sweetness and steel.

31 MARCH

2pm David Bailey—he's such an open, kind, funny, vulnerable soul. Maybe these will be some of the most honest pictures of late. Although he says 'I don't like taking pictures of people I like . . .'

1 APRIL

10ish Walking up Portobello Market in the sunshine with Isabelle [Huppert]—I feel like a tourist. She bought earrings then on to Conran—I bought a gift item, she bought cups and saucers.

---

[1] American journalist (1951–); Gail Gregg was his then wife
[2] Irish writer (1944–)
[3] American writer (1948–)
[4] English actor and satirist (1936–1998)

6 APRIL

Dublin.

8pm Irish Premiere.

Why was it so dark? So late starting?

Feel like an elder statesman reading the letter from Mike [Newell].

10.30 Dublin Castle. In the retiring room (H[ugh]G[rant] perkier).

Late → Lillie's Bordello.[1] Dark, noisy and restful.

7 APRIL

10am Wandering the Dublin streets before getting back to the Shelbourne for 11am to find—!—Neil Jordan and Stephen Woolley re *The Big Fella*. Will I do it? Lose weight? What other commitments?

11.25 → airport and the plane home.

Later pm—The Almeida.

John-Ross—the full pyromaniac—lights a match, it catches—before long the contents of the fire basket are ablaze. But David carries on (almost) regardless—apart from a 'Jesus' when the flames are 3' high . . . Eventually Rebecca and team come on with extinguisher.

10 APRIL

1pm Lunch at the Pelican with Peter Barnes [playwright]. It's like taking the plug out and letting the bile all dribble down to some low-down space. Before he flies off to LA and 'meetings'.

12 APRIL

11 To James Roose-Evans[2] who is recording interviews for the book he has been commissioned to do on Richard Wilson. A happy morning talking about someone I love, admire and have a huge debt of gratitude to, with James R.-E.—grace, wit, intelligence.

2.15 To RADA. Council gathered for the Lottery Assessment. More wit and intelligence although not from some members of council who have crawled out of the dark ages.

16 APRIL

10 Watching *Persuasion*. Roger Michell [director] has done a fine job of demystifying, but has allowed some of his actors to perform as if they were in Portobello Market. The clothes don't allow it—her sentences don't allow

---

[1] Club modelled on a Victorian brothel

[2] British theatre director (1927–). The book was *One Foot on the Stage*.

it. She writes *irony*—love stories of the middle classes, not social realism. I want to know what's happening to these people's hearts and minds not whether they had dirt under their nails. But he's a fine director in spite of all of that, because his eye and mind certainly *live*.

20 APRIL

(Somewhere in here the deal is done for *Michael Collins* or *The Big Fella*. So—back to Dublin.)

22 APRIL

At the show tonight—Richard Wilson, Neil Pearson, Bob Crowley, Ros March,[1] Sophie Thompson,[2] Fatimah & Caroline Holdaway. Audience a bit like a football crowd, dropped coins, a rolling bottle, whistling at the end. But they loved it.

To the Mercury. All of the above plus cast. The worst service—so bad the waitress was laughing. What else could she do?

23 APRIL

11.30 To Anthony & Carolyn Minghella to talk with them and Irène Jacob of *Wisdom of Crocodiles*. She's off to the BAFTA awards tonight with the most wonderful, clear, *comme ci* attitude. She has the same reservations about the part in *WOC*. It just needs nursing now. Anthony also treading through early minefields with *The English Patient*. People in offices with opinions.

25 APRIL

Collected [at Plymouth station]. 20 mins drive to the location. At lunchtime the trailer fills up with Imogen Stubbs, Gemma Jones, Emma Thompson—Imogen & Emma all Austened-up. Gemma in hiking boots . . . Spend the pm doing hair and makeup. Writing this at 7.20pm. Still no sign of the makeup test I've come to do . . . Somewhere around 8 we do the required stand up, sit down, look left, look right in a somewhat tight atmosphere not to mention coat. Gently humiliating. Back to the hotel. A drink with Hugh G., Imogen & Kate W.

26 APRIL

9.35 Train back to London.

Still feeling faintly depressed by yesterday. So much attention to 'The Look'. What about 'The Content'?

---

[1] British actor Rosalind March
[2] British actor (1962–), sister of Emma Thompson

And what about creating a working environment with Ang—who, reading between the already apparent lines, is used to 'conducting' his actors, rather than nurturing.

Hugh G. says they are having 'worst notes' competitions. Fairly typical Grant-Activity. However 'that was dull' does not sound too helpful.

29 APRIL
Last matinée. All four boys are here. And quite right too. The play is handed over beautifully. Why is it that matinées often produce the best work? Afternoon ease, I suppose.

8pm and a truly glorious last performance, full of freedom and new thinking. Sometimes I watch this and cannot think *how* it came together. At the curtain call all 7 boys came on to much cheering.

2 MAY
A 6.15 wake up for my first actual day on *Sense and Sensibility*.

Makeup and hair becomes a gentle negotiation—hair, especially. Heated rollers eventually wins.

And the day is spent walking out of this beautiful church towards Luciana Arrighi's[1] thatched barn and hayricks in green, green fields. Tea in the small hotel nearby . . . Kate W. looking so beautiful in her gilded wedding gown. Emma T. with her eyes everywhere. Harriet W. & I uncool enough to admit just enjoying being here.

Drinks in the bar at 8pm—Emma, Imelda, Hugh L[aurie], Hugh G., Gemma Jones, Harriet, Kate W. Hugh G. his usual snappy, sharp, acid self. In to dinner with 2 x Hugh, Harriet & me. Fortunately the conversation moves away from gossip and we talk of British & US film production. Too much irony? Hugh Laurie turns out to be an action movie freak. Hugh G. is fascinated by figures, fees, %.

4 MAY
I'm beginning to get the hang of Ang. He came by to have a chat. 'What are you going to do as Brandon?' I can only show him and talk in generalised terms. By the end, he and everyone seems happy. And I can go to Plymouth for the 6.35 → London.

Reading obituaries for Michael Hordern—my mind goes back to Stratford 1978 when he was as angry as I was, but warm, funny, flirtatious, no-nonsense. 'I'm not much of a company man.' Dinners chez us, Eve [Mor-

---

[1] Australian-Brazilian-Italian production designer (1940–)

timer, M.H.'s wife] waiting outside theatres at curtain-up, Michael saying that theatre came a poor third to fishing and planting his onions.

5 MAY

7.30 Odeon Hammersmith or Labatt's Apollo as it is now known for Mary Chapin Carpenter. She comes on at 8.30—polished, professional, blonde hair swinging over her shoulder, guitars switched on cue. Maybe once or twice does she make time relative to her interpretation. At all other moments it passes. She moves effortlessly from one song to another. In her dressing room afterwards—cool, professional, untouched.

7 MAY

6ish To Mum. Watched truly awful VE Day concert from Hyde Park. All those showbiz right wingers. Ute Lemper proving yet again that she isn't Marlene Dietrich. Elaine [Paige] *not* doing her own stuff, stuck with Piaf. Cliff Richard telling us that 'today made him realise how much he owed all those brave men and women . . .'

10 MAY

And another day not called.

Lunch on the set. Then into boots and breeches and off to the stables. Marcus is not the smoothest ride—a tank. A reluctant tank. Every stride has weight in it. Which makes him very tiring to ride. After ½ hour I'm knackered.

12 MAY

Another 7.30 wake up. Another day not being used.

The sun shines. They do something else. The clouds come over—they do something else.

Maybe rent a car. The licence is out of date. So it's wait.

13 MAY

7am call—and finally I'm on . . .

As it turns out the scene becomes a nightmare of rushed decisions, manip-ulations, too many looks. It isn't thought through so time is wasted on fixing the horse to the post in a totally unnecessary way . . . Which means that acting is out the window . . . I end the day feeling humiliated and angry—but I can't show it. Words are expressed to Lindsay Doran [producer], however. But that's the scene. Forever. It's no way to work.

Later to Emma's party. Fight through the (real) depression and dance.

14 MAY

Emma, Gemma, Greg [Wise] and I go off for a 3 hour cliff-walk. This was really spectacular. England, my England. So beautiful (mixed up with cara-van parks, garden gnomes, mini-waterfalls—so English). We walk in twos, threes, fours, singly . . . Emma still likes to be the Boss.

15 MAY

An alarming morning—my first with a group of actors, a scene and Ang. He opens himself so wide to be available to others' ideas and a vagueness can creep in. Suggestions are made, the scene relaxes and yields and good work is done. And his taste is a permanent guiding light.

Late night [call] to USA—the *Die Hard 3* Saga. It's a disgrace that work can be regurgitated in this way. Do I take on a major studio? Of course not. I don't have the energy, never mind the money.

16 MAY

The *Die Hard 3* Saga goes on. Litigation lawyers now come in.

Watching *The Politician's Wife* on Channel 4. Compulsive viewing—especially if Juliet's character starts to kick back. Ghastly script, but hugely enjoyable.

17 MAY

Lunch in a pub car park. Ang has revealed a deep affection for desserts and all things sweet. I bring him all 3 puddings on a polystyrene plate—lemon meringue pie, profiteroles and Banoffee pie. Ang heaven. I ate 3 satsumas.

20 MAY

Breakfast at the hotel with Lindsay—we talk of optimists/pessimists and the paths that either create for themselves. Rima throws quizzical glances at me.

22 MAY

This was a day of such contrasts. As ever I wonder what lessons life is attempting to hand out.

Brandon in the reeds, Brandon sitting alone in a boat, walking with his dog, riding his horse—a chance to find his centre in some extraordinary locations. Leaving me introspective enough without coming back to the hotel to hear of all the Cannes/*Carrington* events.

Will this prove to be *the* big mistake of my working life?

23 MAY

9.35 Train to London.

Ruby comes over and we go to the Agadir for dinner. Fine and dandy for stories of LA. Less so for Ruby's analysis of our current sense of each other. The lesson of course is not to take close friends for granted.

24 MAY

Harold Wilson has died. The tributes are generous and lucid and human especially from Barbara Castle and Tony Benn (who reminds us that he *included* the Left rather than sidelined or expelled it—'A bird needs a left wing and a right wing to fly' Ian Mikardo[1]). What they don't say is that to those of us who were teenagers in 1964, it was such a Brave New World and a government filled with brilliant minds and new ideas. A real sense of revolution. And as Barbara Castle said—'If he hadn't resigned we may never have had to endure Thatcherism at all.'

29 MAY

And, almost inevitably, J.P. wins the gong at Cannes.[2] What the fuck are the lessons? Say 'yes' more often. Don't second-guess so much. You made the decisions for some maybe very wrong reasons.

Whatever—it produces a very quiet day. I'm sick of getting thumped like this. But maybe it won't stop until I stop brooding and prevaricating.

31 MAY

Montacute House, Somerset.

Sunny, sunny day.

Various scenes. We solve them together. And in 3 cases one shot.

Later and the strangeness of this life—sprayed with water, in between takes, with the contents of an Evian spray can, surrounded by the National Trust stewards.

1 JUNE

The day starts with radio reports of Christopher Reeve's accident—chilling, focusing, terrible.[3] It makes us all acutely aware of today's last shot.

Later, Gemma & I get into the coach and go with the clappers. Swiftly

---

[1] Labour MP (1908–1993)

[2] Jonathan Pryce, for playing Lytton Strachey in *Carrington*

[3] American actor (1952–2004), best known for playing Superman, paralysed in a riding accident

followed by Mark & I galloping down the drive. 4 times. Thank God we separated the reins . . .

Dinner at the hotel. Flowers on the table. Imelda makes us weep with laughter at the stories of dope scones.

2 JUNE

Hugh Laurie & I talk of the *Wanda* sequel [*Fierce Creatures*]. He'd been asked, decided to say no in the end, now much self-torture & schadenfreude. This rings a bell . . .

3 JUNE

The rain pours down—perfect for the shots which remain.

Greg and I carry Kate in turn across the sodden lawn. A piece of green string is stretched to guide our progress.

Then some waiting. An opportunity to start reading Tim Pat Coogan's book on de Valera[1] which is terrifically well-written and entertaining.

5 JUNE

Today I felt a schism appear—not permanent, but just my own desire to focus more on the work than on having a lovely time. I notice actors being treated somewhat lightly. Scenes put together moment by moment rather than taking a look at the whole scene first.

6 JUNE

Back to London on the train with Gemma.

7 JUNE

7.45 Ambassadors w. Angela Pleasence to see *Killing of Sister George*. In case we are so mind-numbed by the production the play's title is projected on to the front drop. Some really terrible work going on. But, of course, direction-less. Not that Miriam [Margolyes] can be easy *to* direct.

19 JUNE

This was a tough day. I kind of knew it would be. Antagonism and negativity took familiar toeholds and this was added to far too much schoolmarming from Emma. I cannot puppet this stuff. Or any stuff. Liz Spriggs[2] noticed the nerve-endings and her arms slipped round my waist.

Later a drink in the bar with some of the sparks [electricians] was a real plea-sure. They so enjoy their life and the people they meet. Not a trace of cynicism.

---

[1] *De Valera: Long Fellow, Long Shadow*
[2] Elizabeth Spriggs, English actor (1929–2008)

20 JUNE

A freer day, lighter breezes around the brain.

22 JUNE

The square in Salisbury with the cathedral floating up behind us. As ever, words that seem so manageable on the page become intractable in a take. And with this one, a casual 'Sorry, can I go again?' means a major realignment of carriages, horses, extras, an army . . .

Find a print in a Salisbury bookshop. The end of shoot gift panic begins.

And Major 'resigns'. It's called 'courageous'. Fresh from all my de Valera reading I'd call it 'clever', 'well-judged', 'cunning'.

23 JUNE

Once again, the tightrope walking. Suggestions are treated just too much like irritations. And this is *not* an atmosphere for confrontation—and if it were forced, Ang would collapse from wounded pride, honour, everything.

3.23 Train to London.

25 JUNE

These are the CUSP days on which a life hinges. Left? Right? Straight? Winding?

Rima decides not to come to the Directors' Guild dinner—so wisely—I take Louise Krakower. What the hell is this event about?? Obey your instincts in future—DON'T go.

How can Cinema be celebrated by [John] Boorman rambling, Zeffirelli not communicating. And so on. As soon as the last speech descends we escape . . .

26 JUNE

7.20am pick-up to go to Heathrow and Dublin.

As I got out of the car [in Dublin], there is Julia Roberts, upstairs to find Liam [Neeson] & Aidan [Quinn]. Neil Jordan arrives a few minutes later—we all sit down and talk through the de Valera scenes. Neil is his usual jitterbugging self—like a grasshopper nipping from topic to topic.

27 JUNE

9.45 pick-up to go to [the *Michael Collins*] offices for a read through.

Stephen Rea's warm heart fills the room. Some great faces everywhere. Neil reads the stage directions and sings, and makes occasional yelps and stops to talk about a set—so excited by it all.

A bit of a dash to airport to get the 2.45 plane.

29 JUNE

To Shepperton . . . Of course, the set, the newspapers, the TV and every-where is obsessed with Hugh Grant and his Sunset trick . . . [1] What can you say? Except as I said to Emma 'There but for the grace.' At the moment I think it follows on too perfectly from the notion of a world feeding on itself in the most gourmandising way. So many column inches, so many other things we should concern ourselves with.

The scenes feel as if they are being ticked off now . . . Ang seems nervous. He probably needs a hug. Like Hugh.

5 JULY

Ruby calls. She's with Carmen du Sautoy[2]—eventually they come over and we go to Café Med. Great, honest talk with old friends—same old topic of What are we doing—where are we going? But knot-releasing all the same.

9 JULY

1pm To Richard Wilson's for his birthday lunch party . . . Idyllic stuff. Were it not for the increasingly repetitive angst of How Much Has Been Drunk?? It means late-night rowing—pointless silences.

12 JULY

7.45 Dinner with Barbara and Ken Follett. Ken, as ever, starts the evening with a jolly insult about my work—it seems to be a reflex action. Barbara seems v. tired. (Later she confesses to having been working until 3.30am.)

19 JULY

To Kensington Council Chamber. When Rima speaks they all shut up. MP to be . . .

23 JULY

9am A glorious ride through glorious countryside. Pity my horse is called Wogan. But he's high, wide and handsome and when he wants to go he's a Force 10 gale.

Home to messages from LA saying that *Awfully Big Adventure* has been well reviewed but is doubtless too dark to succeed.

---

[1] He had been arrested in Los Angeles with a prostitute.
[2] British actor (1950–)

8 AUGUST

To . . . Dublin. And the Shelbourne. Catch-up-fast time. Hire a video recorder, read the books, get under Dev's[1] skin. Hopefully.

9 AUGUST

8.45 pick-up → the set . . . The reconstruction of O'Connell Street is quite brilliant. Post Office, Mansion House, cobbles and—frighteningly—the platform for Dev's speech. But it's OK (I think) the drive down the street is first to ease me in.

All day the crowds grow and grow—rumour has it that 2000 more were sent home. That leaves 2–3000 inside all staring at me since Neil [Jordan] comes to announce that the speech is first. Is it his nerves that make him question the hair, the costume, the accent, the *everything*???

In the end he's happy and we just do it. No rehearsal. Just do it. Which is why the resentment about 1st class, 2nd class treatment of American & British actors rankles. It will *never* happen again. But there's no denying the buzz of it all.

10 AUGUST

10.30 pick-up to the set. Photo call for the Irish press. Julia Roberts a mite pissed-off at being kept waiting . . . She should have tried yesterday's gauntlet ride.

11 AUGUST

Lunchtime-ish at 'The Highest Pub in Ireland (sic)'. Foxes. The Highest? The most full of bric-a-brac, or junk, certainly. Including some Dev front pages and a Victorian potty, screwed to the wall . . .

12 AUGUST

Taxi to the airport for the 12.30 → Cork. Delays, hanging about, sitting on tarmac. Eventually we get there and fart about trying to find the hire car.

A staggeringly beautiful drive to Cork (and onwards). The Brown Pub in the grey square on the blue, blue day is the last stopping point—a glass of Guinness and then down a lane is Belinda Lang. How did they find this heaven on earth? . . . Picnic on the grass looking up at the hill. Delicious supper. Too much red wine. Bleary-eyed. Bed.

---

[1] Éamon de Valera

17 AUGUST

Wandering around the streets of Dublin—along Dame Street from Temple Bar to Grafton Street, Dawson Street and back, getting keys cut, looking around Brown Thomas[1]—it reminds me mostly of early views of 6th and 7th Avenue in Greenwich Village.

Back to the flat, moulding it slowly to my shape . . . To the set for hair dyeing . . . Back to clean some windows (always therapeutic—instant results). Supper. Early night.

18 AUGUST

The first day on the set with the other actors . . . And the prevailing atmosphere is happy.

19 AUGUST

Waiting for the TV man to fix the video and Rima to arrive . . . Walk around Temple Bar, buy some quite fantastic ham from the Italian deli.

20 AUGUST

Read the Sunday papers. *Die Hard with a Vengeance* opened this week— could describe my attitude towards the 'discussions' with 20th C. Fox.

21 AUGUST

A day of running and jumping . . . Good fun because no lines. A kind of headiness is inevitable—and deepened by a trip to Whelan's for Sharon Shannon. My hero. The joy that empties itself from her CDs is nothing to what happens live. Number after number has the whole body, the whole room moving helplessly with it. And I met her. And kissed her. And asked her to play at our wrap party. And she said yes.

Home to beans on toast.

22 AUGUST

Kilmainham Jail.

2 minutes in one of the cells and I'm starting to get anxious—what must it have been like? Clear enough in *Last Words*—the book given to me by the museum manager. They were all so proud to die. They knew when it was coming [and] what it was for. Strange walking in the footsteps, too, copying de Valera's letter to Mother Gonzaga[2] (he has been told he is to be shot). This

---

[1] Department store
[2] Mother Mary Gonzaga Barry, Irish Catholic religious sister (1834–1915)

is beginning to feel like something I just have to hand myself over to—it will take care of itself. Hidden forces are very strong. I'm sitting in his cell, writing a letter to Michael Collins, the dust filling the slash of sunlight. That glimpse of a changing sky must have meant everything.

23 AUGUST

Kilmainham and the sacristy. Father Benedict would be de Valera if you gave him some glasses. I'm surrounded by people talking of where the host, the genuflexion would be if, and, but, as we try to shape a scene and get a candle imprint in the wax. Difficult and a sudden reminder that heat conducts especially down the handle of a metal key. In the end the scene is sort of stitched together. I hope it has some wit, and that push for full-face was not seen as *pure* ego.

25 AUGUST

Buried all day down in the endless catacombs. Very little room for the easy personal exchanges . . . A bit of High-Nooning goes on—not helped by an excessively silent crowd of jurors (for the scene). The scene is difficult to get hold of anyway and an excessive (and all-too familiar) desire to 'solve' it instantly doesn't help. A mix of concentration, determination and invention produces something *like* the real thing, but tiredness eventually claims the crown as the text turns to intractable ashes in my mouth just as the cameras turn round on me.

3 SEPTEMBER

Gearing up to work on a Sunday is a contradiction in terms. 10.15 pick-up to paint the hair brown again and then many hours in the trailer but at least it's the All-Ireland Hurling final [between Clare and Offaly] and Clare would have been Dev's team. Fantastically exciting game to watch—now *there's* something for Murdoch to promote. Clare wins for the first time in 81 years . . .

The scene is, surprisingly, in a bike shop so a spinning wheel becomes the prop and the metaphor (for my brain trying to forge a connection with my tongue). Not sure it wasn't a bit tricksy and secretiveness must not become Dev's habitual manner but there was a *shape*.

7 SEPTEMBER

7.15 Call. To the Mansion House . . . Some argy-bargy early on about why aren't there any women here. Countess Markievicz?[1] This script is held together

---

[1] Irish politician (1868–1927)

by liberal scrapings of prejudice allied to the fact that the times are so badly recorded, as Neil says. So much is left to hearsay or personal standpoint. We get there, though. In between shots, the usual half-successful attempts to collar Neil and discuss later scenes, or show him contradictory versions. But at least I know now that in some part of his nerve-stillness he is listening. And he lights up all over when he's pleased with the work. A pat on the back from quiet, determined, shy Chris Menges [director of photography] means a lot, too. The day ends well and Neil says (3 or 4 times) 'I'll have a look at that scene, yeah?'

9 SEPTEMBER

To the airport for the 12.45 to London. Stephen Frears there . . . and I hear how well *The Van* is going . . . I still can't think quite what he meant by saying he never understands why people (actors or in this case Chris Menges) want to direct. Does that mean he hates what he does or is he inviolate?

12 SEPTEMBER

12.45 Flight to Dublin.

6.45 pick-up and on to a night shoot at Kilmainham. Sandy Powell [costume designer] has made Dev a fetching coat and bonnet for his Lincoln Jail escape. Much fiddling about with keys and locks and doors then running up the road till 5am by which time it's all happening in a blur. Stephen Woolley says the rushes are great. This is one man (of few words normally) who I believe.

19 SEPTEMBER

1.30 pick-up. Through the Wicklow Mountains to Glenmalure and a thatched cottage by a stream. For the first time Dev in a State scene with the 'Fresh Faced Kid' i.e. Jonathan[1] who's on his third movie this year, plays flute, tin whistle and drums (and sings Gaelic & Rock) has just returned from backpacking in Vietnam, learned Arabic in Egypt, and is, of course, also impossibly good-looking . . .

The scene is snatched at. No proper thoughts AGAIN. Homework and flexibility is what we can offer, but no guarantees as to the mood of the moment. But that is also part of the pleasure of working with Neil. You *have* to yield. He doesn't stand still long enough to have a structured discussion. In a strange way it's quite freeing.

---

[1] Jonathan Rhys Meyers, who played Michael Collins' assassin

21 SEPTEMBER

. . . 6pm pick-up.

Another lump of Ireland commandeered for the Pub and Hayrick [scene]. The town stays up all night to see it. Eventually, my shot is at 4am. Maybe it's just as well. The shivering is fairly authentic by then.

Neil & I and gradually the crew go to the pub for a 6am drink. It becomes a chance for a mutual affirmation of the wish to work together again. My brain had long packed its bags so we may have to have the discussion again with proper sentences.

Bed at 7am.

25 SEPTEMBER

The Treaty Debate. In the Reading Room of Trinity—beautiful octagonal space filled with great faces . . . Dev takes hold and hangs on all day towards evening when the camera comes round. A brief note from Neil and the whole tone shifts to something more neurotic and darker. But it's a long, long smoke-filled day.

Good then to go to Cooke's for a farewell supper with Aidan Quinn. And proper talks with Neil and then Natasha Richardson who is in the well-known shall I, shan't I, dilemma.

And of course Lillie's beckons until it's 4am. Again.

1 OCTOBER

9am The phone rings. It seems only about 3 hours since I went to sleep. It is only 3 hours since I went to sleep. Down to the set to re-do a scene with Liam (off-camera but on-glasses).

Now staging for a Tuesday reshoot. One advantage of this is spending a Sunday quietly thinking about packing, answering letters, moving on.

3 OCTOBER

9.45 pick-up. Reshoot scene with Collins without Liam, with Neil reading in. Chris wanted to re-do the lighting. Fair enough. Actors aren't the *only* craftspersons.

4 OCTOBER

Home to mounds of mail and 24 messages. The phone rings. Emma T. She sounds strange—sort of depersonalised which for her is a kind of contradiction in terms. If only, *once*, she would receive something from a point of innocent joy . . .

9 OCTOBER

7pm *Il Postino*. *Cinema Paradiso* school. At a crucial moment, the subtitles disappeared, and almost wrecked the film. I didn't quite hand myself over to it as completely as I expected to.

Dinner at the Italian afterwards. I landed on the horrendous possibility of a future spent eating in restaurants. Couldn't. Always more fun preparing food in an efficient kitchen and entertaining friends.

12 OCTOBER

9.30 Car to Goldcrest to loop *Sense and Sensibility*. Good to see Ang and Lindsay. An incredibly irritating sound recorder. Complete with acting notes?!? 'Could you put a laugh in here to cover the gap . . .'

15 OCTOBER

To → Mum for a.m. visit including hair-raising trip around the supermarket on her scooter.

16 OCTOBER

Nothing like enough sleep before getting up and checklisting myself out the door, into the car and on the way to Heathrow. Not without hitches. The keys from R.W. The driver leaving me at Terminal 4, not 1 . . . But eventually I'm on the plane with Ian McKellen and St Petersburg here we come. Ian is the best travel companion—funny and generous and curious and as clumsy as me with his fruit juice all over the seat. Lunch is taken in a different area.

17 OCTOBER

Today was re-aligning mixed up with Babelsberg déjà vu, mixed up with costume fittings for a character I don't know yet, so back to the hotel for catch-up time. Which was helpful in terms of clothes if nothing else.

And before dinner Ian & I wandered into a supermarket, niet, mini-market and bought the Georgian wine which can take the blame for these scribblings.

19 OCTOBER

Will I now ever get used to not having caviar for breakfast??

20 OCTOBER

First day shooting on *Rasputin*.

A late start means . . . losing the light so on to the vomit shot—except for the last take, that is. Some HBO whisperings and 'one more take' with the vomit disappearing behind the pillar. Any amount of sex and violence, but no *visible* vomit.

25 OCTOBER

10am pick-up. Shots lost all the time. [Sedmara] Rutstein has recorded 3 songs—some of the day is spent learning the words. Some of it, over lunch, reminding Freddie's[1] mother that he's getting paid so stop complaining . . . Finally hit the set around 6pm. 'We have our instructions,' says Elemér [Ragályi, cinematographer], cryptically. But prophetically. Uli [Edel, director], always in danger of sense of humour absence, is also sounding more & more like a dictator. A showdown may well show up.

Back at the hotel, Diana Quick, James Frain,[2] Peter Jeffrey,[3] etc., etc. have arrived. We all have dinner in the Imperial and laugh. Actors are great people, and special and funny & self-denigrating, so fuck you anyone who disagrees.

26 OCTOBER

The first real scene. After Rasputin's first real healing of Alexei. It's all about manipulating, cajoling, bullying, flattering, whatever-ing the director. Off-set Uli has a vulnerability that shines through his tractor-like nature. On-set, the bark is insistent, humour almost non-existent, manners unheard-of as extras are herded and actors given their instructions. 'You will stand here, you will do this, you will then do that.'

I, of course, respond to all this like a tank running through its gears. A mild confrontation eventually ensues when we test the water of 'Actors are People', mainly because he likes the work, so a moment arrives to explain—as if to a child—how exactly it is being achieved. How will this fadge? At least the bark disappeared.

And the pleasures are that Greta [Scacchi] & Ian retain their wit and good humour as I sail blowsily into the fray. There will be many laughs ahead . . .

31 OCTOBER

Scene between Ian and I. Supported by late script notes—but coming from such a weak, cowardly mouth in production corner.

---

[1] British actor Freddie Findlay (1983–), who played Tsarevich Alexei
[2] English actor (1968–)
[3] English actor (1929–1999)

1 NOVEMBER

In St Isaac's. This gift ($35,000 of it) of a location. I don't think Uli knows what to do with it. Serviceable, clear narrative would be a bonus, but again his panic and insecurities come out as such charmless, mirthless behaviour that it is also counter-productive. We would all be working better if we were really working together.

2 NOVEMBER

I go to the set at 6pm only to be sent home again at 8pm. Somewhere around 10.30 I feel a confrontation coming on, so I go to look for one. Success. Nick [Gillott, producer] & Uli are in the bar. Faffing. 'Out with it' is had by all. Rehearsals are promised. Hallelujah.

6 NOVEMBER

This was the day for singing in Russian to a Russian crew . . . and rowing endlessly with Uli, He Who Waits to Be Obeyed. No process. In his boyish way he just can't stop himself from stopping us if we step outside his story-board.

7 NOVEMBER

Uli finally said it. When I wondered about a camera coming with me across the snow, he says 'Why?' I reply, 'It would have the right energy.' He says, 'I do it in the editing room.'

8 NOVEMBER

The body clock is whizzing, rewinding and whirring. No knowing what time my eyes might click open. Writing this at 8.10am. A brainbox that can't shake off yesterday's 'Why are you doing this movie?'

9 NOVEMBER

The efforts of yesterday turn into the aches, pains and bruises of today. Massage and whirlpool help and then off to the wooden bridge (the actual bridge) for the throwing over of Rasputin. Ten degrees below is a jaw-dropping temperature with gloves and coat off, so I hid in the car as much as possible. I hate last nights, last shots, goodbyes. Casual as possible is all I can do—hard in the face of an outpouring of affection from the Russian crew. Makes me wish we were here longer and with more sensitive leaders.

But the champagne and cake is a happy farewell as the circus moves on. Later . . . Uli lectures Masha & Olga [who are playing two of the princesses] about the history of Russia. Unfuckingbelievable. The almost total lack of curiosity about another human being . . .

10 NOVEMBER

Vienna Airport. Flew out of St Petersburg at 3.15. Now we're two hours back waiting for the 7.50 to Budapest. Totally confused and wondering what I'm doing. This job engages one minute and utterly distances the next. Why do I continually find myself being shunted into the middle of the road?? Is that the awful convergence of Colin Wilson's[1] 2 destinies? Half involved, half outsider—impossible mix or original one?? The above prompted by Natasha L.'s[2] gloom and doom. Drawing ill fortune to oneself then meant that our flight was cancelled. 2 hours later we're on to KLM. Arrive Budapest. Great room overlooking the Danube and Buda.

11 NOVEMBER

Some work on the script. The Nicholas off to war sequence is all wrong.

Budapest has been 'got at'—McDonald's, Burger King, Marks & Spencer. It doesn't have the flowing impossible beauty of St Petersburg but there's something that was obviously unique being ironed out. The hotel is just Budapest, America. Imported phones, lamps, cupboards etc. God forbid Americans should feel they are somewhere ELSE.

13 NOVEMBER

Some days make keeping a diary not only essential but a legal requirement. My hearing has not been right since the shooting of *Rasputin*. Today I asked for a doctor [and] was taken to see a specialist—no burst eardrum but 'acute hearing loss' in the upper register. 4 hours a day treatment (can't) or vitamin pills etc. to regenerate damaged cells—all v. alarming . . . I notice a quiet panic filling the eyes of producers . . . followed by the words 'second opinion'.

14 NOVEMBER

Uli has this irritating ability to look at your instinctive responses and straighten them in the same breath as complaining that it's 'too neat', 'too theatrical'—too something. I am reminded of one of those battery-run toy drummers from the TV ads.

Production designer in the bar later voices the same running complaint— 'It was such a good script'—I keep trying to work out why it changed. When? How? The stealthy hand of the money men.

---

[1] Author of *The Outsider*
[2] Natasha Landau, costume designer

15 NOVEMBER

[Princess] Marisa Scene—Basic Date Rape preceded by the women either washing my clothes, baking my cakes or sewing my shirts . . .

—no opinions, just hero worship. The *Mesmer* echoes resound, the gently reproving faces are a blast from the past, the shrug of the shoulder exactly the same. We hope for the best . . .

'Production' continues to clodhop its way through this experience. Joyce [Nettles] is now fired (after Pat, the attempt on the camera crew & Andy) followed by Hugh Harlow [production supervisor]. They are *all* the people I actually TRUST—is this a coincidence??? A character flaw??

Sheila Ruskin[1] and I, having performed the swiftest seduction scene in history, are fairly plastered by the time we leave the bar.

16 NOVEMBER

—only to pick up where we left off—humping at 8am, cameras and wires everywhere. Taste & judgement & careful placing of clothing.

17 NOVEMBER

The start of the day is promising (the band is a joy—later I discovered that one of the dancers was in tears that her shoulders were uncovered, convinced that her husband would divorce her—Natasha[2] had to move fast with some shawls).

As the day wears on, Uli hits his stride in terms of slowing the work . . . I fall into bed with murder on my mind.

20 NOVEMBER

Charm. Humour. Perspective. Respect for other people. Awareness of foreign tongues, customs. All more or less absent from Herr Director's psyche. But his vulnerability keeps me with him rather than on the next plane.

21 NOVEMBER

Marco Polo with a gang, plus Diana Quick who has flown in. James F.'s last night with us. He's a real representative of his generation of actors. Somewhere covered up is his love of his craft but loud, strong and visible is his knowledge of who's doing what film with who, what the grosses were and how to say Yeah? And Really? As real contributions to a conversation. Or to

---

[1] English actor (1946–). She played Princess Marisa, who asks Rasputin to bless her but before he does he insists she have sex with him.

[2] Natasha Gorina, makeup supervisor

cover up (again) his genuine intelligence and warmth lest they should not be cool qualities. Thank you Thatcher.

22 NOVEMBER

1ish To the hospital for second hearing check. A slight improvement but they want to do 'infusions'. 1 hour a day in the hospital—good luck with that, schedulers.

24 NOVEMBER

Woke knowing there was no way I could work . . . To the set and straight back to bed and boxes of pills of all descriptions . . . This kind of sickness robs you of thought—you are *all* sensation and none of it is pleasant, except a certain relief at being still and warm.

25 NOVEMBER

Ian & John[1] call by having spent 4 hours rewriting two of their scenes . . . Ian calls back later with flowers and concern. He has the biggest heart. Greta told me that yesterday he had visited her and the monologue went 'You don't want those clothes lying there, do you?' 'You don't want all these trays of food left here, do you?' With that room service was called, he hung all her clothes up and then went into the bathroom where he cleaned up, and, Greta thinks, even cleaned the bath. His leaving words were 'You can't get well inside if you're not well outside, can you.' There was only one tray for him to question in my room, but he was certainly looking around.

26 NOVEMBER

Woke feeling lousy . . . What does penicillin do? Mask the symptoms? Kid you?

Rima sorts it out on the phone, of course. 'If it's a virus—no use but no harm, if it's a bacteria it'll help.' I love her certainties.

28 NOVEMBER

The virus seems to have eased and allowed a quick entry to the full 3-sneeze-at-a-time cold.

Watched K. Clarke hurdling through his budget. Good if you are a rich old person owning vintage cars and drinking Scotch—why are we surprised.

Re-reading some pages of this diary is like looking at a graph of an exhausted mind.

---

[1] John Wood, English actor (1930–2011)

29 NOVEMBER

Back to work . . . By an effort of will we make it through 3 scenes (2 of them on one take . . .).

1 DECEMBER

Rima arrives—happy little trot around the streets, buy some shoes at the handmade shop. Some gift items for Greta & maybe Ian.

2 DECEMBER

A day of fairly high temperament—or as Jenny says 'Once you start on Uli, it's amazing how many people have got something else to do.' But it is impossible to ignore his rudeness. 'Move her quicker . . .' 'Her' name is Elena [Malashevskaya, playing Grand Duchess Olga], she's been with us from the beginning. LEARN HER NAME!!!

6 DECEMBER

Another definition of hell. This time a dinner scene in a room full of mirrors with a director who HASN'T DONE HIS FUCKING HOMEWORK. So faff about is the order of the morning.

G.S. has 2 lines and spends most of the day trying to remember them in amongst a lot of queening. Not endearing and deeply remembered. Especially when you have a bunch of text and continuity muddled together. Strangling springs constantly to mind.

7 DECEMBER

10 scenes to shoot (if possible) . . . I watched the plaster/rubber cast of myself (very creepy) being buried & then, later on, burned. Uli, only half-joking, had been looking forward to using me, in person, in the coffin and nailing the lid down (ha ha ha has to be added to this in a Doberman Pinscher kind of manner).

10 DECEMBER

Up to Buda and the Castle to look at locations . . . Now I see one of our problems—Uli's fatal indecision and non-involvement of others. His always shaky sense of humour completely deserts him. Filming is a blinkered, obsessive activity with him, somehow to truly involve others is to confess weakness, or maybe he was bullied, or maybe as John C.[1] was saying his experience of being German with a black Jewish wife makes him even more

---

[1] John Cater, English actor (1932–2009)

defensive. Or maybe he just shouldn't bark. In the car on the way back the unsuspecting driver is yapped at to turn the music off. That's why I fight him and don't love myself for it.

11 DECEMBER

Mind and body getting v. tired. Morning doing prostitute scene with Agnes[1] who is excellent—usual 'could you be provocative' rubbish going on . . .

Later, an Indian meal with Ian . . . Messages saying S&S a treat. I feel a holiday coming on in a big way.

14 DECEMBER

Finally shot the last scene kneeling in wet earth, by the side of a road, dogs barking, traffic going by . . .

Later at the hotel, Ian, Greta and I have some late supper in the Grill. Too late, I discover some edible menu food. Greta is up late. Ian says 'That's OK, you're supposed to look terrible tomorrow.'

15 DECEMBER

Today they shot the Romanovs. Not before I had been to the hospital—no improvement. Now diagnosed as permanent damage. Those words are all suddenly depressing.

Inevitably the wrap party (having been moved to the hotel) moves back to the stage. Sad to finish in such acrimony with producers. In the bar at the hotel afterwards I attempt to talk to Uli about the whole experience—he is immovably certain about his brilliance as a visionary, his tolerance and understanding of actors. He is wrong about nothing, and even does his 'Where is . . .' moments in the middle of something or other I was wasting my breath trying to explain.

Second-rate, says Ian. Infuriating say I.

17 DECEMBER

London.

Rima toddles off to the *Sense and Sensibility* screening. I'm overflowing with cold and post-*Rasputin* confusion and decide to stay at home. She returns aglow, which for this Austen freak-of-all-time is the greatest compliment.

---

[1] Ági Kökényessy, Hungarian actor (1967–)

21 DECEMBER

12.30 To Garfield Davies [ENT specialist]. Identical diagnosis. Permanent damage—nothing can be done. The pills would achieve nothing. Like staring at a blank piece of paper. Can't really comprehend.

25 DECEMBER

Whatever law it is, or thinks it is, which says that families must gather together and get on on a particular day should be repealed or blown apart.

This was the pits.

Alcohol as ever the great loosener of tongues, truths & untruths. It can free and it can destroy. The meal at the hotel was dreadful, appalling service . . . Cold everything, hours between courses. Too much time to drink. Memories of past Christmases.

Rima & I end up, thankfully, alone with some cold meat, a bottle of wine and *The American President*. Appropriate—a film about nothing . . .

26 DECEMBER

A trip to Ruby & Ed's, where, amazement—a hug from Max. A first. We leave him v. happily playing with his Geo-Game and vamoose to Helena & Iain's party. Neil & Glenys, Jonathan & Kate, Susie Orbach, Claire Rayner, Alastair Campbell, Jon Snow etc., etc.—the usual heady mix. BH, what with jet lag and LA-itis—have to be rescued & led to a quiet room. More drink, more tears. A sudden flash of opening a door as a child to find an aunt crying. Christmas, it was, too. Eventually get away to the only real, real thing—my mother sitting at home, not well, but happy to see us. Eventually, join R. & E. & B. at the Standard (local Indian restaurant). Now Miss R. is pissed and voluble and argumentative. I feel like the top of my head is coming off, spinning. Pack.

27 DECEMBER

Painless, easy flight to Toronto.

29 DECEMBER

Straightforward flight to New York. Beverly Penberthy's[1] brother is there to pick us up and take us to Rye—winter wonderland via Disney and Hallmark . . . Beverly later cooks dinner with Martha Clarke[2] as an extra guest. The hearing thing is going to be a battle—it makes me sit 'outside' the conversation . . . But

---

[1] American actor (1932–)
[2] American theatre director and choreographer (1944–)

then so does exposure to the ad campaign for *Sense and Sensibility*—there's no escaping who Columbia thinks is the draw.

30 DECEMBER

am Looking out of the curved windows at the Sound flowing by, dark branches filling the window frames, a clear blue/grey & pale yellow sky—tracking back over this jam-packed year.

Winter Guest Leeds / Sundance / Los Angeles / *Winter Guest* London / Berlin / Blair dinner / Snowdon lunch / ABA premiere / *Sense and Sensibility* / *Michael Collins* / Temple Lane / *Rasputin* / St Petersburg & Budapest / no wonder it had to end with a bang *and* a few whimpers.

Drive into Manhattan alongside the Hudson. Sunny & warm—for all the world, a spring day. Glad I brought the overcoat and scarf . . .

31 DECEMBER

Lazy morning . . . Eventually we head out . . . to meet Liam & Natasha for what turns out to be a wonderful, chatty, friendly lunch—Liam has seen *Michael Collins* and loves it so—ONWARD. Natasha tells us a horror story or two about J.R., K.B., & E.T. and we gas on till about 3.30.

Over the road to Lee Grant's[1] apt at 11.45pm—huge room, lots of people (including G. Paltrow & Brad Pitt) stand around, hold glass, smile, chat, leave with Marcy [Kahan], Pat [O'Connor], M. E. [Mastrantonio], Diana & Richard & R. Visit Marcia's £3m squat.

Bed. Early call. Bye bye 1995.

---

[1] American actor, documentarian and director (born mid-1920s)

1996

15 JANUARY

Lunch at Kensington Place with Hilary Heath. She and Jonathan Powell want me to play whatshisname[1] in *Rebecca*—but it's a 4 part TV. So I said I can't. You may act the same (or better) but somehow TV drags it down. Unless it's a sitcom in the US (Tom Hanks, *Roseanne*) and TV drags *you* up. Impossible conundrum.

7.30 *The Glass Menagerie*.

Another production from Sam Mendes. What is it about him? Theatre is a playground or a wet-wipe of personal therapy, it seems. No real resonance—no sense of the danger of an unpredictable outburst. All carefully arranged. Zoë Wanamaker can look after herself but she needs to be challenged. Claire Skinner[2] can do that standing on her head. It all passes before our eyes masquerading as the real thing.

17 JANUARY

Supper with Belinda & Hugh and Frances B[arber]. An evening of the most *News of the World*ish details. Thank whatever I'm discreet . . . Frances is a life force—tidal waves of laughter and perception. Just don't tell her too many stories; her repertoire is full enough.

18 JANUARY

An appalling hangover—headache, ailing back and neck. The works. Never again.

22 JANUARY

Watch *S&S* in growing dismay. It has been cut to focus only on the women's journey—the men are mindless. Sad—we should care who they are marrying.

---

[1] Maxim de Winter
[2] English actor (1965–)

23 JANUARY

Still brooding, of course. There is a definite sense with *S&S* that all the corners have been knocked off—no eccentricities, no focus on what is *happening* to (particularly) Brandon. We are holding the plot together.

24 JANUARY

Lunch with Kate Ryding at L'Accento. She's deaf in one ear so we make a pretty pathetic sight, picking the seats best for our particular ailments.

25 JANUARY

Michael Collins beckons.

12.50 → Dublin and Ardmore Studios. Neil's hair is longer but his rhythms haven't changed. No sooner started looping a scene than he wants to talk about/show me another. Of course, the looping is all the most emotional stuff. All you can do is get on with it. (Having been told the film is great.) Good group of editors, and we're out of there in an hour. Neil drives us into Dublin—his driving is like his conversation—gear shifts and braking and accelerating in no discernible order. We have a welcome pint of Guinness at the Shelbourne . . .

26 JANUARY

To the airport for the 2.15 flight to London.

Talk to Emma, she's very pro the idea of *Winter Guest* or *Winter's Guest* as the US contingent call it. Siân Thomas is in the front of my brain as my finger reaches for the phone dial. Such clear waters already become murky. But a little determined honesty will help.

28 JANUARY

Talking to Emma T., realise the British Film Industry kicks itself in the face again by putting the *S&S* premiere in the Curzon . . . 560 seats up a side street.

29 JANUARY

One minute talking about film deals, the next about hearing aids and a demonstration of how to pull up your pants with a mechanical gripper.

pm over to see Mum and Aunt Elsie. Who says sisters should get on? But it is still depressing to watch the endless obstinacy and sniping—fortunately with moments of ease and good humour but stubbornness rules.

A welcome evening alone. Salutary to watch the *Evening Standard* Film Awards. Thora Hird emerged with her dignity intact. And she made me laugh. Double hero.

31 JANUARY

Rima's birthday—the day spent organising the evening . . . All down to the always reliable Ivy. I must own part of it by now.

1 FEBRUARY

Leila Bertrand [casting director] comes over to talk through *And All That Jazz* her London-through-the-eyes-of-a-Dominican-girl-in-the-1950s film script. She, John Clive,[1] Thandie Newton all good reasons to be involved. At this stage suggesting a reading is the most helpful thing.

Word from LA . . . that *Rasputin* has been seen and liked.

Two late nights—woken too early—tiredness takes over and signs of how that affects the hearing and seems to focus on the tinnitus. Depressing. And a vicious circle.

3 FEBRUARY

Sandra and Michael Kamen. Supper with Rima, Bryan Adams and Cecilie [B.A.'s girlfriend]. More surprises since Bryan turns out to be a regular guy who worries about buildings and doesn't do drugs. Cecilie is a top—maybe super—model who's in it for a couple of years etc., etc.

At maybe 2am Michael played us the new theme song to the (v. worrying) *Jack* movie. And then rippled through the *Winter Guest* like a spring tide.

4 FEBRUARY

To Mum and Aunt Elsie with lunch. This mental digging and need is odd to watch. Whatever its downside, Mum is looking much healthier. Possibly from bossing someone around or having a rare opportunity to display the diva at her centre. Covent Garden's loss.

And hopelessly touching with Rima & I, hands on the handles of a wheel-chair each, out for a walk around the park, as all four of us pause to look at the magpies waddling about in the sunset.

6 FEBRUARY

To Isabelle Huppert. The easiest person to talk to—full of laughter and the ability to focus on the turn of a sixpence. And curious, too. So un-English. Her courage makes me want to act in French tomorrow.

7 FEBRUARY

7.15 *Volpone* at the National. Gambon magnificent and so wicked. Doubtful that [Ben] Jonson called one of the servants Kevin . . . The production leaves you

---

[1] English actor (1933–2012)

wanting—the set spins, the language flings itself around, the acting is (mostly) brave but there is a general air of UNEXPLORED. Simon Russell Beale has a wonderfully pitched reading. I wish he would find different mouth-shapes.

11 FEBRUARY

As this birthday approaches there is this strong, strong desire to control the past (photographs, old scripts, mementos) or sling it out. *Very* freeing. Look in the wardrobe—if there are clothes which slightly depress you to look at them—maybe out they could go.

Watching tape of Ruby with Roseanne [Barr]—mostly a delight but Ruby should just let them speak. Let's just look at *them*.

12 FEBRUARY

. . . a sad message from Alex Sheriffs.[1]

13 FEBRUARY

Which continues when I phone this morning. Roberta Sheriffs had been taken into St Mary's on Sunday and having not been expected to make it through the night, is still there. But only just—and now they have phoned Alex to tell her she has maybe 5 minutes. I jump in a cab to meet Alex there which we do, on the stairs. Arriving at the ward—Roberta has gone. The curtains are all around the bed, the nurses sympathetic, but going in—gone is the word. If I didn't know, it would be impossible to recognise her. The spirit has truly left this face and body. A sense not so much of death, but of what life *is*, because of its extraordinary absence. Alex combs her hair, over and over, and wipes her mouth, her eyes, kisses her and talks to her. Much more direct than I, who can only photograph it mentally. Forever. The doctor is clear and patient because now Alex needs to talk in details. Then we all go off for an Italian lunch where we laugh as much as we can. Which is a lot.

The value-battles which have somehow been designed for me reach a kind of apotheosis because today is Academy Award nominations day. Let's draw a veil over my own confused response to everything and merely record a happy L'Accento supper with Conor McDermottroe (here to stay).

14 FEBRUARY

Academy nominations for Emma & Kate yesterday but not Ian, nor Nicole K. Crazy days.

---

[1] An old friend

15 FEBRUARY

8pm Hampstead.

Stephen Poliakoff's new play. Absolutely *accosted* by Stephen in the foyer with instructions that I was *not* to give notes to his actresses. How could I? Both brilliant in another of Stephen's trips along the razor edges, the high wire.

18 FEBRUARY

12 Isabelle's lunch at the Ivy upstairs. 34? people round the beautiful oval table. The kind of day you wish would go on and on . . . Other than that— with hindsight, the room full of echoes. Especially of women I have played opposite—and as I look around—Juliet, Fiona, Paola, Harriet, Saskia, Deborah, Beatie, Zoë, Gillian, Anna—it is a source of pride.

20 FEBRUARY

The bar at the Ivy to wait for Isabelle. Bomb scares all over the place— London a fragile place to be.

21 FEBRUARY

2am Judy Hoflund calls from LA for an early Happy Birthday.

The trouble with this job is that you can watch yourself & your friends growing older in full colour, close up. Flip a switch to rewind or fast forward. Too fast forward.

1.15 To Alastair Little for lunch w. Ruby & Suzanne Bertish. Ruby brings me coffee grinder and saucepans—Suzanne a crystal. They're a good balance these two—Suzanne with her beautiful laugh and grounded heart—Ruby whizzing about as ever.

Home to get ready.

6.30 The car is here and by 6.45 we're on the way to the Curzon Mayfair for *Sense and Sensibility* premiere which is a good distraction from the birthday . . . Old friends in new frocks, line-up for Prince Charles (tell him he should have played my part) and in to the film. Terrible sound but cuts apart it's a beautiful piece of work. To the Whitehall Banqueting Rooms for supper—wonderful Rubens on the ceiling—with Richard W. & Isabelle H. in the car. Harriet comes after her show. Jocelyn Stevens'[1] crowd insists that I 'Go on! Say something! It's him! With the voice!'

---

[1] Newspaper publisher (1932–2014)

22 FEBRUARY

A truly awful day after—no sleep, too much wine, unresolved everything; long slow dull pain. A real feeling of why bother? Everywhere is tension from friends to politics. What's going on? Maybe the wind will turn, but at the moment there is a gnawing feeling that this life offers only fleeting moments when it all comes together because the rest of it requires a fitter body and a more grown-up mind.

None of it helped by spending the day alone. Janet comes to clean, the phone rings—agent business, mortgage business. But the contrast to all the glitter of yesterday makes both seem aimless.

Count blessings. Grow up.

24 FEBRUARY

Watch *Shawshank Redemption*. 'Expertly done' would be the review. Not a foot wrong. Classy. I just wish this had not extended even to the immaculate hairdos of all the inmates. When will a director tell a hair person to STOP tidying everyone up—it's an awful reflex action.

26 FEBRUARY

11.15 The car, after a bit of last-minute phoning, planning and parking, picks me up and first stop is Kristin Milward's who is coming with me on a trip to Berlin. Columbia needs me to pick up the Golden Bear. Ang's away, Emma's in hiding or purdah, but it's an opportunity to see old friends.

5pm—Phone interview with the US. And write short speech to be delivered in German.

6.30 Christina, Klaus & Christophe [German friends of A.R.] bring a bottle of champagne to the hotel, then off to the prize-giving. Clamber on stage and receive Golden Teddy . . .

3 MARCH

8pm The Dorchester, to sit around & order room service with Susan Sarandon who has come in to do publicity for *Dead Man Walking*. Susan is a mind on speed—equal emphasis as she skids from politics to her career to Tim [Robbins, her partner] to her kids. Which other mother takes 2 of them river rafting in Idaho?

6 MARCH

2.30 Judy Daish's office—really beautiful space—a perfect frame for Judy's merry, thoroughbred personality.

Later, finishing Draft 2 *Winter Guest*. Some adjusting and maybe Hey Presto. It *is* a great script.

7 MARCH

Isabelle wants an escort for the *Restoration* premiere. I put Hugh Fraser into a tailspin by suggesting him. But he's going.

9 MARCH

3pm *Tommy* matinée. Stunning production. The critics sniping . . . is real anal retention. Just go with it.

5.20 To . . . the Groucho Club to talk with Des McAnuff about his film *Cousin Bette*,[1] which as I said to him is like mixing Feydeau with Ibsen. Is that possible? He's good to talk to, though. Today I managed a *little* less. Filling potential pauses. Sometimes you don't know the end of the sentence upon which you have just embarked. Scary.

10 MARCH

12.15 Car to Grayshott Park [spa]. 4 days away from the phone and the builders. 4 days with no alcohol and limited food. 4 days with regular exercise.

But starting with 45 minutes of face massage and creams & mask. *So* what the doctor ordered that I dozed off and at one point frightened the masseuse out of her wits with a loud snore.

Side-product is that scripts are getting read and letters written. Hallelujah.

11 MARCH

9.30 Dietician—what can she say? It's a ridiculous lifestyle.

10.15 Steam room.

10.45 Massage. And we can. None of your Champney's nonsense.

Lunchtime preceded by swim and hot-tub.

2.30 An hour's coaching on the tennis court. Instant improvement, years of bad habits. Completely whacked.

5pm Cranial osteopathy. Drifting in and out of a kind of sleep/dream state. And when she says at the end 'you're more balanced now' (or somesuch)—I was.

12 MARCH

Lunch is a question of how much can I get on the plate without falling on the floor on the way from buffet to table.

---

[1] McAnuff had directed this adaptation of the novel by Balzac.

5.30 Holistic massage—about as close to sex as it is legal to get here, methinks. She insists on complete nakedness and the hands and oil are SLOW.

Two hours later she's done. I might have enjoyed it but for the ghastly new age 'Relaxation' music and the growing suspicion that she was getting most out of it. 'It's a lovely job—I just can't wait to get my hands on all those naked bodies.'

Very comatose. Pretty damn peckish.

13 MARCH

Today was made somewhat irrelevant by the slaughter of all those children in the school gymnasium in Dunblane. I didn't find out until the afternoon so the Reflexology wasn't complicated by other thoughts, but the Flotation Tank certainly was. My brain fought it all the way trying to make it less self-indulgent, I suppose. What do you mean let yourself go, think of nothing?

If I hadn't been leaving tomorrow, I would have anyway. To do what, I don't know, but just to *join in* again. Taking myself out of it has been very valuable not to say *very* expensive and gives rise to all kinds of examinings. How do you equate a week here with a drama student's living expenses with a jacket for LA with Mum's chair with etcetera etcetera. The truth is, I have been stroked a lot for four days but not by someone I love. And up in Scotland tonight there is all that love and all that loss.

14 MARCH

This morning's TV coverage—and all British life is there. Channel 4 manages to intersperse news reports with silly games—how? BBC is dry as dust, GMTV more alive to the situation, but smug and judgemental with it. Talk of the killer 'burning in hell' helps no one . . . The murderer was also five years old once. Look at him and look at the photos of the children. What happens to us as we move on from their complete innocence—no knowledge of hate, repression, race, responsibility. Just smiling faces—no thoughts beyond the next half hour. Why is it only men who years later pick up the guns? What do we do to ourselves to create these monsters within us? Or is it innate? Whatever, GMTV's simplicities are grotesque.

19 MARCH

10am pick-up for 12.15 flight to Los Angeles.

Ian McK. & his boyfriend Ridian at the ticket desk. Which makes for a really enjoyable flight.

20 MARCH

7.15 Pick-up for *Rasputin* screening. Just as I am about to 'cure' Alexei a voice from the back says 'Is there a doctor in the house? We have an emergency in the foyer.' I nearly got up until I remembered I know nothing. Weird sound. Weird screening. Maybe R. was visiting. Dinner at the Eclipse. I think no one really knows what to make of the film. No wonder—it has been directed by at least a dozen people.

24 MARCH

5.15 Judy at the hotel to go to Lindsay [Doran] & Rodney's house for *S&S* reception. It is a little like a house for an American Agatha Christie film. And it's true—built in the '30s and feeling like a historic monument. Emma & Greg brown & happy.

8.30 To Martha L.'s house for reception for Susan Sarandon and Tim Robbins. There is a growing certainty in the room, the town, the water that Susan is going to win tomorrow. And that's the Oscars—it's not her best performance but it's time. And the Academy has no way to deal with the subtlety of Tim's direction so he *won't* win.[1]

25 MARCH

2pm Meet Ian to drive w. Ridian to David Hockney's studio. It's an industry—offices, files, underlings. Going into a vast studio/exhibition space D.H. is asleep on the sofa. This is a pinch me time, as we go on to his home on Mulholland. All his enthusiasms as his mind bounces around showing us his new things, schemes. He takes Polaroids of the 3 of us and then Xeroxes & enlarges it. Ridian is the lucky recipient. His deafness only seems to increase. His awakeness, his laughter, the colour which he almost swims in, in this house.

5.45 to the Bel Air Hotel to pick up Greg and on to Judy's house . . . The *Braveheart* evening. *Ent Weekly* had thought '*S&S* may have peaked.' What a world. Afterwards to . . . the Columbia party. Noise, cameras, food, drink. A vague sense of disappointment in the room. I feel distanced from it. Emma & Kate arrive—noise, cameras, Emma & Katery.

26 MARCH

9.30 Breakfast w. Anthony & Carolyn Minghella plus their business managers—John and Duncan.

---

[1] Best Film was won by *Braveheart*, Best Actress was Susan Sarandon for *Dead Man Walking*, Best Director was Mel Gibson for *Braveheart*.

Robert Young replaces them—we talk of last night (his film *Usual Suspects* had picked up two).

Julia Roberts comes in looking for Susan's celebration brunch—her waist is the *most* encirclable. On the way out pass Susan who is tired but very OK.

27 MARCH

7am Check out and to LAX with Anthony Minghella for the flight to San Francisco . . .

pm I watched a 4-hour assembly of *The English Patient*. Absolutely exhausting, but riveting, too, in terms of storytelling, coverage, shot-making, acting. The lot. It confirmed what I thought when I read the script—this film will be made in the editing room.

Back home I spew up two responses. Anthony is like a happy dog at his bowl. I can see how obsessive this directing lark might be. Ralph Fiennes, Kristin Scott Thomas, Willem Dafoe and Juliette Binoche all wonderful. Great to see such *intelligent* acting. Not just splurging.

28 MARCH

Back at the ranch (almost literally) Anthony decides to look up A.R. on the internet—368 entries. It's like reading about a stranger. Especially when they write about who I live *next* door to, or don't . . . But mostly they are good-hearted. It's like having a band of cheerleaders, all tapping away into the night.

9 APRIL

7.30 To Santa Monica for *Michael Collins* test screening. And still it's an action movie with not enough politics. Boys Own Revolution. Do the explosions cancel out in art as in life? But it's work in progress, so there's time to help the narrative. Neil sort of there—up and down in his seat. 'Do you have a cigarette?' 'Are you with it?'

11 APRIL

Judy calls to tell me of the *Daily Mail* hate piece. Heigh ho.

12 APRIL

[London]

8pm Michael Kamen's birthday party . . . memorable for meeting Sharon Stone—a truly attractive woman, in the real sense of light in the eyes attractive—and smart and funny. No wonder she doesn't have a man.

14 APRIL

1.15 Lunch at the Ivy w. Peter Medak [film director], Julia Migenes [opera singer], Louise Krakower [film producer], Ruth Myers [costume designer] & Isabella Rossellini. Great to meet Ms R. finally . . . Her beauty is the kind that stops you concentrating on what she's saying sometimes because you are fixated by the shape of her mouth.

28 APRIL

New York.

12 Wyndham Hotel.

A huge shadow casts itself across the day with the news of how seriously ill Diane Bull[1] has become—life in a snap of the fingers. We press on as Jonathan talks to London. It's a luxury working with these people—all with strong opinions and all able to take short cuts so that we gradually rebuild the programme. I worry that there isn't enough humour, though.

7ish Circo—Tina Brown/*New Yorker*/Almeida bash.

A huge crush of people. For most of the evening I only made it to the edge of the throng. Then suddenly the room had cleared. Americans are like that—not the English, we hang on long past the time we're welcome picking at the food and looking for wine in empty bottles.

29 APRIL

2pm Laura Pels Theatre, Broadway & 45.

For a while I thought we might not get through it all—negotiating moves and scribbling them down. By 6 we had finished and went to the dressing room. I could not even remember who entered first by this point. A sandwich was sent for, Natasha Richardson & I went to the supermarket over the road. A quiet trawl through the hurried jottings.

8pm—Performance. First half v. pushed. Inevitably. Fishing around. Who are you? What's this material? Who am I? *Where* am I? But the audience gradually decides to trust it all and the second half is lighter. The balance of the material was fine. By the end it was all very special and joyous.

12 MAY

Cannes Film Festival 96.

. . . to Nice. A car to the Hotel du Cap in Cannes. V. expensive monk's cell . . . it's £60 to have your suit cleaned. A 200F cab ride to the party for

---

[1] English actor (1952–2008)

Kansas City. No one got me a drink but the charm button was in full operation and the final reward was to meet Robert Altman. Human, warm, open, fun. ICON 1. 3am in the bar. ICON 2. Mick Jagger.

13 MAY

12 [midnight] *Trainspotting*. First time up that red carpet. Except we are ½ hour early, so it's not exactly thick with atmosphere. But there at the top is Lord Grade—worth the visit. 89 years old and waiting in the midnight air to watch *Trainspotting*. And so generous in his appreciation. Also there— Damon Albarn, Leonardo DiCaprio, V. Bottomley[1] plus Danny Boyle, of course. The film *is* an advert for drugs. A brilliant one.

25 MAY

9.05 Odeon Kensington. *Secrets and Lies*.

Like watching your own life flash by. Things that aunts did or said and mums never forgot and never talked about leaving you perplexed as you open Xmas doors on sobbing relatives. Tim Spall quite wonderful.

31 MAY

7pm To the Covent Garden Hotel to pick up Laura Dern and on to the NT for *Designated Mourner*. Wally Shawn [the play's author] in the foyer before, at the stage door afterwards and at the Ivy. What to say? I do not know what was going on but it was happening with great style and wit. The Ivy was fun—especially because Fay Presto[2] complete with playing card on the ceiling.

2 JUNE

9ish To Searcys for Brian Cox's birthday party. All human acting was there (including a little boy who was the image of Rima).

6 JUNE

The early morning scratchy throat.

10.15 Ear Test.

The bug starts to wander from the head to the chest.

7pm Dash in order [not] to miss the curtain for 7.30 English National Opera *Fidelio* . . . That 1st act quartet is one of the most beautiful things I've ever heard. David Hockney there and he tells a joke about Degas and the telephone that I still don't quite get.

---

[1] Virginia Bottomley (1948–), then Secretary of State for National Heritage
[2] British magician (1948–)

Later—the Ivy.
and later—Lemsip revisited.

9 JUNE

12 To David Suchet's birthday party dinner . . . Nothing prepares me for the ultimate cute High Street, or David & Sheila's vast, perfect garden. Red check table cloths flapping in the kind of heat that nails you down.

2.45 An undignified exit with Duncan for Susan Fleetwood's[1] memorial service which was fine but nearly ruined by the egomaniac rector of St James's.

10 JUNE

11ish Sharman arrives and we start working through the text and timing the scenes.

12 JUNE

2ish am—call Ian McK. in Los Angeles. He's full of stories—the Indian guru at Goldie Hawn's house. 'Are those Marlboro you are smoking?'

14 JUNE

To Marks & Spencer to find a sweater & dress for Mama.

7 JULY

Emma & Phyllida for tea. This felt a little like an exam. No one's fault but a major career is being handed over for a temporary outing here, and she has a right to feel nervous.

11 JULY

8 Dinner with Michael & Sandra Kamen. Ruby v. funny about her trip to Paris as *Vogue* critic for the new collection. She learnt how to say 'Who the fuck is she?' in 11 languages since she was always put in Seat 1A.

14 JULY

12 Richard W's birthday. His 60th—with friends and filled with his generosity. He should be a grandfather—he loves children so much. Before the party he was patiently organising the toys as the canapes were floating by.

15 JULY

8am Flight to Edinburgh.

Dinner (late) with Anthony, John, John-Ross & David. A phalanx of par-

---

[1] Scottish actor (1944–1995)

ents in the bar. Chinese opposite the Lyceum. Suddenly they have moved from boys to teenagers. John-Ross has a new voice, David found his height, John seems 18 at 14, only Anthony has the same rubber-ball bouncing inside him (only with more room now he's 9" taller).

A message to call Rima. Mum is in hospital. Not much sleep.

16 JULY

A day of hopping about between towns on the Fife coast. Somewhere in here Anstruther and Pittenweem assert themselves in the midst of wondering whether it's all about something simpler, starker.

8ish Dinner . . . with Christian Zanone. Thai. He talks of passing his exams with no work. Subtle changes to his face too. I find myself looking at him as casting directors must look at actors—too much this, not enough that. At least he retains his sweet-tempered side. Talks of playing Malvolio and washing up at a refuge centre in Italy with equal emphasis.

17 JULY

To Loch Lomond in order to rule it out. And on to the West Coast—Largs, Troon, Prestwick, Ayr. In order to scream quietly. Ayr is summer hell. But at Saltcoats there was a wonderful walkway & wall & strange abandoned house which should be remembered.

In essence the Fife coast could certainly work if we keep the camera away from the picturesque and concentrate on rock formations, walls, lighthouse. The writing is crenellated enough.

19 JULY

1.30 To Cheyne Walk and on to Glyndebourne with Barbara & Ken Follett. Ken pissed off because no car/no driver or something. He very much likes things to go according to plan. Champagne & canapes in the car going down etc.

3 AUGUST

5pm St Columba's Church, Pont Street, for Dusty[1] & Jessica Hughes's wedding.

A church, at first seeming an atmosphere-free zone, but in the end its simplicity, not to mention its great choir—some beautiful Mozart—and the picture of Dusty's mother gently disappearing into Alzheimer's as her nurse talks her through the service—made the whole thing rather wonderful.

The reception at Leighton House meant sitting next to Kathy Lette who has to be the world champion flirt.

---

[1] English playwright Dusty Hughes (1947–)

11 AUGUST

1.30 Cab to Ian McKellen's house on the river for Suzanne Bertish's birthday party. Sean[1] is there in high spirits and obviously duck to watering on his film of *Bent*, and Frances Barber on devastating form with tales of Chichester life—NB *never* divulge anything to her that you do not want spread like soft margarine. Even she had to stop Imogen Stubbs with a warning hand when Imogen had started a sentence with 'Strictly *entre nous* . . .'—which we decided was the title of Frances' one-woman show when she has had enough and wants to end her career.

7 SEPTEMBER

10.30 pick-up. 12.15 → Los Angeles.

This is a kind of insanity—a 48-hour turnaround. But there had been a nagging feeling that I should go.

8 SEPTEMBER

3.30ish pick-up for the trip to Pasadena.[2] Louise and Judy both in black. Judy brings a bottle of Cristal and at the time it felt like something for later . . .

Arrive there and hoopla, hoopla. Banks of seats for star watchers, Joan Rivers asking me who made my suit . . . On air & there's Oprah. The jet lag is kicking in, the ceiling is starting to spin a bit, some instinct connected to the Cristal made me try to remember a few thankyou names, and then there was Helen Mirren winning and then the electric shock of hearing your own name. C[hristine] Baranski in gold, a red Cybill Shepherd—the first arms outstretched, the second all reserve. A dazzling blur followed—shepherded through room after room of cameras, microphones, laptops. For TV awards! . . . Then a party . . .

9 SEPTEMBER

Talking to Judy later I hadn't realised quite what a long shot I was.

8.55[pm] → London.

11 SEPTEMBER

9.45 car to Dr Gaynor.

Apparently I am now classed as 'impossible' on the insurance form, so a major overhaul necessary. Interesting and typical that actors aren't indispensable.

Later—to the Art Dept. Bless them—a banner strung across the room. Work going on; steadily becoming the real thing.

---

[1] Sean Mathias, Welsh theatre director (1956–)

[2] A.R. was awarded an Emmy as the best actor in a miniseries for his title role in *Rasputin*.

15 SEPTEMBER

7.45 pick-up → Heathrow and Glasgow. Pick up Seamus [McGarvey, cinematographer] and on to Fife. Walking all over the streets and rocks that will be the frosted life of this film. Seamus' favourite word for all the possibilities opening up in front of him is 'mental'.

16 SEPTEMBER

On to Elie to wait for Emma & Phyllida. It is good to have them here and for them to spend time with Seamus. Of course they all instantly get on and we do the street/rock walk again. This time properly discovering the inside of Chocs 'N Things—which will become a haunt—a throwback filled as it is with homemade chocolates, Jenny's Boilings, Parma Violets and those edible necklaces that my sister used to chew on 'til there was a string of tasty elastic around her wrist and neck.

24 SEPTEMBER

RADA to look at final Vanbrugh model. I went in with boxing gloves on, but the little white box seems to contain the best solutions and Bryan Avery [architect] was genuinely grateful for the intervention.

A rush back to the photography shop for Alessandro & Elizabeth's wedding present and then into the car for the 2.45 → Newark.

On the plane watching *Blue in the Face*—a new hero; the man who takes plastic bags out of trees . . . Then a great *Cracker* episode—camera handled so confidently. I got scared for the second time in days.

Dinner . . . Neil J[ordan]. The human butterfly, spray-gun, jack in a box, grasshopper with a heart.

25 SEPTEMBER

New York.

9.45 → to the Regency for the first day of the junkets. Roomfuls of questions. Julia Roberts there in a corridor with her surroundable waist. The usual mix of questions, the usual avoidance tactics—a slight sense of being perched on my own shoulder.

Lunch with Aidan and Liam, who are studying all the TV ads for the film. *Michael Collins*—the buddy film.

26 SEPTEMBER

10am pick-up. And into the TV interviews. 6 minutes each. Amazing how quickly the questions become standard. What is it like portraying someone who lived? What research did you do? How was Neil/Liam? Were you worried about subject matter? Tell us the history of Ireland and, later in the day, 'Who do you think is sexy in the movies?'

28 SEPTEMBER

7ish arrive London.

8pm Victoria Wood—Albert Hall.

A staggering performance. She delivers the material so fast it could easily be the basis for an all-day performance if she slowed down a bit. Brilliant demolition job on Christmas. Including an alarming reference to *Die Hard* in front of 6,000 people.

4 OCTOBER

Fife.

8.30 Dinner w. Ross, Liz, Seamus, Sharman, Arlene, Steve [Clark-Hall, producer] at the Balgeddie House. This is home now for a few weeks. Country house, huge back lawn, fir trees, comfortable, good food—but 30 mins away from Elie/Pittenweem. This could be a drag.

6 OCTOBER

Sleeping late is sometimes just a matter of limbs which won't move. Which they did at 11.30 when Arthur [Morrison, transport captain] dropped us all at St Monan's for the 3 mile cliff walk to Elie. Breathtaking. Cliffs, rocks, beaches, slopes, expanses, ruins, even a tunnel. Panic, too, that these are all overlooked locations. But maybe not, on reflection. Difficult access, and sometimes too much figure in a landscape.

Lunch at the blessed Ship Inn has Finnan haddock overflowing the plate. Sticky toffee pudding after. How will I survive all this?

11 OCTOBER

10am → Haircuts.

Douglas Murphy[1] particularly stricken by losing his curtains. He's a complicated boy—way ahead of his years in vocabulary, ideas, brain-power but reduced to sitting on the floor with a hat on his head at having his 'fat face' (not true, of course) exposed.

4pm to the office. Emma & Phyllida have arrived. She looks great in *her* new, short hair.

---

[1] Scottish actor who played Sam

12 OCTOBER

To the Golf [Hotel] for Emma & Phyllida's costume fittings. Emma nicks my sweater for the film.

14 OCTOBER

6.25am—The alarm beeps; from elsewhere in the hotel, low voices, creaking floors, distant toilet flushes. It's still dark out, but through the wide sashed window apart from the lights of Glenrothes I can see the sky—frighteningly clear. Seamus will have his nose to the window pane, no doubt.

Here we go!

11pm. Back at the hotel after an Indian meal . . . an amazing day—like the first day at RADA. A calmness has been around me for days—something about being surrounded by the right people at the right time. We got some great shots, missed some. The tide chased us away, the skies beckoned us back.

17 OCTOBER

Impossibly sunny day. We did one shot of Emma crossing the bridge but anything else would have been pointless. In the teeth of some pressure, I asked to move inside.

The rest of the day was saved by ace teamwork. We were up and running by about 2.30pm and by 6.30 had shot most of the bathroom [scene]. Emma fantastic just obeying commands scene by scene. Stand, turn on taps, sit, listen to music, cry . . .

25 OCTOBER

Thousands of feet of film waiting for a seagull to take a piece of fish from Douglas's nervous fingers.

26 OCTOBER

Emma really is a Rolls-Royce. Every detail perfectly angled to the camera. Every thought clear and placed. The job is to keep her vocally centred instead of veering into an upper register which I suspect is where she can monitor herself best.

30 OCTOBER

Rushes look wonderful—Bravo Seamus. (On the way there, help upturn a crashed car. 'Are you Alan Rickman?')

31 OCTOBER

And so to looping. The tide beats us and Emma & Phyllida play the scene with water crashing against the beach and only just out of shot.

And the devil came to sit on my shoulder making it hard to mask my anger at potential cuts and the inevitable compromises of weather & schedules.

5ish. Joan [Bergin] had decorated the bars for Halloween. I was in such a non-party mood and couldn't shake it off.

In bed by 9pm. Shattered and not really capable of talking coherently with Sharman.

1 NOVEMBER

Sleep and the wind blew it all away. And E. & Ph. being wonderful all day. How do they do it? Rigorous *and* good-humoured.

2 NOVEMBER

10ish Finding Sharman in the bar—yes, she *has* been waiting . . . Odd, this stage—when she wants to hang on *and* let go. The bartering of cuts goes on over breakfast.

6 NOVEMBER

Talk to the US re *Man in Iron Mask* movie. *The 4 Musketeers* again?? I suppose they are aiming at *Braveheart*. Depressing. & CAA [Creative Artists Agency] asked when I begin shooting. And Clinton got in again.

15 NOVEMBER

9.30[pm] Rima arrives. As usual, most things calm down.

17 NOVEMBER

Breakfast at Rusacks.

Walk along the *Chariots*[1] beach.

18 NOVEMBER

Hopelessly sunny day. Blue, blue sky. Freezing—but blue. Useless. Except when Seamus can mask off the sunlight.

19 NOVEMBER

A day of hail, frost, freezing wind. The crew stuck outside in it all day . . . A pile of shots to wade through, a pile of cakes to eat . . . the gale rages on . . . What will Mother N. sling at us tomorrow?

---

[1] St Andrews location for the 1981 film *Chariots of Fire*

23 NOVEMBER

8.30 Party at Rufflets. White parachute silk marquee. Great food. Candle-light, ivy, fairy lights, music. We could have danced all night and as I write this at 4.04am we almost did . . .

30 NOVEMBER

Back to Pittenweem for the helicopter shots.

Turns out to be a bit of an 'if only' day amongst other things. If only I hadn't been chicken, I would have gone up in the helicopter earlier and we would have got better shots, better timing. Heigh ho. When I *did* go up, I could slow them down and focus the thing. From then on it was like something from a cop movie . . . By now of course the sun had come out *plus* the road was too narrow to turn round on, *plus* the pilot had to be on his way back to Inverness by 3pm or it would be too dark to land. No pressure. We pointed the camera and hoped for the best. Waved goodbye to Sheila and at 2.50 headed back to Pittenweem. Emma ran along the pier as we flew in and then we circled round to find Gary[1] on the doorstep and then up and away. Exhilarating and mad.

2 DECEMBER

Long scenes. Pages of dialogue. Some good on the spot cutting made them leaner and more specific. Sharman will hate some of the cuts, however.

3 DECEMBER

Dinner w. Emma, Greg, Phyllida & Seamus. The young journalist sits out-side reading a book. At some time I suppose this girl was at university and full of ambitions.

4 DECEMBER

Emma's last day. And to all intents, Phyllida's. Joan [Bergin] & Gabriel [O'Brien, wardrobe manager] had made Elspeth & Frances dolls with much loving care. They were presented—all tears and hooting laughter in the kitchen set.

6 DECEMBER

Arlene looking beautiful in her red & gold tablecloth but it must be way below freezing outside. Ellie says 'But if the heaters go on we won't see the smoke on her breath.'

---

[1] Scottish actor Gary Hollywood (1979–), who played Alex

9.35 Last shot on Arlene. Last shot on film, followed by 30 seconds silence for 'atmosphere'. Interesting 30 seconds that. A moment for what the hell was that? Then hugs, champagne—all in freezing cold, as Arlene glided through the studio set in a towel.

7 DECEMBER

Emma called. I said 'You should direct', she said 'We have to grow up a bit first.' Stamina—that's what you need most.

Wrap party . . . Great to see Douglas Murphy and Sean Biggerstaff[1] again. Not so great being cornered just when you would wish to be free. *But* on time and on budget. Bed at 4.30am. It's what *that* book says—Rima calms me down.

11 DECEMBER

To Dr Gaynor to reassure myself I do not have frostbite (two toes refusing to un-numb).

7pm To Nicole Farhi's Christmas party . . . David Hare has not so much softened as melted with the marriage and now the lucky sod is off to Peru & Colombia for Christmas.

30 DECEMBER

Mum is in hospital again.

31 DECEMBER

Belinda & Hugh for New Year's eve supper. Right & proper—old friends on the move. Their last celebration in this house as our neighbours . . . And Lily more and more the growing girl and problem child. Lovely food. Good talk. Friends.

---

[1] Scottish actor (1983–)

1997

1 JANUARY

A new year starts *not* in the Caribbean—lying in bed, wandering about the flat, opening cupboard doors, finding moth holes in a suit.

Half my brain shuffles the deck of the film [*The Winter Guest*]—keeping it fluid in my head, at least.

4 JANUARY

1.45 train to Leicester and the General Hospital. Mum fast asleep as we walked into the ward. Nudged her gently awake, surrounded her with chocolates and biscuits, watched her doing some embroidery, listened to the cries of the old woman down the ward as she was changed (?) moved (?) whatever happens behind the curtains—'NO! NO! Mama! Mama!' Otherwise a peaceful time—she seems calm and rosy.

6 JANUARY

6.30 *The English Patient* . . . Bravo, Ant. May you win everything with this huge achievement.

7 JANUARY

7.30 *A Doll's House.*

From the second she catherine-wheeled on stage Janet McTeer[1] was giving one of the finest performances I have ever seen. Not a generalised second, not a dishonest moment, always listening, always responding. Glorious work.

---

[1] English actor (1961–)

17 JANUARY

12 BA flight to Los Angeles. Watched *Brassed Off* and *Lone Star*. Poles apart.

19 JANUARY

3pm Car to Judy, then to pick up Louise and on to the Golden Globes. Ian McK. won, we won, I won ...!...! Flash lights, speeches, uneaten food, Stephen Rea, Brenda Blethyn, seeing Anthony win best film—Hollywood hoopla.

Some dark rooms or tents filled with flowers and people standing about. Met Geoffrey Rush and his wife[1] who seem tense and a bit complicated. I think she hates her role as side-dish.

23 JANUARY

Somewhere around 12—back home.

The rest of the day, having started *The Road Less Travelled* on the plane, watching myself not 'delaying gratification' as usual. Not that there's much gratifying to delay—the fridge is empty.

But I managed to find enough enjoyable jobs to do which avoid sitting down and dealing with mail and scripts.

The book is right—do the difficult stuff *first*, otherwise you waste so much time avoiding it.

1am finds me answering mail.

24 JANUARY

A screening [of *The Winter Guest*] at 1pm. Some good some not. Still a worrying tendency to miss the emotional undertow. Or is that just personal taste?

30 JANUARY

One of those big days when you feel alternately very grown-up and small boy in the corner of a room full of adults.

9am To Channel 4 ... and the first screening for the money people. We watch mostly in silence (I of course imagining proper colour, music, etc. and etc.). Some quiet laughter floating up from the grey suede seats. Afterwards a really *dangerous* silence in the elevator. 'Really powerful,' says Sharon H. Bless her. In the office I break it—'So say anything you like.' So he did.[2] All day spent pulling shards of glass from my insides, but

---

[1] Jane Menelaus, Australian actor (1959–)
[2] David Aukin (1942–), then Head of Film at Channel 4

of course it was the best thing. Now the adventure begins. Be reckless, find the film.

31 JANUARY

4.30 The Home Office to join Chris M., Harold Pinter, Denis L[awson] & Sheila G[ish], Richard W., Frankie de la T.[1] and friends to protest at the continued imprisonment of the political refugees in Rochester Jail—all on hunger strike. Eventually some photographers straggled along. We froze. Michael Howard flipped through his rollerdesk.

8 FEBRUARY

To Leicester. Mum surrounded by drips and her face covered with an oxygen mask.

9 FEBRUARY

The morning in the hotel reading the papers cover to cover.

To the hospital. Michael, Sheila, David & Chris there. Rima arrived later.

Mum convinced that the doctor is deliberately mistreating her and the other patients because 'he wants to be leader of the Tories' and knows of Rima's political ambitions . . . It's funny, but very distressing to think this is all swimming around in her head, making her unhappy.

10 FEBRUARY

Mum had clearly had a bad night . . . The doctor holds out little hope, but this amazing spirit blazes away inside the dizzy spells and straining breaths.

11 FEBRUARY

To the hospital.

Writing retrospectively during all this is pretty impossible. The highs, lows, noise, quiet all create an endless graph that takes no notice of diary dividing lines.

Back to London.

12 FEBRUARY

8pm Train to Leicester.

Spending the night at the hospital flats after hanging around the deserted cafeteria. They're holding down a male patient in Ward 20 who screams non-stop that he's being murdered. So there we are, brothers, sister together in what felt like Czechoslovakia.

---

[1] Frances de la Tour, English actor (1944–)

13 FEBRUARY

Mum is now having very peaceful, watchful times, but interspersed more frequently with struggling for breath. The doctor talks of administering Diamorphine. And does so. Which started a new scenario. Sleep, fluttering eyelids, faraway gazes.

Lunchtime to the local shopping precinct (very Poliakoff, windswept, depressing) to find some clean underwear & socks.

Eventually common sense sends us to Gyngell's for something to eat. It's part of Premier Lodge Hotels—my feet walk automatically to Reception and book us all in. Hot showers, towels, TV.

After supper and back to the Hospital . . . As we arrive Mum wakes but it's from a Diamorphine sleep. She's gazing at the ceiling—something fascinating up there beyond the veiled eyes. It's the deepest kind of heartbreak to watch.

14 FEBRUARY

Sheila's birthday—Mum asks for a photo of all of us—Polaroid the only word to spring to mind. Some value from yesterday's lunchtime trip—a Dixon's. Bought a Polaroid, took the photos, put them in plastic frames, propped them up on the cabinet after Mum watched them developing. Sheila gets the Polaroid camera as a birthday gift. Writing this in the welcome peace of the lunchtime sleep break. Lights out, curtain drawn, only the insistent buzz & burr of the nebulisers and oxygen masks around the ward. Mum's eyes open & close, her chest rises and falls—all of it inventing a rhythm moment by moment.

Supper at Gyngell's—Valentine's night in the restaurant/bar/children's play area/whatever. This extraordinary concoction only the English could dream up. From a distance the saxophone and vocals with digital back-up make 'Lady in Red' merge seamlessly with Kenny G as breaded this or tikka that hits the table.

15 FEBRUARY

Breakfast is a more civilised affair. A few people, the sun on the grass outside, coffee, eggs & toast. Unspoilable. Even with the won't-go-away press nonsense about playing Dr Who.

A pattern is emerging. A little chat, some smiles, some vacant looks; we sit, read, go into the day-room, have a coffee, talk to the nurses, sit some more. Mum is peaceful sometimes, agitated at others. She is given nebulisers, and more injections. Through it all, moments of such sweetness shaft through.

Yesterday's smile inhabiting the corners of her eyes and mouth. Today, again, she looks around and counts the four of us sitting there. Her kids. What she said. But today she is talking very little. She counts, and looks, and sleeps.

16 FEBRUARY

Writing in retrospect.

Rima and I both sleepless.

At 7.15 there is a knock at the door—from Michael's voice (or maybe it is from the knock) I knew that Mum had gone. Michael just capsized into the room, desolate that she had died without us. But it could have happened while we were having a cup of tea, in a corridor, turned away for a second . . . But of course nothing takes away that shaft of guilt. We all pull ourselves together and drive to the hospital, where Joyce the nurse is waiting. It was as she turned away for a moment. Mum snatched her space. I have tried to rehearse the inside of my head for months now and as I write this I don't know how much I have accepted, but walking behind those closed curtains and seeing her yellowish face and still, still body is not something you can ever be ready for.

17 FEBRUARY

11.30 Just made the train to London. This was a ride I *had* rehearsed. Sitting there reading quietly as the fields flashed by.

18 FEBRUARY

To the funeral directors with David and Michael.

A day of trying to pull various threads into one cord—church, cemetery, Kew, minister.

At 3pm we went to Kew—a beautiful room. Again I feel the nerves of someone imposing my taste on a roomful of people who probably are expecting low voices and ham sandwiches when I'm proposing a string quartet playing Gershwin and fish pie. It's a beautiful day and we open the french windows onto the lawn and walls and all will be forgiven.

Found 'Barry Island'[1] to read at the service. If you can get through it . . .

19 FEBRUARY

7.30 David & I go to see Rev. John Simmonds—his house is a perfect Methodist vicar's set. Talk about Mum and visit the new Rivercourt Church—unrecognisable really. Scenes of one's youth cannot come flooding back as it has all changed. Or been given a makeover more accurately.

---

[1] Poem 'Let's Go to Barry Island' by Idris Davies

20 FEBRUARY

1.30 Lunch at the Atlantic. I just listen to it all. Oscar chat. Like there will be next year.

23 FEBRUARY

The roses which Lindsay & Hilton sent have given such pleasure. The mixture of colours and smells are so beguiling you find yourself trying to commit every shade & congruence to memory.

PS: Phone message to say I won the SAG award.[1] That's from actors.

25 FEBRUARY

2pm To Kenyon [funeral directors] in Rochester Row via the church opposite. Which was a surprise pleasure with its piped music.

Mum looked fine in her dress. Complete and OK with the world.

26 FEBRUARY

Mum's funeral.

Which should or might be two dark and heavy words. In fact it was a day of flowers and lightness, shafts of sunshine hitting the lawns, Rivercourt filled with daffodils.

Much thanks to Rev. John Simmonds, whose light but focused touch meant that everyone knew why they were there.

It was absolutely about Her, for Her, her picture on the table at Kew, Porter, Gershwin sidling forth from the string quartet. In the end, a real celebration—with people going home clutching flowers and in a way, happy.

You were honoured, Mum. With Love.

19 MARCH

11.30 David Aukin & Allon Reich [film producer] from Channel 4. They know they're walking on eggs, but actually we make a few great strides. And I make a few more cuts . . .

20 MARCH

Looping with Emma & Phyllida—some nightmare stuff for both of them which they buckle down to with almost unfailingly good humour. I don't know how they do it . . . I remember some past tantrums in the studio—microphones hitting the deck etc.

8.15 → Belinda & Hugh w. Ruby. Too much wine. Again. And a run round

---

[1] For *Rasputin*

some familiar houses. But these are friends I love so it doesn't matter—and sometimes real comic energy is released. Rare and wonderful.

24 MARCH

2am Watching the Oscars.

Who's there. Who's not. Who wins. Who should. Who shouldn't.

And what did they wear?

But Bravo Ant, Saul, Walter.[1]

26 MARCH

7pm *King Lear*, NT.

Richard Eyre all over the place again. *No* idea what he was aiming at. Ian Holm wonderful in the detailed, small stuff but too aware of the mountains others have climbed instead of scaling his own slopes.

4 APRIL

2.30 Screening.

Late start. Lousy sound. The music like the afterthoughts of a coke-head. The Finance sit there like M. Rushmore. An Absolute Hell.

7 APRIL

Somehow things seem to pull themselves together (in the cutting room sense). Why is it taking until now to find freedom with this film? The feeling is of having possessed it entirely and of now letting go. Something like learning to yoyo.

9 APRIL

Long call from Anthony Minghella. He's back in the Real World of car insurance. And spends time strengthening my resolve.

Later sorting through fan mail—a letter from a woman who has watched *S&S* and wants to know if in England we still bow to each other on entering a room.

12 APRIL

Mezzo for lunch.

Andrew (from *Rasputin*) is spotted across the restaurant floor. After waving, his companion in leather cap smiles, comes over, and at the last minute

---

[1] Walter Murch (1943–), American film editor who won alongside Anthony Minghella and Saul Zaentz for *The English Patient*

I realise it's Christian Slater—which means that Radha B.[1] is there. As they leave she ignores me in such an overt way, I was actually shocked.

13 APRIL

To 175 Old Oak Common Lane.[2] David, Michael, Chris and I start opening drawers, looking at photographs, discarding, keeping. Nothing which retained any memory had been thrown away. Old light bulbs, ribbon from presents, all the birth certificates. A life made tangible wherever you turned. Mum's certificate for her piano exams tucked in amongst some underwear; my old drama group photos under the stairs. Incredibly touching things like the letter to Kevin Costner's wife with its simple statement of loneliness. We sat in the garden and had lunch together. These are things to hang on to.

15 APRIL

Much more work needed on the music.

18 APRIL

8.30 Roger Graef's[3] birthday party.

A conversational pizza. Helena Kennedy & Iain Hutchison, Janet Suzman, Peter Eyre,[4] BBC people, newspaper people, Eve Arnold,[5] etc, etc. Very 'Eve of Blair/Stalin on the Throne'—so different from '92. If the Tories win no one will be depressed this time, just resigned or on a plane.

25 APRIL

2.30 RADA Council. Attenborough, as always, astonishingly in command of the facts. We all toddle behind in his wake.

27 APRIL

5pm Royal Albert Hall—w. Tara.

Bettina Jonic singing Weill, Heine, Brecht. Bettina is her own biggest fan—and rightly so. Rare to watch a real artist like this. You don't have to speak fluent German to sense the undertow of exile & alienation.

---

[1] Radha Blank, American filmmaker (1976–)
[2] A.R.'s mum's house
[3] British documentary maker (1936–2022)
[4] American actor (1942–)
[5] American photojournalist (1912–2012)

29 APRIL

6.15 Car to the Albert Hall for BAFTA.

Saw Kate W.—couldn't kiss her or her makeup would be ruined; stood behind Diana Ross to present award—couldn't stand too close or would have been surfing on the train of her dress. Gave award to Anthony M. . . . Sat at table w. Ken Loach who showed how to stand up for royalty without seeming to . . .

30 APRIL

8.30 Columbia TriStar—Mike Newell's screening of *Donnie Brasco*. Brilliantly directed and shot and acted. Mike enjoying himself hugely.

1 MAY

Election Day. The sun blazes.

10.30 To Helena K. & Iain.

And the party begins. All I can think as the seats mount is '*Someone* say thanks to Neil Kinnock.' All the time people cheering, laughing and some crying. Endless choruses of 'I can't believe it.'[1]

2 MAY

The Sunniest Day.

Sent flowers to Neil, Barbara Follett & Peter Mandelson. All we can think of is this day 5 years ago. Everything *so* different. Finally a feeling of the country breathing. Long may it last.

7 pm Peter M. calls by to say thank you for the flowers. Says he burst into tears when he saw them. I asked him how he feels. 'Weird.'

15 MAY

12 Michael Kamen.

Thank God Scott came over in the afternoon to referee. This is easily the toughest relationship on the film. Michael is kissed with genius but it is like trapping a butterfly. Wayward, unfocused, utterly specific, instinctive by turns. Clinging on to some calm and aided by Scott's steering, we get some wonderful results and somewhere in there Michael enjoys it. On the way home, I realise I'm dragging through uncharted waters. It is not customary working like this . . . mea culpa.

---

[1] Labour, led by Tony Blair, won in a landslide.

16 MAY

8am pick-up → Luton Airport → Venice.

Paul Allen's[1] Extravaganza.

17 MAY

6am While I can still remember. On the flight here Bryan Ferry, Mimi Rogers,[2] Dave Stewart, Geena Davis, Sydney Pollack, Jerry Hall, Siobhan Fahey[3]—an extraordinary weekend begins. How could I ever have thought of not coming? It's not just the biggest name drop ever (last night the above joined by Robin Williams, Barbara Hershey, Michael Keaton, Monica Seles, John McEnroe, Albert Brooks,[4] Jim Brooks,[5] Carrie Fisher, Ruby, Fran Lebowitz, Michael & Sandra K., etc., etc., etc.), but writing this at 6am on the balcony of the Londra Palace Hotel looking at the length of the Grand Canal as it is swept gently into life . . . it is also a weekend stuffed with indelible pictures. Last night at the Scuola Grande San Rocco, Tiepolos & Tinterettos everywhere, Albinoni and Vivaldi underneath. Red velvet & Harry's Bar.

17 MAY

7.30 Champagne is delivered to the room as we chase a bit to get ready— and it begins. To the lobby and out to the gondolas (more champagne on ice). The convoy glides off to the Palazzo where trumpeters, a fire-eater and dancer greet every arrival. Names announced at the door, Paul Allen & Monica Seles greet us, everyone looking glorious masked & feathered. Upstairs dinner goes on and on, opera is sung, Santana plays a floor higher with Dave Stewart, Noel Redding,[6] John McEnroe & Paul A. & Harry Shearer[7] as backing group.

Later the Piano Bar. Patti Smith sings to me.

18 MAY

12 Bags downstairs and a boat to Cipriani for brunch. John & Di Carling [old friends] pop up in the lobby—it's her birthday. Very levelling in the circumstances—as in Peter Gabriel, Trudie & Sting, Eric Idle, David Geffen, Barry

---

[1] One of the founders of Microsoft
[2] American actor (1956–)
[3] Of Banarama, the then wife of Dave Stewart
[4] American actor (1947–)
[5] American director, producer and screenwriter James L. Brooks (1940–)
[6] Bass guitarist with the Jimi Hendrix Experience
[7] American actor (1943–)

Diller,[1] Laurence Fishburne, Penny Marshall, Terry George [nightclub owner], Maggie Renzi[2] and on and on. Everyone with a specific image to hang on to.

4.30 Into a boat → Aeroporto for the flight to Nice and London.

21 MAY

A trip to the dry cleaner's is good for clearing the brain.

6 JUNE

Michael's music all over the place in tone, warmth, clarity etc.

We will have to re-record.

23 JUNE

11ish To Whitfield Recording Studios for another day of teeth pulling with Michael & Steve.

2 JULY

12ish Ruby comes for script inspiration—Jennifer Saunders is not coming up with the goods fast enough. Rubes, impatient as ever for RESULTS, understanding nothing as ever of PROCESS is already flipping through the metaphorical writers' version of *Spotlight*.

3 JULY

2.30 to Video City to collect and then deliver a TV to Arwen Holm in St Mary's Hospital. She was in a side room having her hair done—lying covered in plastic with newly blackened hair. The whole process requiring great invention by the hairdresser who talks cheerily of her work in hospital morgues. 'I like it—they can't answer back.'

6 JULY

Long phone call with Ruby. There is so much history here I think we should just absorb that and get on with it. Ruby seems to want to analyse. I don't think that will go anywhere but inwards.

10 JULY

On the way to find a taxi, bump into a guy handing out promotional cards— they go flying, he looks at me with such violence and says 'pick them up'. Something in me—for once—didn't argue. Agree how clumsy I was but that

---

[1] American media executive (1942–)
[2] American film producer (1951–)

it wasn't deliberate and walked quietly away. How things change. I know I was a second away from real hard-core assault.

14 JULY

7pm Festival Hall for *Guardian*'s summer party. Absolutely fascinating. Degrees of leglessness unknown other than to journalists.

29 JULY

To 11 Downing Street and Gordon Brown, Chris Smith[1] and Tom Clarke's[2] homage to the film industry. Talk about the usual suspects . . . At one glorious moment we were taken on a scuttling tour of No. 10 and No. 11—the Cabinet Office, Dining Room etc. before the gaff was blown and we scurried off.

3 AUGUST

3 To see Arwen at St Mary's.

4 AUGUST

A day when events, phone-calls frustrations and unalloyed sadnesses & pleasures trip over each other . . . as we try to sort out a holiday and checking the sub-titles. David eventually gets through to tell me that Auntie Elsie died this morning. No point now in writing anything for yesterday's entry—it would seem more like foreboding. But I did sense something *was* worryingly wrong.

5 AUGUST

7pm Chelsea Cinema—*Mr Bean*.

   Sit in (doubtless) wrong seats with Mel Smith & Rowan Atkinson behind us, so laughs are forced in order to send OK messages backwards. Ate whole packet of M&Ms.

13 AUGUST

Talked to Peter Mandelson about being beleaguered. He sounds genuinely depressed, and it has been an onslaught in the press. I talk of heat & kitchens but didn't get round to the fact that he should recognise how he brings it on himself to a large degree.

14 AUGUST

7.55 Flight to Rome.

   11.20 Claudio collects us and drives us calmly and swiftly to Todi.

---

[1] Labour politician (1951–), then Secretary of State for Culture, Media and Sport
[2] Labour politician (1941–), then Minister of State for Film and Tourism

8.30 Dinner at the hotel. Eventually. It only took him ½ hr to bring the menus and ½ hr to serve some food.

15 AUGUST
Drive to Assisi.

Lunch by nose-following, down some steps, along an alleyway . . .

After lunch to San Francisco and the line of glorious Giotto frescoes on the life of St Francis.

20 AUGUST

Rome.

We clambered out of bed and made it to the Sistine Chapel queue at 8.30am. It already wound around the block for 150 yards. But getting in was fairly painless . . . I wish I had the nerve to just lie on the floor and look at it or [on] some trolley on wheels, maybe much as Michelangelo did. Stroll out feeling like a great big human being.

3.40 → London.

26 AUGUST
9.30 Alastair Morris for *Winter Guest* photo shoot. He's being paid a shit-load for 3 hours' work that Emma doesn't really want to do. She sees the artwork (current) and points straight to the image I prefer of the 2 of them. 'What's wrong with that?' What indeed. Alastair is charming, efficient and as I thought the wrong photographer for something which needs to be fresh and full of subtle attitudes. He is classical and controlled. Short of having a clause in the contract I don't know what to do.

27 AUGUST
8.45 pick-up to Heathrow. Find Phyllida & Emma. Find plane to Venice . . . Happy flight, happy boat trip to Gritti Palace.

9pm Taxi to Danieli. Emma is a bit will-she, won't-she today. A bit of gentle persuasion gets her on to the water taxi and off to Ed & Kevin's dinner party.

28 AUGUST
a.m. at the Hotel des Bains—manage not to recognise Jane Campion as she says hello. At first think it's Streep with a haircut but think, no she's in Ireland—who is it? The chair of the jury, no less.

1pm Lunch around the pool of the Hotel des Bains. Arlene, boys, parents . . . Jane Campion . . .

8.30—9 Another walk to a scaffold. The evening in a way wrecked by Ruth Vitale [film producer] telling me of mixed reviews & Ed thinking only of the marketing meetings.

The film is milky and the sound all over the place—I watch it in total, helpless capitulation.

At the end of the evening I am filled with something unnameable but dark. Fine Line [production company] are already unsure of what to do with their eyes—a common attitude of non-culpability is asserting itself. Sometimes I truly hate this business.

29 AUGUST

Very sleepless. The deepest sadness, now depression, settling way down low in the pit of everywhere. Elastoplast—whatever, needed to drag it all up and out for an afternoon of interviews.

First an 11am chat with Judy & Patrick. Something has to be said about *Holy Man*. How much more work can I turn down?

Meanwhile mixed reviews as far as I can tell. Some of them get it. Some of them not. Start rearranging the inside of my head. Again.

I need *months* off.

30 AUGUST

Lunchtime in the Visconti Salon with the bird-filled terrace outside and Venice beyond that. It all seems like a ludicrous backdrop to the endless questions and camera-clicking. How alarming to take Venice for granted.

Home to news that Mary Selway[1] is in hospital having put her nearly new hip out. A horrible story of agonising pain and delays. I feel guilty—I persuaded her to come.

31 AUGUST

The unnameable prevailing still, slow sadness is given an absolute shocking identity when Sean and his family arrive for breakfast and tell me that Princess Diana is dead. For a second or two I thought it was a word-game or strange joke. No—here on the terrace of the Gritti Palace, glittering in the sun and clearly one of the most beautiful places in the world, the news is brutal and true.

Emma, Phyllida, Rima and I go to the Accademia in a daze, but it is the

---

[1] English casting director (1936–2004)

best thing to do—look at the Carpaccio, the Tintorettos, Veroneses. Phyllida finally caves in—you never know with her, all smiles and all heartbreak at the same time. The 3 of us go off to visit Mary in hospital. She's smiling in a body cast (once we get past Nurse Ratched thanks to Emma's diplomacy) and 6 seats are coming out of the plane on Monday.

5.30 Boat → airport and private jet/cars to Country House Hotel land.

1 SEPTEMBER

The hotel grounds stretch away, forever England . . . Lunch at a brilliant country pub, a breathtaking helicopter ride to Heathrow, a car that once belonged to Queen Elizabeth is waiting to take Rima home, Air Canada all charm.

The newspapers are thick with it. Pictures of Diana crowd the pages; flowers carpet the streets. It is true—a light has gone out. A legend begins.

The 4.45 becomes the 5.30 to Toronto. I hope I can handle the next few days with something free of noise and bullshit.

2 SEPTEMBER

Awards & screening. What simple words for such a major Horror Show. Arriving, there was already something chaotic in the air. Then, the shunting & shoving started. Such rudeness by the festival director (echoed by chatting to Rod Steiger in the wings) and a lesson in how *not* to show this film—discord, unsettled audience, noise.

3 SEPTEMBER

Spoke to Ruby—eloquent as ever about Diana.

A photo that is beyond horror in *Le Devoir*. → 9.45 Los Angeles.

Talk to Steiger on the plane. Or rather, listen. And why not? I wish I had a tape recorder. He talks much of Brando and of having met him in a Chinese restaurant in Montreal for the first time in 44 years. Of Brando saying to Val Kilmer 'I don't like your voice, I don't like your face, I don't like your acting, I don't like you . . .' He talks of live TV and the man in the aeroplane scene who forgot his lines and came out with 'This is my stop I get out here.' At 35,000 ft. of the studio executive who said 'Can you do a Southern accent?' (*Heat of the Night*—Academy Award). A reservoir.

4 SEPTEMBER

Read *Holy Man* again—it's an obvious NO. Hand another job, another pile of cash to another actor. Where is the sense in all of this?? *Variety* review is apparently 'GREEEAT'. Grudging would be my word.

5 SEPTEMBER

At Roland Joffé & Susi's beautiful Bel Air house, we settled down to watch Diana's funeral. From about 11pm—5am we hardly spoke. It is not just hindsight which suggests we were watching something extraordinary. The images compelled real focus as they happened. The single toll of the bell every minute; the absolute involvement of the people across sex, age and colour made me watch it in such a highly concentrated way—Remember this. Remember this. By the time Charles Spencer spoke we were watching history shift and stir and the future may have reshaped itself. King William at 25 with his father tucked away at Highgrove deadheading the roses? Quite spectacularly moving the whole thing—even Elton John got away with it. The applause and flower-throwing adding impromptu to detail. People were left standing around outside the Abbey, the Palace not wanting to let go. Wonderful that someone so laughingly direct could gather these souls up like this.

7 SEPTEMBER

The Mark Hotel and then to dinner. Coco Pazzo—horrible East Side, deadly swank. And Paula Poundstone [stand-up comedian] comes over from a Billy Joel type table to enquire as to who I am . . . Breathtaking rudeness but then later the manager slides by to say she's paid our bill.

9 SEPTEMBER

To Boston and a day of interviews. OK apart from a depressing insistence on talking about *Die Hard*. I can see the twisted, mangled tag lines—Die Hard Softy.

19 SEPTEMBER

Dinner with Liam & Natasha and John Cleese, Ewan McGregor & Eve [Mavrakis, his wife], George Lucas & Mia, and Natasha's sister Katharine. Mr McG. is self-involved to a jaw-dropping degree but like a child, so it's somehow not repellent. But how will these people grow into anything at 35 or 40? It is scary how much they *have* to trade on a light-voiced, light-hearted, light-headed 20-something.

22 SEPTEMBER

8 To Orsino w. Michelle Guish for dinner with Lindsay Doran, Emma, Greg, Kate W., Imogen S., Emma J., Pat Doyle[1] and eventually, Trevor Nunn. Autograph hunters' fantasy—even the waiter was auditioning.

---

[1] Scottish composer of film music (1953–)

Much talk of who doing what, but as ever, the best bit was Pat and his stories. His royal family talks could go on a loop tape and I'd be happy. Trevor looks at him slightly bemused—how could someone be this talented and I don't know who he is?

24 SEPTEMBER

7.30am Missed the alarm, missed the car maybe. Phone calls, new car, new time. Wet clothes in dryer. Rethink. Repack . . . Forgot the Gatwick monorail and endlessness of it all. Made the plane with 10 mins to go . . . Watched *Trees Lounge*, Steve Buscemi's beautiful film. Complete re-think on the init-and-direct question although it has such a central quietness you forget anybody is acting or directing something. V. inspiring.

28 SEPTEMBER

[Camden, Maine, re: *Dark Harbor*]

  4pm Everyone comes over to read, eat, drink, hang. Some fittings. The reading is a strange, disembodied experience and I lose all connection to the script and have to lie like mad to Norman Reedus[1] who wonders ½ way through if it's a good idea. He reads beautifully—and X.M. will work fine. As I said yesterday it's Polly[2] and I who have to do the coal-mining.

29 SEPTEMBER

Dark Harbor—First Day. Slipping and sliding. In the rain. Inside the head. Adam [Coleman Howard, director] is all applause, noise and enthusiasm. Probably mistakes my quietness for disapproval, but standing in the pouring rain needs some stillness to bear. Long lunchtime chat with N., who has had a life. Tennis champ, living on an Indian reservation, Tokyo, Spain & Tooting Bec. I'm dazzled by his openness. He could achieve anything with it. How on earth does LA understand him? Polly is quietly heroic all day too. How can I love these two people so quickly? The script still needs vacuuming. The bedroom needs heating.

4 OCTOBER

Standing in a forest being sprayed with lukewarm water so that pyjamas and dressing gown are soaking. In the cold morning air. And because my mind is not in the right place—although in some ways it is, of course—I can't get properly into the scene. Big déjà vu, too, with smoke-guns and mist and

---

[1] American actor (1969–)
[2] English actor Polly Walker (1966–), A.R.'s co-star

watching the DP's[1] nonplussedness as it all vanishes before it has settled. The scene is then played to the background of what seems like a war film.

5 OCTOBER

Raining, raining, raining—especially in my head . . . Eventually, see Tony Blair's conference speech. All NEW, MODERN, REFORMED, CHANGED, like a soap powder ad. It was full of good things but repetitive and straining for sincerity. He has it in bunkerloads but when unmatched by anger or real indignation, he can appear to be Head Boy rather than Prime Minister. You slightly want to pat his head rather than applaud.

6 OCTOBER

Duncan Heath arrives somewhat improbably for lunch from New York–Boston–Portland on his way home. Insane, really, but touching. We talk about *The Confessions* which it seems I am not doing. Can't say I'm that worried—it should be a New York Jew. But what is happening inside my head—recklessness? carelessness? Or some new, better stuff? Where I don't obsess . . .

A truth, of course, is that when I am preoccupied with one individual, everything else seems secondary. Idiotic.

7 OCTOBER

Sitting in the Rotunda all morning—the lunch scene. Joined by the fly population of Maine.

Later the Suncream Scene. Pretending to know how to work a laptop.

10 OCTOBER

Out on the dock and screaming around the bay in the motorboat. Authentic thrills. And nearly spills, as we hit the wake of the camera boat. But all in glorious slowly-settling sunshine (after a morning sailing in the mist) until the boat hit a twig, complained and stopped. Ignominy is a rope towing us into Camden Harbor. Until 10pm I wait to do an eventually aborted shot.

11 OCTOBER

And now the tiredness from Toronto plus delayed action from the boat is really kicking in and as the day progresses it's an ugly tiredness which has everyone asking if I'm OK, and I can feel the authentic acting *animal* swishing its tail.

---

[1] Director of photography

Not healthy, not productive but it isolates a problem—namely that *isolation* of playing scenes when you & the person you are in love with have no scenes between the two of you to refer to. Everything is supposition. This makes the brain very insecure and the spirit undernourished.

Lindsay & Margaret are there on return. Bless them, they have cooked duck & chocolate soufflé and there's some great red wine. After they go to bed, I went to Waterworks at midnight. A wise move—dancing and talking & singing and laughing—antidote to much if not all.

13 OCTOBER

The Golf Scene. Pulling some teeth. Frustrations. Manoeuvrings. Adam is full of perceptions and full of control mechanisms. Do I see myself? Is that what is putting a band around my brain by 5pm? Something weird is going on and it needs to be lanced. Thank goodness for Polly, the straightforward, giving girl who called—was anyone tapping that call?

16 OCTOBER

Writing this and slow-churning. On the boat all day, playing a sleepy mist scene to the sound of fog-guns. Polly and I inaudible to each other. She and Norman go in the freezing night-time water.

17 OCTOBER

One of the worst all-night-awakes of recent memory. Thank God the day is spent inside a '60s Mercedes with rain pouring down the windscreen . . . On other fronts, something less gut-wrenching descends like a comforter. May it last.

18 OCTOBER

As horrible as yesterday was, today was a stretched out pleasure. Playing parts of Górecki's symphony helped set up the sinner scene, and the rest of the day Polly and I lay in a big squashy bed pretending to be asleep. Filming bliss.

Later to Café Miranda for supper w. Polly, and then the inevitable Waterworks. *Soo* loud but the dancing sweats some of the wine and chicken away.

Adam is like an ever-fretting, boiling-over, alka-seltzered glass of life, love, indiscretion and openness. I can only hope all his boundless enthusiasm is well-placed. And that the vibes have roots.

20 OCTOBER

What the fuck is all this insomnia—the pillow? the mattress? The whole Feng Shui of it all?

Anyway—a morning at the house waiting for the eventual 2.30 call. We are in the kitchen for the first morning-after scene—cigarette magic trick.

And after driving home, laughing, a kiss is returned.

21 OCTOBER
The dreaded Scene 77. Thirteen pages of text, noise, small room and increasing heartache. Somehow, there are some takes we can use.

22 OCTOBER
The day of all the reverses throws me into a cocoon of silence. I watch myself in this pointless activity. It does have a huge effect on people—they are confused, I am confused. All the time the ache gets bigger. At this point I don't know how to deal with it. Punishment comes with the fight—cuts and bruises everywhere. I can see where the word 'difficult' comes from. Why is this destructive side so unstoppable, feeding so voraciously on itself, victor in absolutely nothing. It's just a *film*.

25 OCTOBER
Nasty, cold day on the beach, a hastily rehearsed scene throws up resentments about divide and rule techniques. Water round Walt's[1] ankles. Déjà vu.

Later, at . . . dinner with Adam, Jeff [Roda, producer] . . . It's like a spider's web and after dancing till midnight, one of those all-back-to-Room-138 escapades which ended with lights out and pile of bodies on the bed. I crept away later than I should have . . .

26 OCTOBER
11 Headache. Heartache.

27 OCTOBER
A day in the rain. Only more so. Breeds temperament. Why can't I just get on with it? Polly is amazing in that way. And I'm not even the wettest . . .

29 OCTOBER
In the living room with a cardboard box and two live lobsters, elastic bands round their claws, accusing eyes peering up.

Later in the day an exit on to the porch means a sudden collision with the bell that hangs (way too low) from the ceiling. 20 mins later we're on our way to Pen Bay Hospital with a cut across the nose and an ice pack. And it's

---

[1] Walt Lloyd, cinematographer

all true—20 mins more of form-filling and office work before a glimpse of a nurse or a doctor. But then they are fine and felicitous, guarding against concussion, dizziness etc., etc., etc.

30 OCTOBER

Very difficult to describe in coded form except to say various takes of Scene 105. Once the hair and costume had been decided we basically got on with it. At times the temptation was to stop in the middle and just say Who's kidding who here—this is mutual isn't it? Was it? Wasn't it? Will I ever know.[1]

1 NOVEMBER

Writing this as the wind attacks the house, having run away from the wrap party. I'm not sure who is angry at who—I certainly feel a little mislaid . . .

The scene today was tough. Mostly just arriving at it. Adam's stubbornness is like treacle on the stairs, a roadblock. All I want is some *narrative* not endless rationales.

We get there. And it's one of those scenes the crew describes as 'amazing'.

But now I'm tired of the cold shouldering mixed up with the kiss on the cheek. Of course, it's all about my needs. But, fuck it, I've given this film a ton-load.

2 NOVEMBER

Clearing up. Getting out. Driving off.

7.30 Dinner at Reidy's for cast and crew. A happy necessary time. Still can't get it right, though. Somewhere in my speech the word love is mentioned. Later, hands are held, but more misconnections. I think at this point I have to give up. Dizzy.

3 NOVEMBER

The last day. Last shots. Norman disappears to the airport—his black eye still in place. Had to bang on his door & head massage him on to the set. I go on walking into buildings, from buildings & cabs, along streets, up stairs until 'that's a wrap'. All kinds of mixed feelings, as ever, only this time *so* on the line, on the edge.

13 NOVEMBER

[To LA for the filming of further scenes for *Dark Harbor*]

The day the rain came. The beginning of El Niño? Eventually we start

---

[1] A.R. is here referring to filming with Norman Reedus.

on the car crash stuff in the middle of this Mexican district. The telegraph wires have several pairs of sneakers hanging from them. Apparently this means drugs are obtainable in this area—one shoe for dope, two for crack etc.

14 NOVEMBER
Sitting in the car on the low-loader all morning. Silly but funny and a very good humour pervades. Until the teamsters decide to strike . . .

22 NOVEMBER
Lunchtime around the pool with Greg & Em.

We screened *Winter Guest* at CAA. Pretty damn scary and thank you Fine Line for a shitty print, out of date grade and no song. But they liked it (they really liked it) and we sailed on to Goldfingers. Noisy, small, dark, two girls in gold paint, not enough food but everyone danced and drank till 2.30 . . . Collapse.

4 DECEMBER
3pm and I know I've just been talking to *National Enquirer/News of the World* not the *Guardian*. Horrendous, intrusive, entirely centred on sex life. It gets worse as I think about it afterwards.

6 DECEMBER
2 David & Chris, R. and I go to the cemetery. Mum's birthday today. We planted some bulbs and primroses and hung a Christmas holly wreath. It looked a bit mad but pleased with itself.

Then to Nan & Grandad's. Some artificial flowers have crept on to the earth. Awful. After we drove to Auntie D. & Uncle V. for tea and fruitcake. And photos of the 50th party.

7 DECEMBER
Jean Anderson's[1] 90th birthday party. She's a lesson—still wondering about the next job, still betting on the horses. Miss out on lunch, though; the car to Heathrow is there at 1.30pm.

8 DECEMBER
The phone rings and a voice says 'This is David Mamet', and then I spend ten minutes telling him why I probably won't do *The Winslow Boy*.[2]

---

[1] English actor (1907–2001)
[2] Mamet was writing and directing a screen adaptation of Terence Rattigan's play.

16 DECEMBER

3.45 *Today Show*—Jill Rappaport. God, what a lot of hair.

17 DECEMBER

1pm Lunch Trattoria Dell'Arte. Peter Travers [film critic]. Fun. He's very focused and generous and I could feel the journalist in the gossipy questions slipped in between the professional concerns. Laura Dern tucked in a booth on the way out helpfully calls *WG* 'a masterpiece'.

   8 *WG* screening—Ken's[1] speech curled my toes—references to no one earning more than $150,000 . . .

19 DECEMBER

8.15 Dinner at Erica Jong's . . . A roomful of very witty and probably vulgar people being rather polite all evening.

21 DECEMBER

8.15 *Good Will Hunting*.

   Ultimately a bit of a let down. Matt Damon is a really fine actor, however. But the film feels as if it is looking for a sense of purpose, or that it has too many. And Robin Williams is too sweet from the word go.

25 DECEMBER

Christmas Day in Wyoming [with Judy Hoflund]. Coming downstairs to people hidden behind flying wrapping paper, mounds of Barbie and fluorescent plastic. These girls so spoiled the word has no meaning. Later in the day Rosemary stands in the middle of it all wanting 'something to do'. Charlotte's main dream had always been 'a lollipop'.

   6.30 Dinner's on the table. Reto [the cook] and I negotiating our way around Judy's obsession with oven temperature. She had promised us a wonderful cook and then wouldn't let him do it. When it does all magically arrive on plates it is delicious, original and Reto is exhausted.

   Later—watching *Wings of the Dove*. I have only a question mark as a response. Who are these people? What product are they advertising?

26 DECEMBER

To Calico for a family meal. Reto had been ready to cook but I don't think Judy can stand the competition. Crazy, really—is she checking the restaurant kitchens? No. What does she give the girls for breakfast? Chemically flavoured & coloured 'cereal'? Coffeemate. Back home watching Kennedy

---

[1] Ken Lipper, producer

Center Awards. Dylan in a black suit & ribbons. What next as he sits next to Charlton Heston . . . ?

27 DECEMBER
To New York.

Exodus with many bags . . . Jackson Hole Airport [Wyoming] looking bleak and dramatic and snow-swept.

31 DECEMBER
To Edna O'Brien at the Wyndham . . . Edna spotted Pluck U the chicken shop on 2nd Avenue.

9 To Nick Hytner [theatre director] in the Village. He calls it 'The House That Ho Chi Minh Built'.[1] Very focusing. Stunning views of Manhattan. A real fire. I feel like I'm *in* a magazine.

11 To Susan Sarandon & Tim Robbins on 15th Street . . . A great accordionist plays with Tim & a friend. Another stranger sang 'In the Midnight Hour'. Emily Watson & husband Jack [Waters], woozy with jet lag, come with us.

1.15am Back to the Mark. During the evening the *New Yorker* review of *WG* (it has the lingering radiance of art) was quoted. 'Disastrous,' says Edna O'B.

---

[1] Because of the success of *Miss Saigon*

1998

The *Winter Guest* — Los Angeles — Golden Globes — Brussels —
Tokyo — Issey Miyake — South Africa — Pittsburgh, *Dogma* —
Kevin Spacey — Pittsburgh, *Dogma* — Frank Sinatra —
Los Angeles — *Dogma* — Eddie Izzard — Concorde — Tuscany —
Antony and Cleopatra — Alaska — Helen Mirren —
Cape Town

1 JANUARY

Edna called to say that she was 'never drinking again'—or something like
that—and was currently eating a bowl of porridge.

2 JANUARY

7pm To Kennedy and BA Sleeper Service. Not.

5 JANUARY

Phone, phone, premiere tickets, friends, donations, LA (Golden Globes).
Kath Viner[1]—who talks to me *slightly* as if I'm interviewing her.

8 JANUARY

7pm car to Odeon Hammersmith (w. Rima & Miranda Richardson).
Decided to tackle initial atmosphere head-on at the microphone and refer
fairly directly to shitty reviews. I think it helped. At all events, the audience
relaxed and united and it was v. v. special atmosphere.

Later to Belinda's. 3am and she's talking and cooking! Pasta.

9 JANUARY

The whingeing has started. New York, here I come . . .

11 JANUARY

It has been hellish and perplexing reading some notices, avoiding most—the
complaints are beginning to be predictable. Too theatrical, nothing new to
say. All focusing on negatives. All missing the point. Why does it not at least
occur to them that it is intentionally non-naturalistic, that the film is about
something age-old, that needs repeating.

---

[1] Katharine Viner, British journalist (1971–)

15 JANUARY

12.30 To St George's Hospital, Tooting, to see Pat Doyle.[1] His knowledge of what is happening to him—the morphine to combat the pain from chemotherapy; the daily obsession with his 'count'—is awesome. And still he is funny and *curious*. Emma arrives in the See You Jimmy hat & we take Polaroids.

3pm Nicole Farhi shop in Bond St. Came away with a suit, shoes and 2 things for Rima at some sort of knockdown price. Will I wear this suit more than once?

16 JANUARY

10ish Ruby arrives, finds me in dressing gown and disappears for croissants. Talk of awfulness in the Seychelles and the *Apocalypse Now* of it with her parents.

17 JANUARY

10.30 pick-up → Heathrow → LAX.

18 JANUARY

3.30 pick-up for Golden Globes.

Madhouse of plates being whipped away half-finished lest they still be there for the broadcast; movie stars in vastly expensive dresses they can only wear once; name dropping on a big scale—there and at . . . the CAA party— Gus Van Sant, Matt Damon (I was fairly drunk, grabbing his lapels to tell him he's a really, no *really* good actor), Minnie Driver, Lauren Bacall, Shirley MacLaine (she loved *The Winter Guest*, my hero), Winona Ryder, Joan Cusack (squished in a lift—could we work together?), Kevin Kline. Giving the Golden Globe to Alfre Woodard[2] was *BEST*!

22 JANUARY

11.30 Back in London.

25 JANUARY

South Bank Awards on TV—Peter Hall rightly says both parties wonderful about the arts in opposition. He's right. It won't do.

10.27 Eurostar to Brussels. This could become a habit. Everything they say is true. Speed, soundlessness smooth as silk and straight into the centre of Brussels. Roll on Paris.

3pm Interviews—a strange green room cum bar hidden inside a shopping mall that has the air of an upmarket Leningrad.

---

[1] He was diagnosed with leukemia.
[2] American actor (1952–)

27 JANUARY

Having woken at 5am the day looms ahead full of stifled yawns and sentences without verbs. But the morning interviews are full of bright edgy questions. This makes the job so much lighter, easier. Otherwise I could supply (or even fax) some standard answers to the six ever-ready questions.

pm More stuff as they edge ever closer to *Die Hard* & *Robin Hood*. They are like tired dogs with a very old slipper.

7pm Screening, which was ace. Even the screen covered in Flemish & French subtitles didn't stop it getting across the red, red seats. Standing ovation.

Radio interview after screening. She risks garroting by starting 'Usually you play . . .'

10 L'Huîtrière with Neil [Kinnock] . . . Neil managing to cover 12 topics at once but threading through it a growing savaging of New Labour. 'Kicked out if you don't go to the gym 3 times a week.'

31 JANUARY

→ Heathrow → Amsterdam.

1 FEBRUARY

→ Tokyo.

Weird. Getting off Amsterdam flight there's King Constantine and Queen Anne-Marie of Greece. Getting on Tokyo flight, he's there in the cabin. What are the odds?

2 FEBRUARY

Arrived Tokyo.

7pm Dinner w. Ninagawa . . . Always hard to unpick through the formalities. Ninagawa always so contained, so focused on the work. He asks me to act again & to direct a Shakespeare.

3 FEBRUARY

Interviews all day. Next time—there really is no need for the interviews to be 50 mins each. It's just knackering. But there's a disarming tunnel vision about the Japanese—these quiet, small people throwing up this enormous city, churning out product, quietly, ceaselessly.

8.30 Dinner w. Issey Miyake . . . [1] He's charming, funny and open. Gives me a book of Irving Penn photographs of his clothes. Thank God I had taken the Martin Parr[2] book, although first instincts to stagger across the seas with

---

[1] Japanese designer (1938–)

[2] British photographer (1952–)

the Damien Hirst book would probably have been better. The thought, however, definitely counts in these situations.

4 FEBRUARY

Alarming first TV interview—'the mother and daughter have one expression when they go to the seaside and a different one when they return—how did you make them change their expressions?'

6 FEBRUARY

9.52 The bullet to Kyoto. Well-named this train. So fast you travel with a gentle underflow of nausea. Inasmuch as you can grab any image as Japan flashes by it looks like one vast 3D electrical circuit. But it's a beautiful train. I look forward to the day British Rail has an electronic noticeboard, quiet audible announcements and a ticket collector who bows to us as she leaves the carriage.

11 FEBRUARY

A day of No's.

Uneasy making. A quiet depression.

Further Academy stupidity—the total omission of any nomination for *The Ice Storm*, next to nothing for *Donnie Brasco*, *Boogie Nights*.

Don't be too much of a downer, don't open too early in the year.

13 FEBRUARY

3pm to Hazlitt's to find John Hurt and then to Groucho's and then to the Atlantic Bar.

Taxi to Habitat. Whizz round the bathroom cabinets. Taxi home. Watching the *Dark Harbor* shots. V. depressing . . . 20lbs too depressing.

24 FEBRUARY

9pm The Ivy w. Adam & Polly and with perfect *Hello* magazine placing—Fergie chatting to Elton John with Jeremy Irons & Sinead Cusack across the room. Adam agog . . .

4 MARCH

6.30 Car to Heathrow for 9pm flight to South Africa.

6 MARCH

Streaming with cold/flu/whatever. Life can become another TV set, another hotel room however much the sun and swimming pool say Cape Town, South Africa.

7 MARCH

9 Screening *Winter Guest*.

Like watching it through the bottom of a beer glass. It is so hard for the film to work under these circumstances. Does music work through static? Does a painting work if you have a headache?

8 MARCH

10.30 Q&A on *WG*.

I have a feeling that people don't know quite what to ask since they probably didn't like it very much. Not *all* of them as I gradually discover, but enough.

9 MARCH

9ish *Die Hard*. Ten years on. It still works like none of the others. Real energy, perfect camera work, wit and style.

10 MARCH

9 *Under the Skin*.

This is something very special. No wonder [the jury] gave it the main prize at Edinburgh.

14 MARCH

6.10 → Johannesburg / 9.15 → London.

One of Liza Key's madcap outings. At one point everything lost—the keys, the parking ticket, my wallet. We get lost. Nearly. At one point she asks hopefully 'Can anyone see an airport?' But the drive is spectacular—along the Indian Ocean—and shocking—the townships and shanty towns just a crazy collage of cardboard and metal bits and pieces called home. Lots of washing flapping bravely in the dirt. How would you send a letter here? 300th shack on the left of the freeway?

15 MARCH

Ruby and the Spice Girls on TV. What? Who? Why?

17 MARCH

11.30 → PITTSBURGH.

Watched *Regeneration* on the plane. Curiously uninvolved, uninvolving. Not stealthy enough or cold enough or sharp enough. Smooth, slow and brownish—Sunday TV. Except in the last minutes. *Something* epic started to happen.

We stopped in Montreal for an hour then on to Pittsburgh and the William Penn Hotel. The burst through that tunnel still as thrilling.

18 MARCH
[Filming of *Dogma*]
11 Costume fitting. Versace rules. Abigail[1] is obviously v.v. good. She doesn't put a foot wrong in terms of shape, line, texture. And she's willing to listen.

3pm Read with Linda Fiorentino. Also meet Jay (Jason Mewes[2]) and assume like an idiot that he's Kevin's assistant then recognise him from *Chasing Amy*. Foot deeply in it. Linda thinks this is hilarious. She's everything she looks and sounds—smoky, dark, a coming-on disposition. Somewhere in the middle Ben Affleck crashes in, later Jason Lee and later yet Matt Damon. The room is suddenly full of baseball caps, popping cans of water/iced tea/whatever, peeling oranges, potato chips, cigarette smoke. We bungee-jump our way through the script. Chaotic, free fall, Linda resolutely giving nothing . . . which we discuss somewhat in the Steelyard restaurant later. Everything slows up or opens out here and we have some really interesting, open chat. They are all bright, funny, passionate people. And vulnerable. Some eyes soften I'm glad to say.

19 MARCH
9 Kevin Smith has the strangest way of running a rehearsal. Matt and Ben seem to take it, so when in Pittsburgh . . . We spend an hour reading newspapers, chatting, sitting, waiting . . . for breakfast. No explanations or attempts to pull us together. Then we do this sort of show and tell rehearsal. Get up, go in the middle and do your scenes. Kevin just watches, says 'sweet' and at the end of a scene takes photographs on his digital camera. Jason Lee throws himself at it, Linda beyond laid back.

3pm Linda and me. Where Kevin gives line readings or says up a bit, down a bit on odd lines. It has its own *real* charm. He wrote it. He hears the tunes.

Supper in the room. Strange, dislocated perplexed state of mind. Sometimes one feels like the milk bottle without which the rocket can't take off. But that would be negative thinking so away! with it.

---

[1] Abigail Murray, costume designer
[2] American actor (1974–)

20 MARCH

6.45 Drive to Pittsburgh Airport for 8.05 → New York.

Somewhere around 10 arrive at the studio for prosthetic making.

To the Lombardy Hotel.

21 MARCH

2.30 *The Big Lebowski*.

Like its title sounds—sprawling. Jewels in amongst the box of chocolates and other such mixed metaphors.

26 MARCH

10.15 Car to Newark Airport for 12.14 flight to Pittsburgh.

3pm Wardrobe for costume fitting. Would like to drop 10lbs overnight. Starvation diet before Wednesday.

31 MARCH

To the set, the church.

George Carlin and the Buddy Christ[1] figure both on great form. Carlin improvising brilliantly with the extras. Should have taped him. An echo of the day when Gore Vidal joined us, in Pittsburgh, on *Bob Roberts*.

1 APRIL

7.30am pick-up to the set and all day in the Mexican restaurant.

A six page scene to start the film. Reminders of day one on *Michael Collins*. Here was another cliff face only this time involving the daggers-drawn battle between memory and any kind of freedom. Somewhere in there the 2 shots, the one over-the-shoulder and the close-ups, there were moments when it took off but always with the slight frustration of not really being able to make it a scene between 2 people. So much plot to get over. And fast.

Kevin seemed to be flushed with happiness at the end of the day. Hours skate by at times like these. 7.30am pick-up finish at 6 pm.

Linda has this volcano of brilliance rumbling quietly underneath the persona she brings out and applies to every line. Seductive, dark, throaty, eyebrows arched, eyes rolling. All fascinating and all wrong for this character. But it ain't my place to say anything. I must be learning.

---

[1] Scene in *Dogma* in which a cardinal attempts to rebrand Jesus Christ

3 APRIL

Spoke with Mike Nichols who issued invite out to Martha's Vineyard. Certainly. Happily.

2.30 Pick-up for car to JFK and 5pm → Heathrow.

6 APRIL

8 *Closer*.

A cast trapped by their director.[1] Who is also the author. Same old problem. Frances Barber talks of being unable to step outside Patrick's notes. And it's true—you can see the lines sitting on the page.

To the Ivy & Teatro. Someone should do tests on Frances—to measure how laughter makes you healthy because something must be counteracting the wine intake. A hasty escape from Teatro when the *Daily Mail* slides into the cubicle, along with Caroline Aherne.

11 APRIL

Discovering exactly what I earned on *Judas Kiss* (the movie) was a bit of a shock.

13 APRIL

The Iceman Cometh.

Kevin Spacey is the acting equivalent of a champion surfer. He makes everyone else look effortful. Even if he also carries a slightly self-satisfied air.

19 APRIL

Watching the BAFTA awards. Like watching from Mars. Where I speak only Martian. At least *Titanic* went home empty-handed.

But, yet again, apart from Sigourney Weaver, so did *The Ice Storm*, a continuing injustice in the nonsense of these ceremonies. *Winter Guest* keeps good company. And avoids a deeply tacky ceremony which at times shamed all those present.

25 APRIL

12.25 → Pittsburgh.

27 APRIL

1pm Costume fitting. Issey Miyake has sent two garments from Outer Space—a little *too* far out for this film.

---

[1] Patrick Marber

4.15 To the doctor to deal with the nose bleeds. He cauterises (another word for hurts).

8.15 Jeff[1] comes to re-dye my hair.

30 APRIL

A rehearsal. At which Linda asks for 2 lines out of 5. Has she looked at the scene apart from on the drive in? I am catapulted into a dark and frowning place—silent with resentment at having to work solo. Again. And so—a long day with a pile of lines and [a] scene that's all about prosthetics and 80lb wings. The latter is a unique experience. When they're down it's like a magnet pulling you against the wall and as the minutes turn into half hours the weight and the harness play games with the memory. Pain versus concentration. And *still* Linda blows her lines. Kevin does notice. And asks me if there's a problem. What can you say?

1 MAY

Vince[2] and his team paste me into my false crotch and away we go with a cinema first. Full frontal no frontal. Everyone takes many snaps which will doubtless wind up on the internet.

Somewhere during the day someone mentions this great dermatologist Linda has been to. Off I trot to 3pm appointment. Dr Nancy Nieland[-Fisher] promptly informs me I have rosacea, psoriasis and acne and here are your prescriptions for these ungetriddable ailments. Great.

5 MAY

Meet Alanis Morissette. She's in the makeup van having flowers put in her hair. Odd this. I have the CD[3] along with the rest of the world. All that angst and rock 'n' roll. Here's this quiet, charming, gentle girl/woman. We wait a lot, shoot a bit. Share a van back to the hotel. Talk about work; what's now, what's next. The Girl Next Door acquires new resonance.

6 MAY

Me and Alanis—comedy duo. Who knew? Laurel and Hardy live . . .

7 MAY

Definite change in the atmosphere—Chris Rock allows himself to be more vulnerable now that Ben A has gone. That's one of the deals with the devil—

---

[1] Jeffrey A. Rubis, makeup artist
[2] Vincent J. Guastini, special effects makeup creator
[3] *Jagged Little Pill*

surrender your peculiarities to the pushy certainties; be seen as often as possible with a mobile phone—right up to a call for 'Action'.

All sorts of stuff released—in the bus on the way back to the hotel Salma Hayek talks of her time in India as a volunteer for Mother Teresa—this utterly beautiful woman talking of wiping up shit and worms and keeping the flies off a dying woman's face.

Alanis had talked only yesterday of being there too.

8 MAY

Pittsburgh will forever be associated with my room at the William Penn Hotel. Car-less, cab-less and on a film which is all about creating a family of any description. I have a feeling that the need is there throughout the unit, but there is a shyness at the top which coagulates unhappily with the arrogance factor and makes visible vulnerability impossible. I'm just not around enough to make a huge difference.

9 MAY

Somewhere on the way back to the hotel, I felt a familiar knife-like pain in my lower back. I know what this means. Five days of pain. The wings have caught up with me.

10 MAY

Trying to move the body out of bed is like a mathematical equation. A slow progression to an upright position and an 8am pick-up by Ratz, the production designer, and off to the flea market.

11 MAY

Woke up at 8 after just over 4 hours' sleep. The pain in the lower back is bad so a chiropractor is called. Maybe not such a wise move. There is a pinched nerve and all around it muscles have put their fists up to defend it.

7.50 pick-up for the 5 min drive to the Station restaurant. Pain starting to dominate every thought and move . . . A bad call was to shoot my close-up at 3.30am because by then my brain had gone. I asked for cue cards. First time ever. Horrible experience. But otherwise no scene and a lot of despair. Pain worse and worse. Standing up from the chair excruciating.

12 MAY

The pain is too gross. Can't film tonight. They shift the scenes around . . . Doctor comes and gives pills for spasms and pain. Somewhere in here, had a massage. Watched TV standing up.

13 MAY

To the hospital for X-rays. Fortunately, no disc problems but muscle spasms are eased by a brace (which I probably should have been wearing with the wings anyway).

15 MAY

A day when the pain lessens gradually and then just when you're feeling confident, stabs you hard.

Clearing up. Clearing out. Moving on. Again.

Listening to Sinatra songs all day on TV. Even the dreaded 'My Way' is coated with that amazing voice, although the utterly unpredictable phrasing is better heard in 'All the Way' or the spider's trap of 'I've Got You Under My Skin'. Someone dies and for a while you stop taking them for granted.

16 MAY

11.50 to New York.

20 MAY

9am Flight to Los Angeles and the Mondrian Hotel.

21 MAY

9am Lasse Hallström. Gentle man. V. intriguing script of *Cider House Rules*. Would not require acting—just getting on with it while the camera has a look.

2.15 Car to looping for *Judas Kiss*. Sebastian [Gutierrez, director] says would you like the good news or the bad news. Turns out there's really only bad news. The Germans & Stefan [Simchowitz, producer] have cut the film to resemble an action flick which means Emma & I are trimmed to the bone (or so it seems). *Plus ça change.*

26 MAY

Pittsburgh.

5.40 is one of those nightmare pick-up times that punish you all day long. Plus the gentle insistent presence of a headache punctuated by sneezing. Just what is not needed.

The scene has a myriad of set-ups and by the early evening is drowning in the daily fly-past up above, the shoot coming alive to the sound of ghetto-blasters.

30 MAY

6.45[pm] pick-up and out to the Star Lake auditorium to walk on water. Which all works fine apart from the by now predictable 3am when the camera comes round, and my brain is frying gently. But there's a vaguely celebratory atmosphere, the lake lit beautifully and as dawn broke we drank some champagne in the makeup trailer and said goodbyes.

To bed at 7am.

1 JUNE
5.50[pm] → New York.

4 JUNE
8.30 Eddie Izzard's show.

He was more openly political than I have ever seen him and wonderful as he skated around from Pol Pot to landing on the moon to puberty.

Later—to Balthazar. Eddie in jeans, T-shirt and 4″ stilettos. A lovely evening.

5 JUNE
As Catherine was saying on the phone this morning, Eddie is one of the people who change the world. And the morning after I feel real admiration for the clarity of his stance, and the shrewdness of his approach. He challenges and reassures at the same time and you can hear the grind and click of rusty minds all over the audience.

6 JUNE
7.30 Wangle my way on to Concorde. Hooray. Ivana Trump adds a bit of dash sitting in front of me just where I can watch her checking her press clippings, tearing bits out, looking through itineraries and then rather touchingly looking long & hard at photos of loved ones before putting them back in her wallet.

20 JULY
7.30 Broadcasting House. Dinner . . . What to say about this? Were we set decoration? Will any of it be of use? Michael Frayn the only real intellectual heavyweight. Richard Eyre v. good as was Jonathan.[1] Harvey G[oldsmith]—opinionated. Simon Russell Beale & I hoping same. Simon Curtis [film director] and Elizabeth[2] think it's funny to tell stories of me in silk pyjamas during the [LA] earthquake.

21 JULY
RADA Appeals Committee.

Attenborough tells horrific tales of Arts Council Lottery funding cut-

---

[1] Jonathan Kent, English theatre director (1949–)
[2] Elizabeth McGovern, American actor (1961–), S.C.'s wife

backs, double-dealings etc., etc. And, consistently, he puts his hand into his pocket to shore the whole thing up.

30 JULY

8 Dinner w. Catherine & David Bailey.

The loft of anyone's dreams. High above King's Cross Station, the rails curving into the arched entrance. Hours of potential pleasure people-watching from this big airy room with its TV den tucked round a corner. They are a great couple. Aside from all the iconic stuff, both very vulnerable and straightforward.

3 AUGUST

HOLIDAYS!

Talk to Helen Mirren who, as ever, is warm, funny, honest, persuasive, understanding, persuasive . . .

12 Car to Whiteley's [shopping centre] (Amex & A&C) and on to Heath-row for supposed 2.10 → Rome. It took off at 4. Livia meets us for (it turns out) her first 'long' drive for 10 years. Never goes on autostradas. So drives slow. Until the full stop. And what looks like a hideous crash six cars ahead. A container lorry stretched and crushed across the road like a huge broken unknown animal. Eventually discover that the driver has been pulled clear and seems OK . . . 2 hours later the crane lifts the entire thing into the air—a massive poetic sight as endless frozen carcasses of meat spill out across the road. Antonioni.[1]

2am. Sit down to pasta & prawns as the crickets do their stuff.

4 AUGUST

5 A drive into Capalbio. Etruscan walls, narrow streets, waiting to be a film set. Or for the tourists to just fuck off.

7.30pm. That's it. I'm doing it. *Antony & Cleopatra*. NT. Helen Mathias. Sean M. Relief.

6 AUGUST

A great happy beach day . . . I'm reading Arnold Wesker's account of *The Birth of Shylock and the Death of Zero Mostel*. I know it was written (it's a diary) in 76–77 but I am shocked by the overall tone. Deification of John Dexter,[2] total fascination with Wesker's own every thought & move. Especial

---

[1] Michelangelo Antonioni, Italian film director (1912–2007), best known for films such as *Blow-Up*
[2] English theatre director (1925–1990)

fascination with the number of times his advice had not been heeded. The amount of input—almost as 2nd director—that had been allowed but mostly the patronising of actors—constantly referred to by their characters' names. Endless references to him & Dexter hissing comments during run-through. Actors are performing dogs—malleable, silly, not capable of rational thought just blind instinct & infuriating inabilities to hear their authors' 'music'. And it comes across as a surprise to find they have private lives. But he does quote John Whiting[1] memorably—'A line in a play holds just so much sense and no more. Just so much emotion & no more . . . The really great actors exercise their own control. They give a line an essential rightness of sense which makes it seem impossible to read any other way. They also make the emotion a kind of atmosphere in which the sense can freely exist. LESSER TALENTS OFTEN TRY TO OVER-HUMANISE.' (p. 108)

8.30 Spoke to Paul Lyon-Maris. Something about the NT contract. Will do *Antony & Cleopatra* for about £100 per performance. Tell that to those opera singers. Patrick Proctor[2] will do the poster.

9 AUGUST

11ish to the beach. Finishing the Wesker diary. Contradictory, irrational, pointed, exact, self-delusory, honest, self-important, fickle—whatever adjective suits—apply. And ultimately so disrespectful to actors. We should *all* be engaged in an activity which 'gives away'. Here, too much is 'on show'.

11 AUGUST

8ish Dinner at Monte Po. This is like a chapter from Evelyn Waugh. The Greenes. Graham[3] & Sally and their children Matt (screenwriter, Los Angeles), Charlotte (the homemaker) and Alexander. This breathtaking house, every corner filled with effortless taste and abundant eccentricity. Candle-strewn tables, a disco upstairs with the children dancing behind a shadow-lit sheet. And the cook quit at 5pm. Hat, bag, case, the lot.

17 AUGUST

First day rehearsals *Antony & Cleopatra*.

Rehearsal Room 1 and a time warp image of a circle of cushions on a collage of Turkish carpets. But it's not a bad thing to be thinking of Peter Brook and 1978 especially because whatever else Helen and I will never

---

[1] English actor, playwright and author (1917–1963)
[2] English painter (1936–2003)
[3] Graham Greene (1936–2016), British publisher

fall into the alarmingly cold space that Alan Howard and Glenda Jackson inhabited.

Anyway, a few familiar faces . . . are there and lots of strangers with great faces. Trevor Nunn greets us with a big hug and a hello speech surrounded by the NT staff and then Patsy R.[1] gets us breathing before Sean starts. The rest of the day is picking the text up in forefinger and thumb for examination.

Tim Hatley shows us the set, David Belugou his costumes. First alarm bells. I hope unnecessary—but how will we make this personal and not epic given that golden wall, those clothes?

19 AUGUST
5.30 First run (words) of Act 1. Too much acting from me . . .

20 AUGUST
Sean handles rehearsals beautifully. Honest, fun, denying the power of his role, really. 'I can't *direct* unless you show me something'—or words to that effect.

21 AUGUST
11.30 26 Manchester Street and Patrick Proctor. (Suddenly there's a reason for a diary.) Dressed immaculately (was it a paper hanky tucked into his pocket?). And however drunk he is—and he is—he knows he's wearing a Versace tie. The drawing time amounts to about 15 mins during the next hour, interspersed with several large whiskies. But whenever, as he lowers himself on to his stool his eyes focus murderously on to me, lines come out of him on to the canvas . . . that are ravishing. He insists in his utterly aristocratic way on lunch. At Odin's—full of Peter Langan's drawings & paintings. Beautiful Laura Knight, Hockney and across the way—Proctor.

24 AUGUST
A session with Patsy and in roughly 20 mins she sorts out the 'fogging' vocal problem. Surprise—I'm not breathing properly (1) and (2) drinking enough water.

8 To Sandra & Michael Kamen for Sandra's birthday. And in view of Sandra's recent aneurysm and operation it's great to see her cutting a cake, answering the door, *anything*. George Harrison there trying to find a corner, a hallway, anywhere but the middle of the room at, God forbid, a party. I can see his point. He seems incredibly genuine and open.

---

[1] Patsy Rodenburg, British voice coach (1953–)

25 AUGUST

Reading through Act 2. Something light and generous takes hold and all of Sean's work & methods over the last 10 days pays off. As he said afterwards it was simple and direct and *modern*.

26 AUGUST

Strange to feel this company getting closer and closer but somehow Helen and I remain on the outside. With Finbar.[1] Involved, committed but outside. Make of it what you will.

27 AUGUST

9.45 There's no solution to where's the taxi? Except the fantasy of the NT sending a car. Ha. So—late again.

pm On into the wondrous depths of *Antony & Cleopatra*. Evening reading in a circle, in a monotone, the jaw drops.

Supper at home. Packing.

28 AUGUST

TO ALASKA!

12 Alaskan time. Arrive Juneau Airport.

1.30 Deliver surprise of the year to Mary Elizabeth [Mastrantonio] on the set . . .

3.30 River rafting. Wind, driving rain, talk of 'How not to fall in'—we nearly chickened out, but didn't and are glad.

30 AUGUST

7.30 Drinks in the Red Saloon before 8.30 dinner & Alaskan totem rituals in completely designed-and-built-from-scratch top floor, over-the-pool venue . . . The constant sense of who's sitting where beginning to wear me down. Robin Williams arrives—his usual, disarming, shy, unpushy self and makes an example of everyone. Dance till late while Rima 'Scrabbles' in the bar.

31 AUGUST

8.30 Wake. Pack.

And the long goodbyes.

Through all the unbelievable work and care and attention to detail it's hard to let go and just enjoy it. A gift others possess. This year's guest list [at Paul Allen's party] included—Francis Ford Coppola, George Lucas, James Cameron,

---

[1] Irish actor Finbar Lynch (1959–)

Neil Jordan, Jim Sheridan,[1] Terry George, Jeff Goldblum, Candice Bergen, Annabeth Gish,[2] Ed Begley, Dave Stewart, Deepak Chopra, John Richmond,[3] Noel Redding, Dan Aykroyd, Robin Williams, Patti Smith,[4] Jennifer Saunders, Ade Edmondson, Clare Peploe,[5] Douglas Adams, Quincy Jones, Carrie Fisher, etc., etc. All mixed up with scientists, architects and Belfast family members.

1 SEPTEMBER

RETURN FROM ALASKA.

11.30 (Managed some sleep) . . . Car back home. Change. On to NT arrive 3pm. Straight into reading Act 3. Use it, I thought, and the spirit was accurate but the eyesight was weak.

2 SEPTEMBER

Finishing the work-through of Act 4. Odd flicker of shapes, cohesions, threads appear through the jet-lag recovery. Sometimes I speak, for a long time I'm silent. So much so, that Helen wonders in her easy non-judgemental way if I'm OK with the process or find it boring? Nothing could be further from the truth. I just lose myself in possibilities with this glorious play. Talk about 'mouthed to flesh-burst gush'.[6]

3 SEPTEMBER

Lunchtime—looking at Patrick Proctor's finished work. It looks like a portrait of two 14-year-olds. Not far wrong.

7 SEPTEMBER

First day of moving the play. By late afternoon—alarm bells. These weeks of detailed text work and now a day of some v. good work but no real sense of sorting wheat from chaff. So in there is some terribly demonstrated work and bad verse speaking. The set proving to be as awkward as I had feared in terms of creating a dynamic set of entrances and exits.

8 SEPTEMBER

Better. I'm a dog with a slipper in the morning. I can feel all the new separate energies flying around. Helen, if offered no other option, does a solo act. One small suggestion and she transforms spectacularly. Instinctive genius.

---

[1] Irish playwright (1949–)
[2] American actor (1971–)
[3] English fashion designer (1960–)
[4] American singer-songwriter (1946–)
[5] British screenwriter (1942–2021)
[6] From 'The Wreck of the Deutschland' by Gerard Manley Hopkins

17 SEPTEMBER

Working through the 4th Act am . . . and Sean is worrying about the impenetrable lyricism of this part of the play. It forces me to analyse aims—specific feelings, actions. And in the following run-through a lot becomes clearer, more direct. Sean is a big pile of Kleenex—and honest to himself ever, tells us how moved he was. It is in a way, a warning. Don't sit back on it.

23 SEPTEMBER

These have been difficult days, running scenes with that awful grasping sense of the text. So—no impetus inside. And listening to text being chopped every which way, so no impetus outside.

The only solution is to *stop* and *teach*. I sound and feel so reactionary but it is like a knife in the stomach when Shakespeare is rewritten or ridden the wrong way. He makes it easy (or easier) if you think *on* the line.

6.30 Fittings. The mustard suede is on its way out. Hallelujah. I would have been a face with no body.

28 SEPTEMBER

Run through Act 3. Ohmigod.

29 SEPTEMBER

Starting Act 4. Learning lines a little ahead of myself here. Recipe for panic.

30 SEPTEMBER

Oh God, let me lose this script.

1 OCTOBER

3 hours' sleep and a run. Thank God for experience (of a kind) otherwise I'd be reaching for the hand-gun.

5 OCTOBER

7pm First run—Act 1.

Sean's happy. It feels like a mess to me. Except for Helen who is free, creative and flying. An afternoon of Katia C.[1] and her intense missing of the point exhausts me.

6 OCTOBER

These are the tough days. I can feel myself not exactly closing off from the company but concentrating so hard that chatter disappears.

---

[1] Katia Caballero, playing Octavia

The Thidias Scene is the first big Waterloo. You just have to say these words over and over so that the knowledge sinks deep.

7 OCTOBER

2.30 The first run-through. An out of body experience. Full of heroics, dumbness, company things, solo things, conclusive, inconclusive. But a basis. For tomorrow. And an excuse for getting fairly blasted in the bar afterwards.

8 OCTOBER

Hung over in a major way.

3pm The Tech starts. Memorable moment in the wings as Helen says 'I'm so happy . . . all I dreamed of as a girl was to be a queen in a big theatre . . .'

9 OCTOBER

Hung over in another major way.

The day spirals on, the costume gradually appears, the character gradually disappears; hairpiece is tried. Much hoopla from the rest of the cast. Only question marks from me.

10 OCTOBER

Like a car crash we get past the interval and on into the second half. My questions are getting larger & more urgent. Where is the music? Where will the story be? Time and again where is the exactness?

11.30 In the bar. Everybody is good humoured. Helen and I quietly hoping there will be a dress rehearsal.

11 OCTOBER

11am–7pm and at the close we are still in Act 4. A kind of calm terror looms at the prospect of a public performance tomorrow night. Armour seen for the first time . . . Why? Could it not have been made in week 3 or 4? It's a prop. Now they have to duck and dive all day tomorrow as we all face the prospect of public improvisation for close on 4 hours. The music appears in arbitrary strokes. The lighting will be an instant surprise.

12 OCTOBER

7.15 and on . . .

1200 people watching a dress rehearsal and only the second-ever run of the play. Utterly terrifying. And I will always think—destructive. But, of course, we have to turn it to our advantage.

13 OCTOBER

Second performance.

It grows. And shrinks. But it has started to find its space.

14 OCTOBER

Still hideous nerves. It's so big, this play. And this theatre.

Later talking on the doorstep with Helen & Sean. His vulnerability in spades. But so? Directors, I think, aren't allowed that. They should only encourage, challenge, reassure. *Never* look for validation.

15 OCTOBER

The gremlins arrive.

Skidding on water.

Road trips on the breakers.

The sword falls from its scabbard and is revolved off.

Antony killed himself with Eros' sword tonight . . .

A corporate members' do in the Olivier bar. Followed by a too-late session with Helen and some LX guys.

17 OCTOBER

1.30 First matinée.

Somewhere around 6.25 . . . Sean comes in, looking wired. He doesn't drink but I found myself looking at his can of orange juice wondering about the effect of carbonated water. For some reason he was on the attack. 'Would it hurt you to show some fucking charm?' I was stunned, asked him not to speak to me like that, he nearly stormed out. I said just give me the notes, this is the first time you've mentioned this, I'm piecing the part together etc., etc. The evening show was a step forward but as I write this I'm still bewildered. Had people been nagging him? What? Ian McK. & Charlotte Cornwell came round having loved it. Were they sent too?

18 OCTOBER

A day of relative stillness. Sleep. Newspapers. Planet Organic. Cappuccino. Ironing the odd shirt. Answering mail. Cooking supper. Thinking. Thinking. Rima, blessedly and unsentimentally, with me.

20 OCTOBER

7pm Press night.

As per usual everything heightened. Therefore—high energy, high focus, not as free as it should be.

Later to Soho House.

21 OCTOBER

And then the morning quietness which means the press is not good. Eventually I hear the tentative messages and get the picture.

7pm Second performance. Not easy. Nothing discussed. Is this a good idea? I don't think so. Major cut inflicted during the show so I pour blood until plasters are slapped on.

22 OCTOBER

Here we are again. Major avoidance. Major silence. Appalling how Good/Bad determines everyone's response—like it's some club to which you have admittance, or not.

7pm Actually, a show full of good things. And lessons. Don't push so hard throughout. Find things. Let go. Led by Helen—the freest soul.

23 OCTOBER

7pm The other side of the coin. Young actors playing their own isolated ideas—no sense of status (of character). In the Thidias Scene I hit Ed[1] twice. Wrong, wrong. But when Antony is in that kind of rage and is faced by such insolence it is almost unavoidable.

25 OCTOBER

Another heavy silence hangs over the grey, grey day . . . By now this means only more bad press . . . OK—on through the next 6 weeks.

26 OCTOBER

7pm These are the tough shows. Everyone knows what has been said. No one refers to it. Except at the interval (after a shaky first half) there's a very touching, anonymous note from the company sending love and loyalty.

At the end of the show, Sean knocks. Unaware of what it might have been like for an actor tonight when it is pointed out he says 'What about me?' Oh Sean . . .

29 OCTOBER

2.45 Company call.

Sean tells us how important a time this is for *him*.

30 OCTOBER

Maybe it's time to try and let go. Antony would. Stop holding on to the problem.

---

[1] Edward Laurie, playing Thidias

4 NOVEMBER

This just feels impossible. But somehow it happens. Belinda & Hugh are there and full of disbelief of the reviews.

Working through a dizzying band of tiredness. Some things released, some trapped. A swift cab home—some simmering anger from a phone call to Paola Dionisotti (not her fault—just articulating friends' lack of faith—YET AGAIN).

6 NOVEMBER

This one was tough. An incipient cold/flu/thing threatens. Worse—bone crushing tiredness and an awareness that there is a price to pay for a night out.

10.45 With a bit more nerve I should have gone to Langan's Brasserie . . . with Patrick Proctor & friend. He *loved* it. Bless him.

10 NOVEMBER

Mistaken purchase of *Time Out* . . . forgetting inevitable discovery of theatre review. How trashed can you be?

13 NOVEMBER

7 . . . Ed punches me, so I kick him, he kicks me again, I kick him again . . . Drama centre . . .

14 NOVEMBER

6am What is this destructive force within my body that makes me wake at 5.30 knowing that I have two shows today? Malevolent and unfair.

1.30 and 7pm with a 2 hour break. Dizziness, yawning and eventually at around 9.30ish a sudden burst of energy. From where? Finbar thinks I put him down with 'Thou art a soldier only . . .' These sensitive souls around whom Helen and I are like bookends.

18 NOVEMBER

Helen says she's nervous. I worry that she's starting to shout her way through it.

19 NOVEMBER

A blessed 1½ hours' sleep, somewhere between 9 & 10.30.

Tonight remarkable for the woman with flash camera—3 shots in the first ½ hour.

→ Back to the world of 'well done' from Danny, Leila, Emily, Tom. But not Arlene who clearly thinks she's seen something else . . . Bless her . . .

20 NOVEMBER

Long phone call from Ian McKellen. Gee-ing up, reminding, empowering, focusing. He's currently rehearsing *Present Laughter* 'without a director'.

21 NOVEMBER

Spent some time flipping back through the pages of this extraordinary year. Some 27 plane rides . . . *The Winter Guest*, Japan, Spain, South Africa, *Dogma*, Pittsburgh, *Antony & Cleopatra* . . .

The odd moment of peace in Tuscany. Like living in a watershed. Or so, I am sure, it will prove.

1.30 The long slog begins . . . The matinée has a freewheeling thing that feels good. After, Vivien H.[1] brings round some professor of drama in Hawaii who says I have some 'moments' that 'show potential'.

26 NOVEMBER

A real need to sleep as long as possible.

7 The show is all fits and starts, pluses and minuses.

11.30 To Sheekey's. Richard Wilson and Anna Massey. A depressingly chill air over their response especially after last night. How volatile an inexpertly directed show is, how much it depends on the spit sharp energies of its actors. Still I attempt to articulate the positive, how negative has this experience been?

28 NOVEMBER

. . . a happy audience. More and more people saying 'What were they talking about?'

1 DECEMBER

1.30 The curse of the matinée. From which it is hard to recover.

7 This is an endurance test. One scene at a time, conserve energy where you can.

3 DECEMBER

And the last performance. Just to help it along—a barracker is in the audience apparently shouting 'Rubbish!' at one point and then 'Quiet, ladies' as Helen & I are kissing. Removed at the interval.

---

[1] Scottish actor Vivien Heilbron (1944–)

4 DECEMBER

Bed at 7am.

Woke at 12.

To the theatre to clear out the dressing room. Turns out to be a 2 hour job.

7 DECEMBER

First night home just making supper, watching TV. Helen is right—I miss Antony. Or the idea of him. The reality is just too tough. But moments recur. And the defensiveness mounts.

10 DECEMBER

Talk to Helen. News comes of *Sunday Telegraph* hate piece. Fax sent to Dominic Lawson [editor].

11 DECEMBER

Morning dealing with ICM, Keith Shilling [lawyer specialising in privacy law], National, Thelma re *Telegraph* and now *Daily Mail* pieces. Total lies. Invention. Malice.

13 DECEMBER

3pm To Richard & Ruthie Rogers'[1] for their 25th wedding anniversary.

18 DECEMBER

Conor McDermottroe comes by. We wander to David Wainwright—Ruby had said of her gift (metal-framed mirror) 'take it back to DW if you don't like it'. DW says, 'We haven't stocked this for 6 months.' The penny drops. I think this mirror used to hang over her kitchen fireplace.

20 DECEMBER

7.30 To Lindsay & Hilton.

A real sense of who came to see A&C and who didn't. Curious how these things matter.

22 DECEMBER

4[am] pick-up for Heathrow.

6.20 Flight to Cape Town.

Impossible to sleep.

Watched *The Mask of Zorro* with swords & masks but Ms Zeta-Jones jumps off the screen.

---

[1] British architect Richard Rogers (1933–2021) and his wife, British chef and restaurateur Ruth Rogers (1949–)

23 DECEMBER

8.15am or so arrive Cape Town.

Taxi to the house.

Lovely house, splash pool out front—hammock looking straight at Table Mountain; inside every room full of wonderful witty ceramics—Marmite pot full of walking sticks, huge balsamic vinegar bottle etc., etc. I immediately collide with coffee table and start breaking things. What is it with me?

1999

11 JANUARY

6.30 Miranda Richardson picks me up—off to Camberwell Art Gallery for the Julian Schnabel show. He's there, and a charmer. The room is packed with young people in black—nobody looking at the paintings, which are huge and looking at us actually.

8.45 To Pharmacy for a drink.

9.15 The evening has terminal cool. At the Campden Hill Square house there are Schnabels, a Bacon, a Warhol, some Basquiats. Terry Gilliam arrives with Johnny Depp. As we leave the party, Depp is in close conversation with Kate Moss who has suddenly materialised. I feel like I'm walking around in a magazine.

15 MARCH

12.05 → Flight to Los Angeles.

Galaxy Quest.

16 MARCH

9am pick-up. Plaster cast to be made of my head. As usual the experts are charming self-effacing people utterly confident of their craft. This is the second time I have had my head encased in plaster or goo (*Rasputin* was the first). It is a very disconcerting experience. You have to talk yourself out of panic or fainting. Can't see, hear, speak or move. The stuff (same as dentists use) is cold, then warm as it sets—temperature and consistency gradually changing as your world closes in.

19 MARCH

8 onwards (we arrived 9.15) Ed Limato's[1] party. Absolute 24 carat Hollywood. Faye Dunaway, Warren Beatty, Jack Nicholson, Madonna, Emily Wat-

---

[1] Talent agent

son, Holly H., Catherine Z.-J., Michael Douglas, Nicolas Cage, Minnie D., Rupert E., Carrie F. etc., etc.

21 MARCH

4pm → Dan and Barbara's [old friends] for Oscars 99 TV Fest. Apart from its sheer length this was suffused with an air of something manipulated, cynical and insincere. Knowing too much about G.P.[1] doesn't help. Memories of *Out of Sight*, *Dancing at Lughnasa* etc., etc. abound. Real acting rather than the demonstrated neon-lit stuff that gets awards. Often.

24 MARCH

6.15 pick-up for the 7.55 flight to New York. 3 minutes down the road I remember my shirts and jackets are still in the closet at the 4 Seasons.

25 MARCH

6.30 First night—*Closer*. This is the difference between here and London. Outside the theatre there are cameras, TV & flashbulbs. Inside Judi Dench sitting in front of me—elsewhere, Harrison Ford, Uma Thurman, Ethan Hawke, Kate Moss etc., etc. The production still doesn't fly—Patrick won't let it. Natasha and Rupert Everett very good. Anna Friel amazingly first time on stage. Ciarán [Hinds] yelling a bit. Natasha doing the star bit way too much with dressing room lists and celeb table at the party. Went to Café Loup with several of the above. Kate M. very sweet and vulnerable—a victim of the crap which Natasha craves. Depressing.

29 MARCH

3pm Mike Nichols' to talk about *Betrayal/The Real Thing*. Lindsay still not getting any keener, but thankfully she's as articulate as ever about it. A reading is arranged for Wednesday.

31 MARCH

Talking to Bob this morning I discover that the *Betrayal/Real Thing* double bill is intended for off Broadway. I still have a hankering for *Private Lives* on Broadway.

Gramercy Park Theatre for reading of *The Real Thing*. I enjoyed letting rip on this part and the play has subtle painful threads running through it. I should have done it in 1984. Now? Lindsay not keen. Mike N. *very* keen.

---

[1] Gwyneth Paltrow, winner of Best Actress in a Leading Role for *Shakespeare in Love*

1 APRIL

6.15 pick-up for 8am flight to LAX.

4ish Rima arrives from London. We struggle together with the mechanics of the house—esp the insane TV system.

3 APRIL

Waiting for the pool man, the satellite TV man and Lauren the cleaner to make their separate arrivals so as they could sort out my life. Also drive to Sunset Plaza Drive to see possible rental. V. clean, new-pin, soulless.

26 APRIL

Galaxy Quest.

5.45 pick-up and the Dining Room scene.

This is tough stuff—not made simpler if no one drives the car, be it director or leading actor. Also having to deal with a bowl full of leeches and centipedes who, unsurprisingly, do not wish to remain in their watery abode and proceed to wreck the scene by crawling up, out and all over the place.

6 MAY

3.15 pick-up → Burbank Airport for 4.45 flight to Grand Junction, Utah, and drive to Green River. The town is one big truck stop. Dozens of motels, places to buy steak, frankfurters, ice cream, watch satellite sports in bars.

8 MAY

Working in Goblin Valley.

This amazing place. Wind and seas have eroded the valley into something akin to the Chinese soldiers' tombs, only here it's those mushroom/goblin/penis shapes that create a dizzying maze all over the valley—especially as it looks more film-set planet than real planet. But 'exposed' hardly describes it. Wind and sun rule.

9 MAY

5–7 Rehearse at the Comfort Inn. Actually 'rehearse' is so far from the right word. Cue monologue might be better.

10 MAY

6am pick-up for a day in the wind, the dust and the red dirt. And the other side of the coin. At the end of the day Sam [Rockwell] says 'Sorry.' I say 'For what?' 'I just don't want you to think American actors are wankers.' Which, of course, I don't. But Tim [Allen] has this perverse need to needle, antagonise, provoke, demoralise—he just thinks he's being funny (maybe)—which just slows everything down and leads to zero concentration. I feel like a reactionary.

The wind & dust & sun make me feel like an invalid with a red face.

11 MAY

This was one of those utterly glorious Mother Nature days—blue skies, mountains and NO wind. The landscape looks like a cut out.

But still—Tim takes every opportunity to belittle. Finally, there is so much chatter and noise that I can't hear 'action' and step away. 'Oh, Alan has a little problem.' 'I don't have *any* problem.' 'Oohh.'

And doubtless, a seed has been sown.

13 MAY

9ish To Sigourney's room for fried chicken with Tony [Shalhoub] & Mark [Johnson, producer]. Some 'political' chat which makes Mark look nervous. (He already looked nervous since Sigourney's room is a palace in Green River terms.)

14 MAY

pm 'I thought that was great' (Dean).[1] 'Well, fabulous concentration' (Me). Which were brave words but had an amazing immediate effect. Oh, this complex chemistry. Young actors looking for moments, close ups, Tim by turns pugilist and wild animal.

17 MAY

9 Tamarisk w. Dean, Jerzy[2] & looking at storyboard. Dean is easy going in capital letters—whatever his inner terror, horror, whatever, his demeanor is that of a slow cowboy song. As I listen to them all talk I can't feel the weight or energy of a decision. But something progresses apparently. Maybe this film is becoming itself without us noticing.

18 MAY

Grand Junction for the flight to Salt Lake City and then Los Angeles. Said au revoir to Tim before leaving—touching that he says he'll miss us. 'I've grown attached'—there has been a sea change recently in noticing the spaces that each of us needs and should allow each other. Genuinely I was able to say

---

[1] Dean Parisot, director
[2] Jerzy Zieliński, cinematographer

that I knew how he felt. In a week we have, I think, a really healthy respect for each other which was frighteningly absent at first.

23 MAY
The long trek home.[1] 10.30 and into the cars to Nice airport, London airport and then Virgin to LAX.

24 MAY
In the morning Sigourney is amazed by my with-it-ness. As am I . . . But it's a little like madness when you mess around with sleep and travel zones—at least for ½ the day I can put one word after the other. Later on, my legs start to leave my torso.

26 MAY
The Rock Monster Speech, which whenever I let it float through my mind, or worse, tongue, seems laboured and deeply unfunny. Something, however, stops me from forcing it and lo and behold by adhering even more strictly to the written text it seems to work. Seems to . . .

28 MAY
Hallelujah. A day off. A day free of chicken head. A day of chicken head to be free of me.

4 JUNE
Hawaiian Day on the set. And Tim has to motor a scene which is the heart of the movie. And he does it beautifully.

6 JUNE
Tony Awards. There was a messiness about it all—the patronising air towards Arthur Miller, names being fudged, the sense of give it to the American choice if possible.

8 JUNE
Another day in the corridors of the space ship.

9 JUNE
8pm Dinner with Mel Smith. Jet lag or illegal substances? Hard to tell, but v. good to see him and fall instantly into the shorthand of an old friendship.

---

[1] From Cannes

10 JUNE

8.30 pick-up.

Longish wait in the trailer. Which I like—plenty of channel-hopping and jigsaw-finishing.

11 JUNE

8am pick-up.

Oh boy. Writing this at 1.10am. We finished at midnight after flying by the seat of various pants day. Beginning in my trailer with Dean & Tim. Almost a waste of time as Tim spins off into a rant and eventually is clawed back. I know now that he won't be landed without a fight. Huge budget. Impatient producers. Actors & directors fashioning a script at the last minute. Then the day was like a 12 hour scrum ending with Sigourney's transparent manoeuvrings to get in the shot or create her own shot or whatever. It's so transparent she might as well announce it over the Tannoy.

14 JUNE

7pm *Buena Vista Social Club*. What a joyous film. Total collaboration. Brilliant musicians in their 70s, 80s & 90s are rediscovered by Ry Cooder and Wim Wenders records it. Heart-stopping music. Heart-stopping people.

8 JULY

Heigh ho. Still it's the kick, bollock and scramble school of writing. Wind up outside the sound stage with Dean & Sigourney stitching a scene together. In comes Tim and it's like a nailbomb has arrived. When the initial dust settles we then pull it all back together again. Until Sigourney walks into a steel pole and, touchingly, becomes a 12-year-old.

20 SEPTEMBER

8ish Dinner w. Ian McK., Edna O'B., Suzanne Bertish, Neil Tennant, Martin Sherman,[1] Penny Wilton.[2] A gentle, homely evening. Ian cooked and gave away books, mementoes as he packs for a year in New Zealand, and the house waits to be ripped apart.

30 NOVEMBER

7.30 *Mamma Mia*.

This was good fun, but could easily be sensational. Some real choreographing (rather than the dated TV variety show spins and finger snapping) would help.

---

[1] American dramatist (1938–)

[2] Penelope Wilton, English actor (1946–)

The Ivy—Lindsay awaits. Heroically. Since she's working tomorrow. I'm a bit concerned about her—she looks preoccupied, dispirited underneath her perennially brave & beautiful exterior.

4 DECEMBER

I have spent the last few mornings snatching moments to read David Hare's *Acting Up*. He says he has decided not to edit with hindsight, but I wonder if he knows just how transparent it is? More self-involved than any actor I have ever met, but then I suppose if I kept a diary about my decision to write a play maybe the parallels would get closer. He describes me as the V. S. Naipaul of acting—hardly able to do it at all. That, of course, is not unconnected with the decision not to do *The Judas Kiss*.[1] He forgets that I would have done it if he had written a First Act. It remains, however, a huge ambition to work with him. His cool candour is a breeze.

5 DECEMBER

9am → to Heathrow and 10.55 → New York.

7 DECEMBER

Waiting at the elevator with friends—none other than Sarah, Duchess of York, who looks at me and yells 'Eric!' as in Idle . . . Must call him.

10 DECEMBER

8.30pm Lupa—170 Thompson Street. Excellent food, good wine and company. Nick Hytner arrived later but I was in my 'escorting Edna O'B. role' so left a little earlier than I should have. She complained in the taxi that Nick had no curiosity about any other human being, that a smugness had settled over him. But then, that's an epidemic.

17 DECEMBER

Los Angeles.

8pm Little Door—Marcia, Tim, Dan O'Connor & Barbara, Maggie & Scott & Dexter Fletcher. Seamus McG[arvey] and Stephen Frears (who at the end of the meal says, predictably, 'Do you need any money for the bill? No—you're in a hit film, aren't you?') . . . The general assumption that I will pay the bill is beginning to pall a little, however.

---

[1] Play by David Hare about Oscar Wilde—not to be confused with the film *Judas Kiss* that A.R. appeared in in 1998

18 DECEMBER

9–6 PRESS DAY.

Unremittingly tough. Although the journalists are very generous of spirit. They all seem to love the film.[1] Hang on to that thought. Sometimes one is articulate, ten minutes later blathering.

19 DECEMBER

2pm Screening. Terrible sound for some reason makes the comedy harder to land. The audience goes wild at the end but they were never quite together. Not helped by the crass editing, of course. I notice *more* cuts this time.

7pm Dinner w. Sigourney, Dean & Jed [Rees]. Stories of great notices are not helping lift my leaden heart. Here we go. AGAIN. This is so boring. Let it go. Move on. Don't angst over what you can't change. Too many films have the same battles. At its heart *GQ* has an innocence they could never understand.

20 DECEMBER

8am → LAX.

10am → NY AA [American Airlines].

There is the gradual realisation of having been shafted. Again. Almost all of my (Alexander's) moments in the driving seat have been removed to effectively give Tim a clear road. It's not *just* about length. Or 'rocket-ship rides'.

26 DECEMBER

New York.

4ish Ang Lee arrives with Haan and Mason, his sons, later joined by Jane, his wife. Ang maintains his legendary (to me) reputation for elbow-off-the-table plain speaking (you look good—better than you did on *S&S*) but all in all it's another lovely day, with the Long Island Sound and its spreading sunset to cast a beautiful glow.

28 DECEMBER

9.10 → London . . . We're not properly tired so fiddle about with opening mail etc. until about 2am.

---

[1] *Galaxy Quest*

31 DECEMBER

4am awake . . . Thinking . . . is that even the word for this activity? Into my mind (or what passes for it) comes a quote from Mandela: 'Harder than changing the world is changing yourself.'

8 Ian McKellen's party.

Friends and strangers.

David Foxxe, Armistead Maupin, Dena Hammerstein,[1] Martin Sherman. The house beautifully lit and decorated—wonderful food and wines. The last gathering before the builders and decorators move in. As midnight approaches, coats are gathered and we all clamber on to the roof . . .

---

[1] British actor, writer and producer (1940–)

2000

1 JANUARY

We watched 2000 arrive with the river spread out below us, a piper played on a balcony nearby and fireworks dolphined above the skyline from Tower Bridge, Greenwich and Docklands.

6.30am Home . . . Clearly something stilled any violence in the streets, everywhere there was celebration and thoughtfulness. A reflection which slid on into today. All day. So that we didn't want to *do* anything.

Bumped into P. Mandelson & Reinaldo [his partner] in Westbourne Grove. He was eating a choc-ice and trying to rent a video. *Tea with Mussolini.*

Quiet supper at home. Although with hindsight another party would have been a good idea . . .

2 JANUARY

Later am . . . Jet lag, of course, but also brain scramblings. Of late, this diary has become not so much a trial but almost an avoidance and at best a record. If there is a resolution knocking around just now it's not about the diary as such (although it would doubtless be affected) but to stretch the boundaries of all relationships, try not to leave so much unsaid, put it in a note *WHEN I THINK IT*—maybe as Ian McK. says succumb to the laptop and thereby the email. Braver, less enigma, let it all just HAPPEN. Be more known. Cut away the negatives. Say what you mean. Be clear & decisive.

2pm Harriet W. (CBE . . . !) & Peter [Blythe].[1] Some lamb casserole & Christmas pudding, a lot of wine and dates. Many reminders of old friends,

---

[1] English actor (1934–2004)

simple pleasures, and Mandela's creased but curious & playful face bookends it all (BBC TV).

6 JANUARY

8.15am Julie-Kate Olivier[1] picks me up → the Globe via Helen M.'s house. Poor Helen. Two shows yesterday and we're ringing the bell at 8.45. '5 minutes' says the voice on the intercom . . .

6pm Emma, Greg and Gaia Romilly Wise (aged 1 month). Ms Wise is a beautiful child and a comedian to boot. And boy does she live in a lovely, comfortable home.

8 JANUARY

More or less all day in the Harrods Sale buying late Christmas gifts. Sometimes easy, sometimes headbangingly difficult—not least when clutching six carrier bags, losing one of them, going to lost property, back on to the floor trying to check sizes one-handed when the size is completely obliterated by a price ticket.

10 River Cafe for supper, or so we thought, at 10.15 with Miranda and David Young [playwright]. They eventually arrived at 11 (disastrous) with Simon McBurney (happily). We ordered for them earlier in some uncertainty and when the bill came Miranda was in the loo and David was saying thank you before I had even found my credit card. For once, I was a bit pissed off at paying the bill. It seemed close to very bad manners . . .

11 JANUARY

6pm A phone call from Jacky Cukier[2] asking me to come to Paris. I suggest Jan. 21st.

13 JANUARY

To Wandsworth Bridge Road and the lighting shop. Boy, is this a backward area in GB. Try to find a decent lamp . . .

7.30 NT. Fiona [Shaw]'s production of *Widowers' Houses*. Cottesloe. The play is pretty unspeakable but Fifi has given it the full Dostoevsky/Meyerhold/Moscow Arts production. And good for her. This is made for 14–18-year-olds and will of course enrage the traditionalists. Indeed there was some reported spluttering at the end. Margaret Drabble there with Michael Holroyd and was kind and positive about *A&C*. 'It reminded me very much of someone I knew . . .'

---

[1] English actor (1966–)

[2] French director and screenwriter

18 JANUARY

Slept. Woke. Read. Until 4am. Simon [Callow]'s book *Love Is Where It Falls* is breathtakingly honest. Takes all sorts of chances. His recall is staggering—I can't remember what I was doing yesterday. But then Peggy Ramsay[1] is such a spiritual guide. She talks of not trivialising one's life—too many people, restaurants, and of the Krishnamurti-inspired notion of solitude. So that the mind can wander . . .

19 JANUARY

Word has reached me that Jane Lapotaire[2] has had a stroke. This eventually is corrected and as Rima suspected from the collapse/intensive care information, the truth is an aneurysm. Messages are sent, and a call to her agent—she cannot have flowers, does not really want it widely known.

23 JANUARY

1.48 Eurostar to Paris. Taxi to Hotel Raphael.

24 JANUARY

1.15 To Ron & Karen Bowen's [old friends]. Chose a painting. Reminding myself of the Robert Graves poem about 'Vases, words and stillness'. Then to a fantastic Tavola Calda for lunch and on to the Beaubourg and an exhibition devoted to time. Hard to forget the backwards-playing film of cow → steak etc.

7 To Isabelle H. & Roni Ch. for a drink and to meet Angelo, their 2-year-old, for the first time.

25 JANUARY

10.00 Taxi to Paris Nord. 10.15 Coffee with Isabelle D[uBar].

11.43 Eurostar to London. It's a pleasantly disorienting experience, this. Lunch, a newspaper, a script and you're back in London as if you'd been to Leeds. Odd for an islander. We spend all our lives on boats & planes in order to escape. Now there's this little miracle.

29 JANUARY

To John Lewis and the purchase of the BLENDER . . .

8.30 Hampstead. *My Best Friend*, Tamsin Oglesby's play. Deeply unsatisfying production of Tamsin's clearly good play. No changes of gear, little of its comedy, pushing for melodrama throughout . . . Tamsin obviously unhappy about *this* production, but planning another . . .

---

[1] Australian-born British theatrical agent (1908–1991)
[2] English actor (1944–)

9 FEBRUARY

Filing system on the stairs finally claimed its first victim. Me, a tray with plates, bottle and glass (all empty . . .) headlong, or rather footlong, down the stairs. And later a nagging pain to the right ankle.

11 FEBRUARY

11.53 WATERLOO → PARIS → 26 Rue Guynemer—Annette & Saul Zaentz's apartment in St Germain.

16 FEBRUARY

Reading the Oscar nominations. Once again, nothing makes much sense— sixth or otherwise. *The Green Mile* is an *awfully* long film. But it is clear in my mind that however difficult the subject matter the voters need space to cheer and get on with their lives at the end of any movie.

1.30 → Carpeaux exhibition in the Luxembourg Palace Museum.

Walking around and caught in the most all-embracing storm—thunder, hail, snow and eventually, blue skies and sunshine.

2.30 A croque monsieur at the local café.

7.30 Car arrives to pick us up → Ron + Karen and → to Champs Elysées for *Ripley* premiere. This is not a *Green Mile* type movie. This one picks you up and tosses you around from start to finish. Lack of Oscar nominations (or is it my imagination?) means a quiet house and Ant and Matt & the rest seem subdued.

11.30 Dinner at Fouquet's on the Champs Elysées. The food, apparently, was good. The ambience very red plush. Somewhere in here is an agreement that a play will change your life in a way that film never can.

17 FEBRUARY

1.30 [Le] Bristol—lunch with Anthony M., Matt Damon, Carolyn, Max, Gabriel,[1] Saul Zaentz.

Later—a whistle-stop tour of Malvolio with Max for his NYT audition, & shopping with Carolyn.

7.20 *American Beauty*. Ron was right—the endings are all too neatly contrived so that we can leave disturbed but at peace with ourselves—hence the multiple Oscar nominations. All the same—hats off to Sam Mendes. It is full of good stuff.

---

[1] Lebanese-French composer Gabriel Yared (1949–). He was nominated for an Academy Award for *The Talented Mr Ripley*.

23 FEBRUARY

11 Car to Gare du Nord and the 12.19 train to Waterloo.

7.30 *Dublin Carol*—Royal Court. The theatre is stunning. A perfect balance of preservation, restoration and re-invention. It makes one hungry to perform there again. The bar under Sloane Square is a triumph and would be made perfect by the until-now denied access to Sloane Square. It will happen. The play is difficult to hear because Brian [Cox] insists on shouting words for no apparent reason (unless it's the feud he's conducting with Trevor Nunn which he tells us about afterwards).

25 FEBRUARY

7.45 Dinner with Anna M[assey] & Uri [Andres] plus David Hare & Nicole Farhi. Reminded again of how fond I am of Anna & Uri. She for her impeccable manners salted with the fruitiest swear words. And Uri is an inspiration and a lesson. Courteous, kind, vulnerable with eyes that crinkle with concentration, sympathy, total involvement when someone else engages his attention. He's *curious*.

27 FEBRUARY

4.45 Tea with Emma, Greg & Phyllida (briefly) to deliver the dress bought for Gaia in Paris. Gaia already has the most glorious personality—funny, quirky, quixotic creature. Talk of a Tuscan adventure . . .

Home for the last half hour of *Prince of Thieves* which is on BBC1 tonight. *Soo* many waters under so many bridges . . .

6 MARCH

9am pick-up for 10.50 flight → COPENHAGEN.

From around 2pm–7pm working in the downtown studios on *Help! I'm a Fish*.[1]

8pm Dinner in the ex-monastery. Great environment. Awful food.

7 MARCH

am (early) to 11. Thinking, reading, brooding. And eventually leaning towards 'No' on *Final Curtain*.[2] The idea, the personnel are fine. Scene by scene needs more work. Will they get this? Doubtful.

pm → Elsinore.[3] The courtyard all that was open at 3.15 but all rather special, really, in the wind, rain and absence of tourists.

---

[1] Animated movie in which A.R. voiced a character called Joe
[2] Released in 2002, directed by Patrick Harkins and starring Peter O'Toole
[3] The setting for *Hamlet*

8 MARCH

11.15 Pauline Dowd. Harley Street. More antibiotics, more cream. I cannot escape the feeling that it's all more to do with giving things up, not sticking things on . . .

10 MARCH

To Brightwell.[1] The bathroom approaches its debut, its unveiling, its renaissance. After lunch a trip to Do It All to find floor tiles, fire extinguishers, smoke alarms.

12 MARCH

12 To the cemetery w. David & Chris. Where have all the potential flowers gone? (Has someone nicked the bulbs?)

14 MARCH

9.15 Pick-up to Blue Studios, Old Compton Street, to start recording Discovery Channel's Patagonia Eco-Challenge.

17 MARCH

6.30 John Wark down from Scotland for his second RADA audition. As Sharman said, 'a real actor'. And it's true. I don't feel the same nervousness as with Christian & Arlene. John knows where he's going.

19 MARCH

[Re *Galaxy Quest*]

12 Pick-up for drive to Heathrow and 2.15 flight to Hamburg.

Arrive at Vier Jahreszeiten—4 Seasons—a beautiful suite with a terrace looking at the lake and rust/orange roses in two big vases. And some Veuve Clicquot. Like living in an occasional cartoon.

20 MARCH

9.45am Makeup and 10am start of interviews. Generally the questions are much brighter than expected. A relief—it's less tiring when the answers *are* spontaneous rather than *appear* to be. Lunch in the Hotel Grill and hello again to Sigourney. A message on the machine at home from John Wark. He has got in to RADA. So that's 3 of them [from *The Winter Guest*] in the business now . . .

---

[1] Brightwell-cum-Sotwell, a village in Oxfordshire. A.R. and Rima bought a house there for Rima's sister, Francesca.

Later to the Reeperbahn and the Dollhouse. All rather tasteful and innocent. A hand delicately placed over the crotch as the G-string slides down. Incredibly efficient take-overs by dancers, clever lighting, good bodies, middle-class audience.

21 MARCH

10am start. And through to about 1.15pm.

Lunch in the excellent Thai (sort of) restaurant in the hotel . . .

2.50 Back to the grind. And when it's over the familiar sensations. The constant attempt to avoid bullshit, not to be irritated by the labelling, say what you believe etc., etc. always leaves me whacked and empty. Quite close to humiliated. And as I do it I always forget the pay-off.

4.45 pick-up to Hamburg Airport and the 6.10(ish) flight to London. Lufthansa . . . Later, at home, reading an old journal. Stuff from 20 years ago. Scary. And also looking at excerpts from Sylvia Plath's journal. My old one is very pre-movies. Pre-interviews and pre-those more recent books. Much more naked. I can only hope that when I look again at the '90s volumes that I can remember the coded details and the sharp thoughts hidden between the safer lines.

24 MARCH

Dinner at the Bear. A long time since I've seen deep-fried Brie or mushroom stroganoff. Almost expected to hear Steeleye Span on the intercom.

28 MARCH

Lunch w. Karen Moline[1] at Dakota. She seems angrier at life this time. And, as ever, hopelessly indiscreet. God forbid I ever give her information I don't want passed on . . .

8pm Royal Albert Hall for Sting concert. Nitin Sawhney first. Or Knitting Sorbet as the guy at Door 9 calls him. In all seriousness. Suzanne B. and I go to Box 25 which Trudie has filled with food and drink. Perfect hostess as ever. The concert (both halves) is really wonderful. Very moving, really, to hear the sheer number of anthems that Sting has written over the years. And still awake to the innovations of Nitin S.

29 MARCH

8pm Dinner w. Suzanne, Nicky & Edna O'B. Edna the phenomenon . . . Story after story. 'If Pat Magee[2] were here now—he's dead—if he were here

---

[1] American writer and journalist
[2] Irish actor Patrick Magee (1922–1982)

now . . .'; 'May I ask a trivial little question about Juliet & Fiona . . . ?' But a lovely evening. Which I look forward to reproducing *in the country* . . .

30 MARCH

To RADA to see the new building . . . I can't quite shake off the feeling that too much has been smashed into too little space, but at the moment it's all grey cement and no light so it's unfair to speculate. In an ideal world and an ideal building the rehearsal rooms would be bigger with higher ceilings, the Vanbrugh stage would be deeper etc., etc.

1 APRIL

11am To the Millennium Wheel. For a second time. This could become a habit. I can imagine solo trips before long.

5 APRIL

11.45 Dr Pauline Dowd. Mainly memorable this time for finding a horoscope to purloin from the waiting room. It even mentions clutter-clearing, which has been the word du jour for a week now. (Karen Kingston's brilliant book[1] finally finished last night.)

Almeida—*Celebration/The Room* [plays by Harold Pinter]. V. enjoyable evening in all senses. First the pleasure of seeing Lindsay, Susi,[2] Andy [de la Tour] and Danny Dyer on stage together and all very funny, esp. in *Celebration*, and Lindsay *does* pull off *The Room* in spite of her worries. Harold and Antonia[3] are also in—he had thought we were a bit quiet. It's hard to guffaw if you worry that the author won't approve. Still thinking about the plays and about how deep they actually bite, but talking afterwards in good old Casale Franco when Andy & Susi tell of Harold only directing the actor who is speaking . . . Only underlines my belief that writers should not direct their own work in the theatre.

11 APRIL

7 Anna M. & Uri A., Eve Black & David Samuel for drinks before dinner at Assaggi. This is something to do more of. Put together a group of people who *really* have something to talk about and basically listen and enjoy their mingling. David, the brain chemist, Uri the physicist, Eve the Arts Administrator–Marine Architect, Rima and Anna knowing something about all of it. I enjoyed the noise.

[1] *Clear Your Clutter with Feng Shui*
[2] Susan Wooldridge, British actor (1950–)
[3] British writer Antonia Fraser (1932–), wife of Harold Pinter

12 APRIL

→ LAKE COMO.

9.30 Car to Heathrow for flight to Milan, and on to Villa D'Este at Lake Como. Here for the BBDO Ad Agency get-together, bonding thing. Isaac Mizrahi[1] and Ismail Merchant have already spoken. Fairly terrified for a week now but having finally got the opening paragraph, spent the plane ride and then the early evening scribbling furiously and now have 17 pages.

5pm A drink in the bar with Ismail Merchant & Richard his assistant. It's always been a bit of a mystery why I've never worked with this (extremely amiable) man. Now we *all* think that.

Dinner in the Grill. Good food but on my top ten hate list would be over-attentive waiters—I like watching my wine glass get emptier. I am close to slapping the arm of the next waiter who refills my glass after every sip.

13 APRIL

To Regina Room to throw myself to the wolves. A speech I was concerned may only last 10 mins actually ran 45 mins. You can definitely feel the good bits and bad bits and with (now) hindsight the bits I'd rewrite. Doubt whether references to Thatcher went down well with an agency boss who was on Reagan's re-election team. Peter Souter—the UK boss—extremely impressive and says 'Don't suppose we'd get you to do something for us?' Hmmm . . .

21 APRIL

Clearing clutter . . .

Specifically a first go-round at *Winter Guest* papers. And you think—How did this ever happen? How did it start? Look at all the people who became part of it. And then it faded into the past.

6pm *Erin Brockovich* at Whiteley's.

Good for Soderbergh. A film that has gathered a huge audience and that involves from the first frames. Full of beautiful acting (Julia Roberts always underestimated anyway, but here she gets her chance to show how in-the-moment she is). Albert Finney and everyone—smaller parts brilliantly played—clearly happy working with such [a] meticulous, observant, subtle director. And it's about something.

---

[1] American fashion designer

7 MAY

Watching *Close My Eyes*[1] on Channel 4. Brings back all kinds of memories of that hot summer and a vow to lose a stone. At least. In spite of its list of implausibilities, the film still looks good and makes the current crop of Brit-flicks look ridiculous.

10 MAY

Miranda Richardson visited late lunchtime with the mad dog Liv. Who could hardly contain her excitement, and so didn't. 20 mins later the house and garden resembled a rugby pitch . . . Took an hour to find the door wedges . . .

3 To Jim Henson's for a face mask. Third time for this weird piece of sensory deprivation. And I feel the beginning of a sense of panicked responsibility to learn the lines in time.

7 *The Merchant of Venice*, NT. Henry Goodman on another planet (from most actors, but certainly from everyone else on stage tonight). Every line is a thought contained in a body which has a life. Every line is discovered. An acting lesson.

18 MAY

Breakfast at 106. Sara Sugarman[2] sitting there and a chat later. Her film [*Very Annie Mary*] opening in August—she's now thinking of moving to LA. And she's one of the few people who could take her own mix of ambition and anarchy and bend LA to *her* will.

22 MAY

10.10am Pick-up to Pinewood.

Play, Samuel Beckett, with Kristin Scott Thomas and Juliet Stevenson. Anthony Minghella directing us in our big pots.

24 MAY

6.10am pick-up.

On set at 8.30ish after longish makeup. All of us terrified. But because Anthony has a) done his homework, and b) is receptive to what is going on around him—it becomes properly organic and 'found'.

Home at around 7.45pm.

---

[1] 1991 film directed by Stephen Poliakoff in which A.R. starred alongside Clive Owen and Saskia Reeves
[2] Welsh actor (1962–)

25 MAY

6.15am pick-up.

Much less nervous-making. In 24 hours there's a real feeling of a team. Benoît,[1] the DP, grins, and the sound recordist says 'When I read this I didn't know what it was all about but now I think it's amazing.' Juliet is amazing. She's doing a play by night and still manages to be brilliantly ahead of the game in this. Hats off.

26 MAY

6.15[am] pick-up.

Finished around 8pm. This has been a very special time. Pushing the boundaries; testing resources against a great text; knowing that a secure friendship means a relaxed honesty; noticing how K.S.T.'s 'froideur' moves through insecurity to quiet confidence in the course of 3 days; Juliet's real strength.

2 JUNE

11am Lyric, Hammersmith, for run-through of Ruby's new show.

4 JUNE

12.13 Train back to London.[2]

4pm Run-through of Peace Garden concert at Royal Opera House. One of those extraordinary events. Trudie Styler gathers quite a clan around her. As I arrive, Madonna is on stage with an Egyptian band. Trudie trying to be organised but the time is disappearing fast. Vanessa [Redgrave], Alan Bates, Angharad Rees, Simon Callow, Lulu, Jimmy Nail, Bryan Adams, Miranda Richardson, dancers, singers, monks, Can Can dancers (Simon's favourite sight—the monks watching the Can Can). Somehow all these elements sort of gel and we started 45 mins late. But the evening (especially the second half, especially the singers & Vanessa) had some wonderful moments and the audience, thankfully, was alive and warm—not the dreaded mass humourless gathering of the Tory party.

Sights of T.S. [Trudie Styler] with her makeup & hair stylist, v. expensive dresses and the food & drink afterwards gave pause for a little thought . . .

---

[1] Benoît Delhomme, French cinematographer
[2] From Brightwell-cum-Sotwell

5 JUNE

11am To Emma & Greg's to find Catherine Olim & Phyllida & to go for a v. pleasant stroll around Hampstead and the Heath. A sandwich in a side street, a glance in an estate agent's window (or rather a pause while Emma actually goes in and gets details of a couple of properties—oh, you must come and live in Hampstead—and indeed, the leafiness and elegant mishmashery of it all is seductive . . .). Also a trip to the refurbished Everyman Cinema. Great people running it and superb circle seating. A Must Go.

12 JUNE

Stay-at-home night.

13 JUNE

5pm Lanesborough Hotel to meet Mike Binder [film director]. Mostly, I'm trying to figure out whether or not he dyes his hair. Somewhere in there I'm meeting a gentle, determined, honourable man.

18 JUNE

6pm Royal Court for run-through(ish) for—Aung San Suu Kyi benefit.

7.45 Show. Thanks to Philip Hedley's[1] brilliant sense of balance and organisation it was genuinely enjoyable. Mark Thomas (great), Richard W., David Hare, Glenda Jackson, Miriam K[arlin], Tim [West] & Prunella [Scales], Kate Williams,[2] Fascinating A.,[3] jiving Lindy Hoppers (Glenys & Neil K. jiving together at the beginning of the evening before Glenys' terrific speech). Amazing woman in support of amazing woman.

23 JUNE

10.30 Car to Wicklow and Annette Carducci's[4] set.

26 JUNE

9am Pick-up to Carlo Manzi [costume supplier] for second fitting.

27 JUNE

1pm Rehearse.

30 JUNE

9.45 Voiceover to Chechnya documentary. Andrei Babitsky. Reporter Extraordinary.

---

[1] British film director (1938–)
[2] British actor (1941–)
[3] Fascinating Aïda, British comedy singing group
[4] French film director (1942–)

2 JULY

7am Pick-up. Day One. *Gissing*.[1]

A house in South Street, Mayfair. Lunch in Berkeley Square. In and out of a front door with the Sultan of Brunei's cook slamming windows and yelling at having her Sunday disturbed. Probably can't blame her. But as Mike says, London is full of eccentrics. (Just you wait . . .) Sonya[2] gets it together remarkably for someone cast on Friday.

11 JULY

9am Pick-up. And a day of tap-dancing. Figuratively in the morning with Sonya's stripping scene.

Literally pm with the roomful of tap dancers and the rest of us crashing about in our suits, ties and cufflinks.

13 JULY

How did today turn into such a pain? How quickly I lose my equanimity. Concentration becomes silence and at the end of the evening I wind up standing in a corridor defending my 'perfectionism' to the beleaguered director.

26 JULY

7am pick-up.

Today was the day of Matthew [played by Mike Binder] & Gissing throwing each other around the office—but, no real rehearsal; crew watching; no stunt person—so, injured knee which I discover at home later when it just won't bend.

NB *Harry Potter* is offered . . .

6 AUGUST

7.45 pick-up for Scene 86. 5 page horror. Umpteen angles, same speech over and over. Not finished at 9pm. Back tomorrow. But in amongst the humidity and tiredness, some welcome laughter with Caroline [Holdaway], Juliet [Stevenson], Owen [Teale], Allan [Corduner].

8 AUGUST

1.30 Train to Stratford to see Mary McGowan and Sandra Voe in *Henry IV Part 2*.

4pm To Mary's house. She is furious at her sudden physical decline.

---

[1] *The Search for John Gissing*, directed by Mike Binder
[2] Sonya Walger, British-American actor (1974–)

Utterly reliant on the Zimmer frame but of course still the woman who says to a midnight drunk intruder ('I was in the kitchen, couldn't sleep, reading Seamus Heaney')—'Would you like a chocolate?!'

7.30 Swan Theatre. *Henry IV Part 2*. Desperately middle of the road production. High spots fudged → Hal's rejection of Falstaff is an anti-climax ... W. Houston[1] a charismatic young actor who could easily just tread the pernicious water of vanity.

10.43 Dinner at the Duck. A triumph of wheelchair manipulation and Mary was having dinner at a place she 'never thought I'd see again'.

11 AUGUST
12.30 Pick-up to N1 Dance Studios to learn dance for Sharleen's[2] video.

Wrap party for *Gissing*. Chinawhite's. These things *have* to be stage managed, otherwise people sit about moaning that it's no fun. Sadly, they have to be told how to *create* fun. Once they had been herded out of the one penny-pinching room we had been ascribed it all loosened up. But this film, although full of crazy invention that might just survive, was never a model of organisation ...

12 AUGUST
8am Rima off to Heathrow and Tuscany. What the fuck am I doing staying behind?

15 AUGUST
Talk to Paola a.m. and hear of Juliet's brother.[3] This is after Fidelis's[4] tale of a drug-crazed, blood-stained break-in.

1pm Nick Kent comes by and we have lunch at his local pub / restaurant / garden and then to his really beautiful flat. Not so much Kensal Rise as Provence via Jamaica. Then a phone call saying his godson has been arrested for snatching a bag ...

5.30 Pick-up to the car park near Southwark Bridge for the start of the Texas video. Drive-bys on the bridge before heading off down the motorway via 20 bikers and finally ending up in a dawn promenade walk in Brighton. Then to the ghastly Thistle Hotel from 8am.

P.S. Somewhere in here spoke to Judy Hoflund about *HP* and the usual negotiating shenanigans.

---

[1] English actor William Houston (1968–)
[2] Sharleen Spiteri (1967–), lead singer of Scottish band Texas
[3] Juliet Stevenson's brother Johnny had been killed in a car accident.
[4] English actor Fidelis Morgan (1962–)

16 AUGUST

Sharleen fuming about the hotel (condom on the carpet last night . . .). I point out that it will ready her for Poland on Friday. We take off for Beachy Head at sunset.

17 AUGUST

During the night, more motorway drives, eventually fetching up at the petrol station in Bordon (which I hadn't previously noticed). Called Claire and Amy [A.R.'s nieces] to say we were coming but not until at least midnight.

Actually 1.30am. The rest of Texas gathers. They are a really great bunch. Together for 14 years and still enjoying each other, supporting each other. Sharleen clearly a powerhouse but always checking for Johnny's[1] ironic, vulnerable eye.

We tango'd at 4.30–5.30am. Hard to connect brain and legs.

Back to London to put things in bags and generally get ready for the off to Heathrow.

10.50 → ROME → Corrado driving me to Argiano. Judy Daish solves the problem of getting him back by suggesting he drive her hire car back. Perfetto. Can't deal with Warner Bros shenanigans. *Plus* there's a Sesti extravaganza for Cosimo & Paloma[2]—fairy lights, dinner for 50, Tuscan choir, Keith sang, I spoke some Berowne[3] pushed by Sarah (the page flipped open almost at the speech . . .)—a gorgeous evening, generous souls singing to each other.

23 AUGUST

6.30 Pile into the car and drive to Siena to get to Il Campo before dark. To the Patio Bar where, around 8pm, I called LA and said OK to *HP*.

9ish Dinner at Le Logge.

Home at 3am.

24 AUGUST

Around the pool and feeling a bit nothing about *HP* which really disturbs me—or is it because I'm reading Martin Amis' *Experience* which charts A Life . . .

---

[1] Johnny McElhone (1963–), bass guitarist
[2] Cosimo Sesti and Paloma Barcella, architects who helped make livable the house A.R. and Rima bought in Campagnatico.
[3] From *Love's Labour's Lost*

28 AUGUST

12.30 Collect Conor from Buonconvento station.

Lunch in Montalcino. Drive to Montepulciano to find Ant M., Carolyn, Max plus Sydney Pollack & Bill Horberg [film producer].

5 SEPTEMBER

To local winemaker S. Palmucci. High above S. Antonio Abbey—the most spectacular position. (Nearly rivalled by the 5 star hotel currently being developed in a nearby 11th C. castle . . .) & the most spectacular wines—his instructions to pickers was an education in itself.

8pm Dinner in the house. Wonderful fresh gnocchi from yesterday in the bread shop.

6 SEPTEMBER

A day by the pool.

Talking to Judy—the bargaining goes on . . . (*HP*).

Lightning in the mountains.

10 SEPTEMBER

Perfect day. Still, sunny. To the pool. Finish *HP* 1, start 2. There's no denying . . .

11 SEPTEMBER

2pm Romano arrives and the goodbye is as swift and painless as I can make it. Which is not swift and painless enough. This *is* another way to live. And the Sestis know how to pull work and pleasure together in the most passionate, blazing, sharing way. Life is lived, worked and celebrated. And invented, daily. Guided by nature.

21 SEPTEMBER

HARRY P. TAKES OFF.

10.30 Car to MBA for costume fitting/discussion. Measurements from hell after a month in Italy. Waltz around each other—higher collar? Blue fabric? Thinner arms? And off to Leavesden Studios. Chris Columbus [director], David Heyman [producer], Makeup Dept. waiting. Wig? Nose? Discussion and a look at some of the sets and special effects.

3.05 Heathrow to LAX. Dinner at Lily's, Venice, & back to the Peninsula.

23 SEPTEMBER

Bruce Willis tribute, American Cinematheque. 12.45 Lunch at Beverly Hilton and rehearse entrances. Mad afternoon trying to find a pair of shoes.

6.30 pick-up to Beverly Hilton. Red carpet gauntlet and into Green Room. Bruce comes in to say hi. The show is fine and the audience laughs.

Drink at Peninsula w. Louise Krakower, Cate Blanchett, her hairdresser Manny. There is instant rapport with Miss B. What will the future bring?

27 SEPTEMBER

2.45 Arrive Heathrow.

6.30 Car → Belinda and on to Empire Leicester Square for premiere of *Billy Elliot*. This is what happens when the distributors and press get behind a film . . . Jamie Bell is quite wonderful—not a sentimental second in his performance. The film is Stephen Daldry at his most calculating → it is almost as if he has fed the requirements into a computer. The film could have been beautiful but its cynical use of the miners' strike added to a long list of untruths (the boy in the dress, the snowman, the brother's change of heart) make the newspaper headlines—'The Best British Film Ever'—an insult to Losey, Schlesinger, Anderson, Dean, Powell & Pressburger, Newell, Minghella, McKinnon and the rest.

6 OCTOBER

First conversation w. Joanne Rowling. Her sister answers—'She's not here— can I leave a message?' Cackling in the background . . . 'Sorry about that! . . .' 'There are things that only Snape & you know—I need to know . . .' 'You're right—call me tomorrow; no one else knows these things . . .'

7 OCTOBER

Talk to Joanne Rowling again and she nervously lets me in on a few glimpses of Snape's background. Talking to her is talking to someone who *lives* these stories, not invents them. She's a channel—bubbling over with 'Well, when he was young, you see, this that and the other happened'—never 'I wanted so & so . . .'

8 OCTOBER

2pm Ruby, Ed & kids → Harbour Club. One of Max's friends is an indication of what's to come. 'Are you Snape?'

10 OCTOBER

HARRY POTTER BEGINS.

8.30 Car to MBA for 9am fitting.

11am Kings X for train to Newcastle, and then car to Alnwick Castle and a (3 hour . . .) makeup for camera test. Criss-crossing of pluses and minuses—pale face = v. ageing; false nose-piece needs heavy makeup etc. General atmosphere is friendly and a mite chaotic.

7.45 To the tapas restaurant with Sean [Biggerstaff] and Robbie Coltrane for many plates of deep-fried indulgences before going back to the hotel for some red wine and a bag of chocolates from the mini-bar.

Hopeless . . .

And *still* awake. TV on, writing this at 3am. Jet lag keeps nipping at the ankles.

Finished *Actors*, Conor McPh. script. V. superior comedy. Very not PC. Actors are idiots and script peppered with 'cunt'.

12 OCTOBER

am Call from Judy in LA which stills the roundabout for a while. Present needs, other people's requirements, destiny, that stuff . . .

12.30 pick-up to the set and putting Snape together. Ultimate result— tighter arms, legs, waist, bluer hair, no contact lenses. But Snape seems to live.

13 OCTOBER

10.30 pick-up. Makeup I may need valium . . . Costume.

27 OCTOBER

11 Angel's—fitting for *Victoria Wood Show*.

20 NOVEMBER

7.30 pick-up. *Victoria Wood Christmas Show*.

28 NOVEMBER

7pm Leila Bertrand & car and → Madonna concert w. Sharleen Spiteri and Richard Ashworth.

Back home, a call from Jim Kennedy and—WE HAVE EXCHANGED![1]

30 NOVEMBER

12.30 British Council for Helena K.'s lunch for Mary McAleese—President of Ireland. Other guests—Greg Dyke, Cherie Booth.

5 DECEMBER

To Harrods for the 10% browse or, in this case, purchase of refrigerator.

---

[1] Re Westbourne Terrace

6 DECEMBER

8 *Madame Melville*—Vaudeville. This was a delight. Delicate, shaded comedy of a rare kind and beautifully directed by the author, Richard Nelson. Irène [Jacob] is quite wonderful and Macaulay Culkin is, as they have said, brilliantly cast.

Later Orso. Mr Culkin is extremely bright, aware of himself and his situation in a touchingly courageous way. 'I was expecting to get slaughtered so I had nothing to lose . . .'

7 DECEMBER

12 To 38WT [Westbourne Terrace] w. Caroline [Holdaway]. Which turns into something traumatic during the day. Caroline's eye is definitely beadier than mine and by the time she leaves she has depressed me somewhat.

Caroline is right—get the basics right before moving in. Her basics are going to cost a bit of a bomb, however, so we shall see . . .

8 DECEMBER

10ish The Ivy. It gets noisier & noisier, some of the food was cold, its days may be numbered . . . Jerry Hall & Mick Jagger there and we chatted (difficult in that decibel-level) as they left.

11 DECEMBER

7am pick-up. Back to *Harry P.* The Great Hall with Maggie Smith, Zoë Wanamaker, Ian Hart, Richard Harris—all in their ways sweet, funny souls. But this is Tick Off The Shots filming—no big speech about the scene and what we're all thinking. Maybe there isn't time . . . Maybe . . . Too many people involved in the decisions. A hat has been made for Snape. A hat? For Snape? Fortunately Chris Columbus is also a sweet, funny soul and you kind of guess what he's thinking, what he wants. Certainly if you step outside that he's in sharpish. So it gets done. And it all *looks* just fine.

12 DECEMBER

Here's hoping that the intense thought processes are making it on to film . . .

14 DECEMBER

10.30 pick-up. Hogwarts singalong.

15 DECEMBER

More Great Hall. More turkey. More Hogwarts song.

18 DECEMBER
Troll in the bathroom day.

20 DECEMBER
The first faxed estimates for the work at Westbourne Terrace . . .

22 DECEMBER
Stay-at-home evening. Is this a flu I see before me?
    Talk to Judy about the *Harry Potter* deal memo which is unsignable.

24 DECEMBER
4–7 Helena K. & Iain H. Reggie N[adelson, American writer] talks of meeting Clinton on the Portobello Road and advising Hillary of knockdown
cashmere prices. 'You're talking my language,' says Hillary. Reggie moves
'like Linford Christie' to meet them in said shop.
    12 Midnight service at All Saints.

25 DECEMBER
3 Mary Elizabeth and Pat. A lovely day with the O'Connors. Food, music,
children. . . . Late-night thoughts are all of moving towards an alcohol-free
month . . .

29 DECEMBER
7.45 Edna O'Brien. In 4 hours or so Edna tells us tale after tale of Beckett,
Pinter—'When I see him on Monday he will say immediately "You have seen
The Caretaker, of course"—"No, I have been away"—"Well, then you have
seen *Betrayal*." The trouble is writers write from pain and Harold has closed
up all his wounds, so all he can write now are these small things.'

31 DECEMBER
David + Christine plus family minus Michael. Show on the roads, horses in
the stables.
    8.30 Pam & Mel Smith. A lovely way to end a year. Friends, fireworks and
singing Beatles, Elton John, Billy Joel songs around the piano.

2001

1 JANUARY

And closing the 2000 diary, noting how this has become more of a note-book, even has a few blank pages . . . Good? Bad? I'm becoming more self-conscious? More closed?

4 JANUARY

NEW HOME—DAY ONE. WE COMPLETE.

   6pm to 38 Westbourne Terrace to collect the keys.

5 JANUARY

To 38WT to meet Caroline. I can feel the cheques flying out of the cheque book. It's still a beautiful space but it needs attention.

9 JANUARY

Harry Potter. 10.30 pick-up. Back to school for the January term.

2 FEBRUARY

7.30 *The Graduate* to see Jerry Hall.

   She is an amazing woman. Onstage you get hints of the offstage warmth.

7 FEBRUARY

First alarming cheque goes off to Caroline. Echoes of 12UA.

13 FEBRUARY

Standby from 11am.

   Fits and starts. Comings and goings. Somewhere in here I'm not shooting today, so the day becomes a walking to and fro tour of Bath.

4.45 Pick-up to rehearse the Classroom Scene. Which has a shape thanks to grabbing a bit of rehearsal yesterday.

14 FEBRUARY

8am pick-up.

This scene put me into a concentration/exclusion zone that I recognise and don't like. It leaves innocent people (makeup, the kids) outside not daring to speak through the wall. But then I decided to get pissed off about the trailers again. This English class system in *all* areas. Who even wants to think about it?

Was the scene OK? Or was I pressing familiar buttons?

19 FEBRUARY

Last day on *HP*.

At the end of the day Hedwig the owl flies the length of the Great Hall and drops the Nimbus 2000 in Harry's lap. Dave, the trainer, hadn't slept worrying about it all. Simple, amazing things.

4 MARCH

To John Diamond's[1] funeral service at Kensal Green.

Helena Kennedy suggested we come. I wasn't sure, once there. It seemed like such a definite, if wide, circle of friends. But it was a calm, orderly, unsentimental service. Which is not to say it wasn't terribly moving. Dominic Lawson[2] read from John's last written words, some of which were very funny but the reference to how he and Nigella 'made each other what they were' struck home. She was looking jaw-droppingly beautiful, smiling and nodding as the crowd filed past. John's friend Charles Elton told of the sadness but hilarity in the room as John was in his last hours. Outside a woman was singing 'people who need people' 'and heaven, I'm in heaven'. It was like a cue for him to reach for his pen.

5 MARCH

Today Ruby and I were all over the papers (from yesterday), I was a question on *The Weakest Link*, the top voice to go to sleep by, and quoted in the trades re Ang Lee. Something's afoot . . .

---

[1] English journalist (1953–2001), married to Nigella Lawson
[2] J.D.'s brother-in-law

28 MARCH

New York.

1.30 La Goulue—Natasha. Her mind is like a collection of animals kitten to viper but all alive and kicking. If only she could lose the anger but who can blame her? She talks of *Private Lives* with Ralph Fiennes. Back at the hotel a message from London talking of—*Private Lives*. With Lindsay Duncan . . .

29 MARCH

6.45 *Invention of Love*. Sitting across the aisle from Tom Stoppard is a bit worrying given jet lag in the dark but although I understood a third of the play it was very moving and Bob [Crowley, set designer] did a great job.

Party in the Hudson Theatre. Ms Paltrow walked in on castors . . .

2 APRIL

6am pick-up for 8.25 → London.

Home around 9pm.

5 APRIL

The first big Premium Bond!

26 APRIL

10.40 → Dublin.

Extremely pleasant suite at the Clarence Hotel with a balcony and view up and down the length of the Liffey.

pm Working w. Alison Deegan[1] [on *A Little Chaos*].

Sometimes a breeze, sometimes like pulling teeth. But her stubbornness is valid—why give in until you understand? And occasionally we crash through to an unpredicted something.

2 MAY

4pm Derwentwater School[2]—what a nostalgia trip. The old junior school indeed . . . And so much of it glued to the memory box. Strangely, it doesn't even seem smaller. Acutely detailed picture of Miss Kendall in her class-room. Her presence, her glasses, her hair—her habit of using handcream after lunch. Her incredibly white hands.

---

[1] Irish actor, writer and printmaker, wife of novelist Sebastian Barry
[2] A.R.'s primary school

3 MAY

The Royal Court. A day's rehearsal of *Plasticine*.

A day and a half for this 33 scene, 33 character play. Well, screenplay. Somewhere between *Trainspotting* and *Shopping and Fucking*. But with a heart and mind of its own. Vassily[1] is from AIDS-ridden industrial Urals, and this is about his life, his town, his country—where simple acts of kindness are misunderstood and greeted with abuse.

4 MAY

4pm Reading.

Heroic stuff from the cast in front of a full house.

8 MAY

Paul Lyon-Maris tells me that the Abbey / out of joint / Sebastian Barry concerted worry is that they are second to *Private Lives*! The Abbey wants to stick to the original dates, which conflict with *HP* 2, which won't declare itself . . . Here we go . . .

pm Talking to Sebastian Barry who is a little more relaxed than I thought he might be, but somewhere in here, of course, he needs the money.

14 MAY

The dreaded Cannes trip is avoided.

26 MAY

12 → Hay-on-Wye.

6pm-ish. Reception. Meeting Germaine Greer. Every question, every sentence is a gauntlet? Exhausting after 5 mins.

8.30 Clinton Lecture. World events domesticised. Made Chekhovian, in a way. 'Arafat wanted to take his gun into the meeting.' ('Never happened' mutters Chris Hitchens behind me), and when Ian—interlocutor—doesn't please him, it's 'Ask a bland question, get a bland answer.' Except that it then wasn't . . . particularly when it hit the Middle East. Anyway C.H. left early loudly opining that 'there wouldn't be any drink left . . .'

1 JUNE

Agree to do Amnesty concert on Sunday with Eddie Izzard.

---

[1] Vassily Sigarev (1977–), Russian playwright

3 JUNE

4pm Wembley Arena. To Eddie's dressing room and then a rehearsal with Vic Reeves & Harry Enfield (for the Monty Python sketch 'The Four Yorkshiremen'). Then on to the stage to run it through and the first sight of that space . . .

7.30 The show. Which goes brilliantly. We have to wait until nearly 11. It is like strolling out on to the scaffold, my script securely taped inside a *Sunday Times Magazine*. The others are wonderful and v. funny. I'm too nervous to corpse. I just stare at them. After, in the bar, talking to Tom Jones. He quotes Dustin Hoffman saying to him 'It's like you open your mouth and an animal comes out.'

7 JUNE

ELECTION DAY.

10.45 To Jon Snow's house. Michael Foot there. A lonely figure, victim of Parkinson's, but still caught up in it all.

8 JUNE

4am to bed.

1pm Ian McKellen—lunch in the utterly remodelled 82 Narrow Street . . . Ian talks about the National Theatre's amazingly blinkered approach to choosing a new artistic director and of the prejudice against Jude Kelly.[1]

13 JUNE

6.30 One Parent Family launch at Jo Rowling's house.

Robbie C., Neil Pearson there plus Meera Syal, Kathy Lette. And Jo Rowling. Who is witty (of course) at the microphone and warm & vulnerable to meet. The house needs the Caroline Holdaway touch to get it finished.

16 JUNE

Mel Smith's 50th. Not. As we found out on arriving and swiftly hid the present. Pam's 53rd.

From then on the usual frenetic mix. Fireworks and Mel playing Petula Clark to Richard O'Brien while Hugh Grant and Patsy Kensit arrive uninvited. Pam, God bless her, remains unimpressed by anything and 2 seconds after our arrival says, 'I've had a facelift—want to see the photos?'

12 JULY

2.30 RADA Council.

Could be paranoia, but I begin to feel pressure to write a big cheque. Cannot explain to them this is not possible or that I have the builders in.

---

[1] British theatre director (1954–)

17 JULY

10 Wallingford—Farmers' Market.

Getting out of the taxi in the town square as the full pig is roasting and the bacon is spitting and the ham is being sliced and the English wine is being poured—all on the same day as Vote 2 for the leader of the Tory Party and the knowledge that they are going down the IDS[1] route leaves one with, as they say, a particularly nasty taste in the mouth.

1 AUGUST

2.05 BA → Rome.

4 AUGUST

Today's marked and controlled by silent brick walls, impasses. Although it's the same old story, there's a danger of real damage.

Reading *Private Lives* doesn't help—indulgent, half-mad creatures that they are.

Pool. Lunch.

10 AUGUST

To the Montalcino Market.

A nasty little prod from the *Guardian* lurks in the cappuccino stop. Why is it all triumphs and tragedies with British journalists? What's so wrong with experiment or then, dare we breathe it, failure? It's beyond schadenfreude, it's as if as a nation we are only happy facing negativity. It's our national security blanket. What did you expect? What did I tell you? There, there; you won't feel the benefit; you did your best; never mind; take care, now.

16 AUGUST

Palio day.

An hour by the pool and then.

12am → SIENA and lunch at Le Logge . . . Then to Colombina (Francesca) and her beautiful apartment with its windows on to Il Campo and as it happened right above the starting line. A fantastic view from 4.30 until 7.15 and the start of the race. The bands, flags, horses, all the time the crowd funnelling into the Campo until the words 'sea of people' actually meant something . . . Typically I missed the start by looking through some binoculars but the race itself is a fantastic sight. As is the whole day . . . After dinner

---

[1] Iain Duncan Smith (1954–), leader of the Conservative Party 2001–2003

Illustrations from Alan's original diaries.
Savouring a perfect day in the park (30 June 2013)

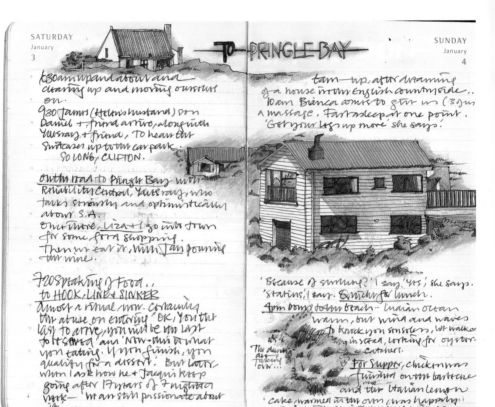

SATURDAY January 3

TO PRINGLE BAY

SUNDAY January 4

8.30am up and about and clearing up and moving ourselves on.

9.30 James (Helen's husband) Ron Daniel + friend, arrive, along with Yusray + friend, to heave the suitcases up to the car park. SO LONG, CLIFTON.

On the Road to Pringle Bay with Reliability Central, Yusray, who talks seriously and optimistically about S.A.

Once more, Liza + I go into town for some food shopping. Then we eat it, with Ian pouring the wine.

7.20 Speaking of food.. to HOOK, LINE + SINKER Almost a ritual now. Containing the abuse on entering 'OK, you the last to arrive, you will be the last to be served' and 'Now—this is what you eating. If you finish, you qualify for a dessert.' But later when I ask how he + Jacqui keep going after 17 years of 7 nights a week— 'We are still passionate about it.'

6am up, after dreaming of a house in the English countryside.. 10am Bianca comes to give us (3 gns a massage. Fast asleep at one point. 'Get your legs up more' she says.

'Because of snoring?' I say. 'Yes,' she says. 'Statins,' I say. Quiche for lunch. 3pm down to the beach—Indian Ocean warm, but wind and waves to knock you senseless. We walked in it instead, looking for oyster-catchers. The dunes are taking over...

For supper, chicken was finished on the barbecue and the Italian lemon cake, warmed in the oven, was happily paired with apricot cheesecake ice-cream..

ABOVE: Holidaying in Pringle Bay, South Africa (3–4 January 2015)

'A delightful evening' in the company of friends (31 August 2013)

On the beach in South Africa (New Year's Eve 2014)

BELOW: Filming 'The Boathouse Scene'—otherwise known as the Death of Snape—in *Harry Potter and the Deathly Hallows—Part 2* (26 November 2009)

On stage: Alan in *Antony and Cleopatra* (1998) at the Olivier Theatre with Helen Mirren and in *Private Lives* (2001) at the Albery Theatre with Lindsay Duncan

As the criminal mastermind Hans Gruber in *Die Hard* (1988), Alan's movie debut, and opposite Juliet Stevenson in *Truly, Madly, Deeply* (1990)

In *Robin Hood: Prince of Thieves* (1991), *An Awfully Big Adventure* (1995) and *Sense and Sensibility* (1995)

As Éamon de Valera in *Michael Collins* (1996), with Liam Neeson in the title role, and in *Dogma* (1999), in which Alan was a fallen angel with a pair of backbreaking wings

In the romantic comedy *Love Actually* (2003) with Emma Thompson and as the much-loved wizard Severus Snape in *Harry Potter and the Goblet of Fire* (2005)

CLOCKWISE: At the premiere of the play *My Name Is Rachel Corrie* (2006), which Alan co-wrote with Katharine Viner, in *Perfume* (2006), an adaptation of the novel by Patrick Süskind, and in *Gambit* (2012), alongside Colin Firth

Filming *A Little Chaos* (2014), which Alan directed and starred in as Louis XIV

Photographs from
Alan's personal
collection, including
two with his soul mate
Rima Horton—on the
set of *A Little Chaos*
and during a trip to
Alaska—whom he met
as a teenager. They
married in New York
in 2012.

we repaired to the Campo for drinks and people watching. Then through the winning Drago district to the car & my turn to drive home.

21 AUGUST

2.30 Drive to Rome.

   6.45 → London.

22 AUGUST

12 and a message from John McGowan saying that Mary has died. In her own favourite word a *great* woman. Her death is a real loss because she was always levelled, focused and inspired. Cigarettes and wine glass always on the go, umpteen books open, only *filled* with life and frustrated by being an 'old wreck'. She was, of course, ageless to us.

7 SEPTEMBER

7.45 Cab to Euston, 8.40 train to Coventry, cab to Stratford and (eventually) St Gregory's Church for Mary McGowan's funeral. Juliet and Hugh there as we arrive and Fifi already inside. Atrocious address by the priest, and the usual interminable mass, but a beautiful, clear and heartfelt eulogy from John, Mary's son.

   12.15 Drive back with Fifi.

   2.30 Rehearsal.

9 SEPTEMBER

8 Michael & Sandra Kamen w. Greg—choreographer. Somehow (by a direct question from Rima really) it becomes an open fact that Michael has MS.

10 SEPTEMBER

pm is weird. First a phone call from Jane L. who keeps asking 'I'm not being aggressive, am I? I've got to tell the hospital if I am.' She basically delivers a monologue about what lousy friends we all are considering what she has been through/is going through, and eventually puts the phone down without saying goodbye. I wrote her a letter saying she was right. She is. But she's also isolating herself proudly but dangerously.

   Then water started dripping from the ceiling via Gilly's [upstairs neighbour] shower. Jimmy appeared with a mop.

11 SEPTEMBER

New York Trade Center Attack.

   11.30 Rehearse. Run Act 1.

   As the dance rehearsal [for *Private Lives*] is about to begin the first report from

New York comes into the rehearsal room. Total shock. All rehearsal becomes an acute, flattening irrelevance but we do it anyway whilst the mind is in limbo.

Eventually back home at 7.30 and just watch it over and over on TV as if to imprint it on the brain, the psyche, the life really . . . That plane was like watching a knife go into butter.

14 SEPTEMBER

11am—3 minutes' silence which we shared with *Kiss Me Kate* cast in their adjacent rehearsal room.

Supper at home. Watching more coverage. Still trying to understand something. Cannot remove the *fact* of 4 million starving in Afghanistan not to mention the innocents in Iraq. There is such political naivety in the US that it only takes one image of five Palestinians dancing in the street to obliterate the bigger picture.

21 SEPTEMBER

8pm First preview.

'This is like drama school,' said Lindsay somewhere in this long day. Somehow, from somewhere reserves are . . . tapped and we get through to huge laughter and applause. Howard [Davies] is glowing with a real pride in actors' courage. He loves actors and takes real pleasure in watching them flex muscles and imaginations—it's incredibly touching when a director shows their vulnerability in that way.

25 SEPTEMBER

Tonight's audience feels wild and almost out of order. They want to laugh at every line.

In Sheekey's champagne is sent to Nick Hytner—it's official—he's the new NT supremo.

28 SEPTEMBER

The show is full of good things—mainly from a lighter, flirtier Lindsay.

2 OCTOBER

The show is Tuesday Bizarre. Lindsay takes Amanda[1] into a scarily down-market area during Act 1. I shouldn't say anything, but do . . . Act 2 is back on track. The thing is—this play doesn't work unless we're talking to each other. As soon as one of us does a number we're in all sorts of trouble.

---

[1] L.D.'s character

3 OCTOBER

9.15 Dr Reid to activate MRI scan re BUPA. Talk of removal of sebaceous cyst & cardiology checks.

10.30 Lister Hospital MRI scan of Rima's knee. 20 mins in the machine listening to my choice from the music on offer—*Breakfast Baroque*.

Shopping for first-night gifts.

3.30 Rehearse.

8pm Packed house and they're off the leash from the word go. A bit of control-freakery from the word go.

4 OCTOBER

Press night. Which goes, seriously, as well as you could expect. Howard rightly warned us of First Night Froideur—people scrutinising or too nervous to support too loudly—and we clamped together as a company and DID THE PLAY. Which is all I ever wanted to do.

5 OCTOBER

In order to avoid the phone take a dazed (not enough sleep—again) walk to 38WT with coffee and muffin in hand.

Back home and there's enough information to know that it's 2 for and one against at this point. God, how I hate their agendas. 2/3 of their reviews are written before they enter the theatre.

7 OCTOBER

Paul Lyon-Maris calls and says the reviews are great. So that strange narrative is played out and we can get on with the run with an official stamp.

10 OCTOBER

Show remarkable for inane laughter from person in the front row . . . Witless, joyless sound that dangerously silences or dilutes the rest of the audience.

21 OCTOBER

Dinner in Sheekey's with Anna & Uri who are so generous about the show. Given that Anna had said she hated the play, the characters, what they stood for etc.—it's a real accolade. Plus it had been a defining image in rehearsals. To make Anna care . . .

23 OCTOBER

David Heyman calls to tell me how brilliant I am in *HP* . . . At home, faxes about the press junket which is huge and impossible. The D.H. phone call was, of course, a coincidence . . .

4 NOVEMBER

6.30 *HARRY POTTER* PREMIERE.

The film should *only* be seen on a big screen. It acquires a scale and depth that matches the hideous score by John Williams. Party afterwards at the Savoy is much more fun.

6 NOVEMBER

66 Harley Street for the beginning of the heart check . . . I like this doctor.

pm On the way in and the *E. Standard* nominates Howard, Lindsay and I.

23 NOVEMBER

8pm Show. Which is more or less trouble-free apart from the wilder elements in the front row. And then the dressing room is like a pub → Kevin Spacey plus friend. The former wearing the backward facing baseball cap.

26 NOVEMBER

11.15 55 Wimpole Street—Blood Test.

 11.30 66 Harley Street—Heart monitor (24 hours).

 12.45 Savoy Hotel, *Evening Standard* Awards.

27 NOVEMBER

2pm 66 Harley Street. Treadmill and ultrasound.

4 DECEMBER

2pm 66 Harley Street. Rodney Foale[1] (I like him) and the results of all the heart checks. All is fine apart from one sheet showing high blood pressure and meaning less red wine late at night.

5 DECEMBER

8pm Show. Charles and Camilla in. The snake is called Charles and the first scene is all about Diana. Of course . . .

15 DECEMBER

Sheekey's. In a day of memorable moments . . . it was capped by having Bill Clinton come over to our table to say hello. I say 'Mr President' to remind myself that he *was* that rather than another actor, the maître d' . . .

19 DECEMBER

Show. From the start Rik Mayall was a big part of the evening. His wonderful, uncontrolled, joyous laugh led the audience and terrified us. But we clawed the evening back.

---

[1] Cardiologist

2002

2 JANUARY

1.30 Dentist. By some miracle there isn't too much to do considering it's been four years.

8 JANUARY

2 Queen Mary's, Roehampton, to see Hugh Cruttwell[1] who, as ever, makes one ashamed of ever complaining about anything. Now paralysed down one side and sight affected but brain as sharp as tacks and heart as unaffected as ever. God bless him.

9 JANUARY

2 Dentist. Bleaching. Ouch.

4 Refit the *Harry P.* costume. A bit of taking in is necessary.

10 JANUARY

Dinner with the glorious Tony Benn plus his daughter Melissa, Saffron Burrows and Mike Figgis. Mike hadn't seen the show (had to picture me in a Noël Coward play, somehow).

11 JANUARY

8 Show. A disturbance in the audience—loud noises, rustling etc. was fairly alarming at the start of Act 2. Both of us thinking it's a madman or drunk but it settled . . . We discovered later, to our chastened spirits, that it was a diabetic having an attack and relatives ramming crisps in her mouth.

---

[1] Principal of RADA from 1965 to 1983

14 JANUARY

Harry Potter 2

   6.50am pick-up (Snape's study).

(except, of course, writing this with the Sunday wide awake at 2am thing)

Nice to see them all again but it's a dreamlike thing, as if it has never stopped. And in a way, it hasn't—and won't . . .

Richard Harris is enveloped in flu—a cue for Maggie Smith to encase her face in a scarf. Through the day little chats about *Private Lives*, although it felt like trespassing. 'That's when Bob[1] was at his maddest.' 'It's wonderful stuff, though.'

Mindblowing exhaustion by the end of the day. Somehow 1 hour's sleep is not quite enough.

   Back to the hotel for a club sandwich, chips, red wine, *Ground Force*[2] and bed.

18 JANUARY

6.50 pick-up.

Olivier Award nominations are in the *Guardian*. Lindsay (twice), Adam [Godley], Emma [Fielding] & I are all there (plus Howard) but these things (part experience, part common sense) are actually rather depressing. So many agendas, so much baggage. Where's Lepage, Deborah W[arner], Fiona? Does it mean don't offend, challenge, upset? *Mnemonic* seems to be award-free too . . .

21 JANUARY

9.15 pick-up →*Harry Potter*.

Made up and ready to go—for a day off camera.

Nothing matters really after the images of the volcano in Goma. People picking their way across potentially deadly lava to get to homes that no longer exist.

23 JANUARY

Sharleen's Burns Night. Much piping and dancing and kilts & tartan—Sharleen, Pat Doyle, Bill Forsyth, Ewan McGregor, haggis, cranachan, as Emma and me go in.

25 JANUARY

8 Show—Coughers from Hell.

---

[1] English actor Robert Stephens (1931–1995). Husband of Maggie Smith, with whom he appeared in *Private Lives* in 1972.

[2] Home improvement TV series

28 JANUARY

8am pick-up → Paddington.

   8.57 → Gloucester.

   On the set (Gloucester Cathedral, that is) we block a couple of scenes and go back to the hotel after lunch (the tent feeling as if it's going to take off in the wind). Emma Watson is unwell so there's nothing we can shoot.

   7 Down the bar to find Maggie S. reading. Ken Branagh joins later and having had Maggie on Cher we are howling at stories of directing de Niro—or first, casting him.[1]

31 JANUARY

Rima's birthday. It's a long time since we've been together on Jan 31st.

2 FEBRUARY

8pm. Lindsay has been throwing up and looks v. pale. The curtain-up is delayed. The audience seems drugged.

   after—Kate Winslet & friend Plaxie . . . then to Sheekey's . . . I think I delivered a somewhat sanctimonious lecture about curiosity v. certainty but then Kate did spend the evening announcing verdicts on everything from ex-husband to George Bush.

17 FEBRUARY

12 David, Chris, Sheila & John—after they've been to the cemetery. Hard to restrain my irritation at S. & J.'s habit of thinking that their girls are still somewhere around 10 years old but resist it I should . . .

   4pm Show.

   A woman in the front row is *very* busy with her bag of sweets.

20 FEBRUARY

Booked Cape Town trip.

21 FEBRUARY

And it's my 56th birthday—how the hell did that happen?

2 MARCH

3pm Show. Jules[2] finding it very difficult to say anything more than how odd it all was. Understandable but sad that she couldn't be generous towards Lindsay. What is the point?

---

[1] Re *Frankenstein*
[2] Juliet Stevenson

3 MARCH

4pm Show. The last show in London. Wonderful that Hugh [Cruttwell] made it. But the show was hanging on to its coattails. Either the head or the body was in the process of going on holiday, or walkabout. Somewhere else, anyway.

8 Sheekey's. Champagne & supper courtesy of Sheekey's themselves.

5 MARCH

7am Cromwell Hospital for orthoscopy on knee. Writing this, still a bit under the anaesthetic. Ivor Slee, the anaesthetist, said (or was it Peter Braid, the surgeon) you won't remember anything about it. True. The whole thing seemed to have taken 30 seconds.

First Conor then Rima come to visit the invalid.

6 MARCH

Woke at 6am. Just for a change. But this 24 hours has been good for script-wading. The knee is pretty painful but will doubtless improve.

Hobble, limp to a car at around 11am after the general all-clear. My instructions are a little contradictory—walk on it, don't use a crutch or stick, rest it, use ice-packs.

8 MARCH

Watched *Gosford Park*. There it is—the script perfectly realised on the screen. And I felt seriously detached. Maybe it's a problem when you don't *really* care about any of the characters. Because try as he might Robert Altman *can't* make us see the story through the servants' eyes. The upper classes will always stop that. That's the point.

15 MARCH

5pm → Cape Town.

16 MARCH

The day spent in various poses of complete exhaustion—part no sleep, part present neuroses, part past recriminations . . . But the body knows this is A Rest and so it happily caves in.

24 MARCH

Waking to more thoughts of how, when, where of having a house here. Made more appealing by the fact that the wind has gone and it's a sunny morning with a calm come-hithery sea.

Maybe it's not such a good idea. How often would we get here? Others would use it, of course, but looking after it?

One of the houses Anna Marie shows us is Christiaan Barnard's. I didn't know he had died. Strange wandering around his home—photos of son and families intact. As we drive away A.-M. tells sad stories of divorce and aloneness.

26 MARCH

To the Pringle Bay Bakery for milk and papers and Oscar winners—it all looks a bit PC to me. A miracle that Denzel Washington mentioned anyone but himself—and there you have it. Awards. For actors. Hours of free TV and some designers pushing their frocks.

30 MARCH

Went for an 8am walk along the beach in glorious morning sunshine, a few mad surfers already in the water for the past hour. Some walkers, some dogs. Back to the house to pack, clear up, cook breakfast. Ate on the verandah, the bacon, eggs, tomatoes, orange juice just lasting the weekend.

As I was cleaning the verandah, a sudden whoosh and a baboon was on the balustrade and then the roof, family members following. A swift door close and minutes later the whole family was next door. I like to think they'd come to say farewell, but suspect the smell of bacon was the culprit.

5pm → Johannesburg.

8.45 → London.

2 APRIL

7.15 pick-up—*HP.*

Up in the Quidditch tower with Miriam Margolyes (about to be OBE and 20lbs lighter—as she tells me in her fairly inimitable way) and Jason Isaacs—who has just become a dad for the first time. The usual nodding-heads-at-numbers scene but quicker this time and we're out of there by lunchtime. Which means I can get to 38WT.

Home for supper and more sorting, rationalising. Finding out how much STUFF I'm surrounded by . . .

5 APRIL

Pack day.

Nigel, Scott and Paul from GB Liners[1] arrive at 8.30am and swing into action. Paper flying, boxes snapping into being all day, a life packed away for a 5 minute drive tomorrow.

Paul says about 10 mins in 'I'm sorry if I keep staring—I'm a bit in awe.' It

---

[1] Removal company

takes me a while to catch on. And then it takes him a minute to catch on that he's staring at someone frazzled, dusty and ordinary.

6 APRIL

THE MOVE.

How could anyone collect all this *stuff*? Or want it?

The inevitable walk round—13 years and a flood of warm images. A flat full of love and very much loved back.

Sleeping at 38WT for the first time. Of course, in the same way that 44 has been punishing us with warped locks etc. over the past few days, now 38 is testing us—no heat and an alarm that beeps gently every 30 seconds.

7 APRIL

1pm The family.

God bless them. Not an ounce of resentment—just wandering around smiling.

8 APRIL

Christchurch, Oxford.

Last day on *Harry Potter* 2.

David Heyman says 'Are you still doing the play?' with his usual charming lack of command of the odd detail. Talk of directors for *HP* 3 reveals that Alfonso[1] is David's choice while Chris favours Ken B. I can only sit & stare.

9 APRIL

It is a great apartment to wake up in—especially when the alarm isn't going off every 30 secs.

6ish and there's a potential flood in the utility room.

7.30 38WT—Wet the new flat's head.

11 APRIL

1.25 → New York.

Watching *The Deep End* on the plane. Everything *Dark Harbor* was meant to be. Tilda [Swinton] amazingly focused and graded performance in a script that must look awful on the page (to continuing mystery of film . . .). Style over content in a way but somehow miraculously more than that.

---

[1] Alfonso Cuarón, Mexican film director (1961–)

12 APRIL

New York.

Realising I left a bunch of clothes in London . . .

18 APRIL

12.30 To the theatre.

7.30 Dress rehearsal.[1]

19 APRIL

1pm To the theatre via Bed Bath & Beyond for more curtains and wicker boxes for Lindsay. As usual—the wrong priorities.

8pm First preview. Gladiatorial—or thrown to the lions.

24 APRIL

8 Show. The shape of things to come. NOT . . . We hope. Bum sound cues and dozy audience (half of it, anyway).

27 APRIL

Not feeling great. Stomach bug? Not to mention the knee.

28 APRIL

6pm OPENING NIGHT—Tough, but Act 1 seemed OK. Act 2 they started to disappear. Act 3 they were already home, then they cheered . . .

In the dressing room—Mike Nichols, Lauren Bacall, Emma T., Tom Hanks, Rita Wilson.

29 APRIL

Reviews all raves, apparently, so now we can just get on with it.

4 MAY

The days are kicking in and lasting too long.

5 MAY

6.15 Wyndham Hotel and some champagne with Edna O'B., or the minx as Lindsay calls her since she tries to prevent us from going to a movie. In vain.

---

[1] After its highly successful London run *Private Lives* transferred with the same cast to Broadway. It opened at the Richard Rodgers Theatre on 28 April and, after 127 performances, closed on 1 September. The reception was generally enthusiastic with one reviewer purring over 'the mutually sublime Alan Rickman and Lindsay Duncan'. The latter won a Tony for Best Leading Actress, while the production was given the award for Best Revival.

Determinedly, I get into the car and off to 12th Street for *The Piano Teacher*. A completely uncompromising film with Isabelle Huppert fearless as ever.

6 MAY

am Tony nominations in and we have 6. I hate all this, especially since Adam & Emma are not in the list. And Helen is, but not Ian etc., etc. Divisive, disturbing, unhelpful.

7 MAY

6am and awake—brooding, writing this and previous page. Finding Christina's note from last summer—

Trust, to go forward, transformation, divine protection, strength, energy, cancellation of the fear of new things, cancellation of the fear of love, relationship, wisdom, intuition, reunion [?] of spiritual creatives and body creatives.

18 MAY

8pm Show.

After which we discover that Nicole Kidman & Tobey Maguire arrived ½ hour late. Why come in?

19 MAY

6.00 Bill Evans [press/publicity] calls with winners losers news.

7pm Café des Artistes w. Lindsay & Bill Evans.

9pm Drama Desk Awards. Our producers are smarmy as ever. Lindsay[1] all dignity intact.

Later Café Lux. Natasha & Liam across the room beckoning me to the losers' table.

20 MAY

6.30 *About a Boy*. The kind of depressing English film where single mothers and Amnesty workers are ugly people in oversized sweaters.

26 MAY

6.30 → Liam & Natasha.

2 hour drive upstate to their glorious house and dinner with John [Benjamin] Hickey & Jennifer [Carpenter] from *The Crucible* plus—oh, Meryl's in there . . . as in Streep. Who turns out to be fun and gossipy. But it's hard—who else looks like Meryl Streep? So you can't quite lose the stare . . .

---

[1] Winner of Best Actress

27 MAY

Lunch on a terrace with the boys and us. Tash is the most miraculous hostess. *Nothing* is forgotten.

4pm Dan Day-Lewis arrives to play tennis.

1 JUNE

2pm Show.

As we came off stage, Meryl Streep is at the stage door. She loved it. Plus
daughter Grace. After the stage door signings, there was a moment when she
was in my dressing room waiting for me to come back . . .

5 JUNE

10am pick-up → *Charlie Rose* show. Who turns out to be exactly what one
had supposed—a great and improvisational listener. This *could* have gone
anywhere.

6 JUNE

8pm Show.

The audience was, as they say, lively.

25 JUNE

Apparently Cher was in. Which accounts for the late start.

16 JULY

8pm Show—Pits audience and, of course, Paul Newman & Joanne Woodward in . . .

27 JULY

8pm Show. Unutterable exhaustion before, during and after. A shame because
the audience was very sharp. Howard watched Act 1 and thought it all fine.
Lindsay's voice started to return in Act 3. But the combination of personal
dramas, antibiotics and the tail end of the run is starting to take its toll.

20 AUGUST

8pm Show.

10.30 Paul Newman, Joanne Woodward. Thalia.

Hard not to just stare in amazement at this wonderful, generous, ego-free,
open, childlike, utterly on-the-ball couple.

24 AUGUST

Supper with Ian Holm . . . Ian does his drunken cowboy—'OK you suckers,
this is a fuck-up' . . .

25 AUGUST

Hugh Cruttwell has died . . . This is a major event for all of us. Happy / sad / enormous / proper.

26 AUGUST

9.30 Dentist. Until 2pm. But Jeff[1] has done a really wonderful job—top half anyway. Bottom half and the lone tooth—gone forever.

1 SEPTEMBER

3pm *Private Lives*—Final performance.

There were a few scary moments but the audience went wild and Jimmy[2] held up a board saying 'I love you very much . . .'

10.30 Café Loup . . . We were sat at a table for 8, right next to the piano. It had Noël Coward's songbook waiting. Emma Fielding picked out and we sang 'Someday I'll Find You' through the red wine haze. IT'S OVER!

11 SEPTEMBER

Decide not to fly home until tomorrow. Everything too rushed and the rush seemed disrespectful. The TV coverage is mercifully restrained and unbearably moving when it is utterly personal—mothers, fathers, children holding up pictures, sitting among the flowers at Ground Zero. And the unalterable sense as the 2,800 names are read out is of world citizens—all those South American, Japanese, Asian, European names . . . And a year goes by and still no one talks properly about it all.

16 SEPTEMBER

LOVE ACTUALLY—first day.

21 SEPTEMBER

11 Tate Britain—Lucian Freud.

Looking at these great paintings it's as if Wagner, Mahler, Elgar were playing loudly. Heroic, isolated, exposed people.

25 SEPTEMBER

9.45 pick-up.

Em & me after the concert. Difficult, subtle, concentrated stuff. The age-old problem of staying innocent whilst the head is full of STUFF.

---

[1] Jeffrey Golub-Evans, New York dentist
[2] American theatrical producer James Nederlander (1922–2016)

Home via Peter Jones (loo brushes) and General Trading Company (a lucky find of a Bathroom Rubbish Container). Such is life off its hinges.

28 SEPTEMBER

8.30 Danny and Leila.

And, as Rima says, Danny talks more and more as mouthpiece of the *Daily Mail*.

4 OCTOBER

Greg Wise was on set but there was no chance to talk.

13 OCTOBER

2pm *Sweet Sixteen*.

Ken Loach's latest and another move towards populism, it seems, although Martin Compston is a remarkable and fine young actor.

21 OCTOBER

8pm Duncan's car to pick me, Beatie Edney and Adam's girlfriend Lucy up to go to Wembley Arena for Coldplay concert. They were really wonderful— every song close to being an anthem already and incredibly moving to see that many people knowing the lyrics. In the bar backstage, Gwyneth Paltrow [married to Chris Martin of Coldplay] introduced herself (more beautiful offscreen) and then [we] met the group in the inner sanctum with Richard Curtis.

25 OCTOBER

2 Brydges Place. Happy-sad talk of Ruby's envy of touring around with friends in a play.

And then there's a cheeky visit to Sheekey's to find a cab, where they sit us down with a bottle of champagne . . . Both Ruby and I can feel a wheel turning. The fascination of 'showbiz' is ever-thinning. The opportunities for only REAL work have to be nourished.

26 OCTOBER

2.30am Before sleep.

This beautiful home must become a breeding ground, a meeting place (although it is probably not rough enough yet), so it has to be inhabited and filled with positive energy, good spirits, rough and tumble.

To Conran to try to find sofa material. Failed.

1 NOVEMBER

The day ends, stupidly, with a row about cleaning brought on by the fine layer, again, of white dust everywhere. Mop and bucket at 1am.

10 NOVEMBER

7pm Royal Court.

Katrin Cartlidge[1] memorial. Gut wrenchingly moving and challenging (so what am *I* doing?) but a real sense of a person still here somehow. Brave, generous Peter [Gevisser] K.C.'s husband singing; her wonderful letter to *Time Out* berating a journalist about a Vanessa Redgrave interview.

17 NOVEMBER

9.10 *Bowling for Columbine*.

This film has you shaking your everything in a numbed *not* disbelief. It's all too true and so well argued. A country kept ignorant and ever fearful resorts to the gun in the name of freedom.

25 NOVEMBER

8.30 Dinner w. Ruth & Richard Rogers—plus Edward & Mariam Said, Daniel Barenboim & Elena, Alan & Lindsay Rusbridger . . . Daunting might be the word. Said, charming, Barenboim alarming, Rusbridger, as ever, it seems, devoid of questions or curiosity or life, really. His wife is like Mrs Mole full of nervous smiles.

3 DECEMBER

Belvedere Restaurant.

Mel Smith's 50th birthday party. Without Pam. Which casts a bizarre shadow.

4 DECEMBER

Talking to Paul Lyon-Maris about *HP* exit which he thinks will happen. But here we are in the project-collision area *again*.

Reiterating no more *HP*. They really don't want to hear it.

7 DECEMBER

Rome.

3.30pm To the Opera House for rehearsal w. Johnny Hallyday[2]—and Mel Smith who finally made it from his film set. Mr Hallyday (remembered well

---

[1] English actor (1961–2002)
[2] French singer (1943–2017)

from youthful days in Paris) is charming and very face-lifted but nothing to what is coming up.

6.30 pick-up Opera House for European Film Awards. Polanski, Almodóvar, Wenders, Jeanne Moreau, Ken Loach, Mike Leigh (with whom we shared a car) & dozens of extremely beautiful Italian actresses.

Later dinner at the Palazzo delle Esposizioni. Mel and Pam hosting a table. Mel somewhat perplexed by the non-response. Why? He misjudged it spectacularly. What can you say? His script was disastrous.

8 DECEMBER
7.35[pm] → to London. Jeremy Irons was in the lounge. Nice to see him & chat of Ireland and last night.

11 DECEMBER
8.45 Sabrina [Guinness] plus car → 5 Cavendish Place for Mick Jagger's dinner party.

16 DECEMBER
Edna O'Brien calls—'Have you seen *Breath of Life*?'[1] She's already appalled and it's only a question. 'No, I haven't.' 'It was so terrible, I thought I might (pause, hesitancy, groping) . . . explode.'

19 DECEMBER
12 Don McCullin[2]—doing portraits now. And strangely the shyest most nervous man—in an incredibly endearing way as he talks of his imminent new baby—'What am I doing? I'm 67'—or his ex-wife—'She's taken everything—I've got to start all over again—I'm off to photograph the Kurds next week . . . this light is fantastic . . . one more roll and I'm out of here . . . sorry to take so long . . . Judi Dench next week . . . I'm no good with women . . . '

21 DECEMBER
Trudie & Sting's Christmas party. Byzantium meets Fairyland. They have built a red, ruched theatre where Richard E. Grant read ''Twas the Night Before Christmas', Zenaida Yanowsky[3] & Andrew Muir danced *The Nutcracker*, the Razumovsky Ensemble played the *Brandenburg Concerto* and Vasko Vassilev[4] prodigied his way through the *Carmen Fantasie*. Around and about all that was fantastic food and beautiful wine & Krug champagne.

---

[1] Play by David Hare
[2] British war photographer (1935–)
[3] French ballet dancer (1975–)
[4] Bulgarian violinist and conductor (1970–)

But perhaps best of all was the chance to talk to Elton John & David [Furnish] about S.A.F.E. [Sponsored Arts for Education, Kenyan charity] and elicit their support.

24 DECEMBER

11.45 Finally make it to the church in St Petersburgh Place—a congregation out of Fellini by Francis Bacon through Ken Loach. But a great organist and very superior choir really letting rip on 'O Come All Ye Faithful'.

30 DECEMBER

12.30[am] Watched an hour of *Winter Guest* on Channel 4. And back into the editing room with that. Amazing how distance lends not disenchantment but maybe internal rhythms change, too little courage (at times), horrible sound—*beautiful* acting.

31 DECEMBER

Selfridges for the presents still to get. Slight sense of panic.

2003

Martin Bashir, Michael Jackson — *Harry Potter* 3 —
Daniel Radcliffe — Tony Blair — Jamie Cullum —
Royal Family — Annie Lennox — John McEnroe — No-wine month —
Paul McCartney — Emma Thompson — Los Angeles — Mos Def —
Something the Lord Made — Antigua — Harvey Weinstein

6 FEBRUARY

Selina comes up trumps with tickets for the Stones concert in LA and alerts us again to the Beijing event . . . mmmm.

1pm Freddie Findlay, now 19, comes round for lunch. Fairly quickly we get to the point. He has been in drug rehab, is now clean for 93 days and his agents have dumped him. That golden 12-year-old still visible behind the eyes, but an alcoholic father and a manic depressive girlfriend are his present.

8 FEBRUARY

11am Phyllida. Late because she went to the wrong address and then wandered up and down Westbourne Terrace looking at doors and in windows until she hit upon the right one. Still one of the most beautiful women on the planet.

Watching Martin Bashir's documentary on Michael Jackson. Disgraceful, self-serving journalism. How much did that cost? Compare M.J.'s actions with those of a million pederasts & paedophiles a day or the thousands of kids dying daily in S.A. from AIDS. Make a film about that with your concerned face.

9 FEBRUARY

1.30 River Cafe. Ruthie & Richard Rogers, Andrew Marr & wife Jackie [Ashley] and children (the eldest at Latymer). Lovely, Sunday afternoon chatter (but not with this lot).

14 FEBRUARY

8am and the phone rings. Judy Daish. Orlando Sesti has been killed in a car crash in Spain. 22 years old. In a way it is like we have been robbed as much as he has. One of those people you watch slightly from a distance—they live life the way you wish you could.

pm. And the madness goes on. Rima's father has died. Not that it wasn't expected—he was 97. But he was their father and the creator of all that Horton-ness.

15 FEBRUARY

12 Duke of York Theatre.

For the march.[1] Except that we didn't make it to the Duke of York—no taxis anywhere. We walked to Piccadilly . . . and joined the march there. At Hyde Park (having seen 1m people behind us) there was Bruce Kent & Tariq Ali at the microphones but Minnie Driver & Tim Robbins to remind us that celeb rules, really.

27 FEBRUARY

→ Bournemouth for Rima's dad's funeral.

9 MARCH

4pm Old Vic / Hugh Cruttwell's memorial.

That it happened was what was important never mind the material although Greg's speech was wonderful as was Geraldine's.[2] And the massed voices on 'A Little Help From My Friends' was the abiding echo.

13 MARCH

6.30 pick-up—*HP* 3. Day One.

3 APRIL

These pages filled with nothing about the war but now they are 15 miles from Baghdad with threats of chemical warfare ahead this seems like a marker point. Rumsfeld has become a hated person (Bush seems like an irrelevance now).

7 APRIL

I don't seem to write much about the war mainly because there is hardly a face I believe. Blair, yes, but his agenda is *sooo* hopeful and idealistic. Forget Bush—just take one look at Rumsfeld and Cheney. What would you sell them? Buy from them?

---

[1] Against the Iraq war
[2] English actor Geraldine McEwan (1932–2015). She was Hugh Cruttwell's wife.

14 APRIL

7am pick-up—*Harry Potter*.

Top table stuff w. David Thewlis, Michael Gambon, Maggie Smith, Warwick Davis.

More of the same really. But what else can you do except get the shots—a choir, 300 children, 1 speech. People reading in the background.

2 MAY

8.40 pick-up.

Corridor with Dan Radcliffe.

He's so concentrated now. Serious and focused—but with a sense of fun. I still don't think he's really an actor but he will undoubtedly direct/produce. And he has such quiet, dignified support from his parents. Nothing is pushed.

12 MAY

1pm Mark Meylan [voice coach].

There are definitely new notes in the vocal range. I hear it speaking, shouting, singing and the title of Kristin Linklater's book is all too appropriate—*Freeing the Natural Voice*. I feel as if I have never used any natural voice, that this noise that people impersonate and which always depresses me is nothing to do with me. Press on.

17 MAY

6pm Car to Chequers . . . Real sense of the shiver of history going through the gates.

7.30 for 8. Arrive to find Ben Kingsley & wife, Peter Hain, Principessa Strozzi, others . . . then Richard & Judy arrive, then Tony & Cherie with 3-year-old Leo in his arms, in pyjamas.

Dinner for 25. Tony hanging around at the door to talk to me. (Was I the only known critic?) I mentioned S.A.F.E., Rima in the Lords and blacklists in the US—not bad for 4 minutes.

On leaving I said 'Well, thank God you're in the room with those maniacs.'[1] He raised an eyebrow or two and said 'Yes . . . it's been . . . difficult.' And we drove away, T.B. silhouetted in the grand doorway in his off-white chinos and blue open-necked shirt.

---

[1] Members of the Bush administration

21 MAY

Evening completely taken over by stupidly picking up a sauce pan by a handle that had been perched over a flame for about 15 mins. Even dropping it as quickly as possible left me with my hand in cold water all evening and holding an ice bag in bed.

2 JUNE

3.30 Car to St James's Palace to rehearse with Jamie Cullum and all the others for tonight's cabaret/after dinner entertainment.

9.35 On stage in front of the entire royal family—40 or 50 of them. The show goes well—Ronnie Barker & June Whitfield walking off with the evening. But the poem plus Jamie's wonderful singing and playing was a happy juxtaposition. Afterwards they all walked in—the pages of a million newspapers. The Queen, Philip, Charles, Camilla (a kiss on both cheeks . . .), Andrew, Anne, Edward, Sophie, William, Zara, Peter etc., etc. . . . No need ever more to wonder . . . And then to the Ritz for much champagne.

3 JUNE

8 Tate Modern Photography Exhibition. Meet Martin Parr—my hero.

6 JUNE

8pm Annie Lennox concert. Sadler's Wells. One of the great voices and one of the great concerts. 'Why' is now a 20th C. anthem. Annie afterwards quiet, curious, gentle, shy . . .

26 JUNE

8.30 Zaika—Dinner for Patty and John McEnroe w. Ruby, Ed, Suzanne, Nicky.

McEnroe is very sweet and loving with Patty [Smyth, his wife] and endearingly unegocentric and polite in other ways. I'm sure he's a great dad and would be a fantastically loyal friend. Who would have guessed? Also—he doesn't mind gossip—*no one* likes Rusedski.

28 JUNE

All day on the sofa, or in the toilet. Thank you Criterion Brasserie, one assumes.

Not to mention their seats bringing the back ache on again. Eating nothing but a bowl of porridge later on.

29 JUNE

Amazingly enough, better.

21 JULY

7.15 pick-up.

Coming out of the hole, fighting imaginary werewolves, etc. Alfonso is looking stressed. Thank you Warner Bros.

27 JULY

1.30 Richard Rogers' 70th birthday party at the River Cafe for hundreds of close friends . . .

30 JULY

7am pick-up. Snape/Lupin Classroom.

The day got off to a fabulous start with the screen guillotining on to my head, a sudden, swift blackout followed by day-long melancholy. *Not* helped by my (fairly innocent) 'Warner Bros won't have that' to the Leonardo Werewolf with genitals drawing. Alfonso was quietly ballistic with me. I love him too much to let it last too long so I wailed off-set and we sorted it out. He's under the usual *HP* pressure and even he starts rehearsing cameras before actors, and these kids need directing. They don't know their lines and Emma [Watson]'s diction is this side of Albania at times. Plus my so-called rehearsal is with a stand-in who is French.

31 JULY

7am pick-up.

Tired, tense, enclosed. Snape-like. Not particularly useful to a joyous atmosphere on the set.

11 AUGUST

8 To Maria Aitken's[1] house.

Edward Hibbert,[2] Patrick McGrath, Edward St Aubyn.[3] To talk about M.A. and P. McG's script for *Some Hope*. My point was that at the moment it has two scripts—*Less Than Zero* and *Gosford Park*. It could be those combined, but not one after the other. They all seemed to take it well. Roll on a second draft.

---

[1] English director and actor, married to novelist Patrick McGrath
[2] British-American actor (1955–)
[3] English novelist, author of *Some Hope*

24 AUGUST

Car to Twickenham and the Rolling Stones concert. Jagger amazing. Energy, focus, voice. Defying every known force that might otherwise drag him into retirement.

10 SEPTEMBER

Finally manage to start a NO WINE month. Stay-at-home supper.

11 SEPTEMBER

Interesting to wake with a clear head.

8.30 Danny & Leila come by for supper. Which was easy & delicious. Especially the amazingly easy lemon sorbet with vodka.

19 SEPTEMBER

5.50 *Calendar Girls*—Whiteley's.

Mostly, I hate *The Full Monty/Billy Elliot/Bend It Like Beckham* version of Britain but at least this one is stuffed with friends all being great—Helen Mirren, Julie Walters, Ceals [Celia Imrie], Ros [March], Ciarán [Hinds], Geraldine [James]—and the story has some inherent shape. And it's true. So it becomes a real celebration. And it's better directed [by Nigel Cole] than all of the above. Clear, witty, honest.

2 OCTOBER

6 To the Royal Court to Ian R[ickson]'s office to meet Cindy & Craig Corrie, parents of Rachel. These are two remarkable people. Gentle, sharp, acute listeners, such grace.

8 OCTOBER

7 for 7.30. Concert for George [Harrison]. Great music & incredibly moving. We measure our lives in Beatles songs as well as everything else. His son [Dhani] is his double. High 5'd with Paul McCartney in the Gents.

9 OCTOBER

Lunch at Harry's Bar for Sting CBE . . . Wonderful speeches by Geldof and Sting . . . Sting's (to music) took right on board the moral dilemma of accepting the award.

10 OCTOBER

9.45 Pick-up to start the *Love Actually* junket.

4pm Golden Square—screening of *Love Actually*. Me, Martine McC[utcheon] and two of her friends.

Actually, she's one of the best things in the film. Unaffected, truthful and direct.

11 OCTOBER

12.30 pick-up → Dorchester.

pm → 6pm with Emma for TV interviews. She was looking great and then worked her socks off as per . . . After a while there was something more duet-like happening. But it's hard for her to relinquish control. Fortunately she's really good at it.

13 OCTOBER

9.30 → Dorchester.

Somehow, for some reason, Emma was on even greater overdrive. I get the feeling that she was on a mission to compensate for my lack of . . . whatever.

15 OCTOBER

5pm Michael Kamen.

Who was in a haze of cannabis . . . and why not . . . [1]

The music needs to go through a sieve and come out attached to the right bits of narrative but he's working on that.

3 NOVEMBER

8am pick-up.

10.55 → New York. Lowell Hotel.

7 NOVEMBER

11.55 → Los Angeles. Four Seasons Hotel.

12 NOVEMBER

Jimmy Kimmel Live! [2]

'So this is a chick flick?'

'No, it's more of a dick flick.'

I got beeped but we were away with the horrors of Toby Keith singing 'American Soldier' only minutes away. I'm on the sofa with a stand-up, a boy trumpeter and one of the Red Hot Chili Peppers. Slightly scary.

---

[1] Michael Kamen had multiple sclerosis and died from a heart attack on 18 November 2003.
[2] *Jimmy Kimmel Live!* is an American chat show renowned for its unpredictable nature.

20 NOVEMBER

Hugo Young's memorial service.

Which in a way I am grateful for. An hour or so in Westminster Cathedral. Some great words, some great music, some space to think about Michael, Gilly, Hugo.

22 NOVEMBER

7.30 Royal Academy of Music. Memorial service for Michael Kamen.

Annie Lennox sings 'All My Trials Lord'. David Gilmour and Bryan Adams sing. The brothers—Lenny, Paul & Johnny—speak. I speak. The girls—Zoë & Sasha—speak. And most memorably, Michael's father—it's like something Shakespeare forgot to write.

28 NOVEMBER

The last week has left me wiped out from putting myself on a kind of hold. No release due to the peculiar pressure that is induced by having to speak at two services. Add to that a skittish relationship with jet lag . . .

29 NOVEMBER

2pm → Baltimore.

5.55 pick-up → Harbor Point Hotel.

pm Watching *The Italian Job* to see Mos Def. Who can act. Very well.

1 DECEMBER

Wardrobe [for *Something the Lord Made*]. Everything is too big.

pm Read through the script.

Mos is an absolute natural and v. smart, but it's not clear how focused.

Move room! Hooray!

2 DECEMBER

7.30 pick-up.

Into makeup for camera tests. Some of which make the heart sink. 'More shading—he's sick.'

Gentle manipulation of the script.

4 DECEMBER

8pm Back at the hotel and a note from Pam Shriver inviting me to the Roddick/Blake charity match in her 'hometown' tonight. Any other time—but I'm whacked.

8 DECEMBER
4.15am pick-up.
   FIRST DAY.
   Which turns out to be an 18 hour day by the time I get back to the hotel.
With a painfully aggravated cartilage pain which keeps me awake.

9 DECEMBER
10.15[am] pick-up.
   Somewhere in here the little speech about letting the actors rehearse.
   Hotel at 11.30[pm].

10 DECEMBER
Robert [Cort] the producer (Central Casting) and I have another of our little
chats. He talks, I listen and then say no . . .

11 DECEMBER
What amounted to a row with Joe [Sargent, director] over his total inability
to let a scene play to the end without talking about a move, a bit of business
or some ill-judged notion. Of course he feels threatened but I'm in a no-win
situation. And Mos is up there in the handlebars.

12 DECEMBER
Robert comes to the trailer to deliver one of his monologues. He does them
often. This one was all about how I was a Rod Steiger (v. temperamental by
the way) and how he could help. All the best notions but if he's not insisting
on a process being honoured—what's the point?

13 DECEMBER
Freezing cold day.
   A walk to the mall in the harbour to Barnes & Noble, thinking mainly
'but books are heavy' so found my way to the CDs. Elvis Costello, Keith Jar-
rett, Youssou N'Dour, Mos Def.

15 DECEMBER
Bits and pieces day.
   Full of my new passivity.
   Of course all it produces is something more bland than it needs to be but
it keeps people happy—ish.
   Although I think the crew relish the challenge.

Bob C.[1] upset that no one seems happy about Saddam Hussein's capture (he's a Republican).

16 DECEMBER

Joe calls with tomorrow's 4.45 call so a planned dinner out is off which leaves me watching Diane Sawyer's interview with George and Laura B. And this is a president. Diane did well, short of being rude—but those little eyes can narrow beyond belief and that little smile can look the smallest, meanest sneer. What a small human being this is. And a tadpole next to the shark of a wife.

19 DECEMBER

11.30 pick-up—was to have been a day off.

12 Long, long wig-cutting session. Plus—a total rewrite of the last scene is handed to me—no warning, no discussion. Totally unactable, written by committee with no awareness of silence or what it is that actors do.

Fuming, fuming until I speak to Eric [Hetzel, executive producer] and we get back to what they had chucked out. A pity that it has to get to me saying 'I'm not saying these words.'

22 DECEMBER

Glorious sunshine all day for umpteen exterior scenes which looked an impossibility on the call sheet. Somehow we made it with a lot of fleet-footed tap dancing on all fronts. What with the holidays, it was all v. good for company morale.

5ish Rima has arrived.

24 DECEMBER

More sunshine. From where?

11 Car to Washington.

Rain, fog. That's more like it.

For what it's worth, sitting in the car I feel I am turning some sort of corner. The past few days—what with rewriting two scenes—that made me surer about adapting a book at some point and letting new things in the door.

Bring it on 2004.

27 DECEMBER

4.30 → Dulles Airport for the 7am → San Juan.

1.40 → Antigua.

---

[1] Robert Caswell, screenwriter

4.30 Eventually make it to the jetty—Barbara & Ken [Follett] waiting to escort us to their truly fabulous house.

28 DECEMBER

Rima & Barbara are perfectly matched at Scrabble and she sorted out the remaining clues in the *Times* crossword.

7.30 To the Hotel for Barbecue Night. Said hello to Harvey Weinstein who didn't seem thrilled to be discovered—or it's my paranoia.

30 DECEMBER

6.30 Another cocktail party—more incredibly rich people in a house lifted from the Hollywood Hills via pharmaceutical millions.

2004

---

3 JANUARY
[filming *Something the Lord Made*]
Baltimore.
Mooching around all day.

4 JANUARY
5.30 pick-up and the continuing madness of shots first, acting second. One
of the scenes appeared to be entirely about Mos and a mop and a bucket.
Even the camera crew entreaties didn't shift Joe. Every take meant people on
their hands and knees towelling the floor dry again.

8 JANUARY

Los Angeles.

A night of vivid dreams. Sitting in some kind of auditorium—fun—and
finding Rima & me in the same row as Bush Snr and family (strangely no
G.W. anywhere). Bush Snr suddenly barks out topics of conversation. 'OK—
what do you have to say on—BEEF!?' I'm nudging R. to speak but there's a
mass silence.

9 JANUARY

Los Angeles.

Oh, my changing eyes and mind re Los Angeles. Still the perennial holiday
town but the celeb obsessed stuff is getting to me in a big way.

10 JANUARY

Los Angeles → Baltimore.

There's this band of always-the-same-ness about LA which is comforting in a way but underneath it is a band of something casual, feral, of-the-moment only, full of eyes staking you out—Are you someone? Were you someone? Do you give off 'any heat at all?' *Might* you? Although that would imply forethought, foresight, a kind of intelligence—and that is ultimately just an animal response—but not an animal that has any dignity or sense of its place in the world. This one has nervous, tight eyes, no sense of home, stays long enough to feed and move on.

11 JANUARY

Baltimore.

Some long chat between Mos and Joe had gone on. Look out of a window and go back to the hotel in full makeup and wait until 6pm to go back for the lecture theatre scene. Which is over at 11pm. So that's another 17 hour day with a close-up at the end of it.

Back at the hotel, there's a movie [*The Score*] with Brando, de Niro and Ed[ward] Norton in. Interesting to see de Niro utterly in control of Norton and utterly fazed by Brando (but was Brando even there?).

Then Larry King has a programme about James Dean. The Real Thing. Truthful, ageless, masculine, feminine. Adored by all.

17 JANUARY

Baltimore.

Day off.

To Barnes & Noble to find more gifts and some Jimmy Scott CDs.

19 JANUARY

To the set at 6.15pm. Dodgy part of Baltimore, Gabrielle[1] has her trousers nicked from her trailer. There's a knock on the door of mine. Outside a ten-year-old claiming to want an autograph.

---

[1] American actor Gabrielle Union (1972–)

29 JANUARY

Baltimore.

Last day.
   3.30 pick-up.
   And an amazingly swift rip through the last four scenes.

30 JANUARY

Baltimore.

7pm Wrap party.
   Hideous—loud (as in cannot hear a word anyone is saying and no one is dancing, so what's the fucking point?). Happily I got there early so there was still some food.

2 FEBRUARY

New York.

8 DEF POETRY. The Supper Club.
   Taping of Mos' HBO show. Marcia Firesten & I two of maybe 6 white people in the audience. It was like a rock concert but for poetry . . .

5 FEBRUARY
1pm Nina Darnton.
   God, will she ever relax and wonder what might happen instead of arranging everything in front of her. With options in case of disaster.
   Version two. Except more calculating, as well. But I love her for her courage. If only it wasn't mixed with being a bit of a madam.

6 FEBRUARY
11 Orso.
   Manage to almost walk past Lauren Bacall on my way back from the Gents. The inimitable voice stops me in my tracks. Sit down and listen to stories of UK/quarantine/dogs.

8 FEBRUARY
Home at 9-ish.
   Rima sick, on prescription drugs and not making a lot of sense.
   Wander round putting stuff in different places, wondering why I didn't stay in New York.

17 FEBRUARY

Michael Attenborough [theatre director] must be one of the most indiscreet people I've ever met—'I'm sorry if X is anyone's best friend but' should be his middle name. And not a good idea to have such open prejudice against actors while in the same room as an actor . . .

20 FEBRUARY

Paris.

6.30 Car to Waterloo Eurostar for 7.30 → Paris.

21 FEBRUARY

Walking, shopping at Issey M.

Gaspard de la nuit/Birthday dinner.

Very good food. Very family-run with someone who needs lessons from Eva at Patio in how to walk up and down your domain dispensing bonhomie rather than quiet alarm. But then the French gave us the word *froideur.*

25 FEBRUARY

Stephen Poliakoff. To dinner at the Cow. He wants to do an interview for the DVD release of *Close My Eyes.* Apart from that his mind as quixotic and lightning sharp as always. The chat has to be so specific otherwise a lazy half sentence is pounced on like a cat with a ball of string.

26 FEBRUARY

4.30 Dr Choy.

Who says (rightly) why is it men who have to get up in the night to pee, why is it that only boys are bedwetters? He thinks we can train ourselves out of this impulse but offers only vague ideas as to how.

27 FEBRUARY

2.30 Oval House, Brixton Road.

Workshop performance of Victoria Wood's *Acorn Antiques* musical. Trevor Nunn [director] was in the corner shop before it started and looked horror-struck that I was coming. After he left Richard E. Grant arrived. But we were, as it turned out, only there to laugh, applaud, and be entirely on their side. Brilliant structure, hilarious show, great songs, wonderful acting.

29 FEBRUARY

Somerset.

A beautiful sunny morning. Walk through the fields, down lanes, to the Margery Fish garden, to the pub for a drink. After, Miranda [Richardson] had taken me around the impending studio and the location of the planned lake. Late lunch after the family who have come to choose a puppy have left. A bit nerve-racking. Like being auditioned.

To London via Basingstoke—one of those seemingly endless Sunday journeys. But the memory of the Yeovil Station buffet lingers. Like something from a '40s film. Long modern counter, fire (false) in the grate.

1 MARCH

8.30 Aphrodite w. Ruby & Ed.

I don't know—Ruby buys a shopping trolley without checking. Ed was only half present—Maddy [their daughter] at home in pain with a new brace. Ruby drank an awful lot for her and it did all end in tears. I found myself staring at a situation I don't want to be part of.

4 MARCH

3pm Stephen Poliakoff—interview for *Close My Eyes* DVD. V. odd having to refer to 'Stephen said . . .' while I'm looking at him. And somewhat to my surprise he segues with slightly surprising (to borrow his vernacular) ease into *Die Hard* gossip. 'Have you told these stories before?' says the marketing director, aquiver.

Car to Olympia [antiques fair]. Bought 4 chairs. And a FontanaArte lamp.

6.45 Lincoln's Inn for Helena K.'s book launch, *Just Law*. And if the people in the room are the usual suspects—rounded up, then I'm v. content to be one of them, in this crazy Britain.

6 MARCH

[RADA away weekend]

Morning session at 9.

Generally this weekend still feels like the staff looking for validation of things they've already decided. There's a reluctance to be self-critical. Blame is such an easy option.

7 MARCH

1pm Joan Bakewell joins on her way to the Bath Festival. She has the perfect balance of curiosity and anecdote, discretion and indiscretion. That's why she's Joan Bakewell I guess.

9 MARCH

To the nursing home to see Auntie D. & Uncle V. The first sight of them is like a rite of passage—in their room, in their armchairs (having walked down a corridor with the smell of urine wafting along with me), both asleep, waxen. Awake, as usual Auntie D. does all the talking—how they love it here, the staff are wonderful, but worry because they've always paid their way . . . Here and there we trade some memories and Uncle V. silently weeps at the mention of people & places gone.

10 MARCH

To Argentina.

   7.15 → Madrid → 11.40 → Buenos Aires.

12 MARCH

9am *Touching the Void*.[1] They had to make a dramatisation because the 2 guys themselves are on a charisma bypass. But the shots are amazing and the ongoing dilemmas jaw-dropping.

14 MARCH

10.30 To the gym to get rid of the Argentinian beef calories.

17 MARCH

A rush through the rain attempting to make it to the auditorium in time for the Brazilian film, but the water is too deep to get out of the taxi—so back to the hotel to pack.

18 MARCH

Argentina.

To Isla Victoria, Lake Nahuel Huapi.

   On the plane to Bariloche—a lettuce sandwich, a roll containing meat & mozzarella with boiled egg on the top, hot tray of pork & prune kebab plus chicken on a piece of toast, all sitting in spinach & cheese & cream sauce; two more rolls, a packet of crispy tostadas and a cream horn with toffee sauce . . .

---

[1] 2003 film about two young climbers, Joe Simpson (Brendan Mackey) and Simon Yates (Nicholas Aaron), who come unstuck while climbing in the Andes

19 MARCH

11am Horse ride w. Marcus the guide and Marianna & Paulo—the only other guests in the hotel. She's a travel agent (how useful), he engineer/farmer. From Buenos Aires. Good thing Rima didn't come—it would have been too hairy for her. Down slopes, cantering, through thick branches, etc. But a dream realised. Riding in Patagonia.

20 MARCH

1pm Boat to the mainland and then to Peñon del Lago. Met by Raquel who says 'Ready for your tour?' Now I understand the meaning of 'seeing something of Bariloche'. Indeed, everything.

pm Rima gets the full birdwatching joy from the gardens outside the room. Ibis and lapwings by the dozen it seems.

21 MARCH

2.30 Car to Bariloche Airport. The point and double-takes and 'It is him!' took on a new edge when one of the culprits was Caroline Kennedy . . . [1]

NB We have talked of not handing over so much of the day to other people, other causes. This trip, this solitude, has reminded me of the time and space needed to be creative. Not to be so subject to others' whims. It will take a real clear out of the cupboard and a real strength of purpose.

22 MARCH

NB cont'd. Currently the phone rings too often and I answer it. Appointments clutter up the work. There should be clearer use of the day. Time to be fit, time to think.

31 MARCH

NB Take these trips more often—you can see the life you are living more clearly. Pack fewer clothes. Heavy suitcases are a misery. Don't slide back into the old habits. If there is a plan—live it.

10.50 Car to Westbourne T. in glorious sunshine.

Immediately unsettled. Unpacking, answering (or opening) mail, email, answerphone. The unutterable clutter of London life. And immediately people want pieces of you . . . watch it like a hawk . . . talking about work is confining not freeing—what does it mean? It all feels like a necessary evil—find myself resentful about ADR[2] and the press requests for *HP* (neither are creative so it's not surprising).

[1] Daughter of JFK
[2] Additional dialogue recording

12 APRIL

Stayed-at-home day. What on earth did I do? Except watch hours of stupid TV which somehow calms the mind in the face of the pile of unread material and the acreage of untapped brain. This has to *stop*.

While the apartment work goes on there has to be some stripping away as well as all that adding . . . If it becomes too much a comfort zone in an indiscriminate sort of way, a torpor sets in. Some rigour needs to be introduced.

8.45 Frontline w. Ruby & Ed.

This is, strangely, a comfort zone. Good and bad that. Old friends mean a space that can be dangerously unchallenging if we just take turns to announce what we're doing. There's so much familiarity but so much that's hidden.

13 APRIL

Swim at the new Health Club. Low lighting thank God. Steam room by the poolside and Starbucks on the way out.

2 Dexter called by for some lunch on the balcony. In the sun. I was being snappy. He looked alarmed.

7.45 *The Permanent Way* NT.

David Hare's play (directed by Max [Stafford-Clark]) about rail privatisation and the big crashes of recent years. Towards the end a character voiced what I had been feeling—'we don't do communal well in Britain'. No—we know how to give orders or how to grovel but getting us to work happily for each other—like pulling teeth. Hence the inevitable existence of the *Daily Mail*—all hate, envy and punishment. It's enough to make one pack all bags.

Later reading Gielgud's letters. Less than 30 years ago and there's nothing like that now. The acting community is all over the shop. Nests are being feathered, careers grabbed at. Must get back on stage and *enjoy it*.

16 APRIL

Figuring out flights/transfers.[1]

2pm Surgery for 4 injections and a prescription for malaria pills. Then I buy up half of Boots.

8pm River Cafe. Alan & Lindsay Rusbridger. Alan is much more relaxed than I've known him. Smaller numbers, maybe. Ruthie's guest list can be

---

[1] Re trip to Kenya

daunting. But her attention to her own detail has her asking us to review her latest waiter's checklist—Piercings? No. Sleeves rolled up? Don't care etc. She also has her verbal no-nos. As in 'enjoy', 'you guys' and such like crap. I was reminded also of the air stewardess who scaled Beckettian heights: 'Would you care for a beverage at this time?'

20 APRIL

Kenya.

Yesterday evening smothered in sadness by [casting director] Patsy Pollock's phone call. Through the tears she leaves a message telling us that Mary Selway is seriously ill—and hasn't long. Glorious Mary.

8.30 → LHR for the 10.25 → Nairobi.

Wrote a bit, read a bit—*The Sea, the Sea* [by Iris Murdoch]. Bewildering, really, cumulatively powerful & disturbing moment by moment in danger of comic melodrama.

Car to the Norfolk Hotel. Time to raid the mini-bar rather than test the rigours of room service. Thus dinner was 1 Diet Coke, 1 packet BBQ crisps, 1 packet cashews, 1 packet macadamia nuts (discarded—honey-coated). Watched Boston marathon [on] TV. Kenyans won everything.

And may these pages catch something of Simon Gray's *Smoking Diaries*— his portrait of the ginger-haired, lounger-thieving New Arrivals seems like something I have actually lived through.

21 APRIL

11.15 → On the plane to Malindi there's a 3-year-old who can really use her crying. Racked with sobs and then the endless pause while she gathers breath, looks around, has a think before *really* letting rip.

12.20 Nick Reding[1] collects and off to find the troupe and my hotel. '£50 a night, will that be OK?' A sentence not often heard. Lunch of fish & rice and off to the performance in a village Disney might have constructed. Band, drums, kids frightened of the camera, as the troupe is encircled by about 500, who listen and laugh as one. So many young girls with the baby sister/ brother strapped to their backs. It is a terrific performance by a very focused group of actors. Afterwards we career down a road to a boatyard café for a cold beer then back to the hotel for a shower.

---

[1] English actor (1962–)

23 APRIL

Mombasa → Nairobi.

7.45 To the clinic, to the apartment, to James' (troupe) house—to the buffet lunch restaurant—to the car pick-up—to the airport—to Nairobi.

Any other time I would be taking it all in with unclouded vision and I certainly did my best to be supportive but the shutters had come down and wouldn't lift. A mood that needs time or a juggernaut to shift.

Reading *Rough Guide*—somewhere in there a fine and accurate description of Mombasa. So much friendlier than the sense (all I can have) of Nairobi which is as screwed up as a city can be. Geoffrey talks to me of driving at night to Nairobi (not a good idea), of nails placed in the road to catch one tyre or another, of beggars holding babies that aren't babies, of never talking to anyone through the driver's window. It's gangland.

24 APRIL

Nairobi → Jo'burg → Cape Town.

At the passport/immigration/whatever desk the woman glances up and says, 'You look too serious to be an actor. You get all the serious parts?' 'Not always.' 'Then the sad ones . . .'

On the phone to the UK—and Mary Selway has died.

28 APRIL

Cape Town.

Lunch with Pearlie Joubert [journalist]—sharp & funny as ever esp. on subject of phone interview with British security forces re her trip to Zimbabwe. 'What would you do if someone pointed a gun at you?' 'Put my hands up, say hello sir, would you like a blow-job, if he said no—run like fuck.' 'This is not a laughing matter, madam.'

29 APRIL

On the plane reading more of Simon Gray's diaries. Very moving about his father and his brother, very funny about his cats and dogs. And the pages suffused with his love for his wife, largely because he mentions her only glancingly—you sense her beauty, and her grace and her laughter.

1.30 After killing some time in Hatchards where an incredibly courteous woman came up and said her simple, clear, heartfelt 'thank you'—to St James's for Mary Selway's funeral service. Sat with Paul Brooke,[1] other

---

[1] English actor (1944–)

friends all over. Simple and beautiful service, the church filled with pink and white peonies, for this great woman.

1 MAY

... a message from Sigourney W. talking about play in New York this summer ...

Also spoke to Ian McK. who had seen *Hamlet*[1] last night and was shocked at the general level of acting. But how crazy to have a profession & a press who are slavering and it's your first real exposure?

3 MAY

9.15 The Wolseley w. Juliet Stevenson and Mark [Shivas]. Not to mention Lucian Freud sitting at the table adjacent ... as was Bob Hoskins ... but L.F. for God's sake—with his beautifully tied tie.

6 MAY

9pm Rufus Wainwright at Dingwalls. Plangent would be the word. And he certainly enjoys making the sounds. A consonant here & there and hearts would crack. Talking to him afterwards he has a high-pitched giggle that comes as a shock.

7 MAY

What dreams. (1) Joan Collins. I'm interviewing her for a magazine about her time at RADA. She arrives in some foyer, taps me on the shoulder—has no makeup on & her hair is streaked grey. (2) Paola Dionisotti. With a length of grey cotton I'm sewing a little triangle of pretend pubic hair on to her trousers/skirt while she tells me of her frustrating time trying to give dialect lessons to some foreign star. [Richard] Attenborough comes in, says we have missed some important lunch.

I think it was the prawns.

13 MAY

7.45 *The History Boys*, NT.

Alan Bennett's new play. A glorious start stuffed with memories of schooldays and teachers. A paean to the most eccentric and gifted of them. Never mind the teachers who have died. I would love to watch this with Ted Stead. Griffo[2] wonderful, Frankie [de la Tour] like an incendiary. Clive M.[3] licking the plate clean.

---

[1] Directed by Michael Boyd with Toby Stephens as Hamlet
[2] English actor Richard Griffiths (1947–2013)
[3] Welsh actor Clive Merrison (1945–)

14 MAY

New York.

Nowadays it's par for the course—not packed at all for nearly 3 weeks away—somewhere in the back of my mind a subliminal knowledge of what has to be clean; not bothering about ironing—the hotel can do that—who is this person??

1.45 car to Heathrow. Crowd outside terminal. Some sort of scare. Anthony M. at check-in. Same flight, instantly reassuring.

6.45 New York.

To the Lowell Hotel.

15 MAY

8 *Jumpers*.

Stoppard bores me rigid again. Essie Davis gives it the star treatment. Simon [Russell Beale] . . . I wish someone would tell him not to be so lovable. It's like he needs a smack rather than a director.

18 MAY

Baltimore.

19 MAY

Baltimore → Los Angeles.

Profoundly hung over. This has to stop. I cannot stagger about like this—head (whose head? what head?) unconnected to neck, legs with a life of their own. Is this what they mean by alcohol being a poison?

21 MAY

Los Angeles.

Brain-tangling phone call where it's hard to frame a sentence let alone get a word in. Some people see the world through such a narrow lens. Widen the fucking aperture and solutions are visible all round you.

The Grove. Apple Shop.

Do I want a computer? Everyone else thinks so. There's someone tapping away opposite me as I write this. I think I prefer pen and paper. No wires for a start.

Talk to Stephen Poliakoff. The *Guardian* wants to do an interview for *Close My Eyes* DVD. Strangely close to the Potter opening . . . I think not.

22 MAY

Los Angeles → New York.

11.10 → New York.

I begin to pick up this journal like a homing pigeon. There's a definite urge to write coming from some left field. Maybe that's the reason for the word processor.

23 MAY

New York.

4pm *Harry Potter* 3. World Premiere.

Arriving at Radio City was like being a Beatle. Thousands of fans screamed as we got out of cars or became more visible. Mostly for Daniel Radcliffe but a rush for everyone. Not to mention walking out on to the stage to 6,000.

Alfonso has done an extraordinary job with this. It is a very grown up movie, so full of daring that it made me smile and smile. Every frame of it is the work of an artist and story-teller. Stunning effects that are somehow part of the life of the film, not show-off stunts. Later back to the hotel w. Eleni & Ariel Dorfman who takes egomania to utterly charming heights. He just *loves* being him.

25 MAY

5.30 Mike Nichols. They've moved upstairs to the penthouse—Diane [Sawyer, M.N.'s wife] was sleeping before the 3am wake-up for *GMA*.[1] Mike poured a couple of Bullshots and we went on to the wrap-around terrace—NY everywhichway—as usual the most all-embracing, civilised, witty, compassionate conversation—Bush, *Antony & Cleopatra*, Pacino, [M.N.'s] new musical, Kate Nelligan[2]—'I think she lost hope'—New Zealand . . . An elegant, verbal slalom. As I left: 'Remember—you're always number one.' And the heart lifts.

26 MAY

11.10 (11.30) → Toronto.

2.15 w. David Cronenberg to Prego for lunch. They say that the atmosphere on his set is always ace and I can believe it. Charm and good humour in spades but unerring eye for the specifics. We talk of *The Sea, the Sea* and seem to be on the same page.

---

[1] *Good Morning America*
[2] Canadian actor (1950–)

7.30 David Young collects me & we go look at his new house. Michael Ondaatje joins to go for drinks.

28 MAY

Toronto → London.

6.15am Heathrow.

Home sevenish. Mail, phone, clothes, email, etc.

I heard yesterday about David MacDonald's[1] funeral.

10am Kensal Green crematorium.

I felt like an observer if not an outsider—I had always found David slightly alarming but then they all were—my Gods of the seventies with their outrageous repertoire and 50p seats. British theatre legend and we *should* be there. Beautiful music, simple service, and then to the Chelsea Arts Club in Michelle Guish's car. Giles H.[2] was looking a bit haunted . . . and there was Philip[3] with his sweet and sourness.

30 MAY

5pm Car to drive to Leicester Square for *Harry Potter* London.

8 Screaming thousands (some since 5am apparently).

9.30 National History Museum for the party. Weirdly there's [a] VIP area which *of course* everybody wants to get into and not everyone can. Not sure if this isn't a little divisive . . .

31 MAY

11ish Orso. On the way in—Simon Gray is sitting at a table. He raises a hand in greeting. 'Mr Nichols,' I say—and it's 2 minutes before I realise. A letter in the morning . . .

1 JUNE

A letter is posted to Simon Gray.

8.30 Brian Cox's birthday party.

Chateau Brian as it's called. Although the Hacienda look is pure Hollywood Hills and rather wonderful in Camden Mews. Lulu there again. Roger & Sue Graef finally succeeded in giving me a lift home not before Ian Rickson talked of a play for me, Frances B. & Miranda. A multi-layered evening.

---

[1] Robert David MacDonald (1929–2004), Scottish playwright and theatre director, Glasgow Citizens Theatre

[2] Giles Havergal, theatre director (1938–), worked with RDM at Citizens Theatre

[3] Philip Prowse (1937–), theatre director and designer at Citizens Theatre

2 JUNE

a.m. listing the possibilities seems like an idea:

Manchester United Ruined My Life

Four Last Songs

Plague House

A Little Chaos

Pas De Trois

French movie

Snowcake

Mrs Farnsworth

The Royal Court play????

8 JUNE

11.30 Mansion House for RADA lunch—1.15 (w. The Queen).

The snapshots would be of milling about, people looking suddenly older, some in hats and palaver, men in red uniforms holding pikestaffs (the ones in glasses letting the side down). A feeling of having to accept our place in the Establishment, or not. Vivienne Westwood was there, for heaven's sake. The Queen in yellow laughing at Richard Wilson. Dickie A. with his finger unerringly on the button, mentioning the D-Day celebrations of Sunday. Working the socks off to enlist Donald Gordon[1] to the cause. But mostly—looking up to the gallery at the T-shirted students looking down—the sense of thirty years. And a shy pride at being there once.

20 JUNE

Home to a phone message from Lindsay saying she was off to the Dylan concert and did I want to come? Did I? It was raining and I was warm. Visions of mud and crowds put the skids on that. But I would have. I called back—she was already on her way. So—hopeless. But the offer to bring Adam Duritz and any stray Counting Crow back afterwards was leaped on and, later, confirmed . . . It was a great evening. From nowhere.

26 JUNE

France.

5am The alarm.

More watering the garden.

5.45am The car.

---

[1] South African businessman and benefactor

6.30am The airport.

7.40 (well 8.10) The flight to Nice.

Once there, the driver clearly has the wrong address. Phone Natasha Richardson, get right address and off we go for the one hour drive to Le Nid du Duc . . . [1] Mythical really and there are already a group of books that speak of it and its heyday in the '70s.

8.30 → St Tropez. Dinner at local restaurant up a side street past the serried ranks of yachts moored, each more bloated than the next, in the harbour facing the cafés.

Back at the house for limoncello, rosé, chocolates and games. Having read some of Tony Richardson's book,[2] I felt we were upholding a fine tradition from the days of Hockney, Schlesinger, Nicholson & Redgraves all.

27 JUNE

Under the vine reading and a phone call from Stephen Boxer[3] telling us that Peter Blythe has died. He'd been ill for a while, no one knew. Poor, poor Harriet [Walter, P.B.'s partner]. She's had enough this year. This awful year.

Dinner at the house. Much talk of how friends & family die, and on to the terrace chatting, listening to Richard Harris singing from *Camelot* and as a 3am reward—banging my head on a doorway and feeling the blood run down my forehead.

28 JUNE

Wake up. Head OK.

Supper at the house—lamb & ratatouille. Delicious as ever. Somewhere over the dessert N. mentions the E tablets she has and L. & R. having declined I join her for a bit of unknown territory. Some initial queasiness and then a lot of affection and chat (Ian McK. on the phone at this point), a walk around the garden, more drinks, more chat, eventually bed at 3am. Wide awake in the oddest way. Still today, accelerating mind. Par for the course, apparently.

30 JUNE

Home again thinking did that really happen? Were we in that glorious place—with all that recent history de nos jours . . . Hockney, Proctor, Vanessa. Lazing & laughing & playacting through the '70s & '80s with Tony Richardson as playmaster.

---

[1] Backdrop to a number of paintings by David Hockney
[2] *The Long Distance Runner: A Memoir*
[3] English actor (1950–)

3 JULY

David and I go to collect Uncle Vic to take him to see Auntie Dolly in hospital. She's less confused now, but it is a fairly unforgettable sight arranging two wheelchairs so that they can kiss each other goodbye.

11 JULY

Last *I'm Sorry I Haven't a Clue* in current series. Oh woe.

Phone call from David to say Auntie Dolly looking seriously unwell.

12 JULY

am Call to say Auntie Dolly has died. So it goes on and on. And only the clichés work. She didn't linger . . . it is better this way . . . well, no there is another way, surrounded by your family, at home. But these days? God rest her soul.

20 JULY

Auntie Dolly's funeral.

1.30 Car to Buchanan Court.

Factions of families gather in the forecourt, lobby and eventually dining room. It's a slow black-clad dance. Nobody knows the steps or the tunes.

3pm The cortege sets off after Uncle Vic emerges with Medea [cousin Eileen] on his arm. He moves slowly on the walker then stops and collapses in tears. It's a family pattern. And he *will* be laughing soonish. At the church Trevor [Arwen's cousin] sits alone on a bench, his black-clad Greek chorus of nieces as far away as possible. The service has an honesty that was good. The pub was basic. Family day out. The worst of it side-stepped.

26 JULY

6.10pm *Fahrenheit 9/11*.

I don't care what they say. M. Moore is brilliant and all the carping from the vested interests cannot detract from the sickening truths that run through this v. important film.

31 JULY

11am pick-up → Chiswick Town Hall. *Vogue* Christmas shoot. Not quite sure how and why I said yes to this.

26 AUGUST

Starting to clear out what might be called the press/PR cupboard. Really rather depressing. Predictably so, I suppose, once one starts to reread interviews, see photographs etc. The brave thing would be to dump it all. I think

I'm moving towards it. Find some kind of essence. A few vaguely sensible sentences, a few unselfconscious photographs. Certainly with all the recent cleaning, the air is lighter around me. I shall persevere.

29 AUGUST
With David to see Uncle Vic. 'Hello strangers' was his fair enough greeting and then he breaks down at the door of the bathroom. Then walks, sits, smiles, breaks down. Clearly takes *everything* in. Chats, sleeps, watches TV. Goes for his lunch.

David & I come home and watch Amir Khan[1] not win a gold medal. Ludicrous expectations but what's new?

2 SEPTEMBER
12 Sarah Shurety, Feng Shui expert. The surname should be a new noun. Her surety left me a bit poleaxed. The space is dangerously awry—something that I have been feeling strongly. Her analysis—too masculine, no resting places, too much metal, water flowing wrongly.

14 SEPTEMBER
Back to *HP*.

7.40 *HP*. Sc. 94.

There could be a new agency called Glorified Extras. It would include Maggie Smith, Michael Gambon, Robert Hardy, Miranda Richardson, Robbie Coltrane, Frances de la Tour, never mind the kids. This is just one of those scenes that goes on and on—something happens—and then it continues with lots of group work and little dialogue.

15 SEPTEMBER
HP.

7am pick-up.

Today we are running *in*to the arena to administer some bizarre liquid.

17 SEPTEMBER

Los Angeles.

19 SEPTEMBER
3pm Judy arrives. Into the limo and to the Shrine Auditorium for the 2004 Emmy Awards.[2]

---

[1] British boxer (1986–)

[2] A.R. was nominated for Best Actor for *Something the Lord Made*, but the award went to Al Pacino.

26 SEPTEMBER

7pm Memorial for Alan Bates. Beautiful man, beautiful occasion. Amazing roll-call of memories—Sheila Ballantyne, Malcolm McDowell, Alan Bennett, Keith Baxter,[1] Eileen Atkins,[2] Frankie de la T[our], Celia I[mrie] etc., etc. His talent deepened all the time. Reminded again that actors have big all-embracing hearts.

28 SEPTEMBER

HP.

7.55 pick-up.

Smacking the backs of Daniel [Radcliffe] & Rupert [Grint]'s heads—doubtless a fuss will ensue about corporal punishment.

29 SEPTEMBER

7.10 pick-up.

Back to the head banging. In a way it becomes an interesting exercise justifying total silence with some mild physical abuse thrown in.

3 OCTOBER

Lunch—Kathy Lette and Geoffrey Robinson.[3]

Maybe only Kathy could put together Bianca Jagger, John Mortimer, Kylie & Dannii Minogue, Helena Kennedy, Frida (from ABBA), Joyce Hytner,[4] plus a bunch of kids, throw in Scrabble and make it all work. Mid conversation Frida suddenly asks 'Do you have psoriasis?' and gives me a telephone number of a clinic she's connected to. Kathy had said in an email she's rather reclusive and interesting.

Later at home, bizarrely, after taking a visiting Sean B[iggerstaff] out for curry, there's ABBA on Channel 5. We wave our arms around to 'Dancing Queen', 'Fernando' and 'Chiquitita'.

4 OCTOBER

A day and a half.

9.30 Goldcrest to do the voice of Marvin in *Hitchhiker's Guide to the Galaxy* which we complete by 1.30. My voice a bit sarf London but me for now.

5 OCTOBER

10.30 Royal Court.

Meeting w. Elyse Dodgson [theatrical producer] and Katharine

---

[1] Welsh actor (1933–)
[2] English actor (1934–)
[3] Labour politician (1938–), married to Kathy Lette
[4] Mother of theatre director Nick Hytner

Viner.[1] Katharine has done some valuable early interviews and collating but is learning about non-linear approaches and non-specific deadlines.

13 OCTOBER

7.10 pick-up for → *HP*.

Off set much utterly unmissable chat between Maggie and Michael about days at the NT, Olivier, Coward, Edith Evans then talk of what's upcoming. 'Serena (Ian McK.) is doing his Dame,' says Michael. At first I thought he'd said '*Arena* is doing the Dame.' 'Judi?' I enquired to blank faces. Once corrected, I proffered, 'That'll be packed.' 'With what?' says Maggie.

18 OCTOBER

HARRY POTTER.

2 words. Completely meaningless ones. Various times, various angles and then we're out of there. This could be stir crazy time.

20 OCTOBER

2.30 → more sitting down in the Great Hall. 'Which expression did you use?' says Maggie. Earlier Zoë had called. Did I think she should play La Poncia in *Bernarda Alba*? I couldn't raise huge enthusiasm. Zoë said Maggie had originally been asked to play B.A. Her responses ranged from 'I don't want to play that ghastly old bag' to 'Whatever happened to light comedy?' To me she said 'I mean, can you imagine me saying "The men are still in the fields . . ."'

21 OCTOBER

6.30 Peter Mandelson's leaving party. Odd to be apologising for leaving as one arrives. Through a glass darkly I lip read Andrew Rawnsley[2] saying 'Quite a week' to Geoff Hoon.[3] Sally Greene[4] chilly as per usual, Gail Rebuck[5] still wants a book.

29 OCTOBER

HP.

9am The Trophy Room—which after a few stories may be renamed the Ben Kingsley Room or as Duncan Heath says later . . . it would be in his contract to make it the *Sir* Ben Kingsley Room. What makes someone so

---

[1] With whom A.R. was working on *My Name Is Rachel Corrie*
[2] British journalist (1962–)
[3] Labour politician (1953–), then Secretary of State for Defence
[4] Chief executive of the Old Vic
[5] Chief executive of Random House UK

obsessed by all that stuff? Not a trace from Michael, Ian, Maggie, Judi etc., etc. The most profound insecurity I suppose.

11 NOVEMBER

HP.

7.15 pick-up.

In Dumbledore's office with Maggie . . . My speech is unlearnable. So some serious laughing goes on. Plus Maggie's stories of the *Ladies in Lavender* premiere: 'Miriam Margolyes looked like a Sherman tank in sequins.'

15 NOVEMBER

3pm Cutter and Gross [opticians] to get Rima an eye test and new glasses. Staggering prices . . .

Today I made the *Vogue* list and was a question on *University Challenge* (they hadn't a clue).

17 NOVEMBER

HP.

7.15 pick-up.

Running in, pointing a wand. Expensive *Dr Who* stuff. Maggie and Michael really beginning to tire now—as in join the queue—of this monumental waste of energies.

23 NOVEMBER

HP.

7.15 pick-up.

For the only Snape v Potter scene of the film and of course I get shafted. First, the line-up at 8 was with a stand-in. Why not tell me beforehand—we are basically rehearsing. Then the announcement which said they were going for a ridiculous number of set-ups. So we all had to be super-on-the-ball, please.

7 DECEMBER

HP.

7.40 pick-up.

Great Hall. Yule Ball . . . An attempt was made to get me to dance. Why? With whom? For what reason? Better to not be there, but if that is not an option then he would, quite unselfconsciously, just observe.

8pm Home to news of inflammatory headlines in the *Independent* re

Rachel Corrie[1] project. Of course the journalist at the Women in Film Awards was from the *Mail* and not from the *Independent* as she claimed.

Later talking to Sigourney about *Mrs Farnsworth* and *Snow Cake*. If our combined wills were enough.

8 DECEMBER
HP.

Two days of just standing very still, applauding twice, and watching the others dance.

But also two days of real progress with the Rachel Corrie piece. So much so that coupled with yesterday's shenanigans—it might even lead us not to include much (if any) of the Gaza material. Her journey seems so detailed already.

13 DECEMBER
HP. LAST DAY?

7am pick-up.

Last scene with Pedja[2] who I rudely described as [like] working with a sideboard on wheels. Nothing to do with him as a (complex, delightful) person but more to do with the way he manages to bang into you at any opportunity.

I feel so shafted on this film with all Mike's[3] best motives. He's under pressure (like Alfonso) and everything is about the shot. We only talk about the scene on about take 4. *Plus ça change.*

2.30 *My Name Is Rachel Corrie.* First reading.

21 DECEMBER
Heathrow → Hong Kong.

2pm Car → Heathrow.

Where we discover that we aren't going to Shanghai (no visa) but can go to Hong Kong. A better option as it turns out since there are four flights a

---

[1] Rachel Corrie, who was born in the United States in 1979, visited Gaza as a student and became involved in the campaign to prevent the demolition by the Israeli army of Palestinian houses. On 16 March 2003, she was crushed to death by an Israel Defense Forces armoured vehicle. Whether this was a deliberate act or an accident is disputed. In 2005, her parents, Craig and Cindy Corrie, filed a civil lawsuit against the state of Israel. That same year, A.R. and the journalist Katharine Viner produced the play *My Name Is Rachel Corrie*. It opened in London and was to transfer to the New York Theatre Workshop but was postponed indefinitely, which A.R. denounced as censorship. Eventually, it opened off Broadway on 15 October 2006, having earlier been part of the Edinburgh Fringe.

[2] Predrag Bjelac, Czech-Serbian actor (1962–)

[3] Mike Newell, director

day to Manila from there. After a bit of toing and froing at Hong Kong Airport . . . we opt for staying overnight. Peninsula Hotel. Spectacular views of the spectacular harbour.

Supper on 28th floor of One Peking . . . They warned us about the spicy cabbage rolls but we went ahead. I managed one, Rima a half. Mouths aflame.

22 DECEMBER
Hong Kong → Manila.

24 DECEMBER
Manila → Amanpulo.

25 DECEMBER

Amanpulo.

Awake at 5.20? Waiting for the dawn—make some tea, watch CNN on repeat, get up, eat mangoes, drink bucks fizz, open presents, go to clubhouse for breakfast, back to Casita to lie on beach lounger, to boathouse to watch children from neighbouring island dance in brilliant red, white, yellow & pink clothes—not a smile in sight but with the lightest of hands and feet, back to the lounger, up to the Casita for pedicure/manicure to the strains of 'That's Amore'—Dean Martin from the Christmas gift CD as I doze fitfully and dream crazily—all the time reading Geoff Dyer's *Yoga for People Who Can't Be Bothered to Do It*—or did I read it? Or did I write it? Must ask him. All lines are blurred. Possibly by how seductive is all this perfection and how—arranged . . .

7.30 Turkey dinner. But boneless with prune? Walnut? Stuffing & mash. Perfect.

2005

1 JANUARY

Amanpulo.

The tsunami[1] stories endlessly coming in on CNN & BBC World. It seems like time is standing still—ironic given the date.

4 JANUARY

Manila → Hong Kong → New York.

7 JANUARY

Heard today that Lord Attenborough lost a daughter and granddaughter in the tsunami.

    5pm Sigourney W. to the hotel for a drink.

9 JANUARY

New York → London.

    9.10 → Heathrow. Being recognised has perks when you are escorted and cosseted like this. And Virgin's flat beds meant that we got about 3 hours' sleep.

12 JANUARY

I had been fairly pissed off at the fact that work[2] had gone on in my absence and without my knowledge but in a way it became very focusing to compare the two edits.

---

[1] On 26 December 2004 an earthquake struck the west coast of Sumatra, Indonesia, generating a series of enormous waves with devastating and far-reaching effect. It is estimated that at least 227,000 people were killed in fourteen countries, the worst affected of which were Indonesia, Malaysia, Maldives, Myanmar, Sri Lanka, Seychelles, Thailand and Somalia. It was the single worst tsunami in modern history.

[2] On *My Name Is Rachel Corrie*

What emerges is hopefully an accurate portrait and something that Megan[1] can inhabit and reinvent.

15 JANUARY
Somewhere this week, Prince Harry goes to a fancy dress party wearing a shirt with a swastika on the sleeve. Idiot. But how predictable to see the tabloids pounce and it is like another tsunami seeing the front pages and headlines cleared to make room.

22 JANUARY
Harrods. Last day of the sale. Time to spend more money. Buy more clothes. And especially an espresso/cappuccino maker.

25 JANUARY
11.30 Royal Court.

Working through notes and alternative versions. The job now is not to lose its musicality whilst allowing some leeway in. The Corrie family are apparently happy, and feel that we have caught the real Rachel. A huge plus.

27 JANUARY
5.30 To David Hare. Who seems to talk about the production rather than the text which is reassuring in a way—and it's good to have those questions asked. In the manner of a scythe.

31 JANUARY
Rima's birthday.

1pm Royal Court—Matt Hood from Equity. The problem of collecting subscriptions when the union is no longer a closed shop, and rich actors say 'Why am I paying this money?'

1 FEBRUARY
7 Chloe Fremantle's private view. Curwen Gallery. Her paintings are like herself contained, courteous, sensitive, searching, full of the past, infused with something less tangible than the present. Alan Hollinghurst was there. I bet he admires their elegance and daring.

24 FEBRUARY
11 Royal Court.

First half—35 mins.

---

[1] American-British actor Megan Dodds (1970–), playing Rachel Corrie

Full of joys. I find myself searching for the political animal and we talk about all of that quite openly.

Lunch.

Second half—50 mins.

Will be faster but it means the whole evening will be 1½ hours.

Clearly work to do but here is the end of a massive first phase. Now it's a period of learning for Megan before we start again on the 7th. Where the personal/political balance will be number one consideration . . .

27 FEBRUARY

Paris.

Late am Carnavalet Museum. Mme de Sévigné's rooms . . .

1.20 To Isabelle [Huppert]'s apartment. For a cup of tea. Brave soul—her home has the decorators, she's trying to pack and she has a matinée.

3pm *Hedda Gabler*. The slowness, the attention to detail, the epic rather than the domestic scale, it all had. It felt like Greek tragedy. And Isabelle was mesmeric & detailed and magnificent.

4 MARCH

12 Cosimo & Paloma.

To talk of Campagnatico which, hopefully, will be done by June. Back to choosing taps and toilets.

7 MARCH

12 Start working with Megan.

Not at my best. And Megan slips so easily on to the back foot—a comfortable place—with one eyebrow raised. But we press on and there are some great discoveries.

9 MARCH

. . . brave, beautiful Sheila Gish has died. It was like a slow crescendo. But so desperately unfair. Impossible to make much sense except the humbling courage.

13 MARCH

5.15 Car → Guildhall. *Empire* Awards. More like 5.40 dash. But all is OK. They haven't sat down when we got there. Kevin Smith, Jennifer, Jason, Matt Damon, Mel & Pam, Helen M., etc., etc., etc. Stephen Frears—of course—

free meal. Made speech, gave award to Kevin. Later took them all to Waterloo Bridge—the only bit of sightseeing they have done in 5 days.

16 MARCH

Second anniversary of Rachel Corrie's death.

12 Meeting with press and front of house to discuss strategy and possible interviews.

Rehearse. After lighting a candle next to some flowers and Rachel's picture.

22 MARCH

Sheila Gish's funeral.

12 St Michael's Church, Highgate.

The applause started as Sheila's coffin—covered with painted sunflowers—came up the aisle. This was totally secular and started off brilliantly by Frankie de la Tour—Shall I compare *thee* to a summer's day? We all sang B.B. King. Lindsay—*Meals on Mules*—wonderful. And so it went on towards the massive applause.

6 No 1 The Aldwych. People still hanging on to each other in the bar when I got there. Then a bunch of us went downstairs for dinner with Denis,[1] who looked calm, watchful and on a nearby, other, planet.

27 MARCH

9am → Toronto.

[Re *Snow Cake*]

30 MARCH

9 pick-up to go trampolining which I seem to have a fairly predictable talent for. Mix dance and high jumping I guess. Unsurprisingly, like skiing, I also sense the thrill of danger and start jumping too high too soon . . .

12 Read through.

3 APRIL

10.35 To rehearsal rooms.

For a day of, basically, letting Sigourney stretch her wings, arms, legs until the point where I had to call her on the incessant rewriting of a script we've just spent a week *writing*. Why oh why do they all do this? It means no value is given to silence or thinking—just fill the air with improvised garbage—always have the last line in a scene.

---

[1] Denis Lawson, Scottish actor and director (1947–) and Sheila Gish's husband

5 APRIL

9 pick-up for trampolining. I could get used to this. The moment where you 'hang' is supposed to be very health-giving.

6 APRIL

6.15 Toronto → London.

7 APRIL

Slept 4 hours. Thank you, little white pills.

7.45 *My Name Is Rachel Corrie*. First preview. I find myself mentally blotting out all the good stuff and focusing only on where it needs to get on with it. But Megan is amazing and there is nothing but massive approval for the work afterwards. Including 'praise indeed' from Edna.

8 APRIL

Kath Viner's piece is in the *Guardian* today and is very good for the whole enterprise. A slight stab of wondering if I have been too self-effacing. But as I keep saying, this is all about Rachel and her family.

3.15 Heathrow → Toronto.

12 APRIL

Wawa [township in Ontario, where *Snow Cake* is being filmed].

5.30 wake up.

6.05 Back to car wreck and the very disturbing sensation of being strapped in upside down in a car. Followed by backward tumbling down a slope. Followed by shock/vomit work.

Back at the log cabin and into the bath. Or more accurately lie down in the shower tray.

14 APRIL

Wawa.

Last night [in London] the audience stood for Megan. She looked at Craig & Cindy and burst into tears.

Spoke to Ian [Rickson] at the Court. He wants to move the show downstairs in August.

1pm Called Megan in her dressing room. Seeming calm. Ready. Proud. Attagirl.

pm As far as accuracy is concerned, working with Sigourney is like working with an autistic. As I told her, the job is going to be about her need for freedom—absolutely right—and my need for tension in the scene as well. Conundrum.

15 APRIL

Wawa.

5.42am. The other person that lives in my brain box is already up and dressed. Metaphorically, since I'm actually trying to get back to sleep. Too much to think about in order to cancel out brainbox person. So light on. Pick up pen. The main superficial brood subject is that S.W. has the personal hair and makeup people and that these ministrations are done in a special raised area in the van. Not sure that this elitism (which I find hilarious in other circumstances) is useful on this occasion.

18 APRIL

Wawa.

Somewhere around lunchtime phone Megan in her dressing room. Saturday pm she was wasted . . . and if there is any future for this show she needs to be paid properly. But the reviews are the kind which begs the show to have a longer life so the pressure will be on.

21 APRIL

Wawa.

Another 14-hour day.

A phone call from Judy Hoflund who is spending the next 6 weeks in England producing a film of *As You Like It*. This was the first time she'd mentioned it. Why do I find this mind-frazzling?

19 MAY

Toronto.

8.45 pick-up.

Filming the goodbye between Alex [A.R.'s character] and Linda [S.W.'s character] was appropriately matter of fact and throat-catching. In a way it matched the mood on the set. When you've all been so close and now you'll probably never see most of these people again. And this has been, with all the high-nooning with S.W., the most incredibly *shared* experience I've ever had. A real *journey*.

11 The worst anti-climax imaginable. Gina [Carter, producer] & Jessica [Daniel, producer] walk towards me, the crew whizz banging behind me, and say 'We're pulling it—it's going to take an hour to light.' If only I had thought more clearly I would—and should—have said 'Liars—it's not about

light it's about money.' As it was we just sizzled & puttered our way to the wrap party in a coitus interruptus daze.

1 JUNE

Vancouver/Tofino.

3 JUNE

Tofino.

Whale-watching trip. One glimpse of a grey whale's back and several spouts of spray.

Back to the hotel pm while Rima is on the birdwatching trail. Watch the birth of new superstar Rafael Nadal known in Spain as Rafa. Even the name works everywhere.

8 Shelter [restaurant].

Really good cooking of the thick-pork-chop-on-mashed-potatoes-plus-asparagus-&-port-jus variety.

Too much of my journals seem to be about food and almost nothing about exercise . . . and the waistline expands . . .

4 JUNE
Tofino → Sooke Harbour.

5 JUNE
Sooke → Victoria → Seattle → Olympia.

2.15 Seattle—Cindy & Craig Corrie there to collect us. And now begins the strange journey past road signs, down streets I know so well but have never visited before.

6 JUNE

Olympia.

9.15 Wander along the boardwalk, Craig coming towards us. A coffee in the market by the water.

'Hey, are you that actor guy?'

Well, that's a label.

'What? Sorry—didn't mean to offend.'

7 JUNE
Seattle → Laguna.

25 JUNE

Laguna → LA.

29 JUNE

Los Angeles → London.

    5.30 Virgin → London.

    Robbie Williams on the flight, presumably free (why would he want the hassle and general bus station of it all?) and on his way to Live 8 concert.

7 JULY

The day the bombs hit London. Absolute pillar to post—from the euphoric yesterday[1] to the numbness of today. A bus and three? four? stations. Hundreds injured and (as of today) 37 killed.

    Bush has the nerve to talk of 'the killing of innocent people' and Blair feels it necessary to use his 'I am moved' voice. Real tragedy wherever you look from whatever angle but threaded with hypocrisy as ever.

    Newsnight has Paxman pressing his tired old buttons in, of all people, Tony Benn who as far as I can see is making perfect sense.

    We stayed home all day. Answered worried phone calls. Watched TV. Stared at it all.

20 JULY

London → Rome → Campagnatico.

    4.30 Paloma plus Claudio, Lia and others are there looking slightly amazed that the house is habitable at all. Paloma with a dab of white paint on her cheek. She and Cosi have done a wonderful job. There's a terrace. There are bathrooms. Storage. It's a house let free.

25 JULY

The others head off to the beach. I stayed to give job list to Claudio. Just as well. As Lia is leaving she points out that the electricity is off. Call Paloma, call Claudio, call Raimondo—who comes and says it's nothing to do with his work. I have Yellow Pages, its ENEL[2]—find ENEL bill, call them, 40 mins later they arrive, slip switch outside and leave. Me none wiser. LEARN ITALIAN.

7 AUGUST

11 Uncle Vic—who apparently is doing really well, but his first words were 'Alan! My, you're getting tall . . .'

---

[1] London had just won the bid to host the 2012 Olympics.
[2] Italian energy company

15 AUGUST

The flight no one wants to make. To Toronto for Luke Greenblatt's funeral. Just before leaving, a message from Kate [Luke's mother] asking me to speak. Spent some of the flight writing it. Which got some of the tears out of the way.

20 AUGUST

→ Barcelona—*Perfume*.

5ish Ritz (but incorporating dispute, now Palace) Hotel.

This could be time for foot-stamping. Certainly a time for yelling 'Hello?' since there was nobody on Reception and the concierge wasn't budging. 'Not *today*,' was the horrified response to a request for a DVD. Lonely little mini-bar, limited room service, polyester pillows.

21 AUGUST

New pillows, extra hangers, DVD player on its way.

22 AUGUST

4pm Riding lesson.

23 AUGUST

Day One, *Perfume*.

24 AUGUST

Late pm pick-up. Rehearsal w. Ben Whishaw and eventually shoot bedroom scenes with him and Rachel [Hurd-Wood]. Tom [Tykwer, director] maintains extraordinary temperament—detailed, enthusiastic, supportive and hallelujah—two [able directors] in a row—*vulnerable*.

Back at the hotel at 5.20am.

25 AUGUST

Sleep till 12.30.

4.30 pick-up.

On Tambo the Big Black Horse. Legs too short to jack-knife me into the saddle.

Home at 2am.

26 AUGUST

7pm To the set w. Rima and Arlene who hang out heroically 1am-ish for dinner. I'm less heroic given the agony of my shoes.

7am Back to the hotel → for bacon & eggs ... Half of my brain says 'stay up—you're awake now'—the sensible half says 'no you're not' and I collapse into bed and sleep until 2pm.

29 AUGUST

3pm Press Conference.

'Rachel, how is it to be so beautiful?'

'Alan, what are the smells of Barcelona?'

5 SEPTEMBER

The town square week starts. Go to the set & watch 750 people get naked.

8.45 Casa Calvet.

Calvet family house by Gaudí. The restaurant is in what were his offices. Utterly beautiful—white tiles, polished floors, wooden compartments, stained glass. Appalling food. Ben (of simple food tastes) gets an unannounced pile of pasta in squid ink.

10 SEPTEMBER

pm Kevin Spacey calls from his dressing room during the tech for *Richard II*. He talks of having loved working with Trevor Nunn, I tell him of walking through a crowd of 750 naked fucking people and the urge to lift a mini camera from the costume pocket. 'Make friends with the stills photographer,' he says, wisely.

They want me to be in Arthur Miller's *Resurrection Blues*, to be directed by Altman in February. Hmmm.

26 SEPTEMBER

Navata (Figueres).

10.40 pick-up and out almost to the French border. Beautiful piece of countryside . . . for the ride into the mountains.

Rambo (my horse) of course gets freaked out by 1½ inches of water (it was a grating last time) so everything is delayed while he is acquainted with it.

30 SEPTEMBER

Figueres (Navata).

3pm Drive to Barcelona Airport.

6.30 → London.

3 OCTOBER

5pm Ann McFerran for an interview—*Sunday Times*.

   Still they want to talk about stuff from 20 years ago or *HP, HP, HP*.

   Should I be surprised . . . ?

9 OCTOBER

8 Dinner for Sebastian Barry, Alison, Chris, Ruby & Conor.

   Pre Booker Prize.

   Sebastian his fluid mix of wise and boyish. 'Get your hands in clapping position' is our concerted advice.

10 OCTOBER

Sebastian didn't win (John Banville did).

13 OCTOBER

7.30 Preview. 'A disaster' strikes Megan in the dressing room. Hardly, but the piece has inbuilt dangers if she sits back on it too much. Tonight was a demonstration of how hard she has to *work* at this piece. One or two sections carry her but the rest is full of ideas and images which have to be realised and shaped here and now.

14 OCTOBER

7 Press night.

   Megan on utterly inspired form. One of the great nights ever in the theatre. A full house completely inside the play with her. I stood at the back [and] glanced occasionally at the concentration on the audience's faces. Made 6 notes. Breathed out.

16 OCTOBER

Figueres.

11.15 → Barcelona.

   8pm pick-up.

   For the torture chamber in a castle (17th c.) which had housed 30,000 soldiers at one time. Now it's home to a big vat of water for Ben to be doused in. Turns out the scene also includes a voice saying 1–2–3 before each dousing. What would Stanislavsky suggest? Somehow we make it through and then there's clapping and goodbye Richis [A.R.'s character] and flowers. Was it paranoia that made me think the flowers were not so much presented as thrust . . .

17 OCTOBER

Figueres.

4am to bed.

8am Hear the cars coming back from the set.

8.30[pm] Wrap party in the Spa Restaurant which actually turned out to be a v. good venue. I . . . was forced into making a speech of sorts . . . Then Ben hits the microphone and says, quite rightly, 'No one's listening anyway—let's get drunk.'

25 OCTOBER

6pm Chelsea College Lecture Hall.

Interview/chat with Andrew Marr. Who is brilliant at simultaneously listening acutely and moving it on before I get too entrenched anywhere. It gives me the oddest sensation—almost pleasant—of being candid *and* discreet.

28 OCTOBER

Los Angeles.

1.55 → Los Angeles.

Judy H. and Bianca Jagger on the plane. They were both at the play last night.

29 OCTOBER

7.15 Marcia collects me and we're off to the Kirk Douglas Theatre for a benefit for the homeless. Alfre [Woodard], Don Cheadle, Eva Mendes, Morgan Freeman, Marisa Tomei, Tim Robbins. And at the piano a few feet away and worth the ticket alone—Tom Waits. V. well put together hour or so of testimonies and T.W. sang 3 songs. I sat sort of floating during 'Waltzing Matilda'.

9.30 Four great words—I MET TOM WAITS. Who turns out to be stylish, gentle (which those plangent piano chords now seem to suggest, totally).

31 OCTOBER

7.10 pick-up. *Nobel Son*. Day One.

3 NOVEMBER

Los Angeles.

To the Park Plaza Hotel.

'Hello Lindy,[1] I'm Alan.'

And straight into sex across the office desk.

7pm Sit at lunch (dinner) with Mary [Steenburgen] & Ted Danson [talking] of things in general and US specific . . . Mary talks of Bill Clinton with real affection and admiration about his lack of vanity and passion for problem solving. Ted with *all* his instant recognisability is all curiosity.

4 NOVEMBER

3 women take their clothes off and we do *in flagrante* poses. 'Hello. Do you mind if I hook my thumb in your G String?'

7 NOVEMBER

A fax from David Johnson [producer] full of his support for *My Name Is Rachel Corrie* and containing news of Maureen Lipman's piece in the *Guardian*.

8 NOVEMBER

In the car on the way to the set I start composing a letter to Maureen Lipman. Doubtless it could become a standard letter.

28 NOVEMBER

12.45 *Evening Standard* Theatre Awards lunch.

Talked to Maureen Lipman about her Rachel Corrie remarks in the *Guardian*—I now have the feeling she has confused the [Royal] Court with the Hackney Empire.

Brian Friel and I exchanged mimes. ME-YOU-WRITE./I-YOU-WRITE./GET-ON-WITH-IT-THEN.

30 NOVEMBER

TheatreGoer.com nominations. We are nominated in Best Solo Performance, Best Play & Best Director.

pm Elyse Dodgson calls to say that *MNIRC* has been nominated for a *South Bank Show* Award—along with *Mary Stuart* and *The Philanthropist*.

The *Standard* is beginning to look plain rude. Or censored, perhaps.

---

[1] Lindy Booth, Canadian actor (1979–)

1 DECEMBER

8.30am. 149 Harley Street, Professor Justin Vale.

Finally all the Doctor's entries from June come to a diagnosis. Call it PC.[1] Justin Vale is clear and hopeful. It's the brain, the will, everything clamps down like the metal sides on those jam jars. He says you won't hear a word. I strain to hear *every* word.

I sat with his receptionist making appointments and getting BUPA clearance. This is all happening on a cloud.

A dizziness and a blackness seems in danger of swamping me. This may be a diary too far.

2 DECEMBER

Talk to Jeremy L. who has been there and is wonderfully calm and sensitive.

A message on the machine from Jeremy—did I want him to come over? A friend.

7 DECEMBER

Enjoyed hanging out at home in a dressing gown for most of the day. This is all a big clue—to stop *running* so much. And to *run* (as in exercise) a bit more.

8 DECEMBER

3[pm] 149 Harley Street. MRI.

9 DECEMBER

Kath Viner calls to tell me that Maureen Lipman has said 'Mea culpa' in today's *Guardian*. Good for Maureen.

15 DECEMBER

6 And finally news from Justin Vale's secretary that the scans are clear.

20 DECEMBER

8pm Sting and Trudie's Russian Imperial party in their new/old house in Queen Anne's Gate. Horse drawn carriages outside (we went round the block later) . . . A snow-covered garden leading on to a snowstorm in St James's Park . . . A caviar corner . . .

---

[1] A.R. was diagnosed with prostate cancer.

22 DECEMBER

The Lister Clinic. Grosvenor Rooms.

To talk through the options. I'm not really any clearer. Each consultant pressing the claims of his own speciality.

6–9 Helena and Iain.

Alastair Campbell on free and easy form. I gave him my little spiel on how I've never met a *curious* politician—one who asks questions rather than makes little speeches—exceptions, on reflection, are of course Neil Kinnock and now I think of it Robin Cook.

23 DECEMBER

. . . the heat has disappeared again.

28 DECEMBER

9.30 car → Heathrow → New York.

30 DECEMBER

11am *Munich*.

It's like Spielberg is already on to his next film while he's shooting the one we're watching . . . so what we get has an aridity to it. And its admirable efforts to be non-judgemental render it soulless.

2006

4 JANUARY

2pm → Nashville.

3.30 Collected and taken to Vanderbilt for pre-op talks and to meet Dr Jay Smith[1]—calm, centred and sensitive man.

5 JANUARY

5am Wake up.

5.45 Driven to the hospital.

6am Pre-op.

This is like a film set. Nothing seems real.

Remembering nothing but with that painkiller high in the recovery room. Attentive, caring people.

To my room. David, the ace nurse awaits. Rima is there (with book).

pm Dr Smith calls in.

9pm Rima goes back to the hotel after we watch with sublime irreverence *Dancing with the Stars*.

The new details *de jour* are all about various pain control positions or drugs and tubes seemingly everywhere.

6 JANUARY

Woken through the night.

6.30am Doctor visit. Begin to feel full impact of life changes.

---

[1] Throughout 2005 A.R. had been receiving treatment for an aggressive form of prostate cancer. It was decided that the best option was to remove the entire prostate, to which end he and Rima travelled to the Vanderbilt University Medical Center in Nashville, Tennessee, where he was operated on by Dr Joseph 'Jay' Smith, one of the leading surgeons in the field.

11 Rima arrives/lunch/some walking.

pm Roxy [nurse] takes Rima to Target to buy food, sweatpants etc.

7 JANUARY

Feeling cold through the night. Stomach tightening.

Amazing what a walk and patience in the toilet will do.

Dr Smith comes by and this literate, aware man asks direct intelligent questions about my work . . . and tells me to stay in another day.

8 JANUARY

5am Patience is rewarded—enough gas to power a brass band.

7 The doctors come round and after dealing with catheters and drainage, finally, nervously get to the point—'How did you do the fall at the end of *Die Hard*?'

Check-out and → Hermitage Hotel for a week in Downtown Nashville. Dr Smith, Tour Guide, says Graceland is 200 miles (too far) away—suggests a visit to Jack Daniel's brewery. Even though it's a dry state, so no free samples.

The hotel fits the bill perfectly. Late pm—wandering the quiet Nashville streets. Very *Alphaville*. The odd guy in a cowboy hat.

'Catheter College' now has a new graduate.

13 JANUARY

A fax from Gina—*Snow Cake* is the opening night film at the Berlin Film Festival. Then a message that *MNIRC* has won Best New Play, Best Solo Performance and Best Director at TheatreGoer/whatson.com awards. So no Friday the 13th rubbish this year.

Grey, rainy day so after a sandwich and coffee hightail it back to the hotel.

This is like being in hiding. Which, in a way, it is.

16 JANUARY

7.45am → Vanderbilt.

Dr Smith pulls out remaining tubes etc. and rips off plasters. All with his trademark air of quiet dignity and sustained wisdom.

17 JANUARY

Reporting in some triumph to Dr Smith that it was a dry night. Standing up and moving around are the problem areas. But he seemed pleased, and it means I could dump a lot of the packages.

Rima doing rest of dumping, sauntering innocently towards public garbage bins.

3.25 → Nashville to LaGuardia and then → Mercer Hotel.

22 JANUARY

London.

At home with a pile of mail.

24 JANUARY
11.30 David Coppard.
   Which contains the piquant info that *HP* 4 paid less than *HP* 3 thanks to exchange rate.

30 JANUARY
Finally, yes to *HP* 5. The sensation is neither up nor down. The argument that wins is the one that says 'See it through. It's your story.' Added to the 7 weeks per film clause.

8 FEBRUARY
Spoke to Andrew Ward[1] and finalised plans to travel to Ullapool for the Great Birthday Escape. Wilderness, old friends who got engaged in our flat, now with 1-year-old boy. Seems like good karma. And train rides. Books and windows.
   Plus—a phone call from Francine LeFrak full of foreboding about *MNIRC* in New York. As I said—it's happening and I can't (won't) cut it. The US fights for free speech but censorship is important, too, it seems.

9 FEBRUARY
7[am] car for 8.55 → Berlin. Regent Hotel (ex 4 Seasons) in the Bentley. (A couple of leaning-on-the-bonnet photos and it's ours for the duration.)
   9 *Snow Cake* opening night film. Berlin Film Festival. And the film *looks good* up there. This little miracle becomes a kind of epic. They listen and laugh and clap loud and long. It's like a row of cherries on a one-armed bandit.

17 FEBRUARY
Call Diane Borger [general manager] at Royal Court with news from David Johnson that Michael Moore has given us $10,000 to hear that NYTW[2] wants to 'postpone for a year', which is euphemism for 'We're getting frightened, no PR firm will touch us and we don't have the guts to just say NO.'

---

[1] An old, Edinburgh-based friend of A.R.'s from his art school days, married to Alison Campbell
[2] New York Theatre Workshop

18 FEBRUARY

Phone lines back and forthing and having to give the news to Megan. Diane is organised, Elyse her usual passionate self, Megan wonderfully calm. David Johnson talks of West End before America, Elyse wants to expose the whole story, Diane wants to tread carefully, Megan will stay strong at the centre. As I said to Diane, we're not living in New York, we don't know the pressures—but a little honesty would have gone a long way. To use the Hamas government as a reason to postpone is ridiculous—how can you guarantee what the situation will be in a month, 6 months, a year or 10 years? Moral cowardice has to be dressed in any old clothes to disguise it. Or is it just fascism? Certainly, censorship is back.

19 FEBRUARY

8pm Euston. The Caledonian Sleeper to Inverness. Supper. A pill, which works for maybe 2 hours. Then the night is punctuated by lurches and ear-splitting alarms.

20 FEBRUARY

9.30—Inverness ½ hour late. Met by nice lady with car for the 1½ hrs drive to Ullapool and the Ceilidh Place hotel.

12.30 Lunch at the hotel with Andrew and Kerstin and Carlin. I really *like* this child.

Drive to the layby at the far end of the towpath to the lighthouse next to the plot of land A&K hope to build on. Windswept and glorious with the Stornaway Ferry passing twice a day.

6pm Andrew collects us. To their cottage for seaweed w. oats/haggis, neeps and tatties. Absolutely wonderful Scottish soulfood. And Kerstin is right about the grain issues. Don't grind until you need to. The stomach has no complaints whatsoever for a change.

21 FEBRUARY

Birthday in a Celtic wilderness.

Andrew took us to see his painting store, played some Martyn Bennett music, took us home to blow out some candles and then we sallied forth on the road to Achiltibuie and nearby beach for wandering and a picnic.

7ish. Dinner at the hotel . . . Later Jean Urquhart[1] joins and, SNP councillor that she is, chat ensues. To bed, feeling that the day had a forward momentum—not sentimental, backward-glancing torpor.

---

[1] Then owner of the Ceilidh Place

27 FEBRUARY

Chat with Kath Viner at the *Guardian*. Royal Court wants to stay neutral.

Rachel Corrie lived in nobody's pocket but her own. This is censorship born out of fear. Whether one is sympathetic to her or not, her voice is like a clarion in the fog and should be heard.

28 FEBRUARY

And stuff appears in newsprint. 'Rickman slams . . .' etc., etc. But basically fair coverage of the situation. *Tim Robbins calls. Do it in LA.*

pm Checking Kath Viner's copy for tomorrow's *Guardian* comment. Requests to give interviews or appear on Dimbleby at the weekend. No to everything. Let's just do the play and let Rachel Corrie speak for herself.

2 MARCH

Most of the day on the phone to Diane at the Court, to Cindy & Craig Corrie, to David Johnson . . . Janine in the PR department 'doing her job' of trying to persuade me to talk to those nice newspaper people. IT'S NOT ABOUT ME I bleat. BUT WE HAVE TO SELL IT they bleat back.

4 MARCH

8 Lindsay & Hilton.

Talking to Diane on the way. She has spoken with Oskar Eustis [NYC Public Theater] who is passionate that *MNIRC* should come to NY if only to demonstrate that single groups cannot close a show.

6 MARCH

Faxes go back & forth from the Court, answering the NYTW website. Now they want it in the *NY Times*.

7 MARCH

Another *NY Times* piece, still landing me & my 'film commitments' with the blame.

8 MARCH

A fax from David Johnson eloquently asking for mercy for Jim[1] at NYTW who may lose his job. This would be distressing for everybody and as David said—it's typical neo-con policy to create unrest and then step back to watch the liberals tear each other to pieces.

---

[1] James C. Nicola, artistic director

Diane . . . just wants Jim to stop talking to the press. And I think there is no way the Court would work with them, anyway. What a sad mess. But worse than that if there was intervention from the Mayor of New York or the Chief Rabbi.

17 MARCH

Talking to Uri [Andres] on the phone. He regrets that *MNIRC* is on again. As Anna [Massey, his wife] later says, 'He's 80'—she says it with utter love and pride but as a helpful explanation, too, with no further discussion necessary. And he's a Russian Jew so I shouldn't be surprised, I guess. For him the past *is* the present.

19 MARCH

Reading Lynn Barber's interview with Vanessa Redgrave it's the same old dichotomy—it's as much about the journalist as it is the subject except the journalist is funny, forthright, perceptive and gets to just leave at the end and have another say until the next one, but at the same time I am seduced by her complete lack of bullshit. Vanessa shouldn't be subject to it, however. She trails greatness behind her. What is Ms Barber's legacy?

24 MARCH

Hear myself agree to go on the 10pm BBC 1 news next week . . . a day after I said no to Celebrity Show Jumping . . .

26 MARCH

Feeling much less confident about talking to BBC News. Whatever the sympathies they will come at it from a negative standpoint and I will be placed on the defensive on a topic I don't have to defend. Plus the danger of internet editing.

28 MARCH

8 *My Name Is Rachel Corrie* first preview.

Megan says she was terrified—you'd never know. And the audience is standing at the end.

1 APRIL

Ruby drives/takes a taxi to meet Sandra Kamen & Annie Lennox & Barbara at the Wolseley. They have been to see *MNIRC*. And have loved it . . . Neil Tennant across the way, Lucian Freud behind us. You're thinking 'I'd be a patient model—I promise. CHOOSE ME!!!' Annie is a delightful soul with such a strong strain of it'll all turn out for the worst . . .

6 APRIL

pm Watching *Perfume*. Tom has made a beautiful film. One is totally unjudgemental of Grenouille (Ben—wonderful). Is the beauty a problem for the sense of *smell*? And *who* is driving the car?

12 APRIL

6.45 pick-up *HP*.

I realise as soon as that [Snape's] ring and costume go on—something happens. It becomes alien to be chatty, smiley, open. The character narrows me down, tightens me up. Not good qualities on a film set. I have never been less communicative with a crew. Fortunately, Dan [Radcliffe] fills that role with ease and charm. And *youth*.

Home moments, it seems, before it's time to get up again.

21 APRIL

7am pick-up.

Great Hall revisited.

Along with Maggie and Michael. Hysterical laughter within minutes—abetted by Imelda Staunton who told hilarious stories of filming with Steven Seagal and meeting Bonnie Zimmerman[1] in the lift on the morning of the Oscars. 'I have to have you in my Diane Arbus movie. You play this character with no arms or legs.'

24 APRIL

11pm The Wolseley w. Ruby. Eventually having steered La Wax away from some cheap Soho dive. She thinks the W. is 'fancy shmancy'. She recants, [and] fesses that she's doing Celebrity Show Jumping. *Plus ça change*.

30 APRIL

10.25 → New York.

4 MAY

9.30 *Snow Cake*.

Slightly murky projection but the film plays beautifully, the audience is quiet or roaring whenever it cracks its whip. The Q&A afterwards is calm & easy—filled with the confidence of having made something decent.

---

[1] American literary critic (1947–) specialising in women's studies

5 MAY

... talking to Rima today—she lost her seat.[1] And that is seriously *their* loss and her freedom.

14 MAY

4 *My Name Is Rachel Corrie.*

Cindy & Craig in.

20 mins late going up—power surge equals blackout.

Megan taps into something very pure—not unconnected to seeing the Corries sitting in the circle together. Beautiful work.

Today the *Observer* talks of a triumphant run—not quite David's[2] words in the hospitality room ...

21 MAY

4 Last show in London. Packed house. Megan started too fast, got into her stride and then the lid came down towards the end. Backstage I discover that the woman yelling at the curtain call had barracked throughout the second half and Megan, understandably, was freaked. A last day marker for New York?

30 MAY

Campagnatico.

Today was my chopping back the garden day. Releasing the fig tree from the confines of the kiwi fruit and on the way, helping the honeysuckle to have a presence and reminding the wisteria who is boss ...

7 JUNE

Campagnatico.

A letter has been sent March 22 from Robert Lepage to ICM saying that the French distributors wanted a bigger name in *Dragons' Trilogy*. It's that moment. I was thinking of Tom Cruise and there he was on Leno looking *so* uncomfortable. You're up, down, in, out—whose whim?

---

[1] On Kensington and Chelsea Borough Council, in local elections
[2] David Johnson (1960–2020), producer on *My Name Is Rachel Corrie*

8 JUNE

Campagnatico.

DIY mode and I sanded and first-coated (a 'protective' substance . . . ?) the table and benches outside.

Second coat and it has altered the look possibly for the better.

13 JUNE

To Marylebone High Street to deal with the rash of birthday/wedding presents.

9 JULY

12 Richard Wilson's birthday party . . . Ian McKellen spoke bravely and well, ticking every Wilson box, then Jennie Stoller[1] and I gave Richard his book of tributes.

7 The Wolseley w. Zoë [Wanamaker] & Gawn[2] and then mid chat/story/slander/hilarity in came Penny Wilton closely followed by Antonia F. and Harold Pinter . . . Will the subject come up? It does and from Harold (who is looking clear-skinned and is unalterably clear-minded not to mention courteous and generous). Do you know my poem 'Democracy' he asks after kind words about *My Name Is Rachel Corrie*? He then recites it for us . . .

Richard and Harold; 2 flag-bearers in one day.

24 JULY

To New York.

2.35 BA → Newark.

On the plane finally reading excellent article by Tony Judt—'The Country That Wouldn't Grow Up'—talks of Israel 'comporting itself like an adolescent', 'that it can do as it wishes, that its actions carry no consequences and that it is immortal'. And this was written way before the horrors of Lebanon.

3 AUGUST

→ Edinburgh.

3am Jet lag—reading Tom Courtenay's book *Dear Tom* sends me hurtling back to the kitchen, sculleries, front and back rooms of my youth—does that explain my pleasure & faint unease at my surroundings now?

11 Train from Kings Cross.

---

[1] British actor (1946–)
[2] British actor Gawn Grainger (1937–), Z.W.'s husband

5.55 *My Name Is Rachel Corrie*. First preview. Josie[1] ticks the boxes with great clarity and efficiency.

8 Shore Bar, Leith, w. everybody. Perfect choice.

Later to the Prestonfield bar. Hoots of pleasure all round.

6 AUGUST

David Johnson called to say we have a great review in the *Scotsman*. This obviously helps him.

9 AUGUST

6.30 Rima off to Italy.

11 AUGUST

Feeling less and less desire to go to Italy this time. Airport chaos aside it feels like more stress, running a hotel and no rest. Added to which they are not starting on the garden . . .

12 AUGUST

Whittington Hospital [London].

5 Max [Stafford-Clark]'s mind as sharp as ever, recall total, eyeline unknowable, left side paralysed. But we all chatted away as if nothing had happened. Which I hope was the point. Max asked pointed questions about Corin Redgrave & talked of Alan Ayckbourn's stroke, but we moved swiftly on.

15 AUGUST

11 Train to Edinburgh.

Some trick of fate led me to read (and just finish) Tom Courtenay's book. Parallels all over the place, though he and I so different. And so similar. Stuffed with mirror images of leaving one career for RADA, telling Mum not to talk to the press, the constant hubbub of relatives, Nan, Granddad, aunts, uncles, Mum in hospital. Guilt. And all as I train to Edinburgh for a screening of *Snow Cake* and tomorrow's *My Name Is Rachel Corrie*. But it's work I'm proud of. And I'm shaped by my family.

7 *Snow Cake* screening. J.K. Rowling, Neil [Murray, her husband], Andrew [Ward], Alison [Campbell].

Dinner nearby—Hamilton's.

Q&A, then the Loft (w. Brian De Palma), then the Sheraton Bar. Steve Coogan there all the while being very brilliant and likeable. But the red wine

---

[1] English actor Josie Taylor (1983–), playing Rachel Corrie

sends me to a place full of sentences and no verbs. How did I make it back to my room?

16 AUGUST

Edinburgh.

1pm Oyster bar [Cafe Royal]. How have I missed this place all these years? A haven. Roy Hattersley comes in and we point & wave. 'Are you still on board or despairing?' 'Worse,' I say. 'It's going to be alright,' he says. Very Brownite, I think.

7 SEPTEMBER
Munich—*Perfume* premiere.
Press . . . 'What is *Perfume* to you?' 'What is your favourite perfume/ smell?' 'What perfume do you buy for a woman?' etc., etc., etc., etc.

9 SEPTEMBER
5.30 Wake up.
6am Cab → hospital.
Echoes of January.
Somewhere in here, pathetic behaviour from the Labour Party—totally out of touch with the real world, institutionalised, cannabalistic, egomaniacal, bitter, twisted and stupid. Charles Clarke[1]—never trust a man with two-day growth, who also stuffs his face that much. Blair, of course, nips off to Israel for a swift bit of statesmanship.

13 SEPTEMBER
9pm Rima back from Italy.

19 SEPTEMBER
3pm *The Queen*. Whiteley's.
Enjoyable voyeurism and Helen [Mirren] really wonderful, but its research is of a tabloid level and not rigorous when it needed to be. Meeting the royal family en masse at St James's Palace was meeting a group of people who actually do have fun together. And isn't it a known fact that H.M. and Philip sleep in separate bedrooms? I suspect that the Queen Mother had more influence even at 90-odd. All in all, involving to watch but it fades swiftly—a shame since there are some zonking issues at the centre of it.

---

[1] Labour politician (1950–) who had recently been sacked from government

29 SEPTEMBER

I am currently at odds with everything, it seems—RADA, the Pinter play, *Snow Cake*, *Perfume* screening, potential personality clashes on *MNIRC* etc., etc. EVERYTHING is or becomes a problem. Why on earth is this? It's even felt at one remove—re Sigourney being treated appallingly by Harvey W[einstein]. So now I want to punish him. Like he'd feel it. . . .

11.15 Car → Heathrow. MOVING ON.

4 OCTOBER

New York.

8 Dress rehearsal.[1]

With some producers, some marketing, some press. Megan way behind her eyes and soul—tiredness. Which defeats her and makes her negative and vulnerable.

5 OCTOBER

8 First preview.

And she's back on form. The audience, however, are worryingly geriatric. A standing ovation would be an impossibility—it would take too long to happen.

12 OCTOBER

Somewhat caught unawares—Rima phones and says 'I'm on the way from the airport.'

15 OCTOBER

7 The opening night.

As good as anyone can expect under NY pressure. Suits and ties and money and influence everywhere. People hanging around in the auditorium talking to the Corries afterwards for a long time.

Later. Balthazar. Where Diane Borger has the first intimation of a 'mixed' (awful word) review in the *NY Times*. Here we go again.[2]

16 OCTOBER

. . . the power of a fucking newspaper hangs over the entire day—the pressure of it visible on Megan's face.

---

[1] *My Name Is Rachel Corrie* was performed at the Minetta Lane Theatre, produced by David Johnson.

[2] The *New York Times* concluded: 'No matter what side you come down on politically, Ms Corrie's sense of a world gone so awry that it forces her to question her "fundamental belief in the goodness of human nature" is sure to strike sadly familiar chords.'

28 OCTOBER
3pm Bree[1]—first performance.

She takes 6 minutes off the running time so I'm miming reins from my seat on the stairs, but the audience stands at the end and her youth & spirit are incredibly affecting.

Rima → Kennedy → London.

3 NOVEMBER
11.05 *Borat*. Utterly brilliant comedy—the whole movie and the performance which is kissed with genius from start to finish.

28 NOVEMBER
New York → Toronto.

6.30 pick-up → *Snow Cake* premiere—in the multiplex.

Roots—for the reception. A 58-year-old autistic woman tells me she's trying to keep her mouth shut. 'I can be too bold.'

3 DECEMBER
6am Jet lag and reading Antonia Quirke's book *Madame Depardieu and the Beautiful Strangers*. It's a joyously uninhibited 300 pages. At times it smacks of being written by a wet and muddy 5th former who has flung her hockey stick across a room, grabbed her maribou-trimmed diary and dived on to the bed to write, write, write.

5 DECEMBER
Premiere of *Perfume*.

The film looked beautiful and 300 people sat mesmerised.

6 DECEMBER
11.30 Car to Pinewood.[2]

Plaster cast of head, weird, buried alive experience—can't cough, see, speak. People slapping on plaster strips which then start to get alarmingly hot. Then singing. I think Paul likes the way I fight back against amazingly rude pianist . . . Start to get a picture of a faded (very) roué. A bit Les Patterson.

11 DECEMBER
London Clinic. Blood test time.

On the way out, there's Andrew Marr on his mobile phone, in a state

---

[1] American actor Bree Elrod, playing Rachel Corrie
[2] Preparations for filming *Sweeney Todd*

about where he's supposed to be and seemingly unconcerned about the fact that he's on crutches with his right leg in a cast. I wait until he hangs up and say 'I'm sure you're tired of answering this—but what happened?' 'Oh, torn tendon, do you know where Cavendish Street is?' I didn't and wished him well, of course outside, turn left, walk 100 yds—Cavendish Street. I looked around and he was hurtling towards it.

13 DECEMBER

Royal Court 50th Birthday.

Rima later said the whole party had a melancholy air to it—she could be right, plus the Court's self-examining doesn't really approve of letting go. We retreated to The Wolseley.

15 DECEMBER

9.45 Pinewood. For a very bad-tempered (me) rehearsal. Too early—no voice—no high notes and the bland insistence that it will be OK . . .

17 DECEMBER

9.35 → New York.

3pm *My Name Is Rachel Corrie*. Bree's last performance. She now owns the stage, and her space. Still too keen to get to the next sentence before she's fully lived in *this* one, but she does some miraculously fresh things. She *went* to Gaza of all of them.

7pm Kerry's[1] last performance. Wonderful talent that she is, she is still young enough to push a little too hard—'I'm going to give *all* of it my *all*' was the sense one had. But she's rivetting and not a syllable is wasted or unexplored.

25 DECEMBER

Millbrook, Upstate New York.

Tash and Liam are, of course, legendary hosts . . . On opening the bedroom door to make an early morning cup of tea—two large stockings waiting for us.

27 DECEMBER

Millbrook.

NY Times dumps on *Perfume*. *Daily News* likes it. No wonder Dreamworks has been like a coy door person.

---

[1] Kerry Bishé, Rachel Corrie understudy

6 Tash & Liam's party. Indian food and charades with Meryl Streep, Bette Midler (scoring . . .), Mia Farrow, Stanley Tucci and his wife Katie, Aidan Quinn & Elizabeth [Bracco, his wife], Allan Corduner. Meryl got *Volver*[1]— mimed vulva. Ms Farrow talked long and expertly about Darfur.

Reading a really excellent How To book in the Neeson loo—*How to Be Happy, Dammit*. Full of good New Year stuff about fears and patterns. The endless ongoing, really. The fear of success creating the circumstances of failure. *That has to stop. Get that book.*

---

[1] 2006 Spanish film directed by Pedro Almodóvar

2007

Richard Wilson — *Sweeney Todd* — Rima's 60th birthday — Harold Pinter — Gordon Brown — Rufus Wainwright — Timothy Spall — Richard Attenborough — Johnny Depp — Ruby Wax — Tony Blair stands down — Campagnatico — Tbilisi — Publication of last *Harry Potter* — Sonoma, *Bottle Shock* — Leonard Cohen — Daniel Radcliffe — New York — Barbara and Ken Follett — Cape Town

1 JANUARY

Home somewhere around 3.30am from Richard's party in the Royal Suite at Claridge's . . . One of those idling New Year's Days walking through the park to the funfair . . . On to Selfridges (ice-cream maker, living for pleasure now) and a cab home in the rain—the funfair bravely ablaze with lights but deserted now. Quick—write a script, get funding, start filming.

3 JANUARY

9.30[pm] Tricycle Cinema. Q&A after *Perfume* screening which seemed to go fine. They had liked the film, the place was full and the questions were mainly interesting and interested.

4 JANUARY

3.30 Claridge's. Rima's birthday party first meeting. Grabbed Feb 3rd and started the organisation process.

5 JANUARY

10 Mark Meylan.

Singing lesson. Absence of alcohol for the last 5 days means absence of dehydration which means much more flexible voice . . . QED.

8 JANUARY

11.40 pick-up → Pinewood. A 'refresher' was the message. Eventually walk into the studio where there is a full choir. Christopher Lee, Peter Bowles, Anthony Head, Michael Harbour,[1] Liza Sadovy and (thank God) Tim Spall. Not to mention Stephen Sondheim . . .

And—SING!

---

[1] Scottish actor (1945–2009)

9 JANUARY

11.30 Mark Meylan singing lesson.

   12.30 → Pinewood.

And basically, sing 'Pretty Women' for Sondheim. Thanks to Mark, high notes were scaled and breathing occasionally seemed like a good idea. Sondheim talks of the judge [Judge Turpin, A.R.'s character] as a much more dapper figure than I see—I can only sense the crumbs, dandruff, dirt under the nails. Obsessive.

17 JANUARY

A swift hour was spent making a table/seating plan [for Rima's birthday party]. It is, of course, not that difficult and one would take the free-for-all approach, but there are 1 or 2 potential collisions, so best avoided, eh??

21 JANUARY

10.45 Car to Sudbury Hill to visit Uncle Vic. I haven't seen him for—probably—a year now and he seems to have aged a lot more than that. At one point he asks me, 'Do you know my wife?' 'Very well, Uncle Vic.' 'I miss her dreadfully.'

26 JANUARY

SWEENEY TODD RECORDING.

   11.30 First recording of 'Pretty Women'. New version—beautifully sung by Johnny Depp. Tim Burton is there. As is—thank goodness—Mark. Plus Mike and other recordist. They all seemed very happy. I felt a kind of euphoric relief in amongst the usual barrage of self-criticism.

31 JANUARY

Rima's birthday.

   am Dressing gowns, coffee, opening presents.

3 FEBRUARY

RIMA'S BIRTHDAY PARTY—CLARIDGE'S.

   3pm Claridge's. To check in and start helping Alex & Lesley as they made the room look like spring had sprung. Really beautiful.

   6.45 Down to the French Salon. What amounted to an army of friends started arriving, beaming.

   8pm Dinner. The food was terrific, the quiz hilarious—people chatting via text/Blackberry/telephone throughout. Smiling faces everywhere. And then they danced. And then Tara, Lesley & Hilton sang. It was a kind of perfection. Even with the panic button of 2 extra for dinner.

Eventually, as tables were being cleared, 40-odd people were persuaded into the lobby for drinks and more talk. Until 4am. No one wants to go home.

4 FEBRUARY
10.30 Breakfast in Claridge's Restaurant.

5 FEBRUARY
PEN TRIBUTE TO HAROLD PINTER.

5.30 → Windsor, and the car ride from there. Into the blackness, with no street lights & no road signs in Windsor Great Park . . .

7.30 Finally arrive, 20 mins late, at Cumberland Lodge. I'm furious, Lindsay remains gloriously polite. She's right because the readings begin 10 mins later and I'm still boiling. *However* the material wins because it's so brilliant and we have a happy dinner. Harold generous and warm and smiling & thrilled that he's doing *Homecoming* on the radio. Harold makes a typically taut and pointed speech about Iraq.

6.30 Rules Restaurant.

Kathy Lette and Geoffrey Robinson's dinner for Sarah and Gordon Brown . . . Gordon seemed very relaxed and immediately asked about Rachel Corrie/Kath Viner. It was Sarah who carried the tension. But then Sunday night out is probably no one's favourite option.

14 FEBRUARY
Stayed in and watched the Brits. Liam Gallagher is a great rock singer but an absolute tosser as a person. Who cares about his little tantrums—come out from behind the hair & glasses and showy walk and witless rudeness.

19 FEBRUARY
Vague sense of watching bits of my life being put on a record player like some album that's as irritating as it is loved. Or it's the mouse in a wheel thing of who is controlling what, here? Not helped by feeling a bit used in the work area and a bigger bit irrelevant in the world . . . This in spite of loving generous phone calls about *Snow Cake*—something I'm proud of and which does have a point. This is one of the more painful paradoxes.

20 FEBRUARY
10.45 → Pinewood.

To practise falling backwards from the barber's chair.

23 FEBRUARY
6.45 pick-up. *Sweeney Todd*.

First day for Judge Turpin. Tim has a joyous soul, though—clear about what he wants, very concentrated but like a child, an indoor firework. And surrounded by the likes of Tim Spall (looking in the mirror as his 'young' wig goes on he says 'Who is it? Is it early Twiggy?').

25 FEBRUARY
7.30 Rufus Wainwright. Palladium.

This was an amazing feat. 2¾ hours of up and at 'em singing with some shocking brilliance from Martha Wainwright sort of tossed in. Kate McGarrigle skipped and sidled on and off as well. Rufus pays homage and lightens the load on himself with flicks of irony. Somehow it was never a camp-fest. Like watching a conjuror.

15 MARCH

Pinewood.

6.15 pick-up.
Old Bailey Scenes.
Which have the all-day pleasure of being with Tim Spall. Apart from his rich & deep talent and his total lack of vanity, you feel his real love of his family and his boat, and he's endlessly funny. Even when talking about signs seen in windows he remembers 'BASKET CASES HERE' at Karachi airport.

21 MARCH
A pointless *Guardian* article about English accents in Hollywood quotes me as using the phrase 'dear boy'. This would never get past my lips. Sledgehammer journalism.

26 MARCH
8pm Supper w. Ruby & Ed.
Ruby's off to the Palace tomorrow as a Distinguished American. She thinks she's parking in the Palace forecourt. We'll see.

27 MARCH
She did.
12.30 Dorchester Hotel.
Lunch for Dickie Attenborough . . . I'm sitting next to him (someone's

mistake? or because I'm RADA vice chair?). At one point, after a speech of staggering insensitivity and irrelevance, he whispered 'Who was that man?' I said 'Frank Carson'.[1] He made a note and blithely included his name in his speech.

28 MARCH

On the set to rehearse 'Pretty Women'.

Good talk to Johnny Depp about his daughter.[2] I gave him a hug and said 'You've been to hell and back.' He talked a bit and we made an even playing field in a way. Out of something real. It was a good starting point as always.

29 MARCH

Happy, concentrated atmosphere. Johnny wears his fame very lightly and has done his homework and is open to ideas. And has plenty of his own. It's all a gradual process of becoming comfortable with the obstacles although one of them is a real threat—my skin starts screaming at the shaving foam after it has been applied, washed off and reapplied 6 or 7 times. By the end of the day the makeup is concealing red blotches and a lot of stinging.

30 MARCH

It has been a pleasure to do the scene with Johnny D. He has *real* concentration and a great sense of humour. Unbeatable combination. And there seemed to be a real buzz on set all day. Bravo, Mr Sondheim. The song never lost its complexity nor its simplicity—either musically or via its lyrics. That *must* be some kind of genius.

16 APRIL

4am Rima gets up and tries to exit quietly.

pm Stories of progress at Campagnatico—a huge structure, some concrete and the fig tree has gone.

27 APRIL

Champaign → Chicago → New York.

On the plane the *New York Times* review of *Snow Cake*. Would have you believe there isn't a laugh in it. Does the act of criticism automatically generate joylessness, a complete inability to let go?

---

[1] Northern Irish comedian (1926–2012)
[2] She had anorexia nervosa.

1 MAY

London.

7pm Umu, Bruton Place.

Ruby's birthday party.

Those three words . . . a ton of generosity but she'd done a deal says the PR woman who totally blanks Horatia [Lawson, journalist] until I mention she's Nigella's sister, then she's in danger of whiplash. Up the other end—A.A. Gill is seated near Jennifer Saunders (who he has slagged off in print). Unsurprisingly, she won't talk to him. It's Ruby's very own A-D list but since no one's introduced to anyone it's guesswork as to status. Bizarre placements create hot and cold patches as possible clues.

3 MAY

7am pick-up.

Johnny's had a late night, everything a bit behind. Made it on set late morning . . . The crew sits behind black plastic wearing paper suits as Johnny and I are sprayed and drenched in bright orange/red liquid. It somehow gets inside the trouser seat as well as down arms, inside shirts and all over Johnny's face. More of the same tomorrow.

9 MAY

6am pick-up.

Last scene. Lying in the gutter, spitting blood, grabbing on to Mrs Lovett's[1] skin as she shrieks 'Die, die, you bastard (or something like that), die.'

Satisfying and a little less wet around the underpants than in the barber's chair.

10 MAY

Tony Blair's standing-down speech—he could have saved himself a great deal of time by just reprinting the lyrics to 'My Way'.

18 MAY

Home alone. Which means drag a ladder out into the garden, bang a nail into a wall, watch it bounce off into the shrubbery (twice), give up, put ladder away.

pm Talking to Adam about *Transylvania Tales* contract only throws up the wholesale Warner Bros rip-off of actors with *HP*. Why create such dis-

---

[1] Played by Helena Bonham Carter

interest for the sake of penny-pinching greed? But then, why waste time asking why?

27 MAY
David & Chris → Uncle Vic at the nursing home. Sheila & John already there. How to make this un-dutiful? Or where we sit in a circle and talk to each other while Uncle Vic watches the TV with the sound turned down. When I asked how he was doing, he said, 'I've been a little browned off, lately.'

4 JUNE

Campagnatico.

a.m. and the workmen are in the garden. Eventually we hear the cement mixer rolling.

5 JUNE

Campagnatico.

Cosimo arrives from Milan and is his usual heroic self—explaining everything, talking to the builders, attempting to sort out the computer, the telephone system, the damp kitchen walls and with the greatest humility showing us his boundless integrity and taste in the whole garden project, which given the anti-earthquake requirements of whichever state committee, has not been problem-free.

11 JUNE
Campagnatico → Rome → London.
   am This is now like running a small hotel, which I have always thought I would enjoy. The clean up and turn around—very basic stuff but therapeutic.
   9.20 On the plane. Re-reading some of this diary. A lot of people, a lot of places. Eating, drinking. Not too much thinking, shaping, doing . . .

14 JUNE

Tbilisi.

2.10 Book Fair. Major *HP* Fest. Children clutching copies and flashing cameras.
   7 QBP (Queen's Birthday Party) at the Marriott Hotel. Donald[1] plays his

---
[1] Donald MacLaren, then British ambassador to Georgia

bagpipes and makes a speech in English *and* Georgian. Later to a restaurant overlooking the river, with Georgian dancing and Donald reappearing with bagpipes. He's a bit of a star, really.

1 JULY

DIET MONTH STARTS TODAY.

4 JULY

8.30 River Cafe . . . Around and about are Tessa Jowell, Simon Schama, Alan Rusbridger, and Ruthie is on duty. Network Central. 'Are there any more *Harry Potters*?' says the Editor of the *Guardian*. 'The last book comes out end of July—it'll be on your front page. World event,' I offer.

6 JULY

Jo Rowling on *Jonathan Ross*—says 2 more people die in *HP* 7.

8 JULY

12.30 Lunch in the Members' Restaurant. Annabel Croft's shared table. Poached salmon and strawberries. All very Wimbledon. Not a black, Asian or working-class face in sight. I fantasise a hundred conversations about garden centres, awnings, golf, children's schooling, insurance, the A40.

The Men's Final. I prefer Nadal's openness to Federer's, well, closedness but it was yin and yang to a kind of perfection.

20 JULY

THE DAY OF THE LAST *HARRY POTTER*.

11.15pm → Tunbridge Wells and Waterstones.

I had guessed at 20 or 30 people waiting for midnight. Probably 300–400. And a queue moving slowly. 1 hour in the queue and it was time for action. Went to friendly security man. 'Have you read the books?' No. 'Have you seen the films?' One of them. 'I'm in them.' Oh yes! There will be mayhem if I go into the queue. 'I'll get the manager.' (Manager arrives.) 'Oh! Hello!'

27 JULY

. . . I have finished reading the last *Harry Potter* book. Snape dies heroically, Potter describes him to his children as one of the bravest men he ever knew and calls his son Albus Severus. This was a genuine rite of passage. One small piece of information from Jo Rowling 7 years ago—Snape loved Lily— gave me a cliff edge to hang on to.

1 AUGUST

Watching, finally, on an impulse, *HP* 4 . . . Beautifully shot by Roger Pratt and full of Mike [Newell]'s humanity. Rima points out that it's the most complex of the books and the hardest to film. So all credit.

5 AUGUST

[Re filming of *Bottle Shock*]

→ To Chicago → San Francisco → Sonoma.

10 AUGUST

9.45 pick-up → Montelena Vineyard, Napa Valley.

pm Silent wine tasting scene with Jim Barrett himself [owner of Montelena]. Total charmer who talks fondly of Steven Spurrier.[1] I reaffirm my intention only to honour S.S.—no stammer and sense of humour intact.

Later pm—the unlikely story of S.S. eating KFC.

11 AUGUST

Sonoma.

Another day at Chateau Montelena. Driving a car which seems to have a passing acquaintance with brakes and then negotiating scenes with Bill [Pullman]. Tricky at times because as he rightly points out my lines have been sculpted and there's a danger of leaving him stranded. But then, as I point out, I am working in 2 dimensions to his 3. But he's a thinking actor and we bash out some kind of compromise.

13 AUGUST

Sonoma.

Day off.

4pm Massage at the spa. Good masseur . . . but too much chat. And he hung around afterwards presumably for the tip I wasn't carrying in the bathrobe.

15 AUGUST

Sonoma.

6.30 Day One—Tasting.

Beautiful but ridiculous location—a 19th century roofless ruin. An old barrel store? Would be an idiotic choice—tasting world class wines in 90°.

---

[1] British wine expert and merchant (1941–2021), the inspiration for *Bottle Shock*

Something of this illogic breeds testiness and a lot of thinking on the feet has to go on plot-wise. Life made generally easier by the presence of the 6 or 7 French actors playing judges. They all live in LA, and see each other all the time at auditions and are wonderfully free in improvisations and generous.

17 AUGUST

Sonoma.

The trouble with vague narrative inefficiency is that my brain goes into overdrive and I lose my sense of humour. Good for getting through the day, terrible for crew morale and very undermining for Randy [Miller, director], I suspect. It's when the shot rules the story that this happens, but without story the shot has no drive or depth.

18 AUGUST
7ish Rima arrives.

19 AUGUST

Sonoma.

10am. A drive into Sonoma town square. An omelette in a side street restaurant right next to Footcandy which had Jimmy Choo and Manolo on sale. Exited with a small bag full of same.

20 AUGUST
9ish Called in for 'I'm an arsehole' scene . . . Still finding it difficult to be Mr Chirpy on set . . .

28 AUGUST
Out to Glen Ellen for my last two scenes. Eliza Sexy Dushku playing the barmaid Joe. (Later in the makeup trailer I read *lead kindly light* . . . tattooed on her hip. 'I got it done in Albania,' she says. 'Thank God they spelt it right' from me.

8 SEPTEMBER
→ London. Home somewhere around 4pm. 2 hours of wading through envelopes, making piles, writing cheques.
A pizza. Some wonderful Georgian wine. Some terrible TV. Bed.
Sleep. Wake. Sleep. Wake.

11 SEPTEMBER

Campagnatico.

Cosimo and Michael were here this morning so we talked of sinks and walls and railings and tables and plants and screening. One day all this will be here. I kept talking about 'an old person needing a hand rail'. Michael said, eventually, 'Who is this old person who's coming?' 'Me,' I said, 'by the time this garden is finished.' It will be good to have plants so that it doesn't look like Hollywood has come to Campagnatico.

13 SEPTEMBER

Campagnatico.

. . . to Kathy Van Praag's house which is everything an Italian house *should* be. Plus the headaches of running and sustaining it.

Whilst there I'm left with the *NY Herald Tribune* while Kathy & Rima go upstairs. A cold shock to read the words *Anita Roddick* in bold black ink. My eyes moved sideways and saw OBITUARIES. A brain haemorrhage at 64. The world is absolutely poorer.

30 SEPTEMBER

8.30 Denis Lawson's birthday party.

Mr Peter Pan. Surrounded by a few Tinkerbells, many Mrs Darlings and a few Captain Hooks. Very happy go lucky party. And Sheila's picture keeps her present at what she would have loved.

20 OCTOBER

6 Leonard Cohen & Charles Glass[1] in conversation and Q&A.

Q: Mr Cohen, would you ever change the title to something else, like *Fulfilment*?

LC: What's fulfilment got to offer?

25 OCTOBER

12.30 RADA Business Lunch. Dorchester Hotel.

The annual gathering of insurance brokers, RADA choir, Dickie A., assorted alumni—rather good food, Nicholas Parsons, True or False game, raffle, auction.

---

[1] American journalist (1951–). They were discussing L.C.'s book *Book of Longing*.

Dickie asking questions about *Pygmalion*, we talk about the vulgarising effect of ITV—flash ads for other programmes while the film is on, credits reduced to illegibility etc., etc.—who knows when this will end. Meanwhile good time had by all.

30 OCTOBER

9am Royal Court Council/Board.

I have been talked into this. Cannot shake off the feeling of 'What am I doing here?' At RADA there has been something to fight for—here, all is rosy, really, and I lose my independence. Heigh ho. We'll see. Give it a year.

9 NOVEMBER

12 Singing lesson.

'Uptown, Downtown' and 'You've Got a Friend' meet with Mark M.'s approval. The masochist before me turned out to be Daniel Radcliffe with, as he said, 'My first 3 day off period in seven years.'

25 NOVEMBER

SWEENEY TODD DAYS.

1.15 Screening of *Sweeney Todd*.

Tim has made a brilliant film. Johnny drives the car and Helena slouches in the passenger seat. A wonderful pairing and Tim doesn't flinch. Ever. Bravo to him for such guts.

26 NOVEMBER

After a bit of negotiation we manage not to do the interviews in a bedroom . . . And the parade begins. Slightly glazed expressions from most of the journalists. 'Tell me about the razors,' says one woman who should be for the chop herself.

6 DECEMBER

New York.

1.30pm Liam–Tash lunch. 55th for which—thank you, gridlock and red lights—we are 15 minutes late. Food wonderful, bill laughable but what the heck, I love these two and it's a relatively small price to chat this freely. In New York. But with Tash there is always a witching hour. Suddenly she's had enough of this moment in her life—a glance at a watch and she's off.

10 DECEMBER

→ London.

9.30am Heathrow.

Home. Sort through the mail. Order a Christmas tree. Go out and buy some supper. Eventually, cook it. Take delivery of Christmas tree. Put lights on. Lights go off 3 mins later. Why? Decorate tree. Bed.

16 DECEMBER

10.15 The Wolseley w. Jane B., Salman Rushdie, Martin Amis, Ian McEwan and 'an American'. As we went to our table Salman got up to say hello. I said there should be a collective noun for their table. Instantly, he suggested 'a remainder'.

17 DECEMBER

7 Ruby in vulnerable mode. Even with all her intelligence, awareness, wit, she still sometimes snatches at life. There's always something, someone better, more amusing, more useful, more status affirming around the corner or met last night or phoning back. Sit still with old friends occasionally.

20 DECEMBER

Today I finished reading Edna O'B.'s manuscript [re Byron]. It's like the craziest fiction. Like someone made a mistake and shuffled 2 or 3 lines together. Tonight she leaves a message saying her publisher doesn't want it. The casual cruelty of it is, of course, Byronesque.

24 DECEMBER

To visit Uncle Vic/take him his Christmas present/assuage-identify some guilt. He was in bed. Fully clothed. I nipped out to find some staff and get him some tea. Apparently he refused to leave the dining room, then refused to sit in his chair. Probing gently, he said it was 'a protest'—but he couldn't remember why. I left him drinking tea through a straw, scanning the TV magazine. That is to say, I escape.

11.30 St James's Christmas Mass. The sermon evoked Stalin as a reason for the need for God. Mostly I was looking at the congregation and wondering why we don't have a local Waitrose.

30 DECEMBER

4 Claridge's. Barbara Follett's birthday party.

Sandwiches with no crusts. Tea. Champagne. And Barbara at the microphone. 'In a minute we will sing Happy Birthday and then everyone *will* dance. I hope.' Ken gave her a (red, of course) Jaguar—parked outside Claridge's. And then they danced together. Like a couple of kids, which is part of their endless and disarming charm.

6 Car → Heathrow.

8.30 → Cape Town.

2008

1 JANUARY

Cape Town—Camps Bay.

5.30—awake. The beach is still gently buzzing. Looking out of the window, pockets of people who've been there all night, some wet, some dry. Back to bed and, thankfully, sleep. Sort of. The buzzing has gradually grown until at 11am, looking out again the grass verge is packed with families—all in from the townships—for this mass day-off party.

3 JANUARY

Pringle Bay.

6am. Exactly. Which means over six hours of complete sleeplessness. The flight? The wind? (Which was brutal.) The food? He swore the coffee was decaf. New Year-itis? The fact that I missed the New Year Moment should not become an emblem or a theme. Rather a sign that life should be specific, not lost in generalised ritual. It's a thought, anyway, in amongst the night's million, repetitive others.

12.30 Ruby, Ed & Max arrive—Ruby all aglow having discovered that Pringle Bay is another Nirvana.

9 JANUARY

Pringle Bay → London.

6.30 Car → Cape Town. Early because roads had been closed.

10.45 Virgin → London. Hello pill. Hello sleep.

10 JANUARY

London—*Sweeney Todd* Premiere.

8.10 on the plane. Something in me—the ADHD perhaps—wants to buy another journal and write the last ten days with a pen that's actually usable. But maybe that would be to heaten up a New Year's first week that started with me in the toilet as it came in and ended yesterday with a major mountain fire.

6pm Car → Leicester Square.

Which seems to be completely filled with cameras, microphones and hands thrusting programmes, books, pieces of paper. 'If you were a pie which flavour would you be?' Inside find Johnny & Tim—already said hello to Helena & Jim in the Square. 7.30 on stage. Then escape to Sheekey's for dinner.

9.15 Royal Courts of Justice for the party which was ace.

14 JANUARY

Louise Bourgeois Day.

Tate Modern.

Before it finishes at the end of the week and it's everything they say. She wouldn't care, of course, about 'them'. Still working at 94 or whatever and not giving a toss about the Venice Biennale. So *completely* creative. The rooms combine and counterpoint. Aggressive and vulgar at the same time. Completely organic and a spirit 'caught', but very vigorous, too. Inspirational.

15 JANUARY

Michael Grandage [director/producer] calls and asks if I'd like to direct *Creditors*—Strindberg—at the Donmar. I wouldn't normally be 'on the radar' of possible directors so it's down to Ian McDiarmid's[1] suggestion. Again. But that's how the system works. It's all about perception.

16 JANUARY

6.30 Warner House, RADA Screening of *Sweeney Todd*. Very rich people do not react to stories/theatre/film like normal people. Fact. They laugh less. Give themselves less. They're hanging on to what they've got.

18 JANUARY

Chicago.

→ Salt Lake City.

To the 8.30 screening of *Bottle Shock*. Which, with all the horrors of see-

---

[1] Scottish actor and director (1944–)

ing a film for the first time, has a growing and undeniably great heart. There are definitely times when a film like this is needed and the audience seemed to agree.

19 JANUARY
Sundance [re *Nobel Son*].

An interview with Ben Lyons [reporter] . . . I would guess he does 92% of the talking.

20 JANUARY

Sundance.

11ish and out into lounge-land. Photos and gifts after a radio interview at the house. Photos and quick chats and a watch I don't want goes to Rachael[1] (later I discovered it's worth $10,000).

2.30 *Phoebe in Wonderland*.

Elle Fanning is some kind of acting animal. Where/how does she know how to do that? The rest of it would be vastly better if someone had asked a few questions. How come the headmaster hadn't noticed rehearsals . . . for a full-scale musical in the school hall?

21 JANUARY

Sundance.

10 To the Delta Bar (civilised) and the $10,000 watch apology session.

22 JANUARY

Park City, Sundance.

Heath Ledger is dead. I met him in NY . . . Quiet, contained and so talented. The whole day is hammered into focus. Movies, movie stars, festivals, interviews, PR people, lawyers, award ceremonies. Whatever.

23 JANUARY
Home somewhere around 1pm. And this may well be the blank page of introspection. If you add that to jet lag and the blues it accounts for a day (afternoon evening) of unpacking, opening letters, throwing away bits of paper, sitting fairly still and now hoping for sleep with the ticking clock next to me.

---

[1] Rachael Taylor, Australian actor (1984–)

24 JANUARY

There is a deep introspection during these days. A feeling of being marginalised by shallow minds. The shallow minds, however, belong to opinion-formers.

28 JANUARY

To John Lewis—now more than ever a temple to what? Common sense; it is what it is; unspiced, unperfumed and I don't think you'd find bright red anywhere in the building—but everything validates the sensible approach to what adorns (wrong word) *complements* your life. We were there for frying pans.

30 JANUARY

6.30 Wallace Collection. PEN tribute to Doris Lessing.

I like her presence—Doris Lessing. Stylish in curvy grey hair and a red velvet dress. Smiling but without wasting a muscle. Juliet Stevenson late but it all worked out OK although I'm not sure this is material to be read out loud.

4 FEBRUARY

HP 6.

Harry Potter and the Half Blood Prince.

Day One.

Thank God I could do the coat up without visible strain at the seams.

7 FEBRUARY

8.15 pick-up.

Car park. Paparazzi. Freezing cloister of Gloucester Cathedral.

A whole new working relationship, this time with Tom Felton [playing Draco Malfoy]. The story of this so-far-6-part epic is one minute there were all these little kids . . . now? Found Maggie in her trailer vulnerable and fuck it—all at once.

10 FEBRUARY

9 Watching the BAFTA awards. The absence of *Sweeney Todd* (enforced) rendered it meaningless. To whom should anyone complain? Pointless unless there's a conspiracy. But year after year these events are given embarrassing and engorged prominence. It's the acting/directing/whatever equivalent of the duck's neck. Force fed to make foie gras.

11 FEBRUARY

At one point, having said how tired she gets, Maggie's hand slips between mine.

12 FEBRUARY

Sophie Thompson brought flowers for Maggie—incredibly sweet of her (and her sister [Emma]—lifelong fans from Jean Brodie days).

3 MARCH

6.45 pick-up.

The Astronomy Tower and the Death of Dumbledore. The scene seems oddly lacking in drama—on the page—but that is absolute cause and effect of screenplays that have to conflate (deflate) the narrative. We don't know—or remember—enough about individual characters' concerns to understand their issues. Or care. To wit I argue (successfully, today) that a line of Snape's 'I gave my word. I made a vow' was confusing and diluting.

'Did you have to say it?' Rima asks when I get home.

'No, but I bet I will tomorrow.'

4 MARCH

Inevitably, having agreed to the cut line all day, David [Heyman] finds a valid (?) reason to 'just try it' on one take. Pressure from where I wonder. It's ridiculous but predictable and I bet it winds up in the film.[1]

10 MARCH

The line 'take out your wand' reduces Helena Bonham Carter to helpless mirth and will be a bit of a Waterloo come Thursday . . . Helen McCrory says she's terrified but fits like a glove with the mayhem. Which includes a few words on Snape's House being designed and built without *any* reference to himself.

17 MARCH

And back up the hillside. Bone-chillingly cold, Helena with cleavage to the winds . . . me uttering the ironic lines 'Yes. It's me. I'm the Half Blood Prince.' We're 100 yards from the directorial tents so 2 takes and we're out of there, one with flames one without. All very coitus interruptus.

18 MARCH

2pm Back to the Grove [Hotel].

The anonymous hotel room, the golf course stretching forever, it seems, out of the window. Then the 1 o'clock news on TV says 'The Oscar-winning director'—and time slows as my brain runs through the Rolodex, *never*

---

[1] It didn't.

coming up with 'Anthony Minghella died today'. This is all completely unreal. Hand goes to mouth like bad acting. Talk to Juliet who is beside herself . . . Then told to go home. Urged on by Juliet we go to the BFI screening at 7.15 of *The No. 1 Ladies' Detective Agency*, Anthony's film in Botswana. And this is his final work—gentle, fable-like, completely faithful (apparently & typically) to the book. Nothing to do with the real Botswana but it's like a signal, a vapour, a whimsy of Minghella.

20 MARCH

On the news two more obituaries—Brian Wilde from *Last of the Summer Wine* is given precedence over Paul Scofield.[1] In one later bulletin, Scofield is not mentioned at all. A sign of these lazy and crass times.

27 MARCH

6.30 pick-up.

In Snape's quarters all day w. Helena and Helen. Interesting to be with the stage actress and the film actress—both a treat but Helen needs and gives, Helena totally self-motivated, it wouldn't matter if you spoke Chinese to her.

5 APRIL

Anthony Minghella's memorial service.

Even writing a day later it's almost impossible to process. First of all, it all felt like a movie set—*so* unreal. Still can't take it in. Then there's the 400 people. Blair & Cherie are there, Gordon Brown is there; looking around is to see a long sequence of close-ups from the industry US and UK. Can't take it in. 3 hours long (with the Mass), it careers from the blurry to the crystal clear, from the incomprehensible to the profound, from near cringe-making to the deeply moving. Ant was never cringe-making but in many ways the service did reflect his many sides. It was definitely about billing and in the case of Renée Zellweger, the cul-de-sac of stardom.

23 APRIL

7.15 pick-up.

Back in the *HP* Bathroom and in Wellington boots when the feet are out of shot. Through the day it's all about this shot, that shot. When Dan is left spinning in his own over-reactive spiral I gently invoke the notion of 2 characters' mutual respect and of time standing still for a second. It works. For a while.

---

[1] English actor (1922–2008)

25 APRIL

Russell Brand on *Jonathan Ross*.

I like Russell, but ohmigod I hate the faux naif thing that's inevitable when quirk meets ambition (see Gervais, R.). Just be honest about it you fuckers. Don't give us 'who me?' bullshit.

27 APRIL

1pm The Priory to collect Ruby.

Hmm. So this is it . . . Big old white exterior, Ruby coming out as we drive up to the main door.

Lunch at Riva, Church Road, Barnes. Back to the Priory for the tour. Yellow walls, claustrophobia, food smells, cheap wood cupboards in the rooms, small TV screens. Activities included Drama Workshop, Assertiveness and Craftworks (for Ruby?). But she battles bravely on, searching for the drug balance. We talk of old friends, the need for less friends, simpler lives, less ego. The constant, we-know-it-already, truth.

28 APRIL

2.30 David Greig.[1] Immediate rapport, I thought. Absolutely on the same page—not ready to make decisions now. Wait a bit. For the energy and specifics of the rehearsal room.

1 MAY

LONDON ELECTION.

8.30 Wake up, of course.

Doze until 11.30. Coffee in the bar. Car at 12. Home. Go out to vote immediately. Woman with blue rosette foolishly asks for our number. 'No,' snaps Rima. 'Oh,' she says. 'Oh well, variety . . .' On the way out she tries again. 'Hope to persuade you to . . .' Foolish. A torrent of (calm) anti–Boris Johnson abuse falls from my lips, emboldened, no doubt, by my quote in today's *Guardian*. The British electorate proving yet again that they never vote *for* anything. 'Someone's doing us down . . . let's disown him.'

3 MAY

Warm enough to sit outside on the balcony. Coffee and Saturday's *Guardian* dull the Boris Johnson nightmare. Fascist mayor of Rome, Berlusconi, Sarkozy, President McCain? Bush still there, Cameron at a gallop . . . God help us.

---

[1] Scottish playwright (1969–). He was adapting *Creditors* by August Strindberg.

9 MAY

8 Dinner. Tim Burton & Helena Bonham Carter. Picked up by Beatie at 7.30pm and whisked to Helena/Tim Land. It has many fairy lights in its world and the garden is a grotto and almost every room is toytown—but theirs is a miraculous pairing with these two utterly open-faced children— faces that have 'can't believe my luck' written all over them.

24 MAY

Sky News is full of anti-Brown propaganda. How depressing the English are . . . Cameron and his little band of droopy drawers are what they deserve.

25 MAY

Campagnatico.

Beautiful, still, sunny afternoon. *Until the phone call from Ruby. She left her passport at home.* Ed drove it to Stansted, but they missed the plane by six minutes. Now they're rerouted to Rome. I call Melanie[1] who finds Alessandro on his way to collect Ruby and Marcia from Pisa. He turns round and heads for Rome, collects them and they arrive at 11.30pm.

26 MAY

Long chat with Ruby about the Priory. In a way, it's a rest home for the unhappily sane, I think.

9 JUNE

Campagnatico—London.

15 JUNE

Absolute joy. Humphrey Lyttelton's *Desert Island Discs* followed by a brilliant tribute programme. Images of a standing ovation at the Apollo Hammersmith after he played 'We'll Meet Again' at the end of their tour. Plus that flowers were left at Mornington Crescent[2] when he died, had us both weeping. Irreplaceable.

Phone call from Randy that *Bottle Shock* has 5 ovations during the screening and I have won Best Actor in Seattle—great for them and the film.

4 JULY

7.45 *Black Watch.* Barbican.

Breathtaking, the kind of precision, rigour and commitment I despaired

---

[1] Melanie Parker, A.R.'s PA

[2] London tube station and the name of a game on BBC Radio 4's *I'm Sorry I Haven't a Clue*

of seeing. Actors who move like athletes/dancers, brilliant direction and design and with enough to say 'it took 300 years to build an army and a few years of the worst decision in western military history to destroy it'.

5 JULY
To bed at 2am. Up at 4.45am. To Heathrow at 5am. It *can* be done.

8 JULY

Campagnatico.

Glorious Tuscan day for our first full day in our *almost* finished home on the hill. Sabrina arrives to tinker with the leaves. Tinkering is what I'm up to in the garden, in cupboards, while Rima reads . . .

9 JULY
These are the days that have been fantasised about. Cool mornings hearing the intermittent door-slams of a village waking up; hot, still afternoons after a plate of melon, prosciutto, cheese and tomato for lunch, and dinner under the pergola watching the endless dissolves of the sunset. It is *all* like a cheap(ish) novel.

pm The electrician man arrives to connect the fridge. Seconds later it is full of wine and beer and there's a corkscrew in the next-door cupboard.

14 JULY
am The mini market, Antonio for citronella candles and the café for panini and cappuccino. Be seen *in* the village, in the shops.

24 JULY
San Francisco via Dallas.

25 JULY

San Francisco.

The hunt for something to cover Madame's shoulders on a cool evening. SAKS. No luck.

26 JULY

Calistoga.

9pm *Bottle Shock* premiere.
It looks and sounds great. And they (the definition of a captive audience) love it. Of course. But justifiably. Afterwards—more wine. And

then we all converge back at the hotel. For some wine. A quiet escape to bed.

27 JULY

Calistoga.

9.30 and no groomer in sight.

11 Located groomer and → Chateau Montelena for a day of press . . . First 'phoner' woman from Hell who has problems with the film's accuracy. The phone masks gritted teeth but I pointed out that we weren't making a documentary etc., etc. and may have suggested that she loose her stays . . .

28 JULY

Calistoga → Los Angeles.

Print and radio round tables. One-on-one with the *Daily News* and *LA Times*. Somewhere right in the middle the unmistakeable rumble. The building shakes and 10 secs later it's over. An earthquake 5.4! The biggest since '94.

1 AUGUST

8.30 pick-up.

10.40 became 12 → Newark.

11ish arrive at the home of Anne Hearst (granddaughter[1]) and Jay McInerney.

2 AUGUST

The Hamptons.

6am A deer is on the lawn in front of the *Gone with the Wind* House, mist lays over the greenness, the sun is fighting its way through the wisteria. A swim in the pool in front of the house.

8pm Dinner. Anne H., Jay McI. and friends. Fairly quickly it became evident that we were—phew!—surrounded by fervent Democrats. It was even possible to share some Middle East frustrations. Some beautiful wines on the table and Jay can certainly get through them.

10 AUGUST

The Revenge of No. 38.

. . . now there's a flood in the utility room, I'm ankle deep in water with mop and bucket. Rima is on the phone looking for a plumber who will come

---

[1] Of media tycoon William Randolph Hearst

out on a Sunday, the cold is streaming happily and my Psion organiser has gone mad so I am without phone numbers or addresses. It is hard not to think the house is angry with us. This, or something like it, happens every time we come home, it seems.

17 AUGUST
Patti Love[1] & Harriet. The Wolseley.

Patti's birthday.

We're in the middle of the restaurant. Harold P. and Antonia are at one table behind us. Lucian Freud & friends adjacent. Dear Fucking Diary. I went over to Harold and said, brightly, 'How are you—it's good to see you.' Harold was quick to remind me that Simon Gray had just died—his friend of 38 years. I blurted—'I was in America.' Harold pretty much snapped as to the relevance—I pointed out there is no news there (Antonia's hand closed over Harold's). He acknowledged this truth and we talked on *Creditors* and Strindberg. The earthquake averted. I like him so much.

25 AUGUST
Creditors Day One.

Read the play. Start laying down some seeming ground rules. Commit to the line. Listen hard. The 3 of them[2] look and sound great. But it's clear where the steering & great changes will have to be made.

27 AUGUST
pm Talk to Randy. *Bottle Shock* is holding up well . . . Could I fly to Chicago maybe for *Oprah* . . .

4 SEPTEMBER
On TV a first viewing of Sarah Palin. Ohmigod. Now the worship of amateurism reaches elections and presidential levels.

6 SEPTEMBER
Creditors.

10.30 Rehearsal room.

Run the play. Or stagger as it says on the rehearsal notice. It was actually much braver than either word. Anna, Owen & Tom have commitment written through them like the ever-ready when you need it metaphor—stick of rock. A lot to process, re-rehearse, develop—but now we have two weeks.

---

[1] British actor (1947–)

[2] Anna Chancellor, Owen Teale and Tom Burke (A.R.'s godson)

10 SEPTEMBER

1.30 Production meeting.

At which, for me, the main point of discussion was Germaine Greer's programme contribution. A polemic against marriage. Just what I was afraid of, so feet were put down.

28 SEPTEMBER

First knowledge that Paul Newman has died. Wonderful actor, wonderful self-effacing man. Honoured his family and his profession. The dinner Lindsay & I had in NY a treasured memory.

30 SEPTEMBER

Creditors. Press night.

And from the start they were *on* it. And so, it seems, were the audience. Afterwards no one seemed to want to go home and the bar was packed with people shining with having seen something v. special from those 3 heroes.

1 OCTOBER

Michael Grandage calls to say everything written in the press so far 'is a rave'. Especially, in the *Guardian* anyway, for Owen . . .

3 OCTOBER

7.30 *Creditors*.

And what the fuck were they doing playing it as if they were at the RSC? Much acting, much loudness. In the dressing room—guilty faces. Felt like Bill Shankly . . . [1]

5 OCTOBER

Creditors seal of approval from the *Observer*. So whatever any opprobrium elsewhere it has been a Donmar hit.

5 NOVEMBER

OBAMA WINS.

3am to bed. And it looks as if the miracle has happened.

8am. Back to the TV screen. It has. 52% of the US had a supreme act of imagination.

---

[1] Scottish manager of Liverpool football club famous for his expletive-riddled reactions to poor performances

6 NOVEMBER
Labour wins Glenrothes with a 6,700 majority. Maybe the image of Cameron and Obama together is too much to stomach.

17 NOVEMBER
4pm Car → Heathrow.
   6.30—New York.

18 NOVEMBER
Hilary Shor [film producer] picks me up to go to Sunshine Landmark/Houston for the premiere of *Milk*—Gus Van Sant's Harvey Milk film . . . The party afterwards at the Bowery Hotel was the autograph hunter's dream. Glitterati out in force. Talked to Lauren Bacall, Stanley Tucci, Jeff Goldblum, Frances McDormand (& Coen Bros), James Schamus.[1] Around and about—Naomi Watts, Natalie Portman, David Blaine, Mickey Rourke.

25 NOVEMBER

Los Angeles.

12 Logan picks me up to go to Enterprise Rent-A-Car. And here's a reason for keeping a journal. Get in car, attempt 3 point reverse, out of car park, shoot forward on v. sensitive accelerator, hit (v. gently) cars in front and behind, and while waiting for resulting paperwork to be completed, listen to phone messages and learn that I am being offered a CBE . . .

27 NOVEMBER
Write, appropriately, a thank-you but no-thank-you note declining the CBE.
   4 Rhea Perlman and Danny DeVito.
   70 friends and family for dinner in their couldn't-be-anything-but-Hollywood home. Room after room, sofa after sofa. Totally relaxed, totally social. Like Rhea and Danny themselves. And these were clearly old friends and their children from way back. Extra special was talking to the amazing Arthur Lessac—legendary voice teacher and now 99 years old.

2 DECEMBER

LA.

Nobel Son premiere.

---

[1] American screenwriter (1959–)

5 DECEMBER

LA.

Early morning silence means, inevitably, the reviews are not good. Here we go again.

Looking back on this trip is going to be formative, I think. Is it possible to spend time in this town remotely productively, adjacent to just the smallest amount of curiosity? All this is certainly exhausting to listen to.

8 DECEMBER

LA.

pm Chat with shattered—in every way—Randy [re *Nobel Son*] . . . What can you say? Wrong title, wrong marketing, right film.

13 DECEMBER

Saturday in New York. In Greenwich Village. In 12th Street between 4th Street and Greenwich Avenue. Total neighbourhood. Cafe Cluny on one corner, the Cubby Hole on another. A walk down to the party shop on Greenwich at 6th to buy tree lights and stuff, then up to Bed Bath & Beyond at 18th, back to Food Emporium at 12th and home to a warm house—it was freezing out there.

18 DECEMBER

2pm Rima from London.

23 DECEMBER

Christmas smash and grab. Bookshop, cake shop, supermarket, bookshop again. Rima off to John Barrett [beauty salon]. None of it necessarily in that order. Bookseller again.

24 DECEMBER

Ian Rickson calls to tell me that Harold Pinter has died. As I wrote to Antonia, one had got used to the fantasy that he might just go on forever. And indeed he will.

26 DECEMBER

1.30 *Vicky Cristina Barcelona*.

Woman's Weekly tosh from Woody Allen.

12.30 The Box. While waiting for the 1.30am cabaret/vaudeville/burlesque Francesca [Rima's sister] showed us the ready for anything loos (padded seat, footrests, horizontal pole, mirror) which probably prepared us for the naked drag act pulling a condom full of pills out of his rear end. It strove so hard for effect it was ultimately rather innocent.

29 DECEMBER
1pm Lunch w. Dan Radcliffe at Cafe Cluny. One minute he was 12 now he's 19. When did that happen? And he's sensitive, articulate & smart. And owns a 3 bed apt in NY.

2009

3 JANUARY

New York.

To Martha Clarke, Connecticut.

11.48 → Harlem Valley–Wingdale.

Martha collects us at the station. First stop visiting Mr Grey, the eye-injured horse, and local horse-whisperer/nurse and her *HP* obsessed daughter. Then to Martha's house. Within minutes of being inside I wanted to live in it, own it, borrow it. Arshile Gorky did it in the '40s and it is utterly covetable—beamed, galleried, windowed heaven . . . Spent the day stoking the fire, surrounded by books. Chicken supper, Martha's magpie mind skittering from passion to intrigue to struggle to passion again.

5 JANUARY

New York.

Lunch w. Theresa Rebeck.[1]

Who tells of the latest scam whereby directors now claim a piece of the writers' financial action on the basis of how they have (as Diane Borger put it) 'fixed your bad play'. Outfuckingrageous.

Maybe it's time actors claimed a piece of the directors' royalties on the same basis.

---

[1] American playwright (1958–)

9 JANUARY

New York.

12 The Box. Extraordinary Japanese dancer and a girl . . . who did a reverse striptease—clothes came from every orifice and shoes from a wig. Unforgettable. Bed—crazily—at 4am.

14 JANUARY

London.

Clearing the decks, rearranging the piles, throwing away the many envelopes. Staring in some disbelief at my Amex bill.

20 JANUARY
Barack Obama Inauguration Day.

3.30 Electric Cinema, Portobello Road, for Ruthie Rogers' Inaugural Day screening party.

Perfect way to 'be there' if you can't 'be there'. Along with Kathy Lette, Ruby W., Danny & Leila, Mariella Frostrup, Eric Fellner [from Working Title], Richard & Sue Eyre, Philippa Walker [Alan Yentob's wife], Jemima Khan, Jeremy King [restaurateur], Debra Hauer [film producer], Tessa Jowell.

Somehow we'd all been so moved beforehand by the idea of it all that it all seemed like a simple progress in a way. And his speech was short on rhetoric, doubtless deliberately, but packed with stuff to think about and teasing suggestions of his priorities.

24 JANUARY
1.30 Scott's. Lunch.

At the next table was an interesting group of ladies who lunch. Lynn Barber, Virginia Ironside, Tracey Emin & two others. Nigella Lawson & Charles Saatchi also there and we talked outside while he had a cigarette. He's a right-winger with a sense of irony. He and Rima already, of course, got on.

26 JANUARY
8 The Wolseley.

As so often, it seems, Lucian Freud at the next table. My basest urges are to say (1) 'Can I have a painting?' or (2) 'Paint me.' Anything, really, to connect with that massive talent.

31 JANUARY
Rima's birthday.

8 FEBRUARY
BAFTA night. Oh God, how many more awards can we give ourselves? On the news Australia burns and Gaza is in ruins.

10 FEBRUARY
7.30 *Damascus*. Tricycle [Theatre].

David Greig's play inspired by his Middle East trips working with young writers and encountering an entirely other sensitivity. Wry, gentle, but uncompromising—like David himself—and an unbelievably accurate cast including someone who said with total believability 'I am a Ukrainian transsexual pianist' and scored on every word.

17 FEBRUARY

New York.

8pm to Minetta Lane to collect Martha Clarke, Suzanne Bertish & Stephanie Carlton Smith [artist]—not before defending de Valera to Frank McCourt on the pavement outside . . .

20 FEBRUARY
Morgan Stanley Children's Hospital on 165th.

Reading stories to a group of 5–12-year-olds and then visiting some kids in their wards. The succession of drip stands and dazed expressions meant that a bit of self-drilling was needed. The desire to just hug them was irresistible except it looked as if they might break.

21 FEBRUARY
Birthday and it's another one but in NY . . .

22 FEBRUARY
The Oscars.

No big surprises except Sean Penn rather than Mickey Rourke. Kate Winslet wins her Oscar[1]—thank God since apparently someone is videoing her kids' reaction at the announcement which initially sounds like a horrible idea but actually—quite right and why not? As ever, anyway, after 3 hours of it all, it becomes embarrassing and pointless and indulgent and embar-

---

[1] For *The Reader*

rassing again. Not to mention the vulgarity of Queen Latifah singing 'I'll Be Seeing You' to pictures of Ant, P. Newman and Sydney Pollack.

8 MARCH
6 To BAFTA.

7 Mark Shivas memorial.

God knows what he would have made of it and of course it should have happened while he was still alive.

9 MARCH
7.30 Donmar, *Be Near Me*.

Ian McDiarmid's play version of Andrew O'Hagan's novel. Elegaic, cerebral, inward, reflective. Like Ian really.

14 MARCH
9.30 *Wall*—David Hare.

Theatre? Lecture? Glad to hear it—could have read it.

17 MARCH
Today one of the saddest, most surreal days ever. An early call from Ralph Fiennes in New York—7 o'clock his time—with 'terrible news'. Natasha has had a bad fall skiing in Canada, thought she was OK, then collapsed. She *is* now brain dead, Liam is flying up to bring her home so that people can say their goodbyes. Just that. All in one simple, devastated breath. When I put down the phone I must have sat in one place for an hour and then wandered. Left a message for Liam. Spent the day answering the phone and cancelling appointments. All in a daze. Absolute unreality. That lass unparalleled, the world's greatest host. Her life, her days, her every minute checked, cross-checked, crammed. Energy, glamour, talent, fury, compassion, generosity, ego, laughter, smoke, intelligence, wisdom, sarcasm, fun, speed, honesty, vulnerability, taste, improvisation, order. In the midst of the deepest laugh she knew how things should be. Except this.

18 MARCH
Joanna—Liam & Tash's PA—calls to say that they will let her go at 6pm New York time.

Midnight and Tash has gone. It's inconceivable that her sheer force will not be around. The chin tipped up, the mind racing for the next topic before the current sentence is finished, the door opening, the welcome immense.

19 MARCH

All day the news broadcasts are filled with her smiling upturned chattering face. Later on Liam, Joely [Richardson] & Vanessa [Redgrave] returning home to an onslaught of photographers.

Today was the Scofield tribute at the National. I couldn't cope. Stayed at home, pottered around, utterly aimless.

21 MARCH

To New York and Connecticut.

6.55 → New York after Rima did some heroic internet booking.

22 MARCH

Tash's funeral. Clear and sunny.

Tash in her coffin surrounded by photographs and posters. She looks like something from a shop window—incredibly shiny, hard and made-up. Her but not her as Laura Linney said. Ciarán & Helene, Meryl Streep, Mia Farrow, Ralph F., [John Benjamin] Hickey, Aidan Quinn, Joely, Tom H., Vanessa, Lynn [Redgrave], Ann Roth[1] as well as Jemma R. and 50 or 60 others. Micheál and Daniel [N.R.'s sons] are not afraid to smile with their friends and seem amazingly unfazed—maybe that's good. Daniel apparently has described the whole thing as 'a fake'. So doubtless something will hit them later, alone. Into the house for lunch and then down to the beautiful little church—turn right past the crowd of paparazzi and TV cameras . . . Deeply personal service—Liam wonderful, funny and open, Vanessa reading the Shepherd from *Winter's Tale*, Lynn the lesson, beautifully—Joely, Carlo (her brother), his wife Jennifer sang, Ralph read a poem about the sun, Katharine mother Grizelda and Franco sang an Italian song w. Vanessa.

Later Liam . . . told us all that because Tash was an organ donor her 'heart, kidneys and believe it or not her liver' had been successfully transplanted. The doctor said she had the heart of a 25-year-old.

23 MARCH

To New York.

7am One of my overriding thoughts from yesterday is that Liam is going to be fine. In a way, even, acknowledging his absolute love for Tash, he will be released. At the viewing yesterday, he even voiced what I have often thought. 'How did this happen? This woman came along and said "Right—we're getting married. We'll have a couple of children and we might as well

---

[1] American costume designer (1931–)

start now."' Conned, in a way, into a life of parties, houses and responsibility. The man who runs with the dog and sits on the riverbank, fishing. He also said after the service 'But you know however much I sighed at "we're going to dinner" I was always the last to leave. So I have learned.'

27 MARCH

Dublin.

1.20 picked up and driven to University College, Dublin.

2.15 James Joyce award. A little like being picked over by serried ranks of medical students but they were open and generous.

4.30 On the road to Moyne, Limerick.

Just enough time to finish *The Secret Scripture*.[1] Boy, will my review be fresh.

6ish Sebastian and Alison and the Old Rectory, Knockananna.

28 MARCH

Late am drive, walk, lunch in a pub in a valley, walk in and around stunning Limerick countryside. Limerick? *Wicklow*. Time to talk to Sebastian about his brilliant book. It begins as lyrical, elegiac S. Barry & consciously moves towards Dickens.

8 APRIL

7.30 *Plague Over England*.

[Drama critic] Nicholas de Jongh's play about the arrest of John Gielgud [re homosexuality]. Some good writing here and there but not a play. Halfway through I thought 'it's a TV film' and then in the interval Neil Bartlett[2] told us that it is to be filmed. Hopefully with Mickey F.[3] and Celia Imrie who both do great work. The reviews outside are excellent. One can only say 'of course they are'.

19 APRIL

Dogma was on TV tonight. Watched as much of it (i.e. as little) as I could bear. Why is the actuality of one's work *so* far from the intention?

21 APRIL

To Pisa and Campagnatico.

---

[1] Novel by Sebastian Barry
[2] British director (1958–)
[3] English actor Michael Feast (1946–)

23 APRIL

Shakespeare's birthday, I suddenly remember. Memories of Stratford, bunches of daffodils in a procession, barracking the South African ambassador.

The Budget. 50% tax rate for some.

Slew of phone calls before dinner. Rima is finishing *Secret Scripture*. 'I *knew* it was him, right at the beginning . . .' I'm shelling broad beans, topping and tailing green beans, snapping asparagus. R adds to roast potatoes (most of which, thankfully, I dropped on the floor) and some unidentifiable fish and that = supper.

28 APRIL

Lunch at Pizza Papageno watching the Pope receiving people at the L'Aquila earthquake site.

2 MAY

Watched *Il Divo*. Brilliantly imagined and inhabited—frustrating to have so little knowledge of Italian political history, but the spectre of Berlusconi invades the whole film in spite of there being only the briefest mention at the beginning.

8 MAY

11.30ish on the road. Livorno → Pisa → Aeroporto. Avis Car return (no scratches). Shuttle bus. So much calmer than the Roma experience. And then madness. Gatwick. On to the train to the South Terminal to get the train. Which wasn't the Gatwick Express. For which you can pay on board. Result— potential fine at Victoria. Not on my life. A Chinese family is just standing at the front of the taxi queue. 'You have to go around,' we helpfully indicate. 'It doesn't matter, we have a baby.' I'm thinking 'Your pram equals my suit-case.' There'll be a fight, we warn him, *just* before noticing the woman in full friend-powered wheelchair toiling through the queue. Welcome to England.

22 MAY

A phone call from Independent Talent Agency.

'Would I get on a jet (private) on Sunday to present an award in Cannes?' Sorry. Party.

7.30 *Waiting for Godot*. Theatre Royal, Haymarket.

Weirdly the first time I've ever seen the play. Alternately soul-*full* and soul-*less* in this production. Hard to believe that two very famous people are waiting for *anything*. But it is an evening full of joys from everyone. Crazy for it to be criticised for being too populist. A lot of it is music-hall. Ian

McKellen full of quiet wonders. Simon Callow unforgettably blind with Ronald Pickup v. moving Lucky.

24 MAY

Ian McK. 70th.

A magician. La Clique. Wall to wall friends. As Ian said—Family. All in his lovely house on the river on a sunny May evening. David Owen[1] was away so his terrace was purloined. Armistead Maupin and Dena H[ammer-stein] appear to have flown in specially.

25 MAY

7.30 Edna O'Brien. The Wolseley.

Edna's very up. Her play (*Haunted*) is getting some great reviews... Today in the *Guardian* she has let it be known that she is 78—impossible to believe. Over dinner we hear of her affairs with David Owen, John Fortune[2] and John Freeman;[3] antipathy with Dena H.; stand-off with Harold Pinter (re Vanity); talking to Beckett on the Underground, being told by Elizabeth Bowen[4] that she was 'talented and mad'.

7 JUNE

Headache, vomiting, exhaustion and a flooded bathroom. Bad combination and a lot of *mea culpa*.

2pm NT. Rehearse Pinter tribute.

Ian [Rickson] at his Buddhist, inclusive best. 'What do you think...?' 'Or do you think that...?' He insists on offering alternatives. I'm not sure why. Just tell us what you want.

7 Performance.

'Oh I love actors,' said Eileen Atkins as we came off. 'They just get up there and do it.' In some cases, brilliantly. In ours—fine from Lindsay & Gina McKee but I was chasing my own tail—aware of how difficult the material is and annoyed at the inevitable generalising.

11 JUNE

Eyes open. I have (from nowhere) a cold. The news all day is of course all about swine flu. 'Don't be ridiculous,' says Rima. 'You'd have to have been in contact with blah, blah...'

[1] British politician Dr David Owen (1938–), I.McK.'s neighbour
[2] English satirist (1939–2013)
[3] BBC interviewer (1915–2014)
[4] Irish-British novelist (1899–1973)

21 JUNE

Didn't have to be anywhere.

See anyone.

Do anything.

The sun shone a bit outside.

The air was cool.

There was plenty of mindless TV to wade through.

A few letters to answer.

Some lamb for dinner.

And the longest day . . .

28 JUNE

1pm Lunch w. Neil and Glenys K.

w. James Naughtie and Ellie [Updale, his wife]. Visited briefly by Rachel[1] w. Grace and later, on his own, complete with wizard robe and broom, son Joe who fires off 25 questions about *HP*. Apart from that utterly disarming episode this was a great and glorious lunch (til 7pm . . .) with so much insider talk that the head still reels. Labour Party hopeless, Gordon won't take decisions, loathing of Hazel Blears,[2] Mandelson (of course), mistrust of Miliband, grudging respect (I think) for Cameron's cleverness. Wonderful story of [Jeffrey] Archer's Madoff-like[3] nature (surprise . . .)—couldn't have been happier. Neil appeared thrilled with our gift of a mint condition *Spitting Image* board game—him, Gorbachev, Reagan, Thatcher etc. 'Oh David Owen, he made a speech the other day, the word "I" every other word.'

29 JUNE

8 Rima off to Italy.

1 JULY

3.30 To UCH [University College Hospital] to visit Miriam Karlin.

Miriam's in a sealed 'container' still furious that she was resuscitated but the anger at that swims in and out of her other topics—Hazel Blears currently tops the list.

She's had a hip replacement, a duodenal ulcer and C. difficile (maybe) and yet she brushes aside all concerns about herself. She wants to 'show off' her

---

[1] The Kinnocks' daughter
[2] Labour politician (1956–)
[3] Bernie Madoff (1938–2021), American fraudster and financier

walking skills and she is vibrantly curious and funny about endless issues. Half dead and more alive than almost anyone I know.

2 JULY

Somewhere in here, finally, the deal is done for *HP* 7 Parts 1 and 2, and people are all carefully left in possession of genitalia.

3 JULY

Tom Burke. To talk about what? Where? How? How long? The respect that he has earned needs to be matched by the work offered. And we could all say that.

7 JULY

5.15 Massive hailstorm and then on the way to Leicester Square (more downpour) for the *HP* 6 premiere. Sodden, happy, screaming crowds— before exiting a back door into Lisle Street and home for a pizza.

9 JULY

HP 6. New York.

   Party at the Natural History Museum.

   The desire to eat and even more get a drink is matched only by the need to bang the 3 Davids'[1] heads against the nearest wall. I get the character development and the spiffing effects (dazzling) but where is the story????

11 JULY

6 Liam . . . for a drink. He seems at peace but there is such an absence. The last time I was in the apartment Tash sat in the same seat as Liam.

14 JULY

Late—reading the programme notes for *Les Ephemeres* it floats through my mind that I met Pina Bausch, I know Ariane Mnouchkine,[2] I have worked with Ninagawa and Sturua[3]—these absolute theatrical heroes who have shaped my imagination and shown me what is possible in the theatre. It was a sudden heat surge of real privilege.

19 JULY

All day discovering in detail how surrounded I am by paper—accountants, banks, electricians, builders, health insurance, other insurance, charities,

---

[1] *Harry Potter* producers: David Heyman, David Yates, David Barron
[2] French director (1939–) of *Les Ephemeres*
[3] Robert Sturua (1938–), Georgian theatre director

theatre boards—all with agendas, annual reports, contracts, invoices—they weigh the house down.

All this being sorted and filed/dispatched against the background of the British Open golf tournament . . . Amazing that so many overweight men can call it a sport. Hit a small ball, walk through some glorious countryside and galleried throngs, hit small ball again.

24 AUGUST

HP.

3 Davids come into my trailer and I have to push the bile back down. Not very successfully. I try to channel the inarticulacy into words like 'process' and 'narrative' and maybe we reach a way forward. Time—even at this stage—will tell.

Costume felt very tight.

27 AUGUST

Supper w. Ruby & Ed.

Ed in mourning as Maddy goes off to university (she's coming back the first weekend) and clearly she still wants to be an actress, so good luck sociology department.

1 SEPTEMBER

3.30 Tea with Miriam K. plus Allan [Corduner] & [his husband] Juha.

Mim can hardly lift the teapot but somehow she's immaculate—hair done, nails manicured, cakes on the table and a dozen topics of conversation, endless curiosity and surrounded by books and her love of Radio 4. And somehow she still has sex appeal—her memories of lovers—'I've never thought of that—I had Mitch[1] *and* Stanley Kowalski'[2] is acute. She's a national treasure on every level.

2 SEPTEMBER

8 Alan Cumming at the Vaudeville.

An indefinable event. Alan has the most undeniable charm and a fund of the greatest stories stemming from a brave and honest place. And the songs are original and challenging. When he says he 'acts' them, however, I suppose I'd prefer a little less acting (the microphone is a near-relative of the close-up)

---

[1] Robert Mitchum, American movie star (1917–1997)
[2] Character in Tennessee Williams' *A Streetcar Named Desire*

and a bit more thinking. Plus the *real* Alan C. has a much darker, more determined soul than he's owning up to and the *real* show might reflect that.

4 SEPTEMBER
7 Ruby—Live at the Priory.

The good news is—it works. But it's still in its birth pangs which means Ruby is nervous which means she uses Judith[1] as a scapegoat. On stage. Disastrous. But she recovers and through sheer courage and acting ability she has the audience cheering. It's a very brave and moving show which needs dials adjusting and then it will be fine, if always fairly unpredictable.

5 SEPTEMBER
At-home day . . . 2 Beatles films (documentaries) and that leaves us wreathed in nostalgia. But we were lucky to have been there then, buying the White Album and listening to it, *knowing* we had just bought an all-time classic. These songs are in our bones now—a harmonic intro, a chorus, a headshake are triggers to an extraordinary montage of memories and images—friends, parties, love affairs, dancing, tight sweaters, trousers tight and wide, short jackets, pointed shoes.

10 SEPTEMBER
3pm David Yates [*HP* director]. For some reason I have lost the edit button in *HP* conversations, and having unerringly spotted a fatal flaw in the Snape/Voldemort final showdown I didn't beat about the bush. David Y., however, does exactly what he wants. There is a *kind* of listening but real stubbornness. A man who nods sympathetically and goes nowhere unplanned or so it seems.

5 OCTOBER
HP 7 Part 2.
Day One.
5am wake up . . . 5.45 pick-up.
The cold/virus/whatever is at its filthiest. All day.
Can't speak. Certainly can't act. Unfortunately required to do both.
8pm Home. *Utter exhaustion.*

7 OCTOBER
6.45 pick-up.

---

[1] Judith Owen, Welsh singer-songwriter (1959–)

Ralph F. fantastically impressive all day long. Free and disciplined and totally Voldemort.

Chat to the documentary team doing a Fly on the Wall—milking the cow one more time.

8 OCTOBER

Re-shot all my lines. Must have been pretty dire Day One.

9 OCTOBER

Re-shot all my lines again . . . Something is *very* wrong . . . apart from the deadly nature of the lines themselves.

15 OCTOBER

James Macdonald [theatre director] talking about *John Gabriel Borkman* and other possibilities.

16 OCTOBER

Message from James Macd. saying (not unseriously) what about Streep and Close?

30 OCTOBER

Dublin.

8.30 Town Bar & Grill.

Dinner w. Frank.[1]

Skating round the *Borkman* topic, but Frank treats topics of conversation like a pack of cards—shuffle, deal, play. And with the associated amount of fun, too. Never so serious that a snicker isn't just around the corner.

31 OCTOBER

10.45 Coffee w. James Macd. and Frank McG.

So the upshot of it all is that, come September [2010], we'll do *John Gabriel Borkman* at the Abbey, Dublin.

3 NOVEMBER

2 Carlos Lumière [photographer].

Ohmigod. A fashion shoot. Mutton dressed as all sorts of lamb is my fear. Odd how uncomfortable I am with this aspect of the job nowadays . . . I felt fat.

---

[1] Irish writer Frank McGuinness (1953–), adapter of *JGB*

15 NOVEMBER

7pm John Mortimer tribute.

And, amazingly—as ever—actors sniff out clues, possibilities and stitch something together. Something rather wonderful and honest and touching. The best for me was watching John's Oxford Union debate with Whitehouse[1] and Longford.[2] Well, his speech, anyway. Lethal *and* charming.

16 NOVEMBER

7am pick-up. *HP*.

To rehearse what is called 'The Boathouse Scene'. Otherwise known as the Death of Snape.

An empty sound stage with David Yates, Ralph and me. David is the most impenetrable mix of sweet-natured and immovable. He prefers, really, to just tell you what the story is, who you are playing, what you are thinking and where you stand, move, sit, look. Ralph and I (in a boathouse) put our oars in and I see David making a huge effort to let us have our heads. We start to get somewhere oxygenated.

17 NOVEMBER

11 Southwark Cathedral. John Mortimer memorial service.

Beautifully orchestrated service (would John think it a deal with the devil to have so many God references? The head religioso referred to him as an Atheist for Jesus). Everyone, appropriately, was there and Neil K. made a speech that knocked any actoring competition out of the water.

25 NOVEMBER

HP. 6.15 pick-up.

To the Flight Shed . . .

Cold, wet, draughty but the crew seem miles away so Ralph and I can just get on with inching our way towards the scene. David Y. stubborn as ever about V[oldemort] killing me with a spell. (Impossible to comprehend, not least the resultant wrath of the readers.)

Great working with Ralph, though. Direct and true and inventive and free.

Back home and Rima (narrative brainbox) says 'He can't kill you with a spell—the only one that would do that is Avada Kedavra and it kills instantly—you wouldn't be able to finish the scene.'

---

[1] Mary Whitehouse (1910–2001), British teacher and conservative activist
[2] Lord Longford (1905–2001), British peer and social reformer

26 NOVEMBER

HP. 6.15 pick-up.

And the scene goes on through the day and the angles and lenses. The Death of Snape. Nearly ten years later. At least it's just down to two actors . . . David is vulnerable and endearing when he's excited. And he is by this scene. It's the absolute example of what can happen when a couple of actors pick up a scene off the page and work with the story, the space and each other. Stuart Craig's[1] Boathouse gave it something ironic and everlasting. As I said at one point to David—it's all a bit epic and Japanese.

1 DECEMBER

To New York.

2 DECEMBER

During the day, we go furniture shopping and discover identical lamps at Wyeth for $7,200 and at Restoration Hardware for $799.

3 DECEMBER

8 *A Steady Rain*. Daniel Craig and Hugh Jackman and a play in there somewhere. Or rather a story on stage. To the dressing rooms afterwards . . . Daniel and Hugh have just auctioned their sweaty t-shirts (AIDS funding) for $40,000.

18 DECEMBER

10 Talk to James Macdonald. An offer will go to Sinead Cusack to start with. He talks of Marie Mullen[2]—I talk of Harriet [Walter].

25 DECEMBER

Walk along the High Line to 20th Street.

29 DECEMBER

Unbelievably cold so that on the way to lunch I turned and walked backwards against the wind, tripped on the mini railings around a tree and took all my weight on my right wrist.

30 DECEMBER

11 To St Vincent's Emergency Room. X-rays and a splint . . . is it a sprain or a fracture? It is *definitely* a bore.

pm The Miele Gasman Cometh. There *is* a leak.

---

[1] *HP* production designer
[2] Irish actor (1953–)

31 DECEMBER

9 Pamela [D'Arc, real estate agent] & Andrew [her husband].

10 The Box—Even madder than usual—meant that food arrived two hours later and voiceboxes severely strained, but there was the reverse strip-tease to compensate along with an amazing gymnast, a trannie with a bottle . . . Pamela danced with a naked man while we finished our strip steaks.

2010

1 JANUARY

New York.

2.45am. Home. Bed. New Diary.

4 JANUARY

A day of waiting for the gasman . . . trying to negotiate the American Healthcare System—everything starts with 'How will you pay?' The hospital for special surgery is calling tomorrow—all this for a nagging but small, residual pain.

5 JANUARY

To St Vincent's for the protracted business—'Go upstairs, fill in the form.' 'Go downstairs—it's $10—come back with the form, collect the CD'—of collecting my wrist X-rays.

7 JANUARY

9.30 Cafe Cluny.

Coffee and talk with Kate Winslet. *A Little Chaos* steps out and glowing, iridescent Kate loves the script so it's a brilliant start.

Later to the Neue Galerie Klimt to Klee via Schiele and Kokoschka.

Then to 145 Hospital for Special Surgery. Dr Hotchkiss instantly reassuring on all fronts.

9 JANUARY

1pm Susan S[arandon]. Zampa. Turns out the split was Susan's making and as ever from the standpoint of her constant 360 degrees wisdom. Maybe Tim sees it differently.

12 JANUARY

BACK to 38WT.

3.30am (8.30am) on the plane a slow but sudden (here comes jet lag) thought that living in New York makes you look at your life in London through different eyes. What to keep, what to discard, where to focus more. Watching time slip, slide and cascade by from two different perspectives.

10ish. Long, dragging journey through jams to 38WT. Which itself has the dark-eyed mournful Cornelia ('I came at 7am') on the other end of all the dust and disturbance.

The contrast with NY is epic. Suddenly, here is a life circumscribed by piles of paper, possessions, STUFF. Immediately, the compulsion is to change, discard, shed, rearrange, dilute, SIMPLIFY.

14 JANUARY

HP.

6.30 pick-up. After a night of not sleeping at all.

Scene 305. In the Flight Shed. Or—The Last Breath of Severus Snape.

The Flight Shed is freezing, slush on the ground—'colder inside than out' says Chris, my driver. Here I am with Dan, Emma and Rupert 10 (?) years on (Emma is here on a break from Brown University), blood all over my throat from an imagined nagini,[1] the three of them still with furrowed brows and panting a bit. Finding it hard to remember any particular scenes over the years mainly because all the decisions are taken in committee rooms and not on the floor. We listen as D.Y. tells us what we are thinking and why (and in some cases recounts the story . . .) and a small piece of something creative caves in.

17 JANUARY

2.45 River Cafe.

Wonderful opportunity to poke David H. about the Flight Shed, nicking props, what would happen if an American actor showed up, absence of producers etc., etc. and all provoked by him arriving with a compliment about the scene w. Daniel . . . I have no STOP buttons with some people. Especially when they're smart *and* dumb and there's no need.

20 JANUARY

James [Macdonald] called. He's offered to Lindsay and Fiona.

---

[1] Nagini, a long, green snake; in *Harry Potter* she is Voldemort's pet.

21 JANUARY

News this morning that I won't be needed on *HP* until March.

IT PRODUCES SPACE IN MY HEAD . . .

25 JANUARY

2.15 Hygienist.

The Cruella de Vil version. If I'm not wincing from the nerves she's hitting, I'm gagging on the suction pipe, whilst drowning in spray. Somewhere through this and the din made by her scraper-tool she's asking me questions or giving me mini lectures about wine, peppermint tea etc., etc. Get me out of there.

7 FEBRUARY

Reading Antonia F.'s book[1] about Harold and she calls her diary her friend. Mine or my relationship with it is often more resentful. A pity and wrong. It would have been great to find something specific and personal about Tash . . .[2]

12 FEBRUARY

Cape Town.

5.30 Car to FUGARD THEATRE.

It's in District Six—an amalgam of a church and warehouse and Mark [Dornford-May, director] has learned from the Royal Court and the Young Vic and left plaster (and ghosts) clinging to the walls. A beautiful theatre, stunning rehearsal room and jaw-dropping roof with Table Mountain as a backdrop. *The Magic Flute* was as transporting as ever—not an egomaniac in sight on stage, and Athol Fugard [playwright] speaking about the building and performers coming home afterwards.

15 FEBRUARY

CAPE TOWN → LONDON.

21 FEBRUARY

9pm Watching BAFTAs.

Jonathan Ross needs better jokes. We need to be less favouring to the US. Vanessa looked wonderful but I have no idea where she was going in her speech.

---

[1] *Must You Go?: My Life with Harold Pinter*
[2] Natasha Richardson

25 FEBRUARY

6.15 Car to Leicester Square. *Alice in Wonderland* premiere.

In the rain. Tough on all the been there for hours fans. Sign/flash/flash. Line up for Charles & Camilla. He—'Are you still on *Harry Potter*?' She—'Haven't seen you for ages.' Then the movie. Absolutely ravishing—strange and deep and complex and beautiful.

26 FEBRUARY

7.30 *Love Never Dies.*

The new Lloyd Webber musical (*Phantom* 2). I think it has a tune that we'll all be singing, another one that has the same opening notes as 'Room With a View', and definitely a couple of knockout leading ladies.[1] Where was the plot?

8 MARCH

11 Ruthie Rogers.

To work through her eulogy for tomorrow's funeral. Rose Gray[2] her 25-year partner. Ruthie—the great organiser—is suddenly terribly vulnerable. She's written a beautiful and funny/sad speech. I buckle down and talk about breathing and highlighter pens.

3.15 To *HP* to rehearse with Michael Gambon.

Fairly quick in and out. It's clear what the scene needs. On the way back to the trailer Michael talks of his fear of learning/forgetting his lines. And then he tells me he's doing *Krapp's Last Tape*[3]—what's wrong with this picture??

10 MARCH

Just me and Michael G. all day. He's vulnerable after his illness and yesterday's primer was no joke for him. The lines are a real problem for him. Technology helps and why not? It's never great when it's just a memory loss—no relaxation, no freedom, no contact. I'd have boards and autocue everywhere. And anyway when he unleashes a bit of magnificence it's effortless and spellbinding.

Michael's stories are wonderful. On Broadway he found a job (no pay) as a motorbike mechanic [with] ENGLISH BIKES to fend off loneliness and boredom. One night doing *Skylight* [play by David Hare] he couldn't open the door to get on. It was kicked down. He climbed over it.

Rima says Ruthie was wonderful at the service today. I phoned, caught R[ichard Rogers].Then Ruthie called back. She had cried when reading it

---

[1] American actor Sierra Boggess (1982–) and English actor Liz Robertson (1954–)
[2] British chef (1939–2010)
[3] A one-man play by Samuel Beckett

to Richard this morning, was nervous in the cab, but calm in the pulpit. Attagirl.

11 MARCH

7.45 pick-up.

In the evening at Godric's Hollow and Snape going into the house to find Lily. Great concentration, great crew all out in the cold until 9.30pm. No sight or sound of a producer and a new low in disgusting food—cornish pasties, sausage rolls, white rolls with other sausages, more white bread with melted processed cheese, all straight from the cheapest bakery, half cold and ashamed of itself.

12 MARCH

The strangest feeling—giving vent to Snape's emotions after years of snappy aloofness. Not funny to have the scene interrupted (without a 'sorry', of course). 'You don't mind, do you?' 'Yes, I *do*.' 'Oh—well don't be like that.' 'You asked if I minded.' 'Yes well I realise now that was my mistake.'

22 MARCH

6.40 pick-up.

Snape the headmaster.

Tortuous dialogue—monologue—slightly brain-frying.

24–25 MARCH

Many angles, different numbers of children, Maggie going nuts waiting.

29 MARCH

6.15 pick-up.

LAST DAY ON *HARRY POTTER*—All a bit hard to believe. I think even Daniel was shocked by the finality. Cameras were everywhere, it seemed (docu ones). 'So how does it feel?' Before you've felt it, before the feeling has a name. 'It's private' I managed 'and I'm not sharing it with that' (pointing at his lens)—sympathetic, empathetic friend this morning, embarrassed nosey parker this afternoon.

Something is in those cans and it is finished. Thanks, Jo.

6 APRIL

10 O'Clock News. Corin[1] died at the weekend. This is monstrously unfair—to pile all this grief on to one family.

---

[1] English actor Corin Redgrave (1939–2010)

7 APRIL

[Re *Creditors*]

4pm A run. And there were some breathtaking things going on, particularly from Anna [Chancellor] who hits levels of freedom that astonish. And when she and Tom [Burke] are hammer and tongs it is, amazingly, just like life . . .

10 APRIL

CREDITORS TO NEW YORK.

11.30 car to Heathrow. 'I hated you in that *Fish Called Wanda*,' says the driver.

14 APRIL

The tech starts. If only it were just a tech—I'm a bit concerned that Owen [Teale] is losing his nerve, added to weird ideas about softening his character. But we plough on through the evening towards an 11 o'clock exit. Technical staff all fantastic—actors feeling their way. Why am I surprised?

15 APRIL

4pm Dress rehearsal No 1.

Finally, Owen joins the play and if this had been an opening night I would have been OK with it.

16 APRIL

7.30 First preview.

Scary, all those people—laughing. *A lot.* When you haven't been expecting it. Rabbits jump in front of headlights for the actors. And they start to push. Moving on.

20 APRIL

CREDITORS OPENING NIGHT.

7.30 Show.

Which started well and then became, probably only to my ears, a touch underpowered. 83% to its usual 100%.

22 APRIL

That New York thing. Rave reviews and the phone rings.

26 APRIL

Witness for the Prosecution.

Happy band gathers, except for Uma Thurman who is 'at the doctors' *with a disc problem.*

1 MAY

am Anna phone call. 'I'm in a bit of trouble . . .' No sleep, blinding headache. Told her to get into a car and come over.

Phoned Dr Barry Kohn. Which hospital? St Vincent's is closed. 60th and 10th—Roosevelt/St Luke's. And then on until 5pm. Saline drips, blood pressure, CAT scans, MRI scan. Nothing sinister there, but the headache won't go. Now they can give ibuprofen and Anna, sure that it is something viral, goes home. No show tonight.

2 MAY

And there will be no show today. Last night Anna had worsened, gone back to hospital. They gave her a lumbar puncture and diagnosed viral meningitis. Which apparently sounds worse than it is—could be a week off but there is no antibiotic only painkillers and rest. After talking to her we decided to collect Owen and take the train out to Beverley and Rye. Glorious sunny day. Owen swam and boated, we sat and read before an early supper at Beverley's club.

3 MAY

Home to news that Lynn Redgrave has died. This is like something Greek. That sweet and brilliant woman.

6 MAY

11.10 Car to Cipriani 42nd Street.

Women Who Care lunch.

Women who care between shopping, lunch and face lifts.

No, but *really* in spite of other distractions.

Back home and the TV tells us nothing conclusive in the UK except a hung parliament and Gordon lost. For once the polls are right & for once the US is fascinated.

16 MAY

CREDITORS LAST PERFORMANCE.

3pm Final performance NY.

Truly, one of the finest performances they gave, and some of the best, freest acting I've seen, anywhere. It seemed as if the entire audience was on its feet.

7 JUNE

John Lewis—the Great Fridge Saga continues. And as of today, has no solution. The computer and a tape measure tomorrow.

10 JUNE

Finally bought a fridge. 10 days' delivery.

22 JUNE

SONG OF LUNCH.

   3pm Niall [MacCormick, director], Christopher [Reid, writer], Emma.

   Trying to find some calm, unadulterated waters amid Em's whirlpools of opinions. *So* talented—*so* controlling, *so* vulnerable, *so* closed. *Not curious.*

27 JUNE

Learning lines for the coming big test.

28 JUNE

A long, long day—fingers crossed in the memory department (metaphor that seems somehow spot on). Emma never falters—always present, always in charge. Later in the day she says she went to her trailer and cried.

30 JUNE

And now the tougher stuff—slow-motion cranking on the narrative. Legs and back ache from sitting at the table for so many hours and with such undiluted concentration. Well, not undiluted. Somewhere in these two days laughter creeps in endlessly. Has to with Ms T. particularly when I am on brain freeze and she prompts me from ventriloquist-perfect mouth. 'Put your hand out.' 'The other one.'

8 JULY

SONG OF LUNCH—FIN.

   6.55 pick-up.

   Hands, eyes, wine, food details with Em. Then more of the same on me. Before the thank-yous and goodbyes as they swing on to flashback 1989.

   4pm Finish. Sweet speech and a bottle (magnum) of Bollinger '99 from Pier [Wilkie, producer] who could hand out some lessons to *HP* personnel.

12 JULY

ITALY.

   CAMPAGNATICO.

14 JULY

6am swim.

   The air and the water are precisely the same temperature and one of the joys of this pool and this garden is that you can swim naked. You, the air, the waking sun and the water.

16 JULY

Volterra.

4 → San Gimignano—And no need—ever—to go again. No life just tourist traps and depressed faces.

5ish Volterra. Sandra finds us at the hotel and takes us into the town for a mini Volterra tour.

17 JULY

Volterra.

To work through what I will do and when. And to get the text of the Dante poem for tomorrow.

10pm in the shadow of the amphitheatre.

Reading 'All the world's a stage' (a miracle no broken ankles walking down the steps in the dark—Francesca in heels—to get to the stage) then, as far as I could tell, Simone did his favourite soliloquies with Francesca as linkperson.

28 JULY

A leak, a puddle, a smell.

29 JULY

9 Guido, the plumber . . .

But first, the 7am cup of tea—remembering instructions not to empty the sink—and my final piece of reading before I pick up, open and slide into the *Borkman* (I have read, digested and responded to a pile of paper maybe inches high on this trip, an achievement) is Evgenia Citkowitz's book of stories. And this is real writing. Every word carved precisely from what?— ether—for its sharpness and texture. And the stories sly, bold and seductive.

30 JULY

THE STORM NEXT DAY.

7am Sitting on one of the dry chairs, inside, in the doorway, because there's no electricity. Anywhere in the village. A big pile of sopping towels waiting for the washing machine upstairs, exhausted candles everywhere, the contents of the fridge staring at the kitchen from the open door, knowing their hours are numbered. The calm after the storm.

From 7–11pm it raged, skipped, tarantella'd, deluged. Magnificent and inventive and, literally, electrifying. Actually de-electrifying. For split seconds every twenty seconds night was day. We were merely its abject slaves, trying to stop the house being flooded. Now, a cup of tea—early morning light and the pigeons lining up on the roof tiles, dumb as ever. They probably slept through the whole thing.

31 JULY

The brain—in LA (ish), some gala thing, actors dressed up-down—like in the audience etc. It's a dream. Opening number (after I have gone to a seat, following Ruby, found it's not mine, walked to the back, declined a young redheaded girl's pick-up on the way, sat down). Large numbers of the audience are on their feet hollering and dancing. I just watch. A group of mostly overweight women—all in blue satin—get upset with me because I won't dance. I beat a retreat outside, where a crowd of paparazzi are on the hunt. Hand up to my face, I push through. One of them gets very aggressive but in a creative way. I stop and aggressively give him a photograph. The others walk off, furious. The End.

1 AUGUST

PISA → LONDON.

4 AUGUST

We make the hideous discovery of the damp patches and bulging floorboard in the bathroom lobby. Rising damp? Cracked pipe? Is there no end to this?

7 AUGUST

1.45 car to Leavesden for the *HP* wrap party.

Almost every expense spared—at least in the food department. At 2.30pm little was left, anyway. We went on the Simulator and the Twister. (Bloody painful.)

9 AUGUST

Watching *Song of Lunch*. Difficult, uneasy-making stuff. Quality of the film aside, it is *so* hard to look at yourself with any objectivity.

10 AUGUST

The seeming diagnosis of cracked pipe means the gentle hum of dehumidifier collecting water from where the pipe had spewed forth for God knows how long.

17 AUGUST

To work with Kristin Linklater [voice coach]. And in 1½ hours she gives me instant re-education. Just need to hang on to a repeatable structure, and not generalise. The sense of sigh in, sigh out for breath is great *plus* feeling sound in the back of the neck and up over the tongue. But a scary blockage in the left ear.

23 AUGUST

10am Abbey Theatre, Dublin.

Day One—*John Gabriel Borkman*.

First person I see in the rehearsal room is Joan Bergin—literally just off a plane from the Emmys. She won. Her third.

Somewhere after James's talk, we read it. The mountain emerges from the mist somewhat.

Tom Pye shows the set—beautiful, cold, transparent. We're all in a deep freeze. Joan's costumes are beautiful and this is just the beginning of the detail, passion & care.

24 AUGUST

Day Two and the onion shows its many layers. The play starts to seem like Beckett's inspiration, yesterday's costumes seem over-elaborate, some of Frank's dialogue a little clunky, I'm questioning the accents, Fi has positioned herself for extra props—the play will tell us what to do and James seems quietly to spot everything.

Early home. No alcohol. Find healthier food will be the mantra. M&S beckons.

29 AUGUST

After a week of no alcohol last night's ever-pouring bottle hits like a truck this morning.

30 AUGUST

Walking across the footbridge (uneven steps) and looking upwards. Next thing on the ground—hard and sudden. And the shock of it stays with me all day. Not to mention the grazed hand and the holes in the right knee of my (irreplaceable) trousers. All day I can feel the thud, the surprise and the vulnerability that I guess comes as you leave way behind the knocks and scrapes of a child.

1 SEPTEMBER

A day off.

They're doing the first act—Lindsay's nervous. Fi has asked for 'stuff' from their childhood to be in the room . . .

Lindsay called after rehearsals to say that the room looked like something out of *Steptoe and Son* but that Fi really does want to engage so all may be well.

5 SEPTEMBER

7.30 Seamus Heaney. *The Abbey*.

Wonderful work, wonderfully read. Brian Friel there too and we gathered around him in the bar. He says he isn't writing any more. I said—'Write me something, ten minutes will do.' The short time demand appeared to whet an appetite.

6 SEPTEMBER

All day a battle with the boring as fuck hearing thing. Every low-level hum—the air-conditioning, the boiler, the railway, the traffic—is like constant rumbling, reverberation. Underwater.

Rehearse . . . A lot of busking going on; no real work happening. A voice, an attitude has been found and posted. Lindsay, of course, the other side of the coin—questing and honest.

Conversation with Fi in the bar last night still reverberates like a drum, too. And underwater will become a distinct possibility.

8 SEPTEMBER

Car to Beacon Hospital [Dublin].

Supposedly for an MRI—no knowledge at the desk, then a young South African woman finds me and takes me for an audiology test (L ear now on a par with R), then we go back down the stairs and I *have* the MRI (head & neck inside the machine—bang bang bang, clack clack). Back to the rehearsal room by 1.

pm Watching—because there is no participating—Fi in full appallingly arbitrary flight. We worked on into the evening to no effect except a *reclaiming* of space by me with an 'improvisation' designed to prove a point.

23 SEPTEMBER

Act 3.

And there is a different Gunhild[1] in the room—stiller, more involved. A little bit—'Do you want me to do nothing? Here it is.'—but it's a beginning . . .

---

[1] Played by Fiona Shaw

27 SEPTEMBER

2pm. Rehearse.

Act 2. The lines all now inhabiting different parts of the body. Part of the process, I suppose.

6 Act 2 run-through.

There is, it now has to be said, so little energy coming from James's chair that L. & F. are in some kind of panic. It is making L. disappear inwards and F. start fighting outwards.

28 SEPTEMBER

10 Meandering, angsting journey through 3 & 4 and now the full James bottomless pit of no response becomes clear. He generates endless discussion—endless—but does not, ultimately, direct.

29 SEPTEMBER

10 Stagger-through.

Maybe an important day . . .

The run-through had some horrors and flashes of what it all might be.

It prompted a gloves-off discussion about the need for James to police, direct. And for Lindsay to step out of the shadow that Fi casts everywhere by her 'energy' ('I pile it on when I think nothing is happening.'), her arbitrary energy, her zero need of another actor all mixed up with her brilliance—in flashes.

Tomorrow is definitely another day and I do feel cleansed by not editing what I said. It may or may not have fall-out. Too late now. And anyway—we're supposed to be grown-ups.

1 OCTOBER

10.30 Run-through.

The beginnings of a cold for me. Nerves piling up. Impossible to allay. Lines disappearing from view for all of us. Not clear which bits work, which don't—James seems blithe in the face of it.

Back at Spencer Dock at 7pm with L. & F.—martinis, red wine and honesty. A plan and onward.

4 OCTOBER

. . . a visit to the doctor, since, on waking, everything in my body wished to remain in bed—sinus infection no. 83, more antibiotics, nose spray, nosedrops. What can they do?

6 OCTOBER

Preview one.

We did it, Ella, we did it.

8 OCTOBER

1.30 rehearse.

7.30 The show—and all sorts of staging pluses, but oh—these terrifying days. From all of us.

9 OCTOBER

4pm Rehearse/7.30 The show.

At which I thought we reached a kind of understanding about Act 3. Out the window by the evening—we were in a Whitehall farce.

2am Back in the apartment with Lindsay & Hilton.

Only one topic of conversation possible, really.

12 OCTOBER

7.30 The show.

We're all fighting tiredness, really. Act 3—Fi is riffing. One does not so much act *with* her as *against* her. In life—a glorious, generous, open, hilarious force. In art—a nightmare.

13 OCTOBER

7.30 The press night.

Which, as they say, went as well as could possibly be expected.

15 OCTOBER

. . . James creeps round the door sidelong, with sidelong smile. Clearly a mixed press reception and reading between the lines and from the silence and absence (apart from Joan B., bless her) the nagging is aimed in my direction. Now I'm feeling like the fall-guy. Let's hope this feeling fades.

18 OCTOBER

Rima went home . . .

6ish and how will this fadge?

F. comes into my dressing room—can we meet tomorrow?—we need another director—this is not BAM[1] worthy—I may have to leave . . . There

---

[1] Brooklyn Academy of Music

is—as usual—no discourse, only a monologue and the performance only compounds fears.

20 OCTOBER

3 Lindsay. Some good moves forward. The bravest soul—with a cold.

7.30 The show and Act 3 continues to step into itself. But *OH*, the absence of a director . . . at this point—*any* director.

26 OCTOBER

7.30 Act 3—a nightmare.

After the show—James full of 'Marvellous and the set will work in NY' . . . OhmiGod.

27 OCTOBER

12 James, The Bar. Fiach's[1] office. James looked like a wounded animal—but then SO ARE WE. I let him have it on the set front. He will (of course) be stubborn.

28 OCTOBER

Fi didn't show up until 4, so no time for anything except (whispered) notes. During the show—a good word considering an audience hell-bent on laughs. There were guffaws and titters on any old line and they thought the play was over on 'Come on . . .' We discovered some new lows in coping.

In the bar, afterwards, rage boiled over and in the face of the Sphinx smile too much—probably—truth. Or not enough. Could be a Waterloo.

30 OCTOBER

2.30 Act 3—a joke (1).

7.30 Act 3—a joke (2).

Somewhere in here—for diary sake—the potential scenario is—L. won't rehearse with one actress while playing with another . . . Could this be the great malicious victory . . .

31 OCTOBER

7 Town Bar & Grill.

Fiach, Lindsay, Fi and I. Hanging on to my hat here—could have become

---

[1] Fiach Mac Conghail (1964–), director of the Abbey Theatre 2005–2016

very nasty. The waves crashing backwards and forwards, directors' names are discarded etc., etc., etc.—all with the elephant in the room which I raised/pointed at when L. & I got home—*Fi wants to go. Let her.*

2 NOVEMBER
6 Dressing room and Fi 'wants to talk in the bar'. She is grey of face.

7.30 The show—if I can do it with this tight band around my head, I can do it anywhere.

10.15 Fi—the schizoid—trying to stay the innocent party, wanting it to be anything other than her decision. We are having *none* of it. 'Fi—you have to go, and tell Fiach tomorrow.'

3 NOVEMBER
7.30 The show and she's off the rails. And in a way, so am I. Dizzy (literally) with it.

4 NOVEMBER
5.30 Company meeting. Of course, Fi arrives last and says nothing. I show her my groundplan sketches. Immediately, she has plans for sweeping her own path on stage . . . At the interval she tells Lindsay that 'Hollywood has been on the phone.' The circus goes on.

11 NOVEMBER
11am rehearse.

Fi wants Gunhild to be loved by JGB. I can't comment, except to quote the text. We argy-bargy away, no one strong enough to call her on it. THE MARRIAGE IS OVER—IT'S A BLACK, BLACK SITUATION AND WE MOVE ON FROM THERE . . . On 3 or 4 (?) hours' sleep I don't have the will but also will not cave in to generalisations.

7.30 The show. And *how* do I do this? Somehow we make it to the end.

Rima has arrived.

16 NOVEMBER
7.30 The show.

Somewhat fuelled by anger at being told about line-endings and complaints at the box office. It would help not to start the play at the back of the stage and then play much of Act 2 facing upstage or into a corner. And how helpful it might be to start such a conversation on a *positive* note. Too much to ask?

20 NOVEMBER

2pm matinée.

The beginning of these last days is always like staring at some impossible slope. We will never climb it—the summit will never arrive. Minute by minute, line by line, it does.

7.30 Last (Abbey) show.

The sense of where this will go (and the places it may never visit) becomes greater as the run ends. Lindsay and I are *on* the mountain.

10ish The Bar.

Massive sense of relief, release and real achievement. Whatever it is we ultimately did—we did it. Fully, committedly.

22 NOVEMBER

London.

Not a foot outside the front door all day.

Somewhere in there, a phone call with Juliet who seems a bit beaten and negative—her life is all about coping—no Hugh[1] (Canada), the demands of the children, no roles for women over 50, re-living her nightmare with F.S. . . . This is sad from someone who used to explode with laughter. The shock (as ever, as *so* often) is the lack of any real interest in other people (in the same profession).

23 NOVEMBER

55 Wimpole Street. Doctor's laboratory. Blood test and reading many magazines, including *Vogue*'s info that Emma Watson was given a vintage Rolex 'by her producers' . . .

3 DECEMBER

To New York.

6 DECEMBER

Russell Brand unwatchable on Jay Leno. The self styling has gone and now it's a man in search of the rest of his career—shorter hair, a sweater and a tie. And he's being adorably eccentric rather than crazed.

---

[1] Hugh Brody, Juliet Stevenson's husband

10 DECEMBER

A Little Chaos.

9.30 The actors start to arrive.

10.15 Kate Winslet arrives. Intimate and strange—to have known her at 19 and watched her become 35.

10.30 *A Little Chaos.* Its first reading.

1pm Barbuto.

Kate, Gail [Egan, producer], Andrea [Calderwood, producer], Alison [Deegan, screenwriter], Rima & me. Still difficult to read Kate. She seems to be moving forwards and backwards at the same time.

19 DECEMBER

Montego Bay, Jamaica.

Good old American Airlines.

1½ hours late taking off (we have a connecting flight), no magazines in rack, only one earpiece working, a meal that defied analysis . . . hell for leather dash at Miami. Which was delayed. No flight attendant. She was on our flight from NY . . . Got to Montego Bay. Found driver. Got to Round Hill [Hotel]. White balustrades, white curtains, white sheets, colonial furniture. Hot tub. Glass of rum in the moonlight.

20 DECEMBER

A day of nothingness, oblivion. Interspersed with memories of the script on the plane—*Extremaduran Portraits*—and reading the mostly excellent script of *Midnight's Children.* The part, however, is over before it's started.

25 DECEMBER

12 o'clock to the beach to wait for the 1pm arrival, by boat, of Santa—he's black with a big white beard and is heard saying (in deep Jamaican) 'Boy, it's hot in your country.'

To the house to open presents.

8 Dinner. Everything available except roast potatoes, brussels sprouts, Christmas pudding and a third candle to see what we were eating.

28 DECEMBER

To Miami → New York.

Down to the office to check out and think deep thoughts about the bill.

10am To the airport. Where we find that the 5.25 becomes the 6.25, becomes the 7.10, becomes the plane without a PA so cannot be announced, becomes the plane whose crew have now (8.30 and counting) been working too long and have to be replaced (9.05) (9.30) (9.55). To get to JFK, however, seemed like an achievement. It was swiftly (well, excruciatingly slowly) crushed by the 3½ hours we had to wait for our luggage. Staggered home from the siege at 4.30am. The flat was of a freezingness forgotten since childhood.

31 DECEMBER
Dame Harriet Walter for goodness' sake!

2011

1 JANUARY
New York again for New Year's Day.

6 JANUARY
BAM. Day One. The tech begins . . . and, ultimately, it was a *happy day*. The body was in massive rebellion as the head tried to keep pace and direct. Had to lie down a couple of times, but as F., L. and I agreed in Lyon later on (whisky sours helping) the H[1] is such a magical space that you can't help feeling lifted, expanded and inspired by it. The play and its language start to come through.

'We have a play,' says F.

7 JANUARY
9.30 at BAM. Tech continues with Act 4.

2pm we got a dress rehearsal which seemed to go well. Howard Davies [director] was happy—we were free and inventive.

7.30 First preview.

Working within and around complete exhaustion, and I forgot to drink a load of water. Somehow (as ever with this) we made it to the end.

8 JANUARY
Show preview 2.

Fighting across some creeping infection. Somewhere, somehow, some real discoveries were made and a very good show. Something special is happening here.

---

[1] Harvey Theater, part of Brooklyn School of Music

10 JANUARY

Late pm mind-numbing offer from Doug McGrath[1] that makes me wonder what agents are for . . .

14 JANUARY

7.30 Show.

A tough one in the scheme of things. Interestingly, not a glimpse of BAM staff . . . You're on your own day of opprobrium in NY.

10.15 Out of the theatre and into a car and home, and watching Critics' Choice Awards—it becomes embarrassing watching the first of many award shows for actors. We are free TV with ads, trading on an embarrassingly repetitive and needy emptiness. No wonder *Somewhere*[2] is ignored.

18 JANUARY

7.30 Show.

2 phones go off—first-scene offender apparently even said sorry. Second scene—front row complete with bag rummaging.

19 JANUARY

7.30 Show.

Feeling as if the virus from hell might descend. Which it did in terms of an audience cougher and fidgeters. Oh God, this endless battle with *oneself*.

20 JANUARY

7.30 Show.

Skittish audience wanting to laugh at almost anything. Before the show mentions of complaints about audibility had been passed on. Felt like I shouted the evening.

10.15 Caffe e Vino.

People have the faces of those who have read a bad review.

23 JANUARY

3pm Show.

Bizarrely, there begins to be a space in my head—when the gremlins and fears are pushed away—that might enjoy doing this play. You have to *hide* the beast, not let it possess you.

---

[1] Canadian actor (1935–)

[2] Directed by Sofia Coppola

25 JANUARY

1.30 Brenda Currin[1] brings her Eudora Welty piece to our kitchen. She is the most wonderful actress but this show needs a physical identity. Made a few suggestions—basic but fundamental.

7.30 Show.

Very vocal audience, not to say skittish (cries of Snape . . .).

27 JANUARY

Walked home [from a lunch at the Savoy] through the snowdrifts, making it, stomach upset in full command, only just in time.

7.30 Show—Ginger tea, ice packs, water all competing to calm an incipient storm.

Somehow the show achieves some power and afterwards Adam Isaacs [talent agent] is full of it all. It's not until later that I realise my own agent has managed to say almost nothing about my work. What is *that* all about?

2 FEBRUARY

7.30 Show.

Anticipation or hindsight—no one should have to do a play like this twice in one day. Voice, body & spirit take a pummelling, and it vacuums up brain (memory) & technique (v. tired). It all becomes about will.

4 FEBRUARY

7.30 Show.

Still battling a virus that threatens.

10.30 Caffe e Vino.

Kristin Milward and friends. Beyond memorable given that a close friend said *nothing* until I was leaving.

6 FEBRUARY

3pm Show. The last one, and a fine one.

7.30 Blue Ribbon Bakery. Hmm. Not where I would have chosen [for wrap party], but it served, I guess. Everybody very hug-and-goodbye. Fi sits down and states her innocence . . .

7 FEBRUARY

7pm BAFTA interview.

Not telling you what props I stole or what Jo Rowling said to me.

---

[1] American actor (1946–)

8 FEBRUARY

7 Car to BAM.

2 screenings of *Die Hard*. Introduce one, Q&A at the other. Who knew? Both of them packed and cheering, adoring audiences.

26 FEBRUARY

How to Succeed in Business Without Really Trying.

Their first preview, and fantastically assured it was. Dan [Radcliffe] sings and dances like a veteran. Still switches off when not speaking and although the dancing is ace, the walking hasn't been choreographed so it's the Dan awkward shuffle. Show him and he'll do it immediately.

2 MARCH

1am The Box.

One of the acts was a woman farting into a microphone on musical cue. Naked of course.

8 MARCH

11.45 Tisch School.

Fine except for the *HP* obsessed question, and the boy who asked me what I was reading. 'You mean novels?' 'Yes.' Nothing came to mind. I read *around* things all the time. Or scripts. Or *avoid* reading it seems.

Pick up suit from the ace tailors on 14th Street and then home for the packing slow marathon.

Sitting next to me on the plane is Roger Waters [of Pink Floyd]—nice, chatty, smart.

pm The usual—sorting, opening, discarding, unpacking, replacing, heaving, rehanging . . .

14 MARCH

The start of domestic clear-out. Is it beautiful? Is it useful? Is there any object which is faintly depressing? Big Victorian rooms demand a lot of *stuff*.

18 MARCH

11.10/11.30 Dr Reid.

Blood tests and then a run-through of the head to toe (literally) complaints.

26 MARCH

Lindsay comes to collect us—car to Piccadilly Circus for the anti-cuts march. Straight to EAT for coffee and a sandwich before wandering down to Trafalgar Square and long wait for the Equity banner. At Park Lane the sight of the

Dorchester proved too much. Lindsay, Haydn [Gwynne] & us went in and had tea, sandwiches (no crusts) and cakes like good socialists everywhere might do at 4pm.

28 MARCH

Neil Walker at the Lister Hospital—checking moles, blemishes, redness, flaking—the topography of my complaining skin. As ever no real answers—creams, steroids—worse before it gets better. *He* has great skin, I notice, so . . .

31 MARCH

Cooked coq au vin while Rima at governing body meeting and damned fine it was too. Not so much dense as fleeting in the flavour department—but springlike.

6 APRIL

10.30 John Gaynor.

A blood pressure test, a stethoscope and a trot round showbiz.

8 APRIL

8 Olly Driver—THE TRAINER.

Tough, as they say, but fair. And all day I could feel things happening—question marks all over the body.

11 APRIL

8 Olly Driver.

Punishing but not killing, and I can feel the benefit through the day—the body wakes up, glad to be involved.

14 APRIL

Watching more of *The Killing*. My mind wanders watching it [so] that inevitably I lose the plot. Rima, of course, *glued*.

18 APRIL

8 Olly Driver

and he's pushing now . . .

3.30 Read through of *Untitled—Gambit*.

Which was many things. Cameron Diaz is the business—open and funny. Colin [Firth] as inclusive and curious as ever.

The script? It should never suffer a table read, because it is all about the reaction shot, the cut and the homage to a certain kind of film. Sometimes it is funny, often it is not—just sounds as if it wants to be. Michael [Hoffman, director] is v. open to change and the work starts here.

7 Olly Driver.

OMG. Not funny after a late night that contained some good wine—albeit spilt (as usual) during story-telling. But he pushes me through it. This couldn't happen without someone at my door.

20 APRIL

Michael very unsure about things. Hesitant to OK something in case something else is righter—a bit unsettling.

Tom C. comes in to chat—about Philip Larkin, Albert Finney, his old dog, his new dog, anathema towards a certain actress (long discussion). He's a 74-year-old kid in short trousers and he's Tom Courtenay, big star from my growing up years.

Watched a bio film about Cameron [Diaz]. V. useful. Working-class girl catapulted into modelling then film and famous boyfriends. It all seems to have taken a minute but it has been going on for 20 years.

23 APRIL

pm *The Killing*. Brilliant, shaming (for UK television) stuff.

24 APRIL

Watch another episode of *The Killing*.

So brilliantly acted by *everyone*, the smallest parts perfectly inhabited.

Only 6 more [episodes] to go . . .

29 APRIL

Olly Driver—getting tougher.

The Royal Wedding[1] invaded the house while Cornelia hoovered and Keith B. cleaned all the windows, we sparkled retrospectively. It is, however, an interesting kind of theatre. Casting crucial, sets a given, allowing for everything from idiotic to inspired. Script? Open to interpretation and history's verdict.

30 APRIL

Go through the last draft of *A Little Chaos* w. Alison.

2 Waitrose.

pm Finish *The Killing*.

---

[1] Prince William and Kate Middleton

The plot often escaped me, but the production values never did and the acting was sensational throughout. Brilliant.

2 MAY
Mim Karlin. Lunch at Denville Hall.[1]

A play could be written—or an episode of *Midsomer Murders* we all decided . . . actors but still lost, old faces staring from wheelchairs. Mim conducts her battle as ever but now it's against herself as she prays for Switzerland and an end to all the pain. Who can blame her? Brian? Barry? Over 90 but perfectly attired—shirt, tie, jacket, serves coffee to the gathered clan— 'Thank you, waiter,' I said. 'Butler,' he snapped—smiling. Dinah Sheridan[2] holds a camera. Is she looking for evidence of something going on?

7 MAY
8 Dinner at our house.

Kath Viner, Ed Miliband & Justine [Thornton, his wife], Miranda R[ichardson], Henrietta G., Ronan Bennett[3] & Georgina [Henry, his wife], Rahila and friend Mary.

As we closed the door having cleaned up—mostly—at 2am-ish we said with one voice 'nightmare'.

The food, wonderful as it was, was on the table at 9.30 and 10.30, embarrassingly late but it was Pakistan-time for Rahila and she was the ultimate perfectionist in spicing. Ed M. was patient, considering he was to be on Andrew Marr in the morning. I was so tired and stressed I could hardly converse.

9 MAY
Gambit. Day One. Night Shoot.

3.30 Pick-up Tyringham Hall, Newport Pagnall.

And the nightmare (sadly not sleep) of night shoots. Creeping exhaustion, combined with no time to eat and forgetting to drink water, which means words turn to mush and taste and judgement fly across the fields of Tyringham.

Fall into bed (Yellow Peril Room) at 5.30am.

10 MAY
Awake at 10.40.

12ish Sitting around the breakfast table with Colin, Cameron, Mike L[o-

---

[1] Care home for people in the entertainment industry
[2] English actor (1920–2012)
[3] Irish novelist and screenwriter (1956–)

bell, producer], Michael H., other producers. Argentina, music, film, train, dialect issues. Happy to pick at food, drink coffee and chat.

pm Karaoke night which will be rendered unforgettable by the slamming . . . of my left thumb in the car door. A long time since I have felt that kind of pain. Faint-making pain. Now for the black thumb, I presume.

Michael H. has that most idiosyncratic mix of decisive/indecisive all at once. A bit unnerving. Somewhere in there, he knows what he wants.

11 MAY

Yep. Black nail. Throbbing thumb. Reinvent method of doing up trouser buttons.

15 MAY

Stay at home day. Steal a couple of lines from Ruby for tomorrow's scene.

16 MAY

5.50am pick-up. But having gone to bed at 11.30 and awake again at 2.30, failing to sleep again—it was up at 5am for one of the toughest days of the shoot. A hillside outside Henley—Tuscany in England all around—me and a bunch of guys in gun-toting outfits, 2 pages of text and much falling over, getting up, dirt in the face, hitting muddy marks, shouting insanely . . . Finished at around 6pm. Could think only of hot bath. In pain from ankles to eyelids.

24 MAY

4.20 pick-up . . . am, that is.

Tiredness and lack of food kick in, especially in a basement with no clue as to the time of day at any point. It came as a surprise to see people having lunch in cafés on my way back to the trailer. It was 3.30pm . . .

25 MAY

6am Wake up to wave Rima off to Italy.

Back to bed until 10.

I had been vaguely looking forward to these auctioneer scenes. Then the old decisive/indecisive gremlins crept in via M.H.—with M.L. breathing down his neck. Net result—a good idea gets diluted into non-energy and the bland soft option has to be shot. Just in case.

27 MAY

Two hospice visits—no other way of doing it, so do it.

3pm Anna [Massey]—St Charles.

Pale, calm and beautiful—and just staring. Looking for a reason, sudden shafts of controversy, as ever. 'I don't think M. is a very nice person.' (I had thought he was a hero of hers.) But loving, too.

5pm Mim—St John & St Elizabeth.

Perfectly made up (someone under orders), ready for all-comers. Ready to talk & laugh though many drugs keep her eyes half-closed. Don't dare to leave too soon, though.

31 MAY

6am pick-up.

Long scene on the sofa in Sh's[1] office. Me, Cameron, Colin . . . Some shaky knowledge of the lines and my close-ups arrive late pm . . . Poor, defensive Michael on receiving end. How can I curb this ability to distance and intimidate? It is *not* helpful *but* it enforces a bit of a process. As in 'Could we just read the scene?' First thing?—when it was all about the shot . . .

2 JUNE

6am pick-up.

No clothes on day.

Well—flesh-coloured knickers on. And it's like they say, after a while you just don't notice. Except in this case, I'm the only one half (7/8th then) naked. It was what it was, but thank you, Olly Driver—even with the absence over the last week, the grind paid off.

3 JUNE

Mim Karlin has died. Talk about a noble spirit. She never made it to Dignitas, but she had the dignity part in spades. Unforgettable times with her celebratory, unsentimental and passionate heart.

6 JUNE

Talk to Philip Hedley about Mim's funeral next week. Something says up the status—make sure someone is there from the RSC and Malcolm[2] from Equity. Actors can do their stuff at the memorial.

8 JUNE

Back to Ealing Studios.

Cameron proves yet again what a gifted comedian she is: innate pace and precision. And truthful with it.

---

[1] Lord Shabandar, A.R.'s character
[2] Malcolm Sinclair, then Equity president

9 JUNE

Reading *Just Kids* and Patti Smith writes about her and Mapplethorpe taking it in turns to go into the Whitney (couldn't afford 2 tickets) and Robert saying 'One day we'll have our work in there.' That's where I met him. At his own retrospective . . .

11 JUNE

Watching a bit more of *Monster's Ball* and Lady Gaga announces her Tisch School ancestry. Now I know that she is to be taken seriously. Because she *trained*. Has a *process*.

12 JUNE

7.30 Stanley Tucci and Felicity [Blunt, his partner].

Glad to see that someone else can have a bit of a kitchen panic. 'Not enough potatoes, make some polenta.'

14 JUNE

Mim Karlin.

10 Car to collect Thelma and then on to Golders Green Crematorium where Philip H., God bless him, is in full control. DO NOT LET ANYONE IN WHO ISN'T DOING SOMETHING. He kept that up until 11.28 when I thought there must be unrest outside. But then the event started, at which point, after 'Fear no more' from me, Philip spoke for 20 minutes . . . Somehow we made it to the end (Helena K., followed by Harriet and Christina Rossetti), no thanks to Jan S.[1] and Richard Digby Day,[2] who also wittered on for many minutes (interspersed by some real wit from Maureen Lipman and Mim's own letters to the *Guardian*).

25 JUNE

Spoke briefly to Anna and David Huggins.[3] He thought she might have sounded a bit confused, thinking it was Uri. I didn't think so—but David said she is sleeping 90% of the time now, and pain free. She will, they think, just stop breathing. Impossible to make sense of most of the day. I put Glastonbury on the TV. Music as ever takes you elsewhere. Rumer, Elbow, Coldplay. Brits rule.

---

[1] Jan Sargent, British director and writer
[2] British theatre director (1938–)
[3] English actor (1959–). Son of Anna Massey.

27 JUNE

8.30 Olly Driver.

And an absolutely killing session. Too late last night . . .

3 JULY

Men's final Nadal v Djokovic.

Unforgettable experience. Unforgettable day of contrasts. On the balcony of the main entrance and then in to lunch at the Duchess of Gloucester's table. Wrong man [Djokovic]—all triumph and ego—won but Bjorn Borg came over and asked for a photograph. 'Are you kidding?' I spluttered. John Major said 'You have given us so much enjoyment.' 'I wish I could say the same of you', was the unstoppable reply. He had the grace to laugh.

Home. Message from Uri—one in Russian—Anna has died.

4 JULY

Kensington Town Hall. Rima becomes an alderman and makes a firebrand speech that makes me very proud of her.

Spoke to David Huggins. Anna's wish was for me to speak about her at her funeral. Now we find a day. Hard for Uri who as a Russian Jew wants it to be soon.

7 JULY

HP 7 Part 2.

It all ends. Part 1.

To Trafalgar Square—which takes an hour.

Once there, red carpets everywhere. A screen, a platform, an interviewer and thousands screaming and singing 'Snape, Snape, Severus Snape . . .' The carpet snakes into Leicester Square for the film at 8pm. I found it unsettling to watch—it has to change horses midstream to tell the Snape story and the camera loses concentration. Audience, however, very happy. Billingsgate later. People still happy, cannot find (or hear) anyone . . .

8 JULY

12.30 Collect Uri and take him to Angelus for lunch. This complex man, lost without Anna, talking of cremation removing the possibility of resurrection; always the right-wing perspective; loving & interested in all things, otherwise.

13 JULY

Two days on scene 125.

Tiredness & tetchiness and an occasional acid tongue.

8ish Dinner in the Brasserie with Colin [Firth], Stanley & Felicity.

This has been a happy team. Plenty to talk about, laugh about. Colin's monologues are entertaining and come from an open heart, and Stanley just loves London and wants to stay.

15 JULY

Up to finish Anna's eulogy in the early morning calm of the dining room.

12.30 West London Crematorium, Kensal Green.

David Hare, waiting outside, says, 'Well, that's Anna—either nothing or Westminster Abbey.'

2pm Anna's funeral. Calm, ordered, classy. Mozart at the beginning, then a prayer, me, Penny Wilton, the priest, Schubert. I think I spoke for about 30 mins. I think it was fine, in Anna's terms.

20 JULY

Gambit. Last day.

The back of the Rolls-Royce all day.

Cameron strikes an amazing balance (which keeps director and producer at bay) of certainty, assurance and seeming control whilst not *really* having done the work, and given the amount of transatlantic travel she's accomplished in recent weeks, it is staggering that she has *any* idea of her lines. Either way, there is no challenge and I even got notes in the face of no discernible flow in our scenes. This, I guess, is stardom and where the money is/has gone.

27 JULY

Uri the inimitable is going to Palermo tomorrow and to San Diego in the middle of August (while we are in Italy) but still leaves with no good-byes. He doesn't get much of England. The funeral was tough for him. 'No open coffin, no last kiss—cremation. No hope of resurrection.' And tonight I hear how confused he was by people laughing (rightly) at the funeral . . .

30 JULY

9.15 Screening in the courtyard [of Somerset House] of *Die Hard*. Thousands of devoted fans all with cushions, blankets, sleeping bags. Rock star time at the microphone. Unmissable. Then dinner in Tom's Kitchen before watching 15 mins in the Square. Beautiful and yet again you see how masterful the film is. Every shot helps the story.

1 AUGUST

Watching the 2 taped documentaries about [Rupert] Murdoch. Heroes are Nick Davies,[1] Tom Watson,[2] Chris Bryant[3] and Alan Rusbridger, I guess, for letting it happen. And boy, is timing all.

7 AUGUST

Campagnatico.

11 AUGUST

Emily Young [sculptor] comes over from Batignano for pork chops and ratatouille and we have a guided tour of her life. I like her, but not *one* question about ours??

13 AUGUST

A walk around the back of the village—old city walls scaffolded, slip/slide down the path that brings you out at S. Maria and up into Piazza Dante for a panini and coffee. Which Claudio paid for . . .

17 AUGUST

7.30 Swim.

8.30 Couple of hours' walk through the Tuscan hills/villages, stony paths and trees. Listen to Will Hutton's rundown on the Murdoch saga—Jeremy Hunt[4] wants [David] Cameron's job (I'd chain myself to a few railings). Alan R. is the real hero, because of his long-term commitment to Nick Davies, etc., etc.

20 AUGUST

97°

21 AUGUST

100°

Like stepping out into an oven but they know how to build these houses. Maybe they watched the pigeons who desert their wires for the branches of pines during the heat of the day.

---

[1] British investigative journalist (1953–)
[2] Labour politician (1967–)
[3] Labour politician (1962–)
[4] Conservative politician (1966–), then Secretary of State for Culture, Olympics, Media and Sport

3 SEPTEMBER

On the plane, finishing Edna's book of short stories *Saints and Sinners*. She paints words, sings them. But, thankfully, gives me the perfect summing up in the last two lines of the last story 'Old Wounds': 'it was . . . something for which there is no name, because to name it would be to deprive it of its truth.'

Home at 4.10pm. In and out of shower by 4.30pm and it's off to Tom Stoppard's party in the Physic Garden in Chelsea. A bomb would have removed most of the British theatre Establishment. I never moved from a patch of gravel. But fun and a bit scary. Dinner at Caraffini . . . partly because I hadn't got near any food at the party.

13 SEPTEMBER

To New York.

Listened to Adele *21*. She's doing what she was born to.

Nathan & Lewis bring me to 321 W. 13th. The road was closed. Now—4 CONED[1] vans, no elevator working. 2 suitcases up 7 floors . . . Where there is no phone, TV or computer working, and a dribble of brown water coming out of the tap.

30 SEPTEMBER

[Re *Seminar*]

Boy, do I have to hold my nerve here. 4 actors who for whatever reason don't insist on examining the reality of a scene, 2 of them explore the sounds they can make, vocal idiosyncrasies they can toy with, a director who doesn't ask questions, but who is full of sensible suggestions. Sometimes the nerve-wrackingness of it melts and we achieve something, so I have to stay open, available, non-judgemental and trusting . . .

1 OCTOBER

12.40 Pick-up to rehearse.

More of the same, I don't get it.

10 OCTOBER

11 Rehearse.

A real need to know the lines, now. Don't waste the hours, mins, days.

11 OCTOBER

12 Exterminator man shines his torch. Examines mattress (no bedbugs), takes away samples.

---

[1] Con Edison, gas and electric company

12 OCTOBER

11 Rehearse. A run. Theresa [Rebeck, playwright] there, and gone, afterwards. No words of encouragement—boy, is *hers* this play. I caught her at the elevator and threw a few grenades into the mix—'It's our play, now.'

16 OCTOBER

11 Rehearse.

Feeling tense and resentful at having to do a run later when there is so much to be bedded in. God, the pressure to *present*, to *display* is appalling.

2pm Run which was chaotic, w. lines disappearing, no shape, Hamish[1] doing wonderful things, Lily [Rabe] still totally on book, Theresa flipping pages . . . me getting angrier and angrier. We did it is all that can be said.

20 OCTOBER

11 Rehearse.

Hamish finally expresses frustration with some aspects of the text—rightly—and we deal with it. Why has it taken so long? The fear factor? Everyone is sealed in by their brilliance.

pm Run the play with some nerve-jangling nips and tucks. We took 4 mins off the running time—but (for this journal only) *still* the self-centred energy, being dazzling on every line, no idea a lot of the time *what* is being said, there's so much *how*. And so much talent, pissing into the wind but encouraged and lauded.

23 OCTOBER

12.30 Onwards. Tech Day One.

Not enough sleep—Niagara Falls in the pipes—so eventually the body/brain disconnect kicks in.

Meanwhile—the set looks fine, the costumes look good, the theatre feels perfect and welcoming, and I start watching myself and the whole situation. It is impossible to tell where the others' heads are at. But maybe it's all practicalities (we had a happy enough meal at Joe Allen's) and the play will re-emerge . . .

26 OCTOBER

8pm Public press.

Which I thought was for 50 people—turned out to feel like a full house and we all braved it through. A lot of supportive laughter, and we rose to it—

---

[1] Hamish Linklater, American actor (1976–)

Lily doing some of her truest work. A lot of complicated cobwebs blew away and it's clearer where the work will have to be put in.

27 OCTOBER
8pm First preview.

Very nervy from the entrance round onwards. The usual battle with my own demons.

28 OCTOBER
8pm Show.

Still nervy, and when a word is fluffed the entire audience exits for a few moments.

Back at home all my silly concerns, and even serious ones, thrown into sharpest relief when Rima drops the bombshell Bo Rogers[1] has died. No one knows why at this point. I used to stare at him wonderingly; his instant contact with children, his total lack of judgement, his great heart. Yet again, left staring into space.

29 OCTOBER
11am pick-up.

After a night of no real sleep—thanks Reggie downstairs for the thumping bass until 6am.

10ish Bar Centrale w. Stan [Tucci] & Rima.

Stan, ever waspish and warm by turns, hasn't much to say about the show. He felt like an alien.

At home Reggie downstairs is having another deafening bash. Doesn't answer the doorbell. No hotels available. Take pill. Earplugs in. And hope.

31 OCTOBER
9am Blood test.

The easiest, quickest and most painless ever.

Before the performance. How do I stop this happening? Panic attack? Fainting? Sweating? Repeating the lines? Heaviness in the arms? Hard to breathe? Concentrate? First part tough, better onwards.

At home—a pair of shoes outside the door. Ralph F. who stayed happily for supper.

---

[1] Son of Richard and Ruth Rogers

5 NOVEMBER

8pm Show.

Apart from another dodgy opening it was a (Sam[1] says) gangbuster show. Brain/body battle throughout—the body had a sleep in the break, thinks it has done its job for the day, checks out of brain connection, shocked to find itself out there again.

8 NOVEMBER

1.30 Patrick Pacheco, *LA Times*.

'Villain' and 'sneer' popped up in his questions, so hopes are low for anything groundbreaking.

11 NOVEMBER

8pm Show.

Not sure where this audience came from but they were nearly out of control.

17 NOVEMBER

Slept on and off till 11. Back to the apartment around 2.[2] Feeling rested but still not well—weak legs and headache.

5pm To the theatre.

Barry K[ohn] arrives, stethoscope finds fluid in the left lung—potential pneumonia. Straight to antibiotics.

Tonight's show—press night—cancelled. The first time, I realise, I have ever missed a show. They are citing 'acute respiratory infection'. Home, dinner, warmth, TV, bed.

18 NOVEMBER

Letting the antibiotics kick in. It is now, officially, walking pneumonia.

5pm To the theatre.

Test out the stage. Rehearse Sc 2 with the others. Green light. Fingers crossed. Prayers.

8pm Show which felt alive and vital, apart from voice limitations.

19 NOVEMBER

2pm Show which seemed fine but total exhaustion by the end.

8pm Show which seemed an impossibility at 6, 6.30, 7. No strength, dizzy, somehow we made it to the curtain call. Problem is, 2 shows have taken

[1] Sam Gold, director
[2] A.R. had been staying the night in a hotel to get some sleep.

it out of me to such an extent that the body may be going into reverse—antibiotically.

20 NOVEMBER

6.30 Opening night.

Which went as well as these things can ever go.

21 NOVEMBER

NY Times praises and whinges. Find out from Sam later that everything else is a rave.

22 NOVEMBER

7pm Show.

Felt back to normal-ish. No more hanging on to the furniture.

27 NOVEMBER

3pm Show—and this audience was at a baseball game. Applauding lines, entrances, exits and, at one memorable moment, farting. Or so it seemed to those of us who couldn't look at each other.

1 DECEMBER

2pm pick-up.

Eye doctor who, after many up, down, left, right, top line, bottom line, red, green?, says—'See if it is worse in 10 days and here's the retinologist you should see . . .'

7pm Show.

Barry Hopkins[1] and friends thought it was 8pm . . .

In the dressing-room—Anna Wintour, Katherine (Anna W.'s charmless daughter and friends), Suzanne Bertish.

4 DECEMBER

Suddenly health descends . . . just in time for the culmination of the show weekend . . .

7.30 Show. Felt like a very dumb audience (as per my pre-show chat with Jeffrey Finn [producer]). Worried that all is comedy/sitcom/undemanding in the publicity world.

13 DECEMBER

9 Retinologist. Who puts endless drops in to dilate furious pupils so that he can shine lights, see round corners and, eventually, pronounce me free of

---

[1] American actor (1953–)

tears, or detachments. Come back in 6 weeks. Home via the tailor, and 13th Street (for the vacuum cleaner).

14 DECEMBER
7pm Show.

A very quiet house, comparatively. But by the end, God bless them, they were on their feet.

16 DECEMBER
8pm Show.
10pm Bar Centrale.

To wait for Robert, Arlene & Chloe Cushman [illustrator] who elect to have little or nothing to say about *Seminar*. The rudeness is mindblowing sometimes.

19 DECEMBER
12.45 Dr Benjamin Asher, who prescribes Chinese herbs, Vitamin D, an injection of something which does indeed have immediate larynx improvement, and he more or less gets rid of neck pain.

21 DECEMBER
7pm Show.

Someone with the most annoying, ever-present and ill-timed laugh was in the front row. Hard for it not to become all you think about.

29 DECEMBER
Can't think what this diary will read like later on. More or less from opening night illness rules. A few blessed days of freedom dotted throughout, but largely a dodgem car situation of avoidance.

30 DECEMBER
2pm Show.

Feeling markedly better. Still a slave to the Kleenex box, but not dizzy. A plus.
8pm Show.

An audience out for a very good time. Literary references sail out the window—but joyous all the same.

31 DECEMBER
2pm Show.

Crawling across the stage by the last scene. Tiredness in every artery, bone and orifice.

2012

3 JANUARY

11am Call Pat Healy [journalist] re *TimesTalks* on Saturday.

The day is then spent organising and persuading. Since Francesca is so ill, it seems to me that Rima should really get on a plane today.

4 JANUARY

am Talked to Rima. She made it—Francesca is still with us—a miracle in itself. Rima, Peter [Rima's brother] and Melanie Parker in Oxford together.

7 JANUARY

. . . an email from Rima—Francesca has died. Hard to believe that such an indomitable spirit gave out. I have talked about her to everyone who would listen. *This is a rare individual who has gone. Pay attention.*

10 JANUARY

3pm Dr Asher.

More pills, a welcome glutathione injection, and very good neck massage.

Then Bloomingdale's to find (found) a coat.

11 JANUARY

7pm Show.

Now it has graduated to nausea. The diary of this production should be sent to *The Lancet* . . .

15 JANUARY

And find news that Elizabeth Pursey has died. She, along with Toshka and Michael McCallion, Robert Palmer and June Kemp are all people who absolutely shaped what I do, what I am doing, who I am.[1]

17 JANUARY

7pm Show. Patchy, disparate audience—laughter pockets, silent people, a major cougher. Not feeling well—again—all through then afterwards. Brooke Shields says 'Thank you.' Weirdness in the air.

21 JANUARY

3" of snow fell last night.

8pm Show. Rufus Wainwright was in—and happy.

24 JANUARY

A strange and interesting day. Early morning news of only technical Oscar nominations . . . for *HP*. Not unexpected, but focusing (pm) to think of the dullard voters—(1) don't watch children's films (2) don't watch a film about Freud (3) don't watch anything by Shakespeare (4) don't watch Charlize Theron playing a depressed woman (5) celebrate (however brilliant) impersonators . . . Something colder and maybe more useful gripped my heart today.

26 JANUARY

3.45 Dr Asher. Who injects me and takes blood. Let's figure this thing out.

7pm Show. The theatre is too hot, and I'm stressed. We yank the audience together gradually.

2 FEBRUARY

7pm Show. Terribly aware of Vanessa's presence in the house tonight. Afterwards—there's Jeff Goldblum[2] and Janice Honeyman . . . [3]

9pm Orso.

Vanessa, as ever, keen to talk about everything except herself. She wants to unknit the play, her experience of it, the audience, Theresa. Somewhere in there, she is figuring out what she *didn't* like—and that's useful at this moment.

---

[1] All the people named in this entry taught A.R. at RADA.

[2] Who succeeded A.R. in the role of Leonard

[3] South African director (1949–)

3 FEBRUARY

4.15 Dr Asher.

Who is perplexed. Aren't we all? The roller coaster of healthy/sick/healthy goes on.

13 FEBRUARY

Do almost nothing day off . . . There is a programme called *Extreme Couponing* that is the end of civilisation. People spend their days cutting coupons from magazines, then go to supermarkets and buy 70 cans of dog food and 30 bottles of Vitamin Water and 80 packs of diapers etc., and store it all at home. In case. But they got it for next to nothing is the point.

17 FEBRUARY

12.30 Car → BAM.

1.30 Dress rehearsal—*Prima Donna* (Rufus Wainwright).

Luscious music, very silly libretto. A glorious soprano crescendo is subtitled 'I'll call the police!' Rufus is there with his crazy laugh.

23 FEBRUARY

4pm Pick-up for the *Charlie Rose* show.

5.15 He arrives. And we settle—well, he has a cold—into the allotted chairs. But he's amazing—notes forgotten, we just chat. And it feels like we could go on for hours . . .

26 FEBRUARY

5pm To Maria Aitken and Patrick McGrath. Jack Davenport joins. They live near Pace University by Brooklyn Bridge—supper in so-so Italian nearby. Funny, charming, witty, generous threesome.

29 FEBRUARY

9pm Bar Centrale.

David Grausman [composer], Bob Crowley. Except Bob is a tart and stayed at another table ('I double booked') for 40 minutes. He missed meeting Lou Reed who was with Kim C[attrall] post *Death of a Salesman*, and who talks like an actor.

13 MARCH

Dr Cahill leaves a message. No signs of anything. Maybe bye-bye amoeba. But whacked out still.

15 MARCH

9 Bar C. w. Kevin Kline.

A last minute, and wise, change, because Greg Mosher [director] and companion Christa joined us and then, all of a sudden, there was Julia Roberts and husband.

29 MARCH

Major event was Meryl was in. Alarm bells for Lily (fled upstairs).

1 APRIL

Last show and party. Well, drinks and buffet at the Glass House Tavern.

3pm Show. And—miraculously—it was one of our best. Apart from a few tears on stage . . . And full flowing ones at the curtain call.

28 APRIL

11.30 Car to South Salem, Westchester, and Felicity & Stanley Tucci.

7ish Meryl Streep arrives. 'That's just where I want to find you,' she says. 'I am making martinis.' Great dinner of rabbit & polenta but even greater chat—the world and all its baggage—that went on at full voltage until 2.30am. Ms S. is truly a force of nature. *Really* informed—even if you don't agree with the information—and eyes, mind and heart.

7 MAY

A day without appointments is a good thing, I discover. Must do more of it.

13 MAY

Toronto.

Leaving New York this time it is hard to shake off a dull, blurred feeling of having been the victim of a quiet but organised abuse. I daresay, as ever, it will turn into something muscle-strengthening, but at the moment I feel diminished by averted eyes and somewhere there are others that are like gimlets with very tight smiles.

14 MAY

Leonard Cohen.

Glenn Gould Prize, Massey Hall.

8.30 Leonard Cohen concert.

Feeling extremely alone surrounded by all these musicians, but an unforgettable experience walking on to that stage, and that reception. The poems work perfectly and L.C.'s words were powerful in my head.

16 MAY

London.

17 MAY

And an awareness, 8 months away in relatively simple environments, of the habit of adding, acquiring where there is no need. The great cull has to begin.

27 MAY

1pm Ruby et al.

Happy chatty lunch (Ed cooked—Ruby received us in her pyjamas with hair full of wet dye and silver foil) in the garden. Sean and Rupert [Everett] like Court commentators or something. Dashing, indiscreet but relentlessly honest. On the way out Ruby claims she asked him about his career. 'Endlessly clawing my way back to the middle,' he said.

3 JUNE

The Queen's Diamond Jubilee. And it's 60 years since the Coronation. My sister in her Queen's outfit, winning the fancy dress competition.

14 JUNE

10 RADA Council.

An outburst—not for the first time—about the amount of four letter words in the evenings! Can't quite believe one is hearing this in 2012, but then we also have a roomful of white middle class people talking about 'diversity' without another representative (apart from Bonnie Greer) in the room.

19 JUNE

Visa finally arrives . . . Heathrow. Uma Thurman in the lounge and on the plane. 'You can deliver, can't you?' says the nearly-due Ms T.

21 JUNE

[Re *CBGB*]

2.00 → Savannah.

24 JUNE
11 Rehearse.

Boy, will this movie find itself in the edit.

The reading is like the movie—flipping the pages of a magazine.

26 JUNE
CBGB.

Largely spent in one of these beautiful old Southern homes, where the crazy owner allowed us to crash a piano down her beautiful wooden staircase. Managed to avoid the stair-rail, but gouged a small hole in the opposite wall.

5 JULY
6.35 pick-up. *CBGB* full throttle.

Quite something to see these 3 kids ripping into the Police's 'Roxanne'.

Keene [McRae] (playing Sting) has a perfect English accent and comes from Alabama. He stays 'on accent' all day for the benefit of one line.

11 JULY
A day memorable for continued camera-hogging by J.B.[1] Somewhere in the afternoon miking-up went on for a scene he had no lines in—OK, but how about some consulting with the 3 other actors?

16 JULY
Finding a calmer centre all day so that Hilly Kristal [A.R.'s character] just behaves. Leading up to the shot for the end of this movie. Wonderful work from Joel [David Moore], Julian [Acosta], Steven [Schub] as the Ramones.

Rima arrives at around 7 → Garibaldi's at 8.

17 JULY
The last of the Ramones today, and the birth of Talking Heads. Both wonderful—and the Talking Heads quite jaw-droppingly accurate. Which is more than can be said for a couple of the wigs . . .

26 JULY
Farewell to shooting in Savannah.

[1] American actor Justin Bartha (1978–)

30 JULY
To New York.

6 AUGUST
Olympic rings.
   Show jumpers!

22 AUGUST
7.30 I Sodi.
   Stanley Tucci, Fee [Felicity] & Patti Clarkson[1] who is so overflowing with compliments that I start to wonder if she has heard about 'Chaos' . . . I was too busy enjoying the food to be concerned.

23 AUGUST
7.30 → New Orleans and the Windsor Court Hotel.

24 AUGUST
Walking up Royal Street—as if it was meant, a jewellery shop. A four-stone citrine ring.[2]
   5.15 to the set/trailers.
   On the way there, the word 'torrential' doesn't begin to cover it. The driver could hardly see the car in front. Filming can't start . . .

27 AUGUST
Hurricane Isaac arriving tonight. Watching the news all a.m. Most every-body else has scarpered. We have an inkling to sit it out. But then comes the warning that the hotel may not cope if the electricity is cut off, so production books us on a flight to Atlanta.
   7pm (7.35) flight to Atlanta and Loews Hotel and pasta over the road—we are the only customers. It's midnight.

30 AUGUST
To New York.
   Delta outdoes itself in naffness—again. After the $25 for a small case → Atlanta, it's now $50 to enter the 1st class lounge. NOT.

31 AUGUST
10.30 David Glasser arrives with a bunch of flowers. The car is downstairs. We drive, on the most beautiful sunny day, to Brooklyn and the Courthouse

---

[1] Patricia Clarkson, American actor (1959–)
[2] Re marrying Rima.

to find David's father (88 it turns out, amazingly, later). He is the wisest, warmest, most caring and listening man. No wonder he is a judge. We were married. A bit like a doctor jabs you in the arm when you're not looking. Then he told a joke, a good one. We walked back across Brooklyn Bridge and had lunch in Barbuto. Everything about it was the way it needed to be.

1 SEPTEMBER

4.30pm R. → Kennedy and Rome.

4 SEPTEMBER

6.10 *Searching for Sugar Man* w. Tara.

Moving and simple documentary about the 'lost' singer Rodriguez. Everything they say is right—he was ahead of his time, his music is wonderful, and his self-possession humbling.

8 SEPTEMBER

1.45 → JFK → back to New Orleans.

8pm Coquette. Dinner with Hilary [Shor], Lee,[1] his family—and Jane Fonda. Who, it has to be said, is vibrantly alive and curious and sexy. She wastes no time in finding out my marital status (on behalf of a friend, Miss F.). Vulnerable, too.

9 SEPTEMBER

The Butler.

8.45 pick-up → makeup for prosthetics test.

That is, I suppose, the point of testing. Specifically so that I can experience the prison of a pile of rubber around the part of my face that I am going to need most. We dump it, and go for something simpler. Jane looks great as Nancy [Reagan].

10 SEPTEMBER

The Butler.

Get to the set and extras are doing that thing that can only be called 'milling about'. Lee cajoling them into feeling high status, and Jane tangibly nervous. As we wait to make our entrance at the top of the stairs I say 'Look at us—a couple of actors playing a couple of actors playing at being in the White House.' She is determined that we should walk down the (3) steps in unison, so she says 'Let's move off on the left foot.' I don't get it right. Probably because we *both* try to lead.

---

[1] Lee Daniels, director of *The Butler*

12 SEPTEMBER

Jane is in the lobby, behind her big black shades with her step-daughter and Carol from Ashé Cultural Center—Jane still inclusive, curious, involved.

Into the staff dinner and a relationship with a group of random extras . . . Oprah's TV crew is there and there is a non-aha moment, when I say no to an interview in Reagan gear. But then pictures from the set are everywhere. Oprah the Grand Tweeter. The day finishes in fine Lee D.-style as we shoot a scrambled, unrehearsed R.R. being sworn in scene. No one's finest hour . . . But Lee weeps as we finish.

13 SEPTEMBER

→ To New York.

8.45. Having written a (hopefully) conciliatory note to Oprah . . .

On the plane. All too easy to hit the Flixster button, which leads you to what everyone is doing, which leads you to Rotten Tomatoes and percentages of people who want to see it, critics who have seen and liked/disliked it. Factor in Oprah's tweeting and there will be opinions before the film is finished.

14 SEPTEMBER

2.15 Car → Newark.

The greeter says 'I was just watching/reading an interview with Oprah . . .' As the last two days have worn on, I begin to wish my note to her had been a little more challenging, along the lines of—if you want to do serious work, don't be a circus act at the same time.

15 SEPTEMBER

Arriving at Campagnatico there is an unnerving sign—in English—saying CONTAMINATED ZONE. Paranoia strikes and suggests this is aimed at English people living in the village . . .

16 SEPTEMBER

Fucking mosquitoes . . . They like all parts of the body and we are low on sprays. Pardon the obsessiveness, but with their energies harnessed they could go for world domination.

28 SEPTEMBER

7pm Stanley & Fee's wedding party.

Shoreditch House.

A small sign of things to come is that almost the first people I see are Meryl Streep and Tom Cruise. Noisy room beyond the rooftop swimming pool in this terminally cool place. Paparazzi outside, of course.

29 SEPTEMBER
3.30 Middle Temple.

Fee and Stan get married.

Emily & Susannah Blunt stop the show with 'Pie Jesu', as does Christina with The Beatles' 'I Will'. Fee beautiful as ever and shining. Stan a bit Stan Laurel-ish with happiness.

The day's line-up has included Meryl S., Colin Firth, Steve Buscemi, Julianne Moore, Bill Nighy, Oliver Platt,[1] Aidan Quinn, Tony Shalhoub and Ewan McGregor. The (rather camp) Blunt Bros could go into showbiz. Our table is quite hard work. Food is sensational. Happy, funny, loving day.

9 OCTOBER
To Frieze Masters w. Taylor[2] who frets a bit about a Zurbarán, a Madonna & Christ diptych, a Lucian Freud, an Auerbach . . . maybe she bought them all. The Zurbarán was £900,000. Saw David Bailey there who said he almost didn't recognise me since I look so old.

7 NOVEMBER
Early am. TV on. Flinch for a half second but—Obama has won. Thank you, USA.

13 NOVEMBER
Pretty much all day on *A Little Chaos*, eventually getting it Fedexed to London. It still lives and breathes in those pages.

15 NOVEMBER
Today an offer [re *A Little Chaos*], dependent on meeting, will go to Matthias Schoenaerts.[3]

21 NOVEMBER
11.30 Matthias Schoenaerts.

So much more open and smiling than I had expected. It's an instant yes, with all the provisos about his youth. His mum came with him and she carries her own charisma. She's a Beckett translator. I talked a fair amount of rubbish, wading through illness, but hopefully we move onwards.

---

[1] Canadian-American actor (1960–)
[2] Taylor Thomson (1959–), Canadian actor and film producer, daughter of Kenneth Thomson, 2nd Baron of Fleet
[3] Belgian actor, film producer and graffiti artist (1977–)

24 NOVEMBER

Finally read the trashing of *Gambit* in the *Guardian*. The only thing bitter experience tells you is that you *will* get over it.

4 DECEMBER

Justin Vale [consultant urologist]. OK. All change. He feels that, though still small, the rise in figures needs some attention.[1]

5 DECEMBER

Tea at the Ritz with Deborah Meaden and Lindsay Duncan. And she's a delight. Incredible enthusiasm for all that she does, alive to all nuances, doesn't waste a second on formalities and we talk so easily that it seems natural to suggest it should be an annual event.

7 DECEMBER

1pm Alliance [Healthcare] MRI.

Would I like classical or chill out music? Chill out, please, classical is too much work.

All too necessary afterwards to go to Selfridges and buy a kettle.

11 DECEMBER

MRI clear. On to David Landau [oncologist].

Later watching Simon & Garfunkel . . . 'Time it was, and what a time it was.'

13 DECEMBER

8pm Evgeny's[2] party at 88 Portland Place in an apartment I covet. Wide hallways, generous rooms and perfect for the likes of John Malkovich, Ruth Wilson,[3] Keira Knightley, Lloyd Webber, Ed Miliband, Nick Clegg, Hugh Grant, Jemima Khan, Tom Hollander, David Frost, Stephen Fry, Kristin S.-T., Edward St Aubyn.

14 DECEMBER

1.15 Dr Landau.

Who sets out the options, which take a lot of concentration. Fortunately, I have Jay Smith to demystify.

Selfridges to buy Christmas crackers.

---

[1] Results from A.R.'s prostate health check
[2] Evgeny Lebedev (1980–), Russian oligarch who part-owns the *Independent* and *Evening Standard*
[3] English actor (1982–)

21 DECEMBER

1.15 Dr Landau.

CT clear.

The lunchtime session was calmly received, but time scrambles the brain and by the evening it was spinning.

22 DECEMBER

Sleeping not too easy, either.

Or meeting people socially.

12 Angelus.

No real appetite, but the afternoon spent at home eventually gets me to a calmer place. Steak supper and watching the Paralympics opening ceremony helped, too.

24 DECEMBER

11.30 St James's.

Midnight carol service, well Mass, really, with its relative lack of carols and abundance of sitting and standing and answering and communion. But we held candles and listened in vain for inspiration from a sermon that threw in an arbitrary reference to Bob Dylan. Something about the road/the journey . . .

2013

A Little Chaos — Ruby Wax — Paris — Kate Winslet — Dexter
Fletcher and Dalia Ibelhauptaitė — Richard Griffiths — Margaret
Thatcher — Helen McCrory — Stanley Tucci — Campagnatico — Andy
Murray — Mel Smith — Venice — Emma Watson — New York, *CBGB* —
Johannesburg — Christmas in the bush — On the Zambesi

7 JANUARY

London.

Which stretched. Machine malfunction, followed by insufficient water. Get
the balance right and it should be a mark and time each day.

8 JANUARY

9.40—until 3pm . . . drinking water endlessly, waiting, eating a sandwich
then eventually home to throw it all up.

9 JANUARY

An improvement. Finished by 11am. Dr L[andau] stops by and deconstructs
the water issue.

11 JANUARY

6pm NT. Christopher Hampton. The Jocelyn Herbert[1] Lecture.

At which Christopher told stories about Jocelyn rather than giving a lecture. I don't think he was given a clear remit. Not that it mattered—he was,
as ever, entertaining.

15 JANUARY

pm. Flattened by tiredness. This is an obstacle course for sure.

16 JANUARY

Finished Phyllida's new book.[2] She has such a sly style—giving you seeming everything, but staying just out of reach. Deeply humane and funny, of
course. And such quality writing talking about her brother.

---

[1] British stage and costume designer (1917–2003)
[2] *How Many Camels Are There in Holland?: Dementia, Ma and Me*

22 JANUARY

Impossible conversation [re *A Little Chaos*] with Alison. I can't think of many screenwriters who would offer 'No. No. No.' to their director and get away with it.

23 JANUARY

Now we hear that Kate Winslet is juggling dates with another film and that Film 4 says NO . . . *The Winter Guest* was certainly green and salad days.

24 JANUARY

Sleeping through the excellence of *Borgen*, wide awake for the mind-numbing horrors of *Question Time*, and then the nightmare-inducing glimpse of *The Jonathan Ross Show* with Eddie Redmayne forced to behave like the monkey at the end of an automatic piano.

27 JANUARY

Watched *Quartet*. Maggie [Smith] and Tom [Courtenay] full-up with class. And Billy Connolly doing some great work, but which OAP home is that? Let's all move in.

29 JANUARY

12.30 Rupert Penry-Jones who is charming and easy and all the things one might expect and also reminds me that he played Louis in *Power* at the National. I remember him dancing—a long and difficult piece of choreography—extremely well. He almost certainly knows more about the period than any of us, but is far too well-mannered to let it show.

4 FEBRUARY

A Little Chaos.

First major production meeting.

7 FEBRUARY

11 Ruby is back from LA, where, contrary to her expectations, she had a blast. Exampled by 2 videos on her iPhone. One, Carrie Fisher demonstrating the new wooden awning her mother (DR)[1] has constructed so that the dog can pee in the rain without getting wet, and No. 2 the Angelyne-alike,[2] in blonde wig, stretch neon-pink outfit, and football-

---

[1] American actor Debbie Reynolds (1932–2016)

[2] Angelyne (1950–) is an American singer (and phenomenon) who was famous in the 1980s for her provocative poses on billboards in California.

sized boobs, is persuaded by mein host to reproduce her (long-ago) *Playboy* poses.

12 FEBRUARY
Blenheim will take care of Versailles and Cliveden's dining room will be Louis' Versailles bedroom. Beautiful. French moulding and gardens outside. We will put scaffolding outside the windows. Perfect.

19 FEBRUARY
News via email that our funding is all in place. Now make Taylor proud. And happy.

25 FEBRUARY
2pm Greek Street. Casting session.

Actor talking to actor while being director. Not comfortable especially when the parts are so small in terms of lines. In the cab home, Nina G[old, casting director] talks of the pleasure of working with an actor/director, so guilt is eased a bit, only to flare up again watching the annual Oscars. This is what I do and we all take ourselves *that* seriously. Because we have to while looking more and more irrelevant to the world at large.

2 MARCH
12 Ellen Kuras [cinematographer].

And here's another global spirit attaching herself to this film. I sat her down to watch the BBC2 Versailles film.

7.30 Savoy Hotel.

Auction dinner . . . For Park Theatre w. Celia Imrie. Disastrous start. The Mall is closed off, arrive at the River entrance; Celia is at the front. There is no indication of which restaurant we are booked into, and no name to refer to. Eventually the guests show up, Celia and I are reunited and we both surf and glide our way through the evening.

4 MARCH
Eurostar → Paris.

Good to see Kate so happy to see Ellen, and for us all to chat all the way to Gare du Nord. Bertrand meets us—great bus—and off to Versailles. No-tourists day, so unforgettably, we had the Hall of Mirrors to ourselves, and a guide who gave us all the facts we are ignoring. Louis watched in bed by 80 people, no dancing after 30, slept alone etc., etc.

11 MARCH

8pm Dexter and Dalia.

Sunshine on Leith, Dexter's new film, which has great charm but is seeking its own rhythm and identity at the moment.

On the way home, pick up emails from Gail [producer] re Taylor.[1] Wobbling. Proof positive. Don't mix finance and friends, and a demonstration of how the rich are corralled by the people who feed off them.

14 MARCH

7.45 pick-up → Chenies with its amazing gardens.

But these are the days for the cold to crawl inside you, indoors or out. Exhausted by late afternoon, feet like ice blocks and longing to sit inside the car with the heater on, and a cup of tea.

17 MARCH

1.30 Belinda and Matt w. David, Edward & Miranda.

Somewhere in here, I found myself in a quiet despair that E. would *ever* ask a question, actually *wait* for an answer and then elicit some more. It is an endless stream of commentary—does it come from a well-worn path? Noël Coward, Gore Vidal, Truman Capote?

18 MARCH

Kate and I walk through the script. And she really takes the time to examine every loose thought, every wayward word. These are the fine tunings now. And we can't lose sight of the drive toward story-telling.

25 MARCH

4pm Met Nick Gaster who will edit. Fortunately, I liked him well enough. Difficult relationship—months together without needing it to turn into friendship. He assumed he had the job, anyway, so it was doubly lucky we got on.

28 MARCH

Home to sad news of Richard Griffiths. Dear Griffo, and the undying memories of him as Pyramus in Stratford making 1500 people weak with laughter when doing almost nothing. Or in *History Boys*, with a tiny inflection. A master.

---

[1] Thomson, re finance for *A Little Chaos*

8 APRIL

. . . the day Margaret Thatcher died. Rima can't watch the coverage, I have a blank fascination at seeing so many years pan across one's memories, along with mindless adulation from being given certainty.

15 APRIL

A Little Chaos—Day One. Chenies.

16 APRIL

6.15 → Chenies.

A day memorable for the beginning of the carriage crash and for hilarity caused by my using the walkie-talkie as a telephone.

Also K.W.'s husband[1] arrived and there was a distinct sense of an onset presence that distracted concentration . . .

17 APRIL

6.15 → Chenies.

Kate gives so little of herself—*everything* as an actor—but there is never a moment where she finds out anything about her fellow actors—or even says bravo or thank you. Strange to witness. Such a deliberately erected wall.

22 APRIL

6.25 pick-up → Ham House.

Into the study.

Writing this at the end of a peculiarly disturbing day. Maybe the room was too small, with too many people or something, but we got off to a slow start and although Kate and Matthias never faltered or lost focus, we were struggling to make the day's shots by the end of the day, even with an hour's overtime. Things definitely not helped by Nick Gaster's visit which was like being given a glass of room temperature water. Just his style, I suspect. But the vapour lingers, and at the point of writing, it is hard to remember that we actually did some good work today.

26 APRIL

End of Week Two.

In the collection room with Matthias and Helen [McCrory] . . . Helen is as wild and unpredictable as ever, but taming her (a little) for a take here and there, and at the same time allowing for some brilliance all of her own, means that with Matthias' mystery and containment there is some great work.

---

[1] Edward Abel Smith, aka Ned Rocknroll

30 APRIL

Wow. A day that threatened to be hellish . . . So not helped by actors not knowing their lines well enough. Strangely unpredictable state of affairs, but it put us hours behind.

7 MAY

Some great work from K.W. and M.S. today, in bed.

12 MAY

12 Ian McKellen. For brunch before he disappears for months to New Zealand and then New York. Always a room full of people happy to see each other and Ian beavering away at the stove.

14 MAY

7.45 pick-up.

Mud bath. In the rain. Rockwork Grove [Versailles] looks like a set for *Mother Courage*. A brilliant one, at that. Steven[1] has such a light touch inside such a self-defeating head. Fortunately he is in a scene with Kate who just copes with anything and everything. We pressed on through the rain and mud.

19 MAY

Much needed day at home. Leafing through the script. Looking for missing beats . . . Getting rid of limescale on the downstairs garden door. And pigeon shit on the chairs. Sitting outside for the first time with a cup of tea and some toasted panettone. Having a roast beef dinner.

20 MAY

Week Six.

1pm Hampton Court.

Oh boy. That was tough. Sorting out coverage and not sorting out Stanley [Tucci]. Who said he had been finishing some writing all day. A constant source of amazement to me is different approaches to the word freedom. Mine is totally connected to the word discipline. Stanley, with all the fervour in his huge heart, said 'You will kill it, if you do this' (do it again, do it again, faster, lighter). I can only say (but didn't, and wouldn't) you can't kill something if it isn't alive.

---

[1] English actor Steven Waddington (1967–)

22 MAY

Storm in the Grove. Three drenched actors and a sodden set. Which years ago, it seems, was an open-air ballroom. Now the (fake) wind is in the tarpaulins and the (fake) rain arcs across relevant (visible) parts of the set. Soon thunder will be added to the (fake) lightning.

29 MAY

10.10 → Cliveden.

Into the King's Bedroom, with Stanley. Who didn't entirely know his not many lines . . . A shame that his curiosity has left him somewhere along the line, but he's had a helluva time and now has a new marriage, three kids, moved to London, new home. Why worry about acting?

7 JUNE

This is our last official day of shooting. Kate is now 16 (?) weeks pregnant and giving everything. By the end of each day she is wiped but still unbelievably focused. Matthias' last day, today, and this sweet, questioning soul melts back to where he came from. And graces his next umpteen projects.

9 JUNE

A Little Chaos—Last day.

Like a relay race with one runner. Kate jumping from carriage to carriage to desk to bath. Lights up, lights down. Au revoir to Kate. She moves swiftly and cleanly on—total commitment to everything. Ned, the children, this film, the next film, the kids' baked beans, throwing [a] party, ruthless emotional commitment, ruthless emotional detachment.

Wrap party. Which turned out to be a joyous thing. Chiswick House. Great venue . . . But all these sudden goodbyes to people who have shared the inside of your head, heart, insecurities, triumphs, have laughed, stared and yawned with you . . . now the strange absence.

10 JUNE

Wow. Like being hit by a train. The whole body in a kind of shock. What *was* that? Well, I know what it was, but not how much the body holds itself in a constant readiness. I guess this is the aftermath of all that controlled tension. No wonder the left knee gave out, and has now joined the right knee in two independent states. Their own pain, rules and barriers.

A day of relentless exhaustion. Falling asleep at any sofa opportunity.

Supper at home after an attack of common sense said 'Don't go out. Have steak and chips instead.'

11 JUNE

Campagnatico.

26 Via Umberto opened its doors and its freshly painted heart and the sun was shining as we changed the cushion covers on the terrace and under the pergola, and opened a bottle of white wine, waiting for the supermarket to open.

14 JUNE

Dinner at Vecchia Oliviera.

As we walk in, the faithful, and brilliant, pizza-maker shows us to a table or rather opens his arms for us to choose, as we are the only customers at 8pm. When Cortado arrives to take our order, I ask him: 'How are things?' 'Everything is difficult.' 'And new people in government?' 'They are all the same.' The walk through this little town is sad—no tables & chairs in the square, shops closed. By the time we leave the restaurant, custom had grown to 8 more people.

16 JUNE

Tied up the new sun blind. Shoe laces—temporary solution.

26 JUNE

Pisa → London.

9am. Cushions put away, suitcases packed, rubbish dumped and on the road to Pisa.

On the plane w. *Guardian* iPad edition. Thank you Catherine Bennett and, as ever, Nancy Banks-Smith (and while we're at it Marina Hyde) for endlessly dipping your pens in the acid juices that hang in the air from Jane Austen and Dorothy Parker. I guess it's a barbed delicacy men don't possess. Or need to develop, given might is right.

27 JUNE

ALC edit begins.

Of course all I could see was what is wrong. How to reclaim some innocence will be the big thing—doubtless through having the guts to show it to others. The headlines are clear—Nick cuts the action scenes really well, but doesn't always know where the heart of the scene is in the talkier moments. We spent the afternoon reclaiming some of that. Whacked by the evening.

2 JULY

I can now feel the film having a life of its own and I alternate between wanting it finished, magically, tomorrow and wanting to sit there for 24 hours straight. I have, however, no idea how this film will lose 30 minutes. I cannot see what can be cut without chopping into the narrative.

6 JULY

12.15 Wimbledon.

Lunch in the dining room with an extraordinary group of champions & finalists—Margaret Court, Billie Jean King, Virginia Wade, Ann Jones, Angela Mortimer, Martina Navratilova, Martina Hingis, Maria Bueno, Christine Truman, Jana Novotná, Hana Mandlíková.

Spent time talking to Maria Bueno, and later Billie Jean King, but mostly with Virginia Wade over tea . . . Of course she has a script . . . But she's interesting . . . So, of course, is Billie Jean. The other treat was sitting next to Miranda Hart—many laughs about being lip-read by idiot commentators.

7 JULY

Andy Murray wins Wimbledon!!!!

12 Kristin Linklater.

Brunch.

This so smart, engaged and curious-about-everything woman. And a Scot, too. So of course she stayed to watch ANDY MURRAY WIN WIMBLEDON. Heart in mouth time for every second, but a real display of courage and focus and accuracy.

18 JULY

1.15 Dr Landau.

All my doctors, and now my editor—a doctor, in a way—are seriously downbeat. Is this a good thing . . . ?

20 JULY

A phone call Chris Gull [old friend]. Almost as soon as he said 'Have you heard the news', I knew he was going to say 'Mel died' . . . Later at home, got an address for Pam. Another heart attack, the day after Snoo Wilson's[1] funeral. Another waste of an enormous talent and great spirit, a couple of Toby Belches, Falstaffs, their laughter always tempered by something else.

8pm Griff Rhys Jones.

His Fitzroy Square home is truly beautiful. Full of Mel's colleagues and friends, it is the perfect backdrop to a spectacular and—I don't know the adjective—person and life.

---

[1] English playwright and director (1948–2013), who also died of a heart attack

20 AUGUST

10.30 Screening for Gail, Andrea and Ray [Cooper, producer].

Sitting alone in the cutting room. Just me and the film. To be remembered above all things—I was moved. Especially by Kate and Matthias at their most open and vulnerable. Clearly, there are choices to be made but having received Gail and Andrea's notes, the crucial things to remember are—I can't make *their* film. And everything in the film is cumulative—information has to be given for the audience to feel *anything*. I loved *Tree of Life*—others hated it. There is no perfect way for all these individuals to have their say. I must listen, ask for what they feel, not what they would cut and edit.

24 AUGUST

Stay at home alone day, apart from the Waitrose expedition in the rain.

Thatcher—The Downing Street Years has proved to be fascinating, with ex-ministers only too ready to tell all. And they cut to her—not a listening bone in her body, eyes flaring instead of nostrils.

29 AUGUST

6pm Rima home. And apart from anything else the bedroom is not half-empty any more.

30 AUGUST

3pm Screening for us.

This was a tougher one. Starting to see more of the rights and wrongs now. The seesaw of choices.

2 SEPTEMBER

10 Dean Street.

Now down to somewhere around 2 hrs 17 mins.

3 SEPTEMBER

Venice.

6.45 Car → Heathrow.

9.15 → Venice.

Then hang around at the Festival desk for ½ an hour before the car to the boat to the Excelsior Hotel. And the camera, photo hordes start locusting.

Escape quickly in a boat to Venice and spend the afternoon wandering, buying an ice cream & a handbag for Ms Rima, before the boat back, a lie-down and another boat ride—glorious one, in a taxi for us alone straight to dinner.

4 SEPTEMBER

10 Walk into 'town' and locust attack. Refuge in a side street after a wander to the beach.

5 SEPTEMBER

Sleep on and off until nearly 10. Pack. Home to a pervasive sense of the irrelevance of it all which we have to take so seriously. The work is the pleasure but then always the judgement, which can strip the pleasure like turpentine.

13 SEPTEMBER

7.45pm Kathy Lette.

Oh Kathy . . .

The guests—Barry Humphries, Terry Gilliam, Helena Kennedy, Ruby & Ed, Ed & Justine Miliband, Benedict Cumberbatch, Jemima Khan, Salman Rushdie. For God's sake. Exhausting just writing that. But good chats with Justine M. (the pressure of it all) and Ed is upright and still looking forward. An inspiration and still curious about everybody and everything.

16 SEPTEMBER

10 Dean Street.

Some BBC notes come through. As Gail says, strange they read like script notes, not edit notes. At all events, quite a few cannot be considered since they refer to a different film . . .

We press on, cutting, tightening, shifting. The BBC note that rings bells is to shake its logical order up a bit. Hard to predict if that is possible.

17 SEPTEMBER

10am Dean Street.

And then notes from Zygi [Kamasa] at Lionsgate. Boy, do you have to be strong in this game. He wants it to be all Kate/Matthias, what's going on in her head and let's watch them fall in love. Everything else is peripheral etc., etc.

Yes, it is a love story. *Yes*, must see the inside of her head. But there has to be a texture and a context for the main narrative.

18 SEPTEMBER

10pm The Delaunay. 'There's someone in tonight I think you might know,' whispered the maître d', like a ventriloquist. 'Oh, who?' 'Emma Watson.'

21 SEPTEMBER

The blessed, to-be-guarded stay at home Saturday. Apart from the food trip to Marylebone High Street. A toaster repair, some great-looking tomatoes and fish pie.

27 SEPTEMBER

12.30 Harvey Nichols. Where they only stock clothes for human pipe cleaners, it seems.

3 OCTOBER

11am Dean Street.

   Run the film.

   First part improving all the time. Desperate need for music now.

   Nick suggests a radical cut which eventually I concede, but when I realise it contains a major narrative and psychological flaw, I got the standard reply 'I don't think people will notice that.' Even later phone calls receive the same stonewalling. This is a relationship in a moment of severe strain.

4 OCTOBER

→ New York for *CBGB* premiere.

7 OCTOBER

2 hours of phone interviews. The same five questions over and over again.

11 OCTOBER

6.30am → Heathrow (2 hrs' sleep).

   Home to shower, get ready to go into Dean Street. Just in time—Nick Manzi's [Lionsgate] notes. How someone I regarded as an intelligent, aware guy can write such illiterate, insensitive crap is a wonder.

16 OCTOBER

7pm 20th C. Fox Cinema. First public screening.

   And yes, it feels slow at the beginning. And the music is *so* missing. And question marks abound. But the audience is very concentrated.

17 OCTOBER

11am w. Nick. More like 11.30, by which time Andrea and Gail were there—full of how 'good the figures were' from last night, and what marks out of ten the actors had. It may have come as a surprise to them how this was received in my corner . . . I made a speech about not being interested, that my job is a delicate balance between manipulation and truth, and that doing that successfully will mean 'good figures', rather than attending to the figures too closely. I was gently banging my head against the wall.

27 OCTOBER

Later, at home, the newsflash that Lou Reed has died. And a memory of the evening at a table with him in Bar Centrale in NY. When he talked so eloquently about theatre and acting. Not music. Not himself.

2 NOVEMBER

12.15 *Philomena*—Gate.

Deeply frustrating. Seeming to ride on (correct) assumption of Judi's greatness allowing quite a lot of script laziness. Watching it is to constantly want to put your hand up and yell 'Excuse me, what about/why didn't she/ why hasn't he???' Etc., etc. We had to go to Jamie Oliver's shop immediately afterwards and spend a small fortune in order to recover.

6 NOVEMBER

Wednesday nights won't be the same once *Gogglebox* is gone . . . It makes me love the British. Just when you think all compassion and fellow-feeling is gone there they all are on the sofa, totally *with* some strangers on TV.

18 NOVEMBER

4.40 Cab → GPO Tower/Philippines Telethon, where—sign of the abject times—phone lines are blocked by girls hoping to talk to—not there—New Direction.[1] Sat with Juliet and caught up, in between the odd call that *did* want to give money. Somewhere in the 34th floor turntable—Jamie Oliver, Andrew Marr, Stephen Merchant, Nigel Havers, Phill Jupitus et al.—all dodging lack of New Direction slam downs.

12 DECEMBER

10am Dr Landau.

Who was happier—almost than me—to record 0.00, and to say that even Dr Reid's 0.03 meant that things were definitely AOK.

---

[1] One of the strongest typhoons ever to make landfall struck the Philippines on 7 November 2013, reducing the city of Tacloban to rubble and resulting in thousands of deaths. A.R. was one of a number of celebrities—including members of the boy band One Direction (not New Direction)—to lend their names to the relief effort.

14 DECEMBER

am Hooray for the NHS.

First sight of trouble, on the phone and round to St Mary's—blood test—maybe an infection, but wheels in motion including talking to Justin Vale. And this two days after a thumbs up.

16 DECEMBER

7 Screening.

Vue Cinema, Fulham Broadway. A cinema in a shopping mall almost on Fulham Broadway tube station.

Horrible sound—music too quiet, sound effects too loud, and an echo. It felt as if it was slow, but the audience was *very* quiet in a good way. Patti Love came and was knocked out and passionate that it should not be speeded up.

18 DECEMBER

9am Lionsgate Office.

Everyone's a filmmaker, everyone's a critic, it seems.

Would Daniel in the lions' den be the image? . . . These are forces that somehow have to be simultaneously accepted *and* resisted.

2.45 for 3.30 Lindo Wing/St Mary's.[1]

Into the laced-up-the-back gown and a side-room, before walking into the operating room, and Justin Vale, courteous as ever, showing me the inside of my bladder on a video-screen . . . After the ambiguities of the morning, facts and lack of agenda come as something of a relief.

19 DECEMBER

11am Abbey Road.

Lionsgate 'loves' the film, and wants to help make it 'the best it can be' (?) and is offering more money & more time for any pick-ups or strengthenings that occur. I am mystified and somewhat confused. We have contained and simplified and now they are saying 'stitch and expand' . . . ? This is unpicking a sweater.

5pm car → Heathrow.

8.40 → Johannesburg.

---

[1] A.R. was having a routine screening for cancer.

20 DECEMBER

10ish → The Saxon Hotel.

High walls, barbed wire, electronics everywhere outside. Inside all is pools and plants and peacefulness.

21 DECEMBER

8.20 → Johannesburg Airport.

A chancer shows us the way to the clinic for the yellow fever injection— 'Give me the blue one (100 Rand)—no the blue one . . .' He got the red one . . .

Then to Maun (1½ hrs) on the 11.40 followed by the 4 seater over the bush to Mombo.

22 DECEMBER

5am wake-up.

This morning gave us a field of 300 buffalo, many giraffes, a rainbow of birds, a 2000-year-old tree (all of them appearing suddenly, as if out of nowhere), elephants up really close and just before lunch, a bunch of lions sleeping it off, while a crowd of vultures hung about in the trees—the remains of last night's buffalo kill; in this case the head and a rib cage . . . And the frantic buzzing of a million . . . flies.

24 DECEMBER

5am Last Mombo trip out.

And before long, with his X-ray vision, Callum [their guide] spots five wild dogs lying in the sun. Once every three months, these sightings. And then begins *the great chase* as we career or pause through the bush following the steady pursuit of lunch/dinner.

25 DECEMBER

7pm Glorious Christmas Surprise.

Dinner in a clearing in the bush. Beef, turkey, big table, candles, and lion roaring nearby . . . Unforgettable. The Mexican couple had asked for a separate table. Even they could see its ludicrous isolation in this special, shared place, and sulkily joined us.

27 DECEMBER

2.30 Flight to King's Pool.

28 DECEMBER

. . . an eventful few hours, chasing wild dogs and eventually finding them with the end of their hunt—an impala. By the time we found them it was just a few bones. Apparently, they can devour the whole animal in 1½ minutes. Then a group of lions guarding last night's quarry—a hippo bloodynecked and motionless under a tree.

29 DECEMBER

6am wake-up.

Out to inspect the hippo corpse and the lions munching away, while 3 hyenas wait.

31 DECEMBER

5-seater—1 hour—to Kasane. Then cab to speedboat, and then 45 min cab . . . to Toka Leya. The Zambesi flowing outside our . . . front door.

4.30 Just the two of us—sliding up the Zambesi, with Donald, the boatman. Unforgettable. The atom bomb of mist coming off the [Victoria] Falls 1¼ km away. Back at 6.30, a swift shower & change. Dinner at 7.15. Done by 9. Utter wimps back to the room with a bottle of champagne. Goodbye & such memories 2013.

2014

Zambia — Cape Town — Philip Seymour Hoffman — Bob Hoskins —
Tony Benn — Ian McKellen's 75th birthday — Campagnatico —
Rik Mayall — New York — Helen McCrory — Richard Attenborough —
A Little Chaos premiere, Toronto — *Eye in the Sky* —
Mike Nichols — Cape Town

---

1 JANUARY

8am Victoria Falls.

Not sure what I imagined, but I did not think that they would seem so close, or that they exert such an immense pull to jump into them. In *some* part of the brain's mindless area. It's all so wraparound. The sound, the spray, the height, the width. An assault on all the senses.

2 JANUARY

To Johannesburg and then Cape Town. Pringle Bay.

Godfrey collects us for the drive around Livingstone, which is the real deal. Especially the market area ... Elsewhere a stall selling secondhand bags. Otherwise every other building seems to be a church, including the Old Capitol cinema.

11ish to the airport. For queuing hell, and the 13.15 to Johannesburg. Route march to B Terminal and the 17.00 to Cape Town. Liza is in the Departures Hall and we slide down to Pringle Bay in her brother's car.

Watched Ruby being both good and hyper on *HARDTalk*.

3 JANUARY

Lunch. A snooze. A walk on the beach with the dogs and it's time to hightail it to Hook, Line & Sinker for dinner lest we incur Stefan's unbelievably well-projected wrath at being late. I got in first to defuse. Temporarily. As soon as the others come in the door 'I thought I said 7.30 ...' But it's all a bit pretend and he soon gets on with preparing an array of squid, prawns, swordfish and others that cover the table. On leaving, he drops the bombshell that this was probably our last meal there. He's retiring in April.

5 JANUARY

Home to the mail, the cold, the everything that is opposite to where we have just been. Sitting watching crappy TV you realise is a kind of 21st century meditation. Your mind is engaged in a nothingness that allows it to wander.

11 JANUARY

12 Years a Slave.

Hmm. A great film, I am told. Would I watch it twice? No. What does it say? Should Chiwetel [Ejiofor] get an Oscar? No.[1] He's in it a lot, looking worried, and breathing heavily. Is that enough? [Michael] Fassbender, however, is *very* fine. Makes you ferret to understand him. Somehow, I was always watching actors, not a story.

23 JANUARY

On the way home, a visit—forced—to Dean Street Tesco. What a dump this chain is. Reduced their staff as much as possible in favour of shoppers checking their own food out, cabinets missing items, one variety of fruit, and a 15 minute wait for one of the few attendants to go get a bottle of vodka. A must to avoid. A sort of shopping equivalent of our shoddy government.

26 JANUARY

1.30pm Taylor Thomson.

Taylor's usual eclectic mix full of who arrives last (Fi, of course) and who leaves first (Cherie & Tony), and the orchestrated conversation in between . . . Tony seems to be behind some shield, and Cherie more vulnerable than ever.

31 JANUARY

R's birthday.

9pm The Shed.

Young, noisy crowd but they found us a corner table so that our combined age didn't embarrass the room.

2 FEBRUARY

The news tells us that Philip Seymour Hoffman has died. This is truly shocking. Apart from the depth and range of his talent, and the sense of him as a leader in the industry, he was also an NY neighbour. Met him once after *Borkman*, at BAM—but saw him having breakfast on 8th Avenue. He was both ordinary and extraordinary.

---

[1] He didn't.

4 FEBRUARY

[Re *A Little Chaos*]

A day at home. And another day of silent . . . cursing at the crassness of the distributors' notions of screenwriting. Nobody tells them how to distribute or market, but the common rule of a very fat thumb is that they know how to adjust a script. I recognise a good idea when I see it or hear it. I also recognise something that is merely adding surplus fat to a lean animal. It will make it move more slowly.

7 FEBRUARY

Screening for Ellen [Kuras, cinematographer], Kate and Matthias. And they liked the film. Maybe even loved the film. Although Kate is straight in with the 'Can't we . . . ?' 'Why can't we . . . ?'

17 FEBRUARY

5.30 Buckingham Palace.

Sectioned off from Thelma into a line-up—Angela Lansbury, Steve McQueen, Jane Horrocks, Lenny Henry, Luke Treadaway[1] to meet the Queen. Who shakes my hand and moves on, as ever.

Then down to the concert in the ballroom—huge, no microphones, people can't hear. Then a voice in my ear—'The Duchess of Cambridge would like to meet you.' And nice and chatty she was, too. A hundred faces to chat to. Impossible.

24 FEBRUARY

10am Dean Street.

I can sense Nick's exhaustion today. He even had a migraine in the afternoon. Mainly, though, he knew it was the Last Big Day and so he just did what I suggested, knowing it had to be passed over for tomorrow morning. I think we made strides, but hard to believe that it comes down to the wire like this and that the main hope is that we hang on to what we had back in December.

26 FEBRUARY

7.30 Dinner w. Patti Love at home. Harriet, Guy [Paul, her husband], A.L. Kennedy.

Harriet unstoppable these days—in a disarming way—in her ability to

---

[1] British actor (1984–)

talk about herself pretty non-stop. She even gave me a birthday book with a feature on her inside. Guy is pretty silent during all of this—looking on lovingly, as do we all. She has however—as his Christmas gift—booked him into Prue Leith's cookery school. (She hates cooking. He doesn't cook but doubtless soon will.)

5 MARCH

We had 2 episodes of *Line of Duty* today. It is excellent stuff—with really interesting, unfussy actors everywhere. And for the most part you can feel—in a good way—the Scandinavian influence. And then a swift kick of melodrama and it's the UK again. But all in all, classy stuff.

12 MARCH

6.45 Latymer Fundraiser.

This really was a time flies moment standing in the same spot in the school hall where I performed 50 years ago, 50 years since 'it rains on the games that we play at Wood Lane' and the shamefully dropped towel. Yikes. Instantly liked the new headmaster. It is a family, this place. The tiled and honour-boarded hall ensures that. My job is to be the occasional reminder that money isn't the *only* consideration.

14 MARCH

. . . Tony Benn has died. On TV this evening, a long tribute with Roy Hattersley still unable to cover his resentment and Neil talking of someone without whom life would have been poorer, but his path would doubtless have been easier. I remember having dinner with him and Melissa after *Private Lives* one night, and saw nothing of what R.H. calls 'hubris'—only gentle curiosity and warmth. And I applaud the courage to an echo.

25 MARCH

9.45 The film starts to re-emerge, new clothes, new hair, new faces. Maybe it is good for it to be unsettled in this way—for a bit—but the post-production gun to the head is a continuing outrage. There is definitely the ART and the PRODUCT.

30 MARCH

1.30 The Savoy.

Kathy Lette and Geoff[rey Robinson].

And a table with a river view. Table talk always good with these two—

veering happily between frolicsome and deeply political. It also turns out that Geoffrey is involved in the call for getting Stephen Ward's[1] conviction overturned, and that he and Kathy are friends with Mandy Rice-Davies.

30 APRIL

Sitting in the Lipsync lobby glancing to the TV screen behind the reception desk. The sound is down, everybody chatting, eating, and I see the strapline that Bob Hoskins has died. Dear Bob—direct, warm, vulnerable and so honest in his talent and everyday. I called Patti Love in the evening. I first met him when they were together. We managed to find things to laugh about.

3 MAY

Popping into Daunt's for a browse, I picked up Lynn Barber's new number.[2] Her interview with Nadal (sprinkled with hints that kept her this side of a libel suit) reminded me to *just say no*.

5 MAY

Bank Holiday.

1pm Recording with Sharleen S. and Johnny.

Great house Ms S. has—opposite London Zoo. And then round the back to Johnny's mews to record the song. In the kitchen, nearly. Nervous-making. A duet—sort of—with Sharleen?? I don't really know if they were genuinely happy. Another example of how useless nerves are.

23 MAY

3pm Lipsync.

Thank heavens. There were bumps and grinds that needed sorting. They were sorted and now—the film is done.

24 MAY

2 *Wolf Hall*.

Watching this as if it is a curious hybrid—I know I am in a theatre, it sounds like a radio play, it *looks* like a book on stage. Everyone else is very happy, though.

7.30 *Bring Up the Bodies*.

---

[1] English osteopath (1912–1963), prominent in the Profumo affair
[2] *A Curious Career*

And then it became more of the theatre. Maybe the confrontations were stronger, or the ellipses more elegant. Ben Miles (playing Cromwell) also seemed to grow rather than hide.

25 MAY

3pm Ian McKellen.

His 75th birthday party.

Sunshine, caviar, the Gormley statue looking endlessly up the river, a *v. good* magician.

And a cab home with Edna, made priceless by her story of the jealous snatching of poems at an Irish embassy do by Fiona S., Seamus Heaney and herself. These 3 reduced to 'It's not fair' stuff.

31 MAY

Campagnatico.

Was in bed when Claudio came to 'trim' the top of the olive tree. He halved it . . .

5 JUNE

Campagnatico.

Sitting and drawing in the garden while back in London there is a screening [of *A Little Chaos*]. Opposite activities, but linked as I watch my hand listen to my eyes in a parallel action to being on set, the editing room, the grade, the mix.

8 JUNE

10pm Pushed by Ms Rima, we go down to the (deserted) square, and into Massimo's Enoteca, for a grappa and to buy some wine. 'How is it?' we ask. 'Terrible' is the obvious answer. We talk about wanting to write to someone— and now WE MUST. It is ridiculous to see a village die like this. Over the years, the garage, the bread shop, the homeware shops, the flower shop, the wine bar. Now the grocery store and the hotel.

9 JUNE

And now Rik Mayall has gone. Rik—always so vulnerable underneath the ringmaster persona. But this is out of the blue. Shocking. Sitting here in the sun, I just cannot take it in. Ruby emails back. 'He was the most beautiful thing I had ever seen. The pain the pain.'

10 JUNE

Lindsay's email tells me that Kevin Elyot[1] has gone, too. As she says, 'He did well, though, didn't he?' Typical Lindsay. Straight to the point. Moving but unsentimental. And Kevin *did* do well.

1pm Sabrina and Tom Stoppard i.e. Sir Tom and Lady Stoppard for lunch. Their first outing having got married at the weekend. Sabrina so happy. 'I love saying "my husband".'

11 JUNE

8.45am Mario, Alessandro's stand-in, collects us for the drive to Pisa.

Earlier, had read various items about Rik. Including an interview with Lynn Barber from 2000 which caught him brilliantly. And the *Guardian* tells us today that his death was as sudden as his energy.

Dear Rik—so out there *and* so private, so wild *and* so vulnerable.

16 JUNE

11am Quo Vadis.

Gail.

So many lines to read between. Conversations with distributors that can only be guessed at. 'They think it isn't a winter film.' 'Maybe better for next year.'

17 JUNE

Barbara [Rik Mayall's wife] called. Asking me to read.

19 JUNE

Rik's funeral.

11.15 The short drive to the church in Dittisham. My God, is Devon beautiful . . . as is the church.

12.15 Barbara and Rosie, Sid, Bonnie[2] arrive and a beautiful and deeply personal service starts. Nearly a comedy exit, as the hearse plus people couldn't make it up the hill . . .

The farm is stunning, and Rik was buried on a hill above it, overlooking the countryside. Ben Elton, Kevin McNally,[3] Rik's brother spoke and a Burns poem was read.

---

[1] British playwright (1951–2014)
[2] Barbara Robbin's and Rik Mayall's children
[3] English actor (1956–)

25 JUNE

To New York.

2 JULY

11 Cafe Cluny.

Jordan Hoffman [film critic] on the 15th anniversary of *Galaxy Quest*, digging away to find clues whether Tim and I had got on or were we mirrors of our parts. What a surprise . . . an angle.

19 JULY

Yes to Toronto [Film Festival]—and finally news today that the deal is done. Kate will be there. Possibly from her own front lawn, with only one toe hitting the red carpet.

20 JULY

To Munich.

3pm Car → JFK and in the lounge is Julian Schnabel[1] w. his assistant Cat. Travelling to Naples . . . tells me of his version of *Perfume* that Bernd E[ichinger, producer] 'buried'. And invites us to lunch on an island near Positano.

21 JULY

7.15 in Munich and in the Lufthansa lounge chatting to Julian S. who is clearly enslaved by his one-year-old son who he is picking up here and taking to Italy. No wonder he makes good art. He is a human being. Jeff Koons, Ai Weiwei. It all comes in threes.

To Naples and the hour or so drive to Positano Le Sirenuse.

22 JULY

7.45 Invited for a drink at the hotel bar w. Richard Gere & his son. He gets waylaid by a rough sea, so we meet briefly in lobby . . . He is warm, smart and open as one would assume.

23 JULY

Giffoni Film Festival.

3.30 . . . for a Q&A with festival participants. Qs from Qatar, Australia, S. Korea etc., etc. Smart and touching. An award that looks like an *HP* prop on perspex.

---

[1] American painter and filmmaker (1951–)

24 JULY

Around 4pm we go with Taylor down to the harbour and get on the dinghy to *Parvati*—the luxury, on-tap cruiser she has rented for the next two weeks. Magnificent journey in and around massive rocks, and settling eventually looking back at twinkling Capri. We are, however, on Tangier time—she didn't tell the chef she was ready for dinner. We ate at 10.30pm. Delicious but ridiculous. We sailed back to Positano and got to our room at 2am.

26 JULY
To London.

29 JULY

An email from Stanley, having just watched the film. He loved it, but I didn't love the fact that nobody asked me. Adam[1] loved it, too, and had better manners.

13 AUGUST
7.30 *Medea*. National Theatre.

Helen McCrory absolutely commands that ghastly space, but the production has no idea what it is aiming for. The leaves falling as Medea exits was the final unnecessary touch.

The Delaunay.

Helen arrives, apologetic about delay. 'The director [Carrie Cracknell] was in for the first time since press night. I thought for a moment she was going to give me some notes. I have directed myself for five weeks.' Oh, Lord.

21 AUGUST
6.40 Heathrow Express for the 8.50 → Pisa.

24 AUGUST

Campagnatico.

Getting home to the news that Dickie Attenborough has died. Dear Dickie.

27 AUGUST

Watching the *ALC* trailer in some horror. The whole film in 2 mins. With stolen dialogue V/Overed. On repeat viewings, I can see what they are aiming at, but watching this version—questionable that I would go and see it. And from Gail, reports of a chocolate box poster image. Here we go.

---

[1] Adam James, English actor (1962–)

31 AUGUST

10am *A Little Chaos.*

Cast and crew screening.

A unique, unnameable experience. Watching something you have made being shown to the people who helped to make it. And knowing that supportive though they may be, they will not tell a lie.

3 SEPTEMBER

3pm *Eye in the Sky* medical. And a pretty full medical it was, too. Including touch your toes . . .

11 SEPTEMBER

Reviews are out. Good, bad and indifferent. The familiar tightening of the brain. The familiar silences from the rest of the world.

12 SEPTEMBER

To Toronto.

13 SEPTEMBER

6.30 To Roy Thomson Hall.

Watch the film.

At the end, after such tangible silence and laughter that came from the whole house, from people who were listening, 2000 people stood and clapped loud and long. Total, uncluttered acclaim for something that had reached them very directly.

25 SEPTEMBER

7.30 Marea w. Mike Nichols.

Listening to Mike spin a verbal nest around past and present could almost become an aim in life. So literate, such enormous breadth of references and mixed in with the damning is also the celebrating. He talks of Philip S.-H.: 'I think I killed him.' Orson Welles: 'So anecdotal & then I had dinner with him & loved him.' Elaine May,[1] Scott Rudin,[2] doing *Our Town*, Streep and *Master Class*, Tony Kushner, being asked to play Hamlet ('God no')—but then he is, amazingly, 83, and as many names that he recalls there are more that he can't.

---

[1] American comedian, director and actor (1932–)

[2] American film producer (1958–)

10 OCTOBER

7.15 → London.

Listened to Ed Sheeran and Goldfrapp (Alison). She could be singing any old words. Not a consonant in earshot.

17 OCTOBER

London Film Festival, Odeon West End.

5.35 Red carpet. 'What attracted you to this project?' times 10.

7.45 Watch the last ½ hour. Wonderful concentration in the cinema. Huge applause at the end.

9ish The Union Club. Friends all seriously knocked out by the film.

23 OCTOBER

1pm Peter Gregson.[1]

I think it is Peter's surface that talks so quietly and laughs at the end of almost every question, and just keeps going, with only a rare question or moment of listening. I think he saves all that for the music.

24 OCTOBER

Very early a.m.

Reading through *Eye in the Sky* and making pictures in my head of every scene, every moment. Some of them being dangerously repetitive, but I guess that's what we are here for now. Sleight of everything.

6.30 Car → Heathrow and the 9.30 becomes the 10.20. Maybe 2½ hours' sleep. Too much turbulence.

29 OCTOBER

Cape Town.

Huge and terrifying problem trying to connect brain to mouth. Lack of sleep on the plane added to 2 hours, wake up, 1½ hours, wake up, led to memory panic.

30 OCTOBER

Occasionally a burst of clarity but an overwhelming sense of surviving, not enriching . . . A very hot, dusty room and a costume that was tight and adapted. No concrete sense of who I was.

---

[1] Cellist and composer (1987–)

1 NOVEMBER

A happy final morning. Glorious Cape Town sunshine as we filmed in an old colonial-type club and then a created-from-nothing toyshop in Church Square. And I was relaxed because it was character, not jargon. I should be more careful to allow more time if this is anything to be repeated.

5 NOVEMBER

London.

Whacked. All day. Even slept through most of my current favourite TV programme—*Grayson Perry: Who Are You?* on Channel 4.

20 NOVEMBER

Mike Nichols has died. He had looked suddenly frail at dinner and lunch in September, but also, of course, everlasting. But that is doubtless because that is what we lesser mortals need him to be. I found a Meryl Streep quote—'He was responsible for igniting people's dreams.' And he joyously kept that flame alight in so many.

25 NOVEMBER

7.30 Fundraiser for Stephen Kinnock[1]—standing for Aberavon. So good to see Glenys and Neil and a pity that Stephen has yet to acquire their microphone skills. Just reading your script won't do . . .

18 DECEMBER

South Africa.

Walking back from First Beach to Fourth Beach, past the fashion shoots and the toe-stubbing rocks and cold-drink sellers and the massage on the beach canopies and the lifeguards under their shelter, and the gulls bobbing, then back again past all of that in reverse. But the sea just kept doing absolutely its own thing. We are specks in its eye.

31 DECEMBER

Blazing hot day on the beach. We escaped to the V&A Waterfront [shopping mall], but it is one of those days when it is too hot outside, too warm inside. A beer, a Coke, a tangerine.

---

[1] Labour politician (1970–), son of Glenys and Neil Kinnock

2015

2 JANUARY

And what did I eat last night? Apart from too much. A stomach upset to start the New Year.

4 JANUARY

6am—after dreaming of a house in the English countryside . . .

10am Bianca comes to give 3 of us a massage. Fast asleep at one point. 'Get your legs up more,' she says. 'Because of swelling?' I say. 'Yes,' she says. 'Statins,' I say.

4pm Down to the beach—Indian Ocean warm, but wind and waves to knock you senseless. We walked, instead, looking for oystercatchers.

5 JANUARY

Grey skies, rough seas. No swimming today, methinks.

9am Croissants and coffee together. Then start at the suitcases, trying to will them to be lighter. Forget it.

5.30 Liza drives us to the airport. The unending mass of Khayelitsha [township] on our left.

7 JANUARY

A start to the Great Clear Out. This may take some time.

Later today—emails giving a rough guide to *ALC* tours, press junkets and premieres. In theory, there is time to spread in Australia, and time on the West Coast if there is no compunction to hare back for the Dublin FF [film festival].

11 JANUARY

3.30 To visit Geraldine [McEwan]. Takes a while to find her, and even then I almost walked past her bed. It was shocking and strange to see that engaged, curious, youthful energy so drained of it all. A sleeping, grey form with her mouth down-turned in sleep. When she woke, gently prompted by Thelma, she looked at me, said 'My God' and stroked my face with her right hand.

13 JANUARY

Now the cupboard-clearing. A career in a cupboard. What to keep, what to dump. Finding letters that should not have been so long lost. Seeing a shape—a shape punctuated by big decisions and leaps into the dark.

15 JANUARY

Rima goes off to Barlby[1] early. The Duchess of Cambridge is coming today. The arch Republican and the Duchess . . .

23 JANUARY

To Paris.

Hôtel de l'Abbaye which has the smallest imaginable room. But perfectly designed bathroom. And is a walk away from Cherche Midi.

24 JANUARY

After breakfast, a walk down Cherche Midi and into Lilith [a boutique]—still there.

25 JANUARY

To London. A swift change of tickets before breakfast, and a car to Gare du Nord for the 12.40 → St Pancras.

27 JANUARY

7pm Ruby.

Some chicken, potatoes and salad and the horror story of her trip to the US. I think she wanted an injection of old times.

28 JANUARY

Fischer's.

Dinner w. Helena and Iain. So many topics to cover, you have to snatch the odd conversational gap to get your oar in. But H. and I.—a couple of

---

[1] Primary school in North Kensington. Rima is chair of the governors.

major life forces covering a 3D landscape, including Helena's Christmas bust-up with Reggie [Nadelson]. Who, frankly, was asking for it.

30 JANUARY

To New York.

Hardly in the door when Thelma calls to tell us that dear Geraldine has died.

31 JANUARY

Rima's birthday.

This morning I spoke to Claudia and Greg [G.McE.'s children] and Lois [her assistant]. Lois tells of the irony of speech therapists sitting at Geraldine's bed talking their talk (literally, I suppose). Lois gently handed over her phone with Geraldine's Wikipedia page on it. The nurse said 'Oh, you used to act. Oh, you were at the National Theatre!' Geraldine said, 'From the beginning.'

3 FEBRUARY

9 Bar Centrale w. Lily and Hamish. A Bar C. night, what with Jake Gyllenhaal and Ruth Wilson at one table, Jagger sitting behind them, Matthew Broderick coming in not far ahead of Glenn Close, etc. But we four made our own fun, thank you.

9 FEBRUARY

To London.

11 FEBRUARY

Desk-clearing.

Sorting details for screening.

News from Australia that the screening has sold out and will I do a second?

Focus [Features, distributors] still drumming their fingers about the US release date.

17 FEBRUARY

11 To Sara Sugarman for the day out to her new home in Sheerness. Which is like driving into a whole different world. Cranes, old factories, chimneys in a wide, low Kent landscape, odd houses dotted around—and suddenly, through a gate next to a huge pile of containers, are two beautiful Georgian terraces. Sara has a house in one, with a long swathe of garden, and interesting neighbours—a view of the sea from the upstairs windows. Her painter

and decorator friends from Wales are living in the house, painting it a wonderful palette of 18th C. pastels. Glorious. Omelette and chips in a nearby pub with its own gangplank down to the tide-out sea.

18 FEBRUARY

1pm Training Committee, RADA.

Constant sense of having to remind them that (1) I am an actor (2) I am a director (3) I trained at RADA and therefore (4) I don't need a lecture. In fact, they should be asking *me* stuff. But we plough on, hopefully.

19 FEBRUARY

9am Phone call w. Australia

All those miles away, and the same six questions . . .

21 FEBRUARY

Glasgow birthday.

9 & Heathrow Express.

11.30 → Glasgow and the Blythswood Square Hotel which is kind of MDF chic. A bit of lunch and then 3pm grooming followed by STV and print.

6pm Glasgow Film Festival—*A Little Chaos*.

Quick introduction and then to Two Fat Ladies with Allan Hunter and Corinne Orton.[1] Nice room, food too complicated. Back to the cinema for the post-screening Q&A which was actually enjoyable. Huge warmth from the audience.

Then back to the hotel to collect Sean B[iggerstaff], Alison C[ampbell] & Andrew [Muir] to go for more dinner to the excellent Ox and Finch in Sauchiehall Street. Almost collapsing from tiredness at the table but good to hear such love for the films—and a pavlova cake was sent out . . .

23 FEBRUARY

Sheekey's w. Zoë and Gawn—and boy, can Zoë sink those martinis, and boy, does she dominate the conversation when she does. Gawn looks concerned, but lets her free, bless him.

24 FEBRUARY

2pm Geraldine's funeral. All day I have been saying—truthfully—that I haven't processed the absence of Geraldine at all. It feels like a mistake, that we were all there talking about her, eating sandwiches and drinking prosecco. And even now, writing this feels fake. Or maybe it is what one

---

[1] Respectively, the co-director and then producer of Glasgow Film Festival

of the people there said—that you feel as if some people in life should be excused . . .

27 FEBRUARY

I googled Jerome Ehlers[1] to see what he had been up to lest we could say hi in Australia. He died in August last year. Tall, skinny, funny, romantic Jerome . . . More not fair.

The rest of the day was at home packing. Going to the cleaner's. Fish pie for supper. Watching *Gogglebox* watching *Wolf Hall*. Failing to sleep much.

28 FEBRUARY

Melbourne via Singapore.

On the way out pick up a *Harper's Bazaar* with Kate looking straight at *me* on the cover.

Watched *Maps to the Stars* and Julianne Moore, doubtless great in *Still Alice*, is *brilliant* in this, a role that would have the Academy voters reaching for their sick bags. Fearless, inspirational Cronenberg. And a portrait of this insane profession—no, the insane abuse of it by what Mike Leigh calls the numbskulls that makes you think of stepping back, way back.

2 MARCH

Melbourne.

After fitful sleep, we eventually got up around 11am. Some coffee, and with *Lonely Planet* in hand, did the tour of Melbourne lanes, and wound up neatly at Chin Chin for lunch where we boldly had their Jungle Curry—or rather, half of it, since the burning mouths would go no further. The paths led naturally to the riverbank by Federation Square (Melbourne has a lovely energy, but terrible architecture) and took the 3.30 ferry up the Yarra and back.

7 MARCH

4pm Miriam Margolyes at The Script.

Miriam, who lives her life and speaks her thoughts *as* they happen. Here and now. The show isn't very good. She is away too much from her partner. Been together 43 years. Israel deserves to be hated. All over a coffee in the street.

12 MARCH

7pm *A Little Chaos* screening. Watching from the back, on the stairs, and oh God, here we go—the let's get back to the editing room sensation. The

---

[1] Australian actor and writer (1958–2014)

audience are very warm, though, and they seem to have a good time during the Q&A, which is the same five questions only longer.

15 MARCH

1pm → Sydney Airport.

   4.10 → Singapore.

16 MARCH

London.

Somewhere around 3am watched *Gemma Bovery*. Beautifully judged version of the Posy Simmonds' cartoon.

Landed at 5am, sped through the dark streets and home around 6am. The usual pile of stuff on the kitchen table, but nothing broken, touch wood. Unpacked, answered mail, fielded press requests.

17 MARCH

12 Westminster Abbey.

   Richard Attenborough's memorial.

A rather unique sensation wandering up the central aisle of that church, crammed as it was on both sides, and through the nave into the choristers' section and altar to find a seat. Between, as it turned out, Evelyn de Rothschild[1] and Lady Annabel Goldsmith[2]. He with no sense of anyone else's space, she with her arm in a sling. I could have wished to be thinner. Thelma opposite, along with Judi & Finty [J.D.'s daughter], Michael & Shakira Caine, Ken B. to my right, the Attenborough family in the choir stalls. Puttnam had the only jokes, Ben K. read *Gandhi* as if he'd written it and I dropped my seating card which E. de R. pointed at, helpfully. Dickie would have loved the music & showbiz of it all. Not sure about all the religion. Went off to the Delaunay for lunch with the Suchets and Sara Kestelman.[3]

18 MARCH

9am Stephen Waley-Cohen[4] who, somewhat to my surprise, invites me to become President of RADA. Some instant instinct makes me decline. 'You need someone with a higher profile.' 'You underestimate yourself,' says Stephen. The resistance, of course, is to being devoured by the Establishment.

---

[1] British financier (1931–)
[2] English socialite (1934–)
[3] English actor (1944–)
[4] English theatre owner-manager (1946–)

19 MARCH

Prague.

5.30 pick-up → Heathrow.

    7.20 To Prague.

Walked across the Charles Bridge and then had lunch on a terrace looking at the river. The rest of the day was a blur, partly because of the endless, blinding flash bulbs as dozens of photographers popped away—pictures that will go nowhere. Press conference, TV interview, getting the award, intro x 2 cinemas for *ALC*, backroom (serious jet lag now) party in staggering municipal hall and the treat of seeing J.-J. A. after 30 years, and of meeting Kim Novak—an interesting, interested delight. 'Jimmy Stewart and I just played together.'

21 MARCH

Up at 6am. Pack, coffee, iPad and great news—Kath Viner is the new editor of the *Guardian*!!! Breakfast at 8am and off to the airport at 8.40 for the 11am → London, on which 'Can I get a picture?' assumes a new low. People queuing to sit down behind a man who is not taking no for an answer. He now has a picture of his grinning face leaning over two seats, somehow adjacent to my pissed-off one.

22 MARCH

A day of a kind of internal collapse, a mixture of aeroplanes, jet lag & depression from days of eating one's own flesh in interviews that have no real motor.

24 MARCH

1pm Goring Hotel.

    'How We Met' interview and photo shoot for the *Independent* w. Helen McCrory. Helen as good-humoured as ever, the photographer, Ben, also—although alarm bells are ringing from makeup and publicist about the lighting. Then Adam J[acques] shows up to do the interviews and clearly has his ideas in place, and tries to bend us to his questions . . . After we have finished, downstairs for lobster omelette.

2 APRIL

Watching the 2-hour [general election] debate on TV, in which Ed didn't disgrace himself, but Nicola Sturgeon walked off with it as I knew she would. Heart to mouth connection.

7 APRIL

2.30 National Theatre.

Tom Stoppard's *The Hard Problem*.

An hour and forty minutes in the dark. A young—mostly—cast that has no idea what they are saying, or why, and so emotion is wiped across the lines in order to make it 'interesting'. Who is to blame for this?

10 APRIL

Paris and back.

5.40am. Finally, I guess, hearing the alarm and knowing that there will be a car outside at 6am. Made it, somehow.

8 St Pancras, and Lorna Mann, Lionsgate publicist, and Eurostar to Paris and a car to the Hyatt Vendôme Hotel. About an hour in the very swish and beige suite they have given me and then Kelly, groomer, arrives, English—in France for 8 years, married to a Frenchman, missing London. Then to TV interviews, lunch with the ebullient Sammy H., the distributor. Print interviews, finishing at 4.20. So really? Why stay? Hightailed it to Gare du Nord and got the 6.40 home.

11 APRIL

8 Dalia and Dexter for dinner with Hugh Jackman, Christopher Walken, Taron Egerton,[1] Iris Berben[2] and Jamie Oliver. With a Lithuanian cook. Yep. That was the evening that was . . .

17 APRIL

The early morning silence that I know well from the past. Eventually something from Paul. We have a fight on our hands . . . People love it. Critics— some won't go there. One, I would hazard, wrote his review before he'd seen it.

3pm Car → Broadcasting House. Edith Bowman & James King [Radio 1 presenters]. Kermode and Mayo interview. And those are two of the positive voices.

8.10 → Curzon, Mayfair, for a Q&A after the screening. 'This film is so beautiful' is the refrain.

24 APRIL

EN ROUTE NEW YORK HAVING BEEN IN BERLIN AND VIENNA.

Hanging about in the Concorde Room for the 5.05 to Newark. And it's

---

[1] Welsh actor (1989–)
[2] German actor (1950–)

clear what has been deflected and on hold as well as totally enveloping—a deep sense of quiet crumbling inside, which re-assembles every now and then and *will* re-form, but into what? Not sure. This [*A Little Chaos*] is the kind of work I make. If I am to be disallowed then—I just stop. But as I write that, it feels like the wrong response. But *some* energy has to come *towards* me, otherwise I am emptied.

25 APRIL

7.30 White House Correspondents' Dinner.

2000 people at the Hilton Hotel and find Kath & the others—*Guardian* staff, Chris Ofili [artist], David Tennant and wife. Obama and Michelle were dots on the horizon that was the top table, but there was excellent people-watching. Al Jazeera announced themselves as fans. 'I like you, too.' 'You do? Everyone here thinks we're terrorists.'

We were a very enjoyable table even including the elephant in the room—my film.

28 APRIL

BAM. Karen Brooks Hopkins[1] tribute concert.

8.30 A real, unexpected thrill to introduce Martha Wainwright & of course Rufus. They sang a duet that was written by their mother, Kate, that was heart-stopping. Some great dancers, a huge Brooklyn choir, Paul Simon, on screen, singing 'Homeward Bound' and—acute for me—'Time It Was' [better known as 'Bookends']. Laurie Anderson—on screen—playing a ravishing violin solo. A beautiful tribute to amazing Karen.

11 MAY

7am → Paddington.

Where—no explanation, apologies, just guards with their backs turned, one of them even smiling—trains are cancelled and eventually we set off at 7.40. Panicked calls to Melanie & BA and it all turns out to be OK. We got checked in and down to the gate 5 mins before boarding.

Mario is at Pisa—gloriously sunny and hot Pisa—and under 2 hours of his chat we arrive at Campagnatico. Which is beginning to resemble the *Mary Celeste*. And over supper, we both gaze at the sunset and the possibility of letting this part of our lives go. Hmmm.

---

[1] President emerita of the Brooklyn Academy of Music

14 MAY

A walk around the village after a long, slow breakfast. The walk has been opened up now. The resting tractor halfway down the hill tells all.

18 MAY

Into the town square to say hello to Antonio and buy lamp bulbs, a torch, citronella candles. To wave a wand—give us six months in the village, a bit of activism on behalf of the defunct terrace—letting Gabi and Servilio's restaurant and cafés in the square . . . the village would live again.

20 MAY

Pack. Clear up. Wash up. Load up the car.

9.30 off to Pisa.

21 MAY

11.30 Dr Reid's nurse yells your name into the waiting room at loudhailer pitch, but then takes blood with hardly a scratch or ouch, and never misses the vein.

26 MAY

Brussels.

12 Car → St Pancras.

Find Katy (Lionsgate rep) and in Brussels → Hotel Amigo. Print interviews until 2pm and then dinner with the distributors.

9.20 To the cinema for the Q&A. Total blackness with a spot glaring at me. A long loud hello from the audience. To me? The film they have just watched? Bed at 2am.

27 MAY

The Hague and Amsterdam.

28 MAY

Amsterdam.

10 Dutch press day. Getting pretty tired now and am dumbstruck at a journalist who says she thought it clear that I saw the story as an allegory about the banking crisis . . .

5pm → The Rijksmuseum.

Vermeer's woman pouring milk and the Rembrandt self-portrait & the portrait of Titus are the stop-you-in-your-tracks pictures.

29 MAY

London.

7.30 Barbican.

Hamlet last week.

Tonight—*Kafka on the Shore* which, having found Edna, both of us thought was going to be Kafka-esque, rather than about a boy called Kafka. Some memorable images, as always, float past.

The Delaunay w. Thelma and Edna and Seumas Milne (Thelma's nephew).[1]

1 JUNE

A tour around some of the available properties in Marylebone, Notting Hill, Holland Park, Chelsea and one on the river all, hilariously, in the £3–4½m range. None of them suitable for one reason or another. One of them, connected to the Southwark agent, was actually in Bermondsey Street (requested) and is unforgettable. A stockbroker from the US, now moved to Monaco, has created a nightclub out of 5 rooms one on top of another, circular staircase linking them, pool table on the top floor, hot tub (of course) on the terrace. Madness, everywhere.

5 JUNE

8.50 Jonathan Mount [estate agent].

And out to Clerkenwell and Shoreditch we go. Some beautiful streets here—but you have to come back on a Friday and Saturday night for a reality check.

7 JUNE

To New York.

8 JUNE

9 Window cleaning.

Rather them than me, with their belts and clip-on hooks keeping them safe.

9 JUNE

12 Steve, TV. The new remote is an instant improvement, and I let him persuade us to a new DVD player & Netflix.

---

[1] And a *Guardian* journalist and political aide

16 JUNE

Joe Neumaier—*Daily News.*

One of the smartest interviews I have ever done. With really good questions.

21 JUNE

Los Angeles.

10.15 Car to JFK.

Nelson takes us on the pretty route—all along the river, down to almost Staten Island. An hour, but a New York I had not seen. At one point, some tower blocks that looked like a Soviet complex.

6 A.O.C. (Where Oros used to be . . .) Dinner w. Marcia Firesten. Why is everything changing for the worse? This restaurant holds so many happy memories from what seemed like golden days in LA—lunches, dinners, the Beverly Center, Fred Segal's [clothing store], sunshine and looking forward. Tonight—food OK, service pushy and customers that are unpindownable.

22 JUNE

9.30 *LA Times* interview (Susan King) and photograph among the plants. Hard work getting her to mine any new territory. The mind was made up . . .

29 JUNE

10 Sycamore Kitchen.

Breakfast then a drive to Canyon, Mulholland and Santa Monica. *Reacquainting.* But a pain in the left arch & calf is nagging, so walking is tough.

7ish Marcia collects me and → 3, 2, 1 (No) so noisy. Escaped across the road to Mozza who had some Sesti Rosso and fine food. On the way, I mentioned the leg pains. Marcia is on to it, making an appointment with the podiatrist and checking with Bart.

30 JUNE

10am phoner to Brazil and then—podiatrist, cardiologist, ultrasound, blood tests—and yes, there is/are blood clots, but small ones in the non-scary veins. Still scary, though, to hear the words thrombosis, clots, change plans etc.

1 JULY

5pm to LAX.

Dinner in the Qantas/BA lounge. On to the plane at 9pm and—*ALC* is showing . . . just to remind me from whence I come. But a sleeping pill takes care of everything.

2 JULY

Home around 5pm to watch Nadal lose at Wimbledon, sadly, but his OCD behaviour could actually be getting in his way now, especially against someone like Dustin Brown who plays from his fingertips, his imagination. So free and unfettered by anything, it seems.

Nothing seemed too wrong in the house on arrival. But wait—yes, the smoke alarm is beeping downstairs and we haven't a clue. Called the fire service. They came and—we thought—dealt with it. Come bedtime, the beep is back. Took the cover off, still it beeped. Twice. Then surrendered.

3 JULY

Appointment made w. haematologist. This crazy-paving diary has that in it today, plus watching Heather Watson nearly become a Wimbledon legend (but play brilliantly, anyway), find batteries for the smoke alarm, answer a mad array of emails, look out the window at sunshine all day, and a torrential storm as we went to bed . . .

6 JULY

The Wimbledon Days. Which keep you strapped to the sofa convinced, of course, that if you change your position, the heeby jeebies will make Andy Murray's next ball go out.

7 JULY

3pm St Mary's.

Dr Shlebak who does the blood tests and gives me a prescription. 3 months of a different pill every day. Blood thinners.

9 JULY

7.30 Guildhall.

Guys and Dolls.

More like 7.45 when we got there given the tube-strike traffic . . . But there were all those familiar tunes to guide us in. Afterwards, Marina[1] said she now knows she never wants to do another musical—'It's all tits and teeth.' With these young actors, though, it's the heightened reality, the ruthless picking up of cues, the squad-like entrances and exits that marks the genre.

---

[1] Marina Bye (1993–), daughter of Ruby Wax and Ed Bye

13 JULY

2.45 The Wellingon [Hospital].

As instructed. And tested.

14 JULY

5.30 Dr Landau, Harley Street.

A different kind of diary now.[1]

7.45 *36 Phone Calls*.[2]

For instant deflection and a chatty time in the bar afterwards w. Jeremy B. and friends.

At home, later, capsizing.

15 JULY

Falling asleep all day, with instant small dreams.

Emails batting away at each other. Take the pills, don't, talk to this person, get permission for them to talk to another . . .

16 JULY

12 To Ovington Gardens.

An apartment with 3 terraces but it feels like suburbia comes to the Brompton Road. Great to be so close to the V&A, the Park and all that, but views of London whilst suffocating . . . ?

17 JULY

8.30 35 Weymouth Street [Hospital].

New faces, one after another, all day. Thank God for the one loving constant.

And somewhere in the pm a pot of hummus and some vegetable sticks was heaven.

19 JULY

And off to the Wellington we go—as dinner was being prepared—for some 'in case' ultrasounds. White, white room, white lights, we try to watch the second episode of *Outcast*.

Came back and ate dinner.

20 JULY

2pm 93 Harley Street.

David Landau introduces us to Tobi (Dr) Arkenau who I like a lot.

---

[1] It is at this point that A.R. learns he has pancreatic cancer.

[2] Play by Jeremy Brock

22 JULY

9.30 Platinum Medical Centre (PMC).[1]

First session.

24 JULY

8 Fischer's w. Ron and Karen Bowen and us. Good choice. Bratwurst (gentle veal and chicken), sauerkraut, potato salad, horseradish, cucumber salad. And two of our oldest friends who can talk about the past like the adventure it *was*.

26 JULY

12 Melanie Parker comes to start the removals and storing. Boxes come, boxes go. We are talking about Eden, her daughter, who is autistic (to some degree, but on the spectrum), and of *how* smart and inventive she is. Inside all the white Muji fileboxes are scripts, letters, notes, research on each project I've been involved with. That's my imagination in those boxes.

29 JULY

9am PMC.

9.30 Dr Arkenau.

10am The car waiting at the corner takes us calmly and punctually to Goodwood races, another first. The main reason for being there—presenting the Sussex Stakes Cup—is switched by the Sheikh of Qatar, and I wind up going down with the CEO of the Savoy Hotel to present the following race's prizes with him. Weird. But lunch was very enjoyable.

30 JULY

20 Montagu Square.

To look at Flat 1 again. After the weeks gone by, this really *is* the perfect place in the middle of a beautiful square and a 10 min walk to Marylebone High Street via coffee shops, cleaner's, a greengrocer, with a farmers' market and Waitrose waiting.

31 JULY

And now WT becomes an edit suite. Of itself. Every drawer, cupboard and shelf to be diluted, stored or given away. Space for a new set of starting blocks.

---

[1] A.R. begins regular appointments for chemotherapy. Concerned that this would result in hair loss, he is given a tightly fitting ice cap—a helmet-like hat filled with a cold gel—that can prevent this. In the event, it proved unnecessary.

2 AUGUST
Cilla Black.[1]

I feel like we grew up together. She was the best of us, but standing next to The Beatles. And her instincts were powerful. She knew she was a star, but she carried self-respect alongside directness and simplicity. It was good to sit down with her at Mel's that Saturday night, and feel only that I wish I had known her better.

5 AUGUST
9.30 PMC.
  Second session.
  Home at 3.30pm. The repetition means an easier response or would do if one medication didn't fight another.

6 AUGUST
The days of trying to steer around yourself whilst behaving normally because there are cupboards to be emptied and boxes to be filled. Still.

7 AUGUST
1.30 Montagu Square w. Caroline [estate agent]. And yes, it is going to be a different way of being in London. But Caroline and I tick away together and edit ideas in and out (don't make a garden room, do redo the bathrooms, our own bed *could* work just fine & maybe upstairs sofa bed) and so on.

10 AUGUST
Another cupboard cleared. Impatient for cupboard boxes now. The flat is getting used to the air blowing through it.

12 AUGUST
Horrifying to realise that so much stuff just gathers itself around you, especially if you have as much storage as we have. Cupboards & shelves full of efficiently filed things we never look at.

13 AUGUST
7pm Moorfields Eye Hospital.

  Mr Mutiq who is fast and expert and charming. And the recent white flashing in the right eye is, indeed, about getting older, or macular degeneration, I think he said. Home to a suitable fish pie.

---

[1] She had died the day before.

14 AUGUST

To Harvey Nichols. Their food hall is now hopeless. Good to know. But we found the right piece of cashmere for Jane.

7.30 Jane Bertish's birthday.

30 friends gathered to surprise someone who would hate it. 'Did I pull a face?' said Jane, later. And it was a sweet gathering of friends. Until I fell down the step into the garden patio just as the cake's candles were being lit. Time to go home.

15 AUGUST

After a pasta and salad supper we watched *Funny Girl* which Rima had never seen. Apart from Streisand reminding me what a great actress she is, I was hooked by the craft of William Wyler—his pacing and cutting, just nudging you along by a finger, or a hand or a wrist.

17 AUGUST

More boxes filled and a fleeting thought about the fact that I haven't looked at this stuff forever, and now it's going from shelf to a box. The bins outside the bedroom window have a tempting air. But then again, editing is going on, and files are being condensed. So maybe there's another stage, in the storage hold.

18 AUGUST

11 Solicitors.

Margaret Lang (will specialist) is in charge of us, and she probes and nudges us towards some sense of the shape of things. (After Stephen Wegg-Prosser [solicitor] has done the same re house purchase . . .)

29 AUGUST

The office looks like a bomb has hit it, paper thrown everywhere, amidst the sound of ripping, as Rima lightens the file load.

Upstairs, a deep breath and the same is happening to all the saved recipes. Now they are in ordered piles. Maybe we will actually use more than 12 of them.

31 AUGUST

8pm Locanda Locatelli.

For an anniversary dinner.

You have to pick your food carefully. Tuna salad means cubes of rather chewy, hot tuna in a pool of borlotti bean purée (stranger still when you eat it) and the portion of kid goat would have fed quite a few shepherds. I can't quite pin down the clientele, either. But you can *hear*, and the lighting is on the food, not the faces. And we were home in 5 minutes.

2 SEPTEMBER

9.30 PMC.

Very beautiful email about *ALC* from Tom Tykwer. A good director understands every nuance of what was being aimed for. What world is this that we try to function in?

3 SEPTEMBER

9am For a touch of normality, the men who service the steam-room are due. And apparently, all is OK.

Spent the day alternately sticking Rima's recipe books together again, and in some kind of order. The chaos is resumed in watching hellish scenes from Budapest station [of refugees] on the news, and the equally hellish vision of watching the prime minister as he attempts to float his little boat on the perceived tides of UK public opinion. Easy, of course, for Nicola Sturgeon to take the high moral ground, but Cameron should, of equally course, seize it.

7 SEPTEMBER

8.30 Waiting to go to PMC and the floor came up to meet me . . . [1]

9 SEPTEMBER

To the Wellington Hospital.

15 SEPTEMBER

Back home.

17 SEPTEMBER

2.30 Physiotherapist.

Who clearly knows what she is doing, but has an ever-present laugh. I decide to look her seriously in the eye whenever she laughs.

19 SEPTEMBER

4pm Margaret Heffernan and her husband Lindsay.

---

[1] He had had a stroke. Rima called 999 and an ambulance arrived within minutes. He was taken first to University College Hospital then to the National Hospital for Neurology. Within a day or two he had recovered, his speech was back to normal and he was able to walk to Carluccio's. Close friends and relatives were now told how ill he was.

Who brought a book about the Eames brothers and a poetry book called *40 Sonnets*. Our friends are so solicitous—as in kind and courteous.

8pm Ruthie/River Cafe takeaway.

And more solicitousness from Ruthie and the River Cafe. Lamb, vegetables, prosciutto, mozzarella & tomato, almond cake, lemon cake, raspberries, figs, peas & miniature plums.

21 SEPTEMBER
12 Liz—speech therapist.

Who is a little scatter-brained and all-inclusive, but tells me to read more.

2pm Allan Corduner calls by with some chocolates and good cheer.

23 SEPTEMBER
9am PMC.

3.30 Sara Sugarman.

Sitting on the sunny terrace with some Ottolenghi chocolate biscuits and a cup of tea, talking about Sara's happiness in Sheerness, and her upcoming trip to Galilee, and her birthday in Istanbul. Life throws up such opportunities when you put out a hand, or take the chance.

2 OCTOBER
7.30 Scott's.

Valerie Amos,[1] Forest Whitaker and Waheed Alli.[2]

3 OCTOBER
4pm Tea w. Ian McKellen and Frances Barber and Sean M[athias] & friend from the US.

5 OCTOBER
12 To Montagu Square.[3]

7 OCTOBER
PMC.

9 OCTOBER
5pm Leila and Danny.

A walk to the Park & the ducks, and back for tea.

---

[1] Labour peer Baroness Amos (1954–)
[2] Labour peer Baron Alli (1964–)
[3] He pressed on with plans to purchase Montagu Square, viewing it with his friend Caroline Holdaway. It took around six months to complete the deal; A.R. never spent a night there.

11 OCTOBER
A walk to the now super-sized Waitrose and back.

12 OCTOBER
A day at home.

13 OCTOBER
2 Arbutus.
   Lunch.

21 OCTOBER
PMC.

22 OCTOBER
9 PMC.
   Blood transfusions.
   7.30 Marcia Firesten's birthday.

23 OCTOBER
8 Colony Grill w. John Hart.

24 OCTOBER
11.30 Sarah, Andy & the kids.
   7.30 Dena Hammerstein at Ruby & Ed's.

26 OCTOBER
At home all day.

4 NOVEMBER
9 PMC.

5 NOVEMBER
Packing for tomorrow.

6 NOVEMBER
4 → New York.

7 NOVEMBER
7.30 BAM—Wendy & David's[1] show?

---

[1] American ballet dancer Wendy Whelan (1967–) and American choreographer David Neumann (1965–)

8 NOVEMBER
Standard [hotel] for breakfast and then to the Whitney—Archibald Motley—the most wonderful, vibrant show.

23 NOVEMBER
11am Picasso sculpture show at MoMA.
   2pm Alan W. and Peter K.
   5pm M. E. [Mastrantonio] & Pat O'C[onnor].
   In bed by 11.

24 NOVEMBER
Ready for the 4.30 alarm call.
   5.30 car to JFK.

25 NOVEMBER
9.30 PMC.

26 NOVEMBER
9.30 Harley Street.

27 NOVEMBER
1pm Chiltern Firehouse w. Judy Hoflund, Tom, Charlotte & Rosemary.

29 NOVEMBER
7.30 Edna—The Wolseley.

30 NOVEMBER
2pm RADA.
   Recording Glenn Gould.[1]

9 DECEMBER
9 PMC.

10 DECEMBER
10[am] 18 Devonshire Street [clinic].

11 DECEMBER
6.30 Siân Thomas.
   Conor & Siobhan.
   52 Dean Street [clinic].

---

[1] A.R. narrated a video for the Glenn Gould Foundation.

12 DECEMBER
12.30 Shoreditch Town Hall.
  2.30 *Dead Dog in a Suitcase.*[1]
  7.30 Lindsay & Hilton.

---

[1] Musical, written by Carl Grose and directed by Mike Shepherd

Appendix:

The Early Diaries

Alan Rickman kept occasional diaries from around 1974 to 1982 and then again, more fulsomely and regularly, from 1993 to the end of his life. What follows is a selection of extracts from those early diaries, which begin after he had graduated from RADA in 1974 and chart his work with the Birmingham Repertory Theatre, Bristol Old Vic and the Royal Shakespeare Company, among others.

C. 1974

Fine acting always hits an audience with the force and oneness of the well-aimed bomb—one is only aware of the blast or series of blasts at the time—afterwards you can study the devastation or think about how a bomb is made. And yet no analogy suffices—the chemistry is too variable to construct an equation: an actor is about the only artist whose instrument is himself. And his instrument is not just for practice and performance—he has to place and use it in his life, too; has to construct a life in which to practise and present that instrument, and his only means is the instrument himself. Menuhin sounds a gong for dinner, he doesn't play it on his Stradivarius. The Stradivarius is polished and locked away in velvet. The actor's instrument is fed intermittently and travels on tube-trains in the rush hour. Fine acting is a bloody miracle of chance, the most fragile blending of time, mood, talent and trust. Too often, all we present is an attempted repeat of a hazy memory of the once we thought we almost made it.

* * *

More and more I think you've either got it or you haven't. What you can be taught is the recognition of having it and the attendant responsibility, or how best to cope without it. And that depends on whether the teacher has it or not. It's self-generating. The more you have, the more you seem to acquire, but unlike money, you don't know where it came from in the first place, and if you think you do, you haven't got it anyway.

MANCHESTER, MARCH 1975

At one stage, here, there was a danger that my confidence had been crushed. Somehow, the experience has been survived and I stand now in a position of arrogant strength. Everything I believe in has been thickly reinforced, not through example so much as the lack of it. People here say all the right things and fail totally to put them on public display, because try as one might it is well-nigh impossible to 'do' this thing we're engaged in—it needs many boring old-fashioned things like application and discipline to be in any sense revolutionary—their complacency breeds only blindness. In the end, they don't want to see because it might bring them face to face with risk, danger, challenge, honesty, daring and the beautiful simplicity which comes from the act of giving yourself over to an image, an idea, a character, a play, an audience.

* * *

Actors are no more innately neurotic than anyone else, but from time to time their senses undergo an overhaul or two, and thus cleansed they are sent out—back into the smog. Result: neurosis. Even if they don't get the overhaul, their possibilities are nearer the surface than with most people. Result: neurosis. (Fed through and by ego which is basically an unanswered mental tension, anyway.)

Constant encouragement is the vital food.

* * *

You can look at the lines on the page for hours on end, watch the meanings and inferences weaving in and out of the words. Speak them and they've gone in an instance.

LEICESTER, AUGUST 1975

Type-casting is a deadly poison.

Acting can be one's life, but that life must be rich enough to support it.

Fight the temptation to disappear into your own subconscious.

LEICESTER, DECEMBER 1975

Theatre is the only LIVING way to say here is you, here is me, this is what we do to each other, this is what we could do to each other. It is at once a celebration and a warning, a reminder and an encourager. So if needs be make it a shop, a bingo hall, a palace or a bus stop. Just make a strong but flexible framework and fill it with the right spirit. See what a child does with a box.

* * *

The thing inside me that keeps me going is like an arrow that begins somewhere in my gut and pushes upwards into my throat and brain. Other people call it self-confidence—but that has not always been there, although the camouflages of doubt, question, insecurity, laziness etc., have given it different shapes. The blunts and blurs seem to have been mostly stripped away now, and it thrusts upward while I'm trying to sort out some kind of target.

SHEFFIELD, JANUARY–MAY 1976
What do I say about this time? A crucial time. Three big parts[1] which have elicited from me some welcome heights and some fairly appalling depths. There must be a basic something which is right because while keeping my mind as open as I can, things are confirmed or developed—never changed (from disillusionment or that creeping disease 'it's a job').

JULY 1976
Piscean by birth—piscean in everything I think and do. My life swims one way, my work the other and yet it's the same breed. The ever-present objectivity—the 'once-remove'—is invaluable to me as an actor (for the most part—the great danger is lack of surprise, but I recognise that) and disastrous in relationships. Either I spend time keeping an even keel so as to avoid obstacles, or I get knotted up with watching, waiting, imposing. Will I ever just Let Be? Who puts this invisible telefoto lens over my eyes? It helps me to see and it makes me blind. What I enjoy as much as anything is to laugh from somewhere way down inside. And that begins to be like buried treasure.

BIRMINGHAM, OCTOBER 1976
Sunday in Birmingham and a distracted sideways glance out of the window. Two women crossing the street towards a row of bollards on the other side, fronting a parade of shops. It reminds me of so many days, particularly Sunday, spent in the streets around my grandparents' house, to all intents and purposes alone in that tin-kicking way that makes a brick wall become

---

[1] The parts were in *The Carnation Gang* by Stephen Poliakoff, *Nijinsky* by Rex Doyle, and Henrik Ibsen's *When We Dead Awaken.*

a thing of great comfort or menace—so deeply do you look into it as you walk its length and breadth. And a flash of knowledge comes with this. That curious sensation I remember being with me all the time turns out not to be simple loneliness although I've always felt 'different'. It was just 'waiting'. For now to arrive.

MAY–JUNE 1977
Birmingham–Liverpool–Zurich–Amsterdam–The Hague–Rotterdam–Eind-hoven–Cologne.

ON THE TRAIN TO BRISTOL OLD VIC, 1 SEPTEMBER
Some opposing forces to think about while working.
The need to simultaneously hold on and let go.
The most inward emotions must move outwards.

* * *

This is my head. It thinks it talks it charms. It worries it laughs it hurts. It has a hundred wonderful tricks. I am proud of it.

This is my body. It is funny-looking. It malfunctions. It looks best in winter clothes. I have as little to do with it as humanly possible. Lucky for my body that I need it to chauffeur my head around. Otherwise out it would go.

BRISTOL OLD VIC, NOVEMBER 1977
Finally, I came here driven either by fear or by unknown forces who, hacking paths through the jungle ahead of me, were unseen. None of the parts played here are approached with the animal joy that may contain the dangers of preconceived ideas. An agonising objectivity has been ever-present (and will prove to have been invaluable). Laertes, Ma Ubu and Uriah are all unfamiliar territories and bravery alone has not sufficed—I need a guide to show me more rewarding routes, dangerous scenery. God knows what the next ten years will bring, but now I must seek out the experts; the brilliant, the open, the challenging ones. To take my objectivity and willingness to them and let them kick it up to the skies.

JANUARY 1978
The mere fact that it is difficult to write anything these days indicates the watershed that has been my time in Bristol. Two curiously conflicting qualities make themselves felt. One—a numbness from the neck down through tapping the same unstocked reservoir—that of blind aggression. Two—a still more ruthless determination to be an ACTOR, not anybody's puppet, or at

most walkie-talkie-doll. I am ultimately the servant only of the play (that, however, implies generosity to fellow actors and willing listener to directors) not of someone's distorted view of my offstage persona.

20 MARCH 1978

This . . . is the first day with the RSC—a long ago dream. The taxi ride to Euston was like seeing one's life flash before the eyes—typically, in danger of missing the train and almost the last image of London was Stanhope[1] where the dream was conceived. Typically, too, the experience is already tempered with too much disillusionment—yet again, you're on your own. Armoured for the fight. Which has something to do with survival, but more with the added courage that a piece of armour gives, towards the day when it can be flung off. Hooray! And Hello! Free spirit. Somewhere between Caliban and Ariel lies Ferdinand.

ANTONY & CLEOPATRA REHEARSALS, AUGUST

Ironic that this is a blank page. To look through this book after the night-mares of the past few months is to wonder where I got it all from. But to be working with Peter Brook makes up for everything and crystallises all. The blank page is the same one that I felt during the first weeks at art school and RADA. In its emptiness it is rich with preconceptions smashed, naivety regained. Space for freedom to make its mark and depart.

Days later . . . but now I see his vulnerability—he is an artist in the purest sense and after eight years of building his own canvases, he has been asked to use someone else's colours, someone else's time scale. Do I sense some panic? A temptation to block in those colours before the areas have been properly defined. Maybe he needs encouragement too.

OCTOBER 8—SUNDAY BEFORE PRESS NIGHT

There are bound to be yawning chasms of unanswered needs with any pro-duction of a play as impossible as this one, but the intense concentration and effort required over the last two months to bring this company and play together, coupled with the mounting pressure of Tuesday night, have brought a kind of blindness in some crucial areas of the play. Crucial because they are at the beginning and the end.

The above tortuous prose stems from what I have to recognise as a severely unsettled state (conversations with Ruby Wax late Sunday night). I

---

[1] Stanhope Theatre, Euston Road, was where A.R. performed in 1965.

have allowed myself to sink into a state of almost unrelievable torpor, where my mind is quite capable of leaving my body to fend for itself entirely. I offer myself no surprises—danger is given a wide berth. Life becomes a series of habits. That voice up there is screaming 'stir yourself'. This must relate at least in part to the problem I am having of getting the speeches past my lips—they are not in the front of my brain, not present. I am an amalgam of nostalgia and ambition. The present is what makes the link. Act.

21 MAY 1979

The dole queue, with the clock at 89 and me at 00, is the present. The RSC is now the past. The future leers at me with several faces. I gaze back, with arms folded and fists clenched.

YOUNG VIC, LONDON, JULY 1979 – AFTER *DESPERATELY YOURS*[1]

I doubt I could turn to directing permanently. Watching a first night is like being eaten by piranhas while surrounded by people taking no notice. No feedback, no release. But there are muscles there asking for the exercise.

NOTTINGHAM, OCTOBER 1979 – *ANTONIO*[2]

A sustained nightmare. But out of it comes the humble need for a director. My third eye has had to grow such proportions that it can now no longer focus on anything. The intense anger has subsided somewhat and at odd moments I can 'catch the energy on its impulsive exits' but my insecurity makes me 'aware' and therefore dampens it before it can really take me on a journey. What I see clearest at the moment are shortcomings and possibilities—the first in abundance and proximity, the second hazy and far off.

In the midst of this was *Thérèse Raquin* [novel by Zola]—and the warm sigh of relief at being surrounded by people who all know what they are doing.

CITIZENS, GLASGOW, JANUARY 1980

A new decade? Still a bit numb from declining the job I came here wanting. But the arbiter was instinct which is some kind of advance. Two other jobs are declined (1) out of respect for my mental health and (2) my self-respect. In many ways I am getting to recognise signs a little more clearly and obey them. In this show I see my present hurdles in stronger focus, too.

None of this stuff should be written in grey, watery, invisible pencil. Looks too much like an apology.

---

[1] Ruby Wax's first show
[2] *Antonio's Revenge*—by John Marston. A.R. had the title role.

CRUCIBLE, SHEFFIELD, FEBRUARY 1980

My life begins to receive injections from this theatre, directly and indirectly. It is good to feel the warm blood of optimism. Having reread some of these pages, the last six years seem to have been a journey towards confusion and some pretence. I'm less 'packaged' but less idealistic. Having a 'career' means being in the race. Nobody ever talked their way to the winning post. Winning post? Stop trying to impress, to catch up. Lead.

THE BUSH, LONDON, JUNE 1980–
REHEARSING *COMMITMENTS* [BY DUSTY HUGHES]

This book is full of 'fateful moments'. One only hopes that the hazy memory of them means that, in turn, they have embedded themselves in the subconscious and that the last few months have been fruitful.

   The Devil Himself [by Severus Rogue] was a pleasure—the pure pleasure of knowing that wonderful material can still feed the imagination, and that added to a mutual trust between performers (fragile as ever), curious magic can still be confected.

   The pleasure now is to work with Richard Wilson, who says 'don't act', 'behave', and a hundred other things which for a long time had only been murmurings from the drama school days.

KENNEDY AIRPORT, SEPTEMBER 1980

The sense bank should be heavily in credit now as I sit here watching an ulcer grow. How differently a group of sights and sounds can lift you. The time in New York is a mirror of its page in the diary. Some lines of clarity and decision, many crossings out and overlappings. Toronto was a release in some ways, a reminder of an old and misunderstood trap in others. But there was a relaxation which allowed me to see the rainbow across the American Falls at Niagara—the yellow plastic-coated creatures climbing their rickety staircase.

   Kennedy Airport—chaos in flesh. Less civilised than those Greek ferries of years ago. Microphones summon the same person again and again to 'the red courtesy phone'—no seats on the 9.15 flight—heart sinks—hopeful passengers ask the same questions of ever-impatient attendants and muzak laughs and laughs up its sleeve.

9 DECEMBER 1980

The radio says John Lennon is dead . . . A lump of my past has been removed. No, maybe more firmly placed. If you look for it, and even like today when you don't, life will tell you things. Last night some theatre awards were shown on TV and I wanted one of them—but with my teeth and fingernails I wanted out. John Lennon's death hits much harder and lower. Just now it seems senseless—let it not be a waste. (I don't want to be forever observing my own feelings like this—but he had the same groans: 'How can I go forward when I don't know which way I'm facing?')

SLEEPER HOME FROM EDINBURGH, AUGUST 30–31 1981 – *BROTHERS KARAMAZOV*

The ironies flowing from the above are infinite. Working with Max Stafford-Clark followed by the indescribable rehearsal period; playing another introvert but giving full vent to the extrovert in me through unstoppable anger. Ultimately, the memory of desolate lunchtimes on Brighton [where rehearsals took place] beach, and opening to choruses of praise. There may still be a real life to be found in this play. We'll see.

NOTES FROM RUSSIA
1AM, MOSCOW, 7 SEPTEMBER

Grab your chances on a trip like this. A horrendous journey which should have taken 3 hours—we arrived finally in our bedroom at 5am Sunday. At 4am we were eating a supper (packed) of 3 hard boiled eggs, 5 apples, soft soft cheese and apple jam. Definitely signs of things to come, as the morning's breakfast of sausage and peas proved. Faced with a bleak Sunday evening of nothing to do, nowhere to go, no one to ask in Moscow, we landed delightfully on our feet in the home of Igor and Tanya & Tanya's mother Flora. Good food, wine, cognac, company and fun. Simple pleasures are the best.

MONDAY EVENING

Who needs to do anything but just listen to the Kagarlitskys? Minds that have been quietly whizzing around the table for years. He[1] says that Brook doesn't know what to say about the world. 'Sometimes history is difficult but heroic, today it is difficult but shameful.' Boris[2] gives Russia 9 years before it throws up its own Wałęsa.[3]

---

[1] Julius Kagarlitsky (1926–2000), Russian critic and professor of European drama at the State Theatrical Institute in Moscow
[2] Russian sociologist and dissident Boris Kagarlitsky (1958–)
[3] Lech Wałęsa (1943–), Polish statesman, dissident and Nobel Peace Prize laureate

THURSDAY

State Institute of Performing Arts. A building swarming with generosity. Students working together so completely that the stage was filled with resonances, echoes and energy that no one actor could ever create. So open it assaulted you and was really very moving. A very different place from Moscow Arts. I could and should have stayed for hours but the pressure of being a tourist was too much and the coach vacuumed us in for lunch and a trip to a monastery . . .

LENINGRAD STATION, MOSCOW – WAITING FOR THE NIGHT TRAIN

Said au revoir to Lena, our interpreter—an extraordinary woman. Black-eyed gypsy with a devastating line in clairvoyancy. She describes herself as 'hypnotic but lonely'. Also says 'You need her loyalty & patience but don't expect all of her love, she can't give it. She'll always be able to take care of herself. When you are cruel, she may say nothing but she remembers everything. When you fall in love, which is often, it lasts longer than with most people but you are suspicious & jealous in love . . .'

The train ride was enjoyable, hateful, interesting, funny, sad & freezing ultimately. Nothing else matters much when you are cold.

LENINGRAD – AFTER PERFORMING *KARAMAZOV*

The 'bravos' lessened by having heard so many of them last night at the Kirov . . . Went through the motions somewhat at the Youth Theatre (Sunday). They were however displaying some open interest in us, which added another tint to the strangely isolationist (strangely?) atmosphere elsewhere. The Pushkin another stunning auditorium . . . followed by some very formal chat—one of the actresses talked about 'spirituality' and gave a consistently inspirited, gift-wrapped performance in the evening. She did, bless her, come to see us tonight. There was not so much as a glass of water available after the show. 'You should have said beforehand.'

AFTER THE DYNAMO TBILISI FOOTBALL MATCH

Georgia really is a different country, full of its own sounds, sights and smells. Subways with weighing machines and weighing-machine minders, weighing humans or sacks of potatoes. Standing in the middle of the wonderful Rustaveli stage. Enveloping heat. Slightly tentative swim in view of sewage possibilities. A hotel only just on its feet. Everyone at the match sitting on sheets of newspaper to protect their hard-won trousers. And the mass tremor of 70,000 people with a series of single responses for an hour and a half. I must come back here to gather more threads—they retain a lifestyle which seems to have the right balance—not dwarfed by buildings—the peasant roots remain and yet in a population the size of Birmingham there are thirteen theatres. Who knows what the truth is, but I've enjoyed any deceptions.

LONDON, NOVEMBER 1981

Karamazov opened in the West End last night. We open at the Bush tomorrow—still the actors have to act as psychiatrist to the director. Our imaginations are the greatest gift he has—where's the threat?

God, if your soul's a mess, the mind goes scurrying around some pretty dark corridors. There is a part of me which has never left childhood—I must somehow locate it and tell it to grow up fast. I shall continue to settle for the nearest womb all the time; relationships, friends, the flat, bed. I exaggerate, as ever, but in recognising that I constantly move in two directions at the same time, I should remind myself that things can be changed. The overriding urge at the moment (which I don't really understand) is to run my arm across the mantelpiece.

JULY 1982

Two days after coming back from Crete & Egypt.

8am—It's a beautiful sunny crisp blue morning, which is a reminder that this book might benefit from being treated as a positive element in my life. A big black line needs drawing across many of the pages.

Afterword

Alan's last diary entry was on 12 December, but he had been getting weaker and writing less for some time. All through the autumn he had been getting more tired, eating less and often feeling sick. But we continued to do most of the things that had always been part of our life. We saw films and plays, met friends, went out to dinner or entertained at home. And Alan still did some work, although the film projects that he had been attached to had to be abandoned.

Alan also spent a lot of time sitting on the sofa and watching TV—his two favourite programmes at that time were *Don't Tell the Bride* and *Say Yes to the Dress*.

Our trip to New York in November was very important. To stay in our flat again, attend the memorial for Mike Nichols and see so many of the friends who had meant so much to us over the years. Alan loved New York.

He went downhill after that. By mid-December it was clear that things were getting bad. He was often in pain, very weak and sleeping a lot. We both knew that he probably had months rather than years but still hoped that the chemotherapy would work and maybe stabilise the tumour. So we continued with plans for Christmas and New Year—Christmas was meant to be with our good friend Sara Sugarman, and others, at her beautiful house in Sheerness. And New Year was going to be in Norfolk.

By 19 December I was convinced that Alan needed to be in hospital, but we had invited his brother David and wife Chris for lunch that day and arranged to see Zoë in a play that evening. And Alan, being Alan, despite being in pain, would not let them down. But I did manage to talk to our consultant, who agreed that Alan would be admitted the following morning. He was.

He never left the hospital after that. We soon knew that our Christmas plans were out (various friends and family came in that day). I think it was obvious to all of them that things were serious. Alan still had hopes for New Year and on New Year's Eve sent me home to pack, but when I returned with our two little suitcases it was clearly not going to happen. He was far too weak.

New Year's Eve was odd. I was there during the day, but Alan was sleepy so I left about 8. He told me the next day that he awoke at 11.50 and was able to watch the fireworks on TV.

The last two weeks of Alan's life were extraordinary. It was clear that he was dying. Our consultant told us that he had been so bad that it could have happened before Christmas. But there was nothing more that they could do other than preventing him from being in pain. Which they did.

During these last two weeks Alan's room was turned into a salon. Belinda had produced a table-top Christmas tree, Emma brought in a standard lamp, cushions and a throw to cover the sofa. And an infuser. Miranda added a window bird-feeder. I was asked to bring in a beautiful table lamp from home.

Different friends came in each day. Sometimes, Alan told me who he wanted to see. Otherwise, they just came in. There was often a lot of laughter. Alan was in bed but always a major voice in the proceedings.

And, in conjunction with our dear friend, interior designer Caroline Holdaway, he planned the décor of the new flat that we were buying. He even added the instruction 'and you'd better put in a bloody cat flap'. She did.

He designed his own funeral. Ian Rickson (theatre director) was put in charge. Alan chose where it would take place, who would speak and what music would be played. Ian and I sat by the bed while he decided which part of his own work he wanted shown.

He was surrounded by people who loved him and up until 13 January was still in control of everything that was going on around him. But he wasn't there after that, and he died at 9.15 in the morning of 14 January 2016. I was there. He wasn't in pain. He just went.

Alan had six months between diagnosis and death, which is typical for pancreatic cancer where the average is three months, because there is currently no diagnostic test and the symptoms are so non-specific (I have become a trustee of Pancreatic Cancer UK in the hope that we can raise money to fund research to develop the diagnostic testing that might have saved Alan's life).

But, to continue, several friends came in that day: Ruby, Helena, Emma, Tara and niece Sarah, and that evening everyone gathered at Ruby's house. Many friends, many memories, many tears and so much else.

Alan was cremated on the morning of 3 February with close friends and family present. The funeral service was held that afternoon in the Actors' Church in the heart of London's theatre district. Ian directed a stellar cast, which included J. K. Rowling. Megan Dodds performed a piece from *My Name Is Rachel Corrie*. The chosen music was 'Uptown Funk' and 'Take It with Me' by Tom Waits. The only piece of Alan's work was from Peter Barnes' *Revolutionary Witness*. We finished with everyone singing 'The Sun Ain't Gonna Shine Anymore'. Then, in keeping with tradition, the Reverend Richard Syms asked us to give Alan 'one last wonderful standing ovation'.

RIMA HORTON

Index

About the Authors

Alan Sidney Patrick Rickman (born February 21, 1946) was an English actor and theatre director. He was a renowned stage actor in modern and classical productions and a member of the Royal Shakespeare Company. In film his best-known work featured roles in *Die Hard, Robin Hood: Prince of Thieves*, the *Harry Potter* series, and *Sense and Sensibility*. He won numerous awards including a BAFTA, a Golden Globe, and an Emmy. He died on January 14, 2016, from pancreatic cancer.

Alan Taylor is a journalist and writer. He was founding editor of the *Scottish Review of Books*. He has edited several acclaimed anthologies, including *The Assassin's Cloak*, a collection of the world's best diarists. He is the author of *Appointment in Arezzo: A Friendship with Muriel Spark* and the series editor of Spark's collected novels.

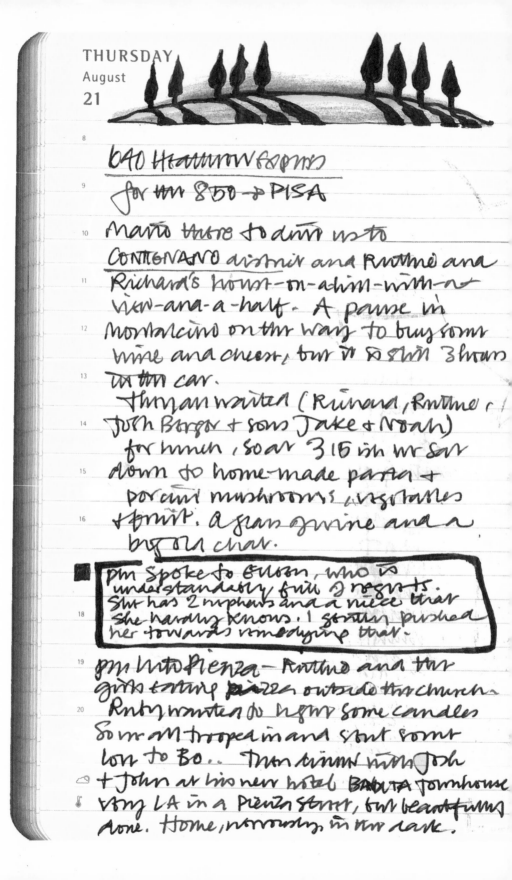

640 Heathrow express

for the 850 → PISA

Mario there to drive us to
CONTIGNANO district and Ruthie and
Richard's house-on-a-hill-with-a-
view-and-a-half. A pause in
Montalcino on the way to buy some
wine and cheese, but it's still 3 hours
in the car.

They all waited (Richard, Ruthie +
Josh Berger + sons Jake & Noah)
for lunch, so at 315 in we sat
down to home-made pasta +
porcini mushrooms, vegetables
+ fruit. A glass of wine and a
big old chat.

pm spoke to Eileen, who is
understandably full of regrets.
She has 2 nephews and a niece that
she hardly knows. I gently pushed
her towards remedying that.

pm into Pienza — Ruthie and the
girls eating pizza outside the church.
Ruby wanted to light some candles
so we all trooped in and spent some
lira to do.. Then dinner with Josh
+ John at his new hotel BADIA Townhouse
very LA in a Pienza street, but beautifully
done. Home, nervously, in the dark.